Britannia's Embrace

Britannia's Embrace

MODERN HUMANITARIANISM AND THE IMPERIAL ORIGINS OF REFUGEE RELIEF

Caroline Shaw

OXFORD
UNIVERSITY PRESS

OXFORD
UNIVERSITY PRESS

Oxford University Press is a department of the University of Oxford. It furthers the University's objective of excellence in research, scholarship, and education by publishing worldwide.

Oxford New York
Auckland Cape Town Dar es Salaam Hong Kong Karachi
Kuala Lumpur Madrid Melbourne Mexico City Nairobi
New Delhi Shanghai Taipei Toronto

With offices in
Argentina Austria Brazil Chile Czech Republic France Greece
Guatemala Hungary Italy Japan Poland Portugal Singapore
South Korea Switzerland Thailand Turkey Ukraine Vietnam

Published in the United States of America by
Oxford University Press
198 Madison Avenue, New York, NY 10016

Library of Congress Cataloging-in-Publication Data
Shaw, Caroline, 1979–
Britannia's embrace : modern humanitarianism and the imperial origins of refugee relief / Caroline Shaw.
pages cm
ISBN 978–0–19–020098–5 (hardcover : acid-free paper) 1. Refugees—Great Britain—History—19th century 2. Political refugees—Great Britain—History—19th century. 3. Humanitarianism—Great Britain—History—19th century. 4. Refugees—Government policy—Great Britain—History—19th century. 5. Asylum, Right of—Great Britain—History—19th century. 6. Imperialism—Social aspects—Great Britain—History—19th century. 7. Great Britain—Emigration and immigration—History—19th century. 8. Liberalism—Great Britain—History—19th century. 9. Great Britain—Politics and government—19th century. I. Title.
HV640.4.G7S42 2015
362.87′80941—dc23
2014040922

1 3 5 7 9 8 6 4 2
Printed in the United States of America
on acid-free paper

Contents

Acknowledgments

The much-missed Susanna Barrows demonstrated to her students that the work of the historian does not happen in isolation. It happens in conversation—in Susanna's case, preferably at one of her renowned soirees. This book is the product of more conversations than I can count.

I am grateful for the constant guidance, support, and criticism of James Vernon and Tom Laqueur, the best duo of dissertation advisors I can imagine. They, along with Catherine Gallagher in English and David Lieberman in history and jurisprudence and social policy, have waded through memos from the archives and drafts of chapters with patience, encouragement, and thoughtful advice. Judith Walkowitz, with whom I had the fortune to work as an undergraduate, taught me how to research in the archives and imparted a love for bringing novels and newspapers into the study of the past. At Berkeley, Susanna Barrows and Tyler Stovall urged me to think comparatively. They perhaps bear some of the blame that this project, which began as a study of 1848, quickly encompassed a few more continents and decades than anticipated.

By its very nature, this work has required me to consult a small army of experts in different geographies and time periods within and outside British studies. David Feldman, Margot Finn, Peter Gatrell, and Carla Hesse—experts in matters relating to different refugee groups in the eighteenth through twentieth centuries—each helped me to contextualize my findings at key moments. I have learned much from the commentary of participants at the American Historical Association's annual meetings, the Berkeley Center for British Studies, the Berkeley-Chicago-Yale-Texas Mellon Consortia on British

Studies, the British studies group at Harvard's Minda de Gunzburg Center for European Studies, the regional and the North American Conferences on British Studies, and the Refugees and the End of Empire Conference at De Montfort University in Leicester, United Kingdom. Among these participants, I am especially thankful for the intellectual generosity of Arianne Chernock, James Epstein, Desmond Fitz-Gibbon, Kevin Grant, Nicoletta Gullace, Darcy Hughes Heuring, Penelope Ismay, Jeff Hoppes, Andrew Keating, Maya Jasanoff, Stefan Manz, Hannah Weiss Muller, Radhika Natarajan, Maura O'Connor, Panikos Panayi, Tehila Sasson, Claudena Skran, Susan Tananbaum, Michelle Tusan, Judith Walkowitz, Keith Watenpaugh, Nicholas Wilson, and Aristide Zolberg. Their comments have been invaluable. The anonymous reviewers for Oxford University Press provided many useful insights. Susan Ferber at Oxford University Press has blessed the manuscript (and its titles!) with her fine editorial intuition.

I am indebted to the many archivists who helped me to access rare books and manuscripts at the British Library; the British National Archives; Bishopsgate Institute; the London Metropolitan Archives; newspapers at the British Library at Colindale; and the special collections at the Friends' House, the British Red Cross, University College London, the London School of Economics, Rhodes House (Oxford), and the University of Southampton. Joan Allen's hospitality and knowledge of the Joseph Cowen Collection at the Tyne & Wear Archives Service in Newcastle salvaged an otherwise disastrous research trip in which my computer died upon arrival. At Bates, Christopher Schiff and Mathieu Duvall lent their considerable technical expertise with images and maps.

The comradeship of colleagues and friends, old and new, has made the otherwise isolating task of completing a book a joy. My colleagues in the history department at Bates have supported my project at every turn. The college's faculty writing group has helped me to think outside my home discipline. Occasional meetups, virtual workshops, and regular Skype dates have helped motivate me while deepening friendships begun at Berkeley with Penelope Ismay, Miriam Kingsberg, and Vlasta Vranjes.

None of this work could have happened without generous financial support from the Mellon Foundation and the American Council of Learned Societies, from Bates College, from the Boyle-Shea Fund for History, and from the University of California at Berkeley's history department, Institute of International Studies' Simpson Fellowship, and Center for European Studies. My thanks to Taylor

& Francis (http://www.tandfonline.com) for permissions to reprint my "The British, Persecuted Foreigners and the Emergence of the Refugee Category in Nineteenth-Century Britain" from *Immigrants & Minorities* 30, no. 2–3 (July 2012): 239–262 as portions of Chapter Two and Three of *Britannia's Embrace*. I am also grateful to Bowdoin College Library, the British Library, the Library of Congress, the Wellcome Institute, Yale's Center for British Art, the Paul Mellon Collection, Yale's Lewis Walpole Collection, and the Yale University Art Gallery for their assistance with and permission to publish images from their collections.

I dedicate this book to my family. My mom and sister, along with extended Shaw and Moodie clans, have provided me with constant emotional sustenance. Ben came into my life at the start of this project and at every turn he has been my first audience and helpful critic. Our Isaac, true to the meaning of his name, has offered laughter as well as love at the most stressful times. Noah, our second son, showed a healthy disregard for academic deadlines with his very recent arrival. My grandmother Sarita's passion for learning has been a life-long inspiration. I will be forever grateful that she got to spend time with Isaac and could catch a glimpse of Noah and of the other baby—the final manuscript draft—in her last days. Finally, I would have loved to talk shop over these past years with my father, Michael. I know he would have enjoyed that I finally came around to studying two of his own hobbyhorses, law and diplomacy, though with my own twist.

Caroline Shaw
Portland, Maine
September 2014

Britannia's Embrace

Introduction
Britannia's Embrace

We cannot entertain . . . any demand for the expulsion of refugees . . . You must be aware that no government which complied with such demands could exist a month in England.

— LORD MALMESBURY, 1852

By the 1850s, the British public was well schooled in the plight of foreign refugees. Activists from across the political and social spectrum helped to spread tales of foreign persecution that invited Britons to imagine themselves in the role of foreigners' rescuer. Britons had reason to take pride in this humanitarian action; the narrative of refuge was matched by new repertoires for refugee relief that made shelter for these particular foreigners viable either at home or under the British aegis overseas. So powerful and pervasive was this morality tale that it developed a life of its own, bending even unsympathetic politicians to its service. Foreign Secretary Lord Malmesbury was himself an unlikely champion for the exiles arriving in Britain in March 1852. As a conservative, Malmesbury's sympathies lay with the reactionary Austrian government, not with the revolutionary Hungarian and Polish refugees who opposed it. In a conversation with the Austrian ambassador, however, Malmesbury had to rule out the possibility of extraditing foreign refugees. He knew all too well that the British public hailed foreign refugees and their rescuers as heroes and took for granted that their government would safeguard them.[1]

The forcefulness of the refugee category represented a wholesale shift in British cultural assumptions. Just a century earlier, few people would have imagined that the British had a moral responsibility to persecuted peoples as wholly unconnected to the English as continental revolutionaries. Until the end of the eighteenth century, refuge had been founded on religious confession. British territory promised freedom of conscience for persecuted Protestants under the protection of a Protestant monarch. As the *Encyclopedia Britannica* of 1796 noted, the term *refugee* referred specifically to the French Huguenots,

Protestants who were forced to flee after the revocation of the Edict of Nantes in 1685. Indeed, the French Huguenots introduced the word into the English language.[2]

By the middle of the nineteenth century, however, the refugee category was, according to the cultural politics of the age, potentially universal in scope. Anyone fleeing unjust governance could be described as a refugee regardless of his or her class, politics, race, or creed. Lord Palmerston's administration won political accolades for rescuing Hungarian exiles from the Austrians after the collapse of the short-lived Hungarian national parliament. American novelist Harriet Beecher Stowe emphasized the heroism of George Harris, the fugitive slave in her bestselling *Uncle Tom's Cabin*, by comparing him to a young Hungarian patriot. The British and Foreign Anti-Slavery Society demanded that the imperial government intervene on behalf of Harris's real-life counterpart, John Anderson, when the American government demanded his extradition from British Canada in 1860 on charges of killing a slave-catcher en route to freedom. Even the little-liked French democratic-socialist exiles in the British Channel Islands vigorously claimed their due as refugees. The day the British stopped recognizing the sanctity of asylum, wrote the editors of the French exiles' newspaper in 1855, the British nation would suffer a loss of honor even more sorrowful than France's when it put them to flight.[3]

This book examines the history of British concern for persecuted foreigners from the late-seventeenth century through the dawn of the twentieth century. During this period, the category of the refugee became potentially universal and provisions for the protection of persecuted foreigners global in scope. While there were other providers of refuge throughout the world, this story is a British one, for it was the British who first and most powerfully incorporated the provision of relief for persecuted foreigners into their national, and then imperial, raison d'être. Refuge expanded in the seventeenth century as a reward for service to the state, but did not remain a quid pro quo for long. Broad normative claims on behalf of foreign refugees instead became associated with national self-image and pride in the wake of the 1814–1815 Congress of Vienna. For the increasingly democratic nation, refuge for an expanding array of foreigners became constitutive of what it meant to be liberal on a global stage.

What is so striking about the British public's commitment to refuge is that it developed at a time when, unlike today, there were no laws distinguishing refugees from other foreign migrants. Although refugees received distinctive philanthropic and political recognition, all foreigners could, in fact, enter British territory freely throughout most of the nineteenth century. In a century of revolutions, only the British government resisted the temptation to institute a restrictive border policy. Even relatively free Belgium, France, and Switzerland—among other places of refuge—periodically expelled refugees in their midst.[4] By contrast, between the lapse of the 1793 Aliens Act in 1826 and the passage of the Aliens Act of 1905, any foreigner—immigrant or refugee—could enter Britain. The 1848 Aliens Act, issued in the midst of a new wave of continental revolutions, expired without having once been invoked. Passport controls, though increasingly strict on the continent, arrived in Britain only in the early twentieth century. Once on British soil, foreigners had little reason to seek naturalization, a cumbersome and expensive process. Refugees and immigrants alike were entitled to relief from the poor law or the workhouse.[5]

And yet, refuge for persecuted foreigners was not simply a byproduct of open-door migration policies. Rather, it was a popular public commitment that activists sometimes anachronistically compared with the biblical command to build cities of refuge or with the medieval practice of sanctuary. Cities of refuge and medieval sanctuaries were meant primarily to ensure that avengers did not kill fugitives before a trial convened.[6] Nineteenth-century refuge was meant to be far broader than these antecedents. It assumed, where its precursors had not, that refugees were worthy of more than a temporary stay of justice. They were to receive the means necessary to ensure a dignified existence in the British Isles or under the British aegis anywhere in the world. More critically still, refuge entailed political as well as humanitarian sympathy and relief. The modern variant assumed that refugees and refuge providers shared in the common cause of advancing liberty worldwide.

This was the ideal, espoused throughout the press and by activists from radical artisans to the Anglican elite. In reality, assistance for foreigners was fickle, as dependent on media sensationalism as modern humanitarian campaigns tend to be. As the fanfare subsided, shared interests could be strained and common cause hard to find. Politics divided liberal from democrat, constitutional monarchist from socialist. Economic competition could pit working-class Britons against refugees just as readily as class sympathies or the bonds of marriage could bring them together.

Despite these less-than-ideal realities, the public interest in foreign refugees had real power. As Malmesbury attested, officials—whatever their politics—were wary of appearing to put refugees in peril. By the middle of the nineteenth century, promises to protect these foreigners extended throughout the colonies and accompanied British missionaries, sailors, and civil servants traveling beyond the boundaries of the Empire.

For activists and public commentators, the liberalism at the core of their humanitarian outreach was part and parcel of their aspirations to reform their own polity. Their liberalism drew a contrast to foreign despotism by emphasizing the rule of just law and liberty of movement. While broader than the classic economic liberalism of Adam Smith, it similarly bespoke a belief that the possibility of national and human progress rested on the freedom and self-regulation of individuals. By the 1850s, members of the conservative establishment as well as the nascent Liberal Party embraced liberal ideology. Liberalism infused the religious writings of middle-class moralists and the efforts of working-class missionaries as they instructed their audiences in Victorian codes of conduct. The project was aspirational. While aimed at self-regulation, the idealized "rule of freedom" could be distinctively unfree, replete with class and racial assumptions about who was or was not ready for self-governance. Indeed, even in Britain, liberal reforms were far from complete in the decades following the 1815 Congress of Vienna when refuge became a cause-célèbre. The franchise in Britain expanded piecemeal over the course of the nineteenth and early twentieth centuries; in 1815, not even the emerging middle class had the vote. The campaign to abolish slavery in the colonies was in full force by the 1820s; yet full emancipation was a painfully gradual affair.[7]

Despite—even because of—the unevenness of their own liberal reforms, Britons of different stripes saw in the foreign refugee the ideal liberal subject: heroic, morally righteous, and independent. While he—and refugees tended to be gendered male in this era—had not succeeded in thwarting autocratic rule at home, he remained an ideal, hard-working subject while in exile. As John Stuart Mill and Samuel Smiles would later celebrate, these were the traits of any good liberal subject; they were the traits that religious missionaries and political and social reformers hoped to impart to the working class at home and to subjects of empire overseas. For Smiles especially, the British had a lot to learn from foreigners on this score; Smiles depicted the Huguenots of the eighteenth century as paragons of industriousness whom all ought to imitate.[8] Refuge for persecuted foreigners, like the campaign to abolish the slave trade and then slavery itself, was thus a foundational act of an increasingly triumphant liberal ideology in a particular nineteenth-century context.

Liberal commitments were not enough to produce a viable humanitarian norm. Imperial command—the financial resources and international clout of the British Empire—made assistance in refugee crises practicable at a bearable cost, affording the space necessary to shelter those who escaped. Power, wealth, and relative security thus enabled the British public and politicians to enact their care for persecuted foreigners. Without these resources, a repertoire for relief would never have developed, and the humanitarian act of refuge would never have gained the traction it did.

Britannia's Embrace offers the first historical examination of the nineteenth-century origins of refuge as a modern humanitarian category. It is not a history of each refugee group that found sanctuary in British territory or in the care of British philanthropists.[9] Instead, it is a study of a culturally and politically powerful commitment and the interplay between this strongly felt moral conviction and the practical vicissitudes that attended it. Refuge as a national and imperial project was itself the product of would-be interventions against oppression that were impossible to undertake, that were too long in the making, or that failed outright. British activists and officials turned to refuge as a second-best alternative: if the dictates of diplomacy meant that they could not enforce liberal justice on foreign powers, they could at least succor the victims of injustice.[10] This consolation prize became a triumphant exercise of humanitarian conscience. This emphasis on shared humanity enabled a diffuse refugee-supporting public, called to arms by the local and national press, to come together across the political spectrum. For Anglican moralists and dissenting Chartists alike, the commitment to refuge became a critical tool in teaching fellow-feeling and propagating a culture and politics of moral imperatives. This project was as imperious and expansive as the liberal ideology of the age. Not surprisingly, then, the refugee narrative, like most forcefully moral imperatives, also distorted reality. It invited the British public to lionize refugees as personifications of liberal virtue and, more often than not, to ignore the ongoing suffering, poverty, and uncertainty that characterized life in exile. As one radical activist bemoaned in 1853, foreign refugees might be free in Britain, but they were also "free to starve."[11]

Public rhetoric in support of refugees and their causes tended to obscure these darker realities. This made sense; propagandists did their best to flatter British hosts, highlighting the contrast between British freedom and foreign despotism. The refugees who spoke to British audiences were a select group; typically English speaking and of elite social origins, they were believed to be the best messengers for their cause. More often than not, it was these activists' voices that British audiences heard. This unfortunate process of marginalization seems to have been intrinsic to the nineteenth-century development of refuge as a humanitarian act.[12] Refuge could become a powerful social force precisely because its narrative appealed to Victorian culture. For activists, charitable subjects who did not fit a set of idealized refugee traits or who elicited the ire of their local hosts became an embarrassment. Those who did not fit the mold were often hastily moved out of the public eye and resettled elsewhere. The Empire offered this social and political safety valve for the British Isles, as it did for tens of thousands of Britons during this period as well. Once dispatched to outposts of the Empire, troublesome refugees could be more readily fitted into the story of successful humanitarian intervention and national pride so central to popular sentiment in the British Isles.[13]

These were the terms on which refuge became a moral norm. Problems with the provision of long-term refuge became impossible to ignore, however, as the political and financial costs of imperial refuge increased in the last third of the nineteenth century. By the end of the nineteenth century, the British became increasingly hesitant to apply the category of the refugee as broadly as they once had. This newfound caution had several sources. One was Britain's changing geopolitical position. While still the global superpower, Britain seemed to be losing ground thanks to increased competition from the United States and a newly unified Germany. Fear for Britain's relative decline made officials, theorists, and the press more skeptical about the possibility of mitigating persecution overseas. As the nineteenth century wore on, this concern dovetailed with Britons' diminishing faith in the possibility of individual and social progress. This shift reflected changing ideas of race and a hardening belief in biologically defined "stages of civilization," but it was not only a racialized one.[14] Officials, once more than willing to equate refugee slaves with political refugees, now became wary of conflating the two. Even political revolutionaries—the core of the refugee category to which slaves had long been compared—lost their romantic luster for many

Britons as their use of political violence intensified after 1870. Could bomb-throwing anarchists be political refugees? Were Irish nationalists entitled to refuge in America in the same way that Hungarian nationalists were protected in Britain? Refugees had long been symbolic of despotism overseas. What happened, though, when they were refugees from British violence or when they threatened the British Empire? What happened when the influx of refugees increased massively?

By the last quarter of the nineteenth century, these concerns, in many cases apparent in the colonies decades earlier, began to impress the metropolitan public as too great for Britain to bear. Officials, activists, and public commentators were forced to examine exactly what constituted viable refuge in their own Empire and under their aegis elsewhere around the world. The ensuing debates dominated public discussion about relief for persecuted foreigners between 1870 and 1905. They produced two seemingly contradictory developments in British refuge. On the one hand, refugees, originally a popular category for humanitarian and political action, were defined and given explicit protection in domestic and international law for the first time. The amorphous "right to refuge" long touted in the British press was at last given shape first in the 1870 Extradition Act and later in the 1905 Aliens Act. Ironically, the language of these laws constituted a triumph for the broad moral standard that had developed earlier in the nineteenth century, though they resulted from a powerful new challenge to the scope of the refugee category. On the other hand, this moment of legal enshrinement had long-term costs. The institutionalization of British refuge in domestic and international law further diminished the moral fervor so central to relief organization. Having recognized the need to treat refugees distinctively, the government turned to new bureaucratic procedures to determine who was or was not a refugee.[15] In the process, public oversight of refugee affairs became increasingly obsolete. While British activists remained integral to international aid work for refugees, by the dawn of the twentieth century, this work was less central to Britons' sense of national and liberal identity. Thus, this moment of legal codification must be seen as something of a defeat for the vitality of broad normative claims on refugees' behalf.

Given the extent of British xenophobia in the twentieth and twenty-first centuries, it may seem difficult to believe that Britain—which now has the lowest per-capita acceptance rate of refugees in Europe—was ever welcoming.[16] Rather than address what attracted Britons to the plight of these foreigners, interest in the history of foreign refugees prior to the Great War has heretofore been subsumed within national accounts of nineteenth-century revolution or the treatment of religious minorities.[17] Important accounts have been written of Italians, Germans, and French in exile and of the persecution of Jews in Eastern Europe followed by their cold reception in the West, America included. In these histories, scholars note that Britain was particularly open to these serial waves of refugees in the nineteenth century, yet they tend to treat this history dismissively. When speaking about popular or national interest in foreign refugees, scholars emphasize stories of public ambivalence or hostility. Historians assume that the British of the nineteenth century grudgingly tolerated the foreigners in their midst, never taking an active interest in their plight. By this account, British asylum was an unintentional byproduct of open-border policies. These policies were so dear to the liberal ideology of the time that officials and the public at large preferred allowing little-liked foreigners to remain rather than regulating movement in and out of the country. More politically stable than its continental neighbors, the British state could afford these liberal indulgences. Unsurprisingly, Britain changed course when the costs of asylum appeared to rise precipitously at the turn of the twentieth century. The British feared for their prospects in an increasingly competitive global market.[18] In this narrative, the British started to take note of foreign refugees at the century's close, as the mass immigration of Eastern European Jews to Britain began. The resulting 1905 Aliens Act marks the beginning of public and state interest in foreigners, and the anti-Semitic and xenophobic distinction between persecuted foreigners and run-of-the-mill immigrants.

These negative accounts, however, cannot help us to understand how relief for foreign refugees became a humanitarian norm subject to formalization in law. As political scientist Aristide Zolberg suggested in 1989, modern refuge developed as would be hosts identified and categorized individuals as refugees.[19] Scholars in refugee studies have offered important histories of this process in the twentieth century.[20] Yet an equivalent account for the nineteenth century does not exist, and the thin understanding of the earlier period shows in the brief "pre-histories" scholars offer of the twentieth century.[21]

Britannia's Embrace seeks to provide an account of the missing nineteenth-century history of refuge and to suggest points of continuity with the twentieth and twenty-first centuries. There is some indication of this alternate account of the nineteenth century in the literature already. As early as 1969, historian Norbert Gossman demonstrated how Chartist financial support for refugees' causes was directed to needy refugees and their families. Bernard Porter, while emphasizing British ambivalence to refugees in their midst, references the scores of refugee relief societies organized in the wake of refugee crises during this period. Historians of Chartism and of radical London have importantly noted the influence of foreign revolutionaries in metropolitan life. More recently, Laura Tabili questioned whether the provinces were as insular as once believed. Her study of foreigners in South Shields demonstrates the extent to which European migrants, many of whom were likely refugees, were integrated into town life in the nineteenth century. This helps to explain the degree to which radical leaders in the region reached out to Polish and Hungarian refugees in the 1850s in the name of the working classes of the region.[22]

The present study draws on these hints in the existing literature and shares their goal of better understanding Britons' complex responses to political upheaval overseas. Yet its analysis goes beyond a history of Britain in an age of revolution and situates the culture and politics of British refuge in histories of human rights and of liberal humanitarianism in the age of empire. Within this second literature, scholars have been considering for some time the relationship between British imperial power, philanthropy, and the nature of British trusteeship on a global scale. As Alan Lester and Robert Skinner have recently highlighted, "humanitarianism was always an engagement in the *politics* of empire and nation."[23] Histories of human rights tend to constitute a separate line of scholarship, focused almost exclusively on attempts to define and codify human rights in the period after World War II.[24] *Britannia's Embrace* aims to bring scholarship on the codification of rights, humanitarian activism, and Britain in the world together. It highlights the sometimes triumphant and often fraught relationship between national and imperial interests, popular moral commitments, and their institutionalization in law.

To tell this story about the evolution of the refugee as a humanitarian category, the chapters that follow are divided into two sections. Part I examines the rise of a liberal, imperial framework for refuge between 1790 and 1860. Chapter One offers a new "pre-history" of modern refuge in British responses to the Huguenot Diaspora and, subsequently, to the victims of the French Revolution's Reign of Terror of the 1790s. Refuge for this latter group was critical in transforming the confessional understanding of refuge. Whereas the Huguenots had been sheltered as fellow Protestants, the French émigrés were all

Catholic, welcomed by Britons despite the fact that Catholic emancipation in Britain remained decades away. Unlikely though it was, this changing rationale for refuge gave the humanitarian category a new, potentially universalist cast. Studied together, both cases establish the connection between refuge and British national identity and highlight the link contemporaries made between refuge and the security of the British state. Chapters Two through Five describe the turn to refuge in the context of the post-Napoleonic world, the appeal of refuge to activists of different political stripes, and the development of an increasingly standardized repertoire for organizing refuge relief that emerged alongside this new humanitarian norm. Flush with the apparent triumphs of reform at home and throughout the Empire in the 1830s, activists highlighted the ongoing evils of illiberal rule in foreign states. The act of providing refuge was a barometer of British difference on this score, and its importance was recognized by Britons across the political spectrum, from the conservative establishment to the radical fringes.

Part II examines attempts to formalize British refuge for persecuted foreigners in the last third of the nineteenth century. The first legal safeguards for refugees in the 1870 Extradition Act and in the 1905 Aliens Act were triumphs for humanitarian norms: in a way never since paralleled in national or international law, they encoded refuge as a right available to those who fit the refugee category. It is a testament to the strength of British liberal humanitarianism that care for these particular people in need became a nation's pride and attained the status of foreigners' right. But these triumphs were short lived, and British refuge's dependence on seemingly abundant resources led to its decline as a popular political act.

In the twentieth century, the violence of total war, population transfer, and decolonization created refugee movements of unprecedented scale. Yet the international refugee regime of the interwar and post-World War II eras did not emerge from a nineteenth-century void. There are important historical continuities in the difficulties inherent in giving practical effect to this once British, now global, imperative to care for the persecuted foreigner. The Conclusion examines the ongoing legacies of the tension between humanitarian movements and the codification of human rights, the ramifications of which continue to be deeply relevant. Nineteenth-century debates over the category of refuge bequeathed to the twentieth and twenty-first centuries the moral possibilities and conundrums that remain so familiar to the "refugee question" and to the quest for human rights in a globalized world.

PART I

The Rise of Liberal Refuge

ONE

Catholic Émigrés and the Protestant Nation

In the fall of 1792, reports varied wildly on the number of French priests and laypersons who sought shelter in Britain in the wake of increasing violence across France. The *St. James's Chronicle* reported forty thousand.[1] Throngs of disheveled travelers hit the southern coast of England each day, hundreds a day in some locations. Samuel Romilly observed in London on September 15, "It is impossible . . . to walk a hundred yards in any public street here in the middle of the day without meeting two or three French priests" who had been forced to flee France after refusing to sign the revolutionary Civil Constitution of the Clergy.[2]

The British public had, by and large, welcomed the liberal constitutional phase of the French Revolution. Most derided early émigrés as cowards who had hastily abandoned their king and country. With the radicalization of the revolution in 1792, however, the situation became dire and English observers grew more sympathetic. Addressing her arguments to the ladies of Great Britain in November of 1793, novelist Frances Burney promoted a national subscription for the relief of the victims of the French Revolution who had fled to Great Britain. Burney announced that aid to these refugees was a national duty: "While to the individual we talk of alms and plead distress, sickness, infirmity; to the community we may be bolder, juster, firmer, and talk of duties." As a nation "so flourishing and happy," Burney rhapsodized, how could British people "see cast upon our coast virtue we scarcely thought mortal, sufferers whose story we could not read without tears, martyrs that reminded us of other days—and let them perish?"[3] Burney's address was hyperbolic. But the sentiments she expressed were shared. Hannah More, Edmund Burke, and others argued that helping these Catholic refugees was the highest level of patriotism. The response was vast. An untold number of British subjects from towns across the southern coast assisted these weary travelers. Local taverns and manor houses became temporary housing. British Catholics, Anglican ministers, and private individuals of all classes came to the aid of the French refugee clergy and laity.

The idea that protecting persecuted foreigners was a national duty was not an innovation of the 1790s. French Protestants—the Huguenots—had received a similar welcome in the prior century. But for Protestant Britain to welcome Catholics as refugees was novel, even revolutionary. In seeking relief for these French men, women, and children—all Catholics—British philanthropists attempted to set aside a deep-seated national phobia of Catholicism in general and French Catholicism in particular. From the Reformation through the eighteenth century, refuge for foreigners had been conceived of as shelter for the Huguenots as well as other continental Protestants from Catholic rulers' persecution. The nation's duty to provide for these particular foreigners followed from concerns for the well-being of the state. French influence had threatened the English (and later the British) state. In the seventeenth century, Louis XIV worked assiduously to promote Stuart Catholicism on the English throne, a threat defeated but not eliminated entirely in the wake of the 1688 Glorious Revolution. Through the end of the eighteenth century, France's connections to Scotland and especially to Ireland continued to endanger British imperial control. While religious confession waxed as the raison d'état, popular anxieties for the integrity of the Protestant nation remained high.[4]

This chapter examines early versions of British concern for persecuted foreigners. It focuses on this expansion of the refugee category from its original application—to persecuted Protestants alone—to include French Catholics. This shift reflected an uneasy mixture of Burney's style of abstract humanitarianism and a more Burkean concern for the security of the state. The expansion of the refugee category bespoke a more ecumenical society in which elite philanthropists increasingly undertook projects to relieve others more distantly connected to themselves. Yet the logic of state security remained remarkably consistent across this early period of British refuge. In the seventeenth century, the threat was confessional; at the end of the eighteenth century, it was political and ideological, epitomized—as Edmund Burke decried—by the chaos of the French Revolution.

The Protestant Refuge

The Huguenots who fled Louis XIV's France joined enclaves of their coreligionists already in England. These communities consisted primarily of Huguenots who fled France at the time of the 1572 St. Bartholomew's Day Massacre, as well as Dutch Walloons who had fled the violence of the Wars of Religion on the Continent.[5] When the Huguenots arrived in England in the mid-seventeenth century, they received succor in the bosom of these continental Protestant churches. The French churches in England became unequal to the task, however, as Louis's dragoons became increasingly relentless in their policing of the Huguenots, sending hundreds of thousands overseas in the 1670s and 1680s.[6]

Though persecuted Protestants had sought refuge in England before, the word *refugee* only entered the English language in the wake of Louis XIV's persecution of Protestants in Catholic France. English hosts self-consciously contemplated what refuge for the Huguenots would mean, the neologism itself reflecting the attention paid to the refugee question among officials and the elite. Providing Huguenots with financial support during the Stuart Restoration was a way for English Protestants to cast their country as the bastion of the Protestant Diaspora at a moment when the religious loyalties of the English state were again in grave doubt. The English Civil Wars and Cromwell's Commonwealth had demonstrated the perils of sectarian strife. Following the fall of Cromwell's short-lived Puritan Commonwealth, the embattled Anglican establishment sought to reimpose religious conformity. The Huguenots were Calvinists and therefore Nonconformists. Nevertheless, their cause reframed the existential battle as one between a united Protestantism and a nefarious Catholicism in a way that could obscure the divisions between Anglicans and dissenters in English civic life. By 1680, this concern about dissent became secondary to a reemerging concern about the Crown's religious loyalties. Charles II, who had restored the monarchical line in 1660, was Protestant. Charles's brother James, the likely heir, was not. Long suspected of papal tendencies, he married the Catholic Mary of Modena in 1673. Capitalizing on popular fears that there was a "popish plot" to kill Charles in favor of James, the nascent Whig party attempted to block James's ascension to the throne with an exclusion bill. After a protracted crisis from 1678 to 1681, they failed to exclude James from the throne. The conflict, however, brought anti-Catholicism to a boil by the time of James's coronation in 1685. In that same year, France's Louis XIV revoked the Edict of Nantes and, with it, the few protections the Huguenots still enjoyed.

Philanthropic concerns about the welfare of Huguenot refugees in these decades also served as Protestant propaganda against Catholicism. In turn, any government equivocation on the refugee question fed English Protestants' worry about the Crown's loyalty to the Anglican Church. Charles II and later James II were trapped. On the one hand, they faced an urgent need to demonstrate good faith to the public and Parliament. On the other, both of them—James in particular—wrestled with their relationship with Louis XIV. Louis was not only a powerful ally who had provided for the Stuart family in their exile and continued to subsidize their courts in England, but he was also their cousin. The mother of the English kings, the openly Catholic Henrietta Maria, was Louis's aunt.

Charles II and his supporters understood this symbolic importance of the Huguenots and other continental Protestants to contemporary politics. The Huguenot plight had become a cause célèbre for Anglican bishops across the country, many of them becoming important benefactors when the French Protestant community could no longer support their growing numbers. Charles could hardly ignore his bishops' concern, especially against the backdrop of the debate over the exclusion bill. To deflect attention from questions concerning his successor, Charles played up his role as defender of global Protestantism. He added continental Protestants to the civil lists, making them eligible for financial assistance from the English Government.

Charles and his supporters also folded relief to foreign Protestants into the pursuit of English trade dominance. The English needed every advantage in their commercial wars with the Dutch, then the world's preeminent merchants. Loyalist papers highlighted the benefits the Huguenots could offer the English if enlisted in the nation's economic and military competition.[7] The King's supporters provided evidence for their claims. Previous settlements of French Protestants had contributed to English trades. Officials hoped these new arrivals—Huguenot weavers, especially—would do the same. After the Great Fire of London and a devastating plague in the mid-1660s, the Committee of Trade had made the same recommendation. According to the committee, the Huguenots would help to rebuild the city, encourage domestic industry, and promote national self-reliance.[8]

In 1681, Charles II issued what would be the first of four national briefs—calls for charitable assistance—on behalf of the newly arrived

Huguenot refugees. This first brief called for a two-year campaign to raise funds across the nation. Anglican bishops, with the help of the lord mayor of London, collected the funds raised at the parish level. For example, Henry Compton, the bishop of London, donated generously to the Huguenot funds himself and issued a circular letter to his dioceses urging generosity. The brief was a success, amassing almost £13,000 in the first two years from individuals and parishes across England.[9]

The Restoration Government and Anglican hierarchy combined forces with the French Protestant churches to distribute the proceeds of the national campaign. Compton and the archbishop of Canterbury, along with the lord mayor, distributed the funds to the most influential of the French Protestant churches, the Savoy and the Reformed Church of Threadneedle Street, both in London. Over the course of the next two decades these concerned parties developed into a three-part association directing the distribution of relief funds. The organization was made up of Crown-appointed commissioners, including members of the Anglican hierarchy and the lord mayor, an English contingent of prominent notables, and a group of French refugees (the latter two groups were nominated by the Crown-appointed commissioners). Together, they doled out relief, guarded against misappropriation of funds, and carefully vetted aid recipients. The relief flowed from these committees to Huguenot communities across England.[10]

The Crown was thus able to broker something of a détente with Huguenot supporters and with the Protestant public more generally. After Charles's death, however, this détente ended. Within months of James II's coronation in 1685, Louis XIV revoked the Edict of Nantes. By the end of the year, approximately 13,500 Huguenots were receiving assistance in London alone. Another two thousand received relief from concerned Englishmen and women at other port cities.[11] The new crisis depleted relief funds rapidly. The Huguenots needed practical support from the Crown once again, and the English Protestant public was paying anxious attention to how their Catholic monarch would respond.

James II continued to provide financial assistance to Protestants on the Continent as had his brother Charles. He hesitated over assistance to the Huguenots in England, however, and the need to act on the refugee question weighed heavily on his new government. James sought to appease both Louis XIV, his cousin and coreligionist, and Parliament.[12] He acknowledged his dislike of the refugees to Louis's ambassadors. There were political risks to an unreserved welcome for the Huguenots. As far as James's supporters were concerned, providing refuge could easily bring political opponents into his realm, bolstering a disaffected Nonconformist population and exacerbating relations with France to boot. At the same time, failing to help the Huguenots would confirm James's Protestant subjects' worst fears about the new king's confessional loyalties.

The Anglican establishment and popular pamphleteers were quick to denounce James's seeming ambivalence to Protestant persecution. James's opponents had argued that Catholic monarchs' persecution of Protestants abroad was a harbinger of things to come in England itself.[13] With James on the throne, Protestant pamphleteers scrutinized his relationship with the French king for evidence of treachery to official Protestantism. Some commentators openly compared Louis's and James's designs on Protestant liberties. One asserted: "If [James II] can prevail in these things to overturn the Civil Government, the Liberty of the Protestant Profession, and of Conscience in all forms, . . . he may as easily destroy it as the French king has abolished the irrevocable Edicts, Treaties or Laws of his Kingdom." After all, those had been "confirmed by his [Louis's] oath, which were as good security to those Protestants as any Magna Charta [*sic*] that our king may make for us."[14]

James II could not ignore the increasing public outcry, and he opened a subscription for Huguenot relief. The briefs of 1685 and 1686, which would not be closed until after the Glorious Revolution, raised a staggering £63,713 by 1689.[15] Relief organizers, however, would limit the proceeds of James's briefs to the relief of new refugees—those who fled France after the revocation of the Edict of Nantes. The move aimed at making the most of limited funds while placating domestic Protestant opinion. Nevertheless, James took the conservative step of requiring that churches distributing aid conform to Anglican liturgy.[16]

This condition on relief unleashed a furious response that united the refugees with members of the Established Church and Protestant dissenters alike. Many Huguenot churches complied with James's demand and adopted at least a veneer of Anglicanism. But they complained bitterly, and a cry of foul play rose from the wider public as well. James's demand fanned popular worries that the religious persecution faced by Protestants in France was also in the works at home. Though James II ultimately reached out to the Huguenots, he was unable to win the trust of the Protestant public. His attempts to enable Catholics to participate in civic life had elicited such fear that he could do little to redeem himself in the eyes of Parliament or the

Anglican elite by the summer of 1688. Indeed, some of James's opponents thought he was helping the Huguenots too much and that the Huguenots were really a Papist fifth column that would aid James in undermining English Protestantism.[17]

Future Huguenot historians would go so far as to claim for their ancestors a central role in bringing about the Glorious Revolution. This is an exaggeration, although Huguenots did march in William of Orange's triumphant armies. Some four or five hundred Huguenots left their shelter in Switzerland in 1688 to join in the battle, accompanying William to England and then on to Ireland.[18] Their pilgrimage from Switzerland to England helped to cement England as the center par excellence of thriving Protestant life.

Refuge under William and Mary reflected this Huguenot service to the new government. Their joint monarchy issued the fourth and last in the series of national briefs on behalf of French Protestants. Once more, the sums collected were respectable. At under £12,000, though, they were inadequate for the refugees' needs.[19] In response, the new monarchs provided for the Huguenots from the royal purse. Mary, and then William after Mary's death, provided them with a substantial yearly fund. This "royal bounty," as it would be called, was used to help the Huguenot community flourish in their new home. In addition to assisting new arrivals and those who fell on hard times, the fund supported Huguenot orphans and the sick as well as Huguenot churches and schools.[20] Parliament cut the bounty in half in the 1720s, a move that reflected the diminishing existential need to support fellow Protestants as much as the easing of persecution on the Continent. Nevertheless, traces of this origin of the modern refugee category persisted. At the end of the eighteenth century, the paradigmatic refugee remained the persecuted foreign Protestant, and British refuge was still celebrated as a means of bolstering the Protestant nation in the face of Catholic foes. French Huguenots remained on the civil lists for more than a century to come. The last pensioner, several generations removed from the original refugees, received governmental funds as late as the 1870s.

Émigrés, Jacobins, and Levelers, 1792–1793

In the early 1790s, reactions to the plight of French émigrés shattered the confessional model of refuge. The core network of refugee supporters who brought the campaign for refugee relief to national attention formed in the immediate wake of the September Massacres

(September 2–6, 1792) in which more than a thousand prisoners of the revolutionaries were summarily killed, many of them priests who had refused to take the oath of the Civil Constitution of the Clergy. Having made a harrowing escape from France, émigré Jean François de la Marche, bishop of St. Pol de Léon began to spearhead fundraising in London that month. British political and social notables flocked to the cause, but it soon became clear that this local munificence was inadequate to the task before them. They needed a national spokesperson and turned to Edmund Burke, whose early public and private interest in the refugees made him a logical figurehead. Within days, Burke issued a public letter to Home Secretary Henry Dundas on the situation in France, particularly the plight of the refugee clergy.[21] Decrying revolutionary violence, he urged the government to assist the refugees. Members of the bishop of St. Pol de Léon's circle followed Burke's letter with the announcement of a public meeting to be held on September 20. By the time of the meeting, sixty-one notables had committed their time and money to the project of orchestrating refugee relief at the national level. They included Lord Sheffield, the Duke of Portland, the Marquis of Buckingham, and evangelical abolitionist William Wilberforce. The list also contained fourteen members of Parliament; a dozen ministers in the Anglican Church; two physicians from the Royal College of Medicine; the lord mayor of London; and several aldermen, prominent bankers, lawyers, and judges.[22]

The resulting Committee for the Relief of the French Refugee Clergy soon became the preeminent voluntary society for the relief of French refugees thanks to the connections of the bishop of St. Pol de Léon and the committee's leader, John Eardley Wilmot (figure 1.1), who had earlier managed compensation claims for the American Loyalists after the War of Independence. A parallel committee for assistance to lay refugees, organized by Sir George Thomas (Member of Parliament [MP] for Arundel), boasted an overlapping membership. Initially, the two groups competed for donors, and several leading philanthropists decried what they saw as a disproportionate concern for the plight of the clergy.[23] Nevertheless, independent local relief committees began to collaborate with the Wilmot Committee, and new local affiliates looked to it for direction. At the end of 1793, the Wilmot Committee merged with the society for the laity. By its close, the Wilmot Committee could boast of backing by the Crown, Parliament, and private philanthropists, the latter ranging from the cultural elite to rural clergymen to the evangelical Clapham Sect.

1.1 · Benjamin West (1738–1820), *John Eardley Wilmot*, oil on canvas, 1812. Credit: Courtesy of The Yale Center for British Art, Paul Mellon Collection, New Haven, Connecticut.

As a group, elites came to identify with refugees and support the Wilmot Committee not on a confessional basis, nor necessarily on a political basis, but on a humanitarian one. This reflected a broader belief that traditional alms provision was inadequate for those at the margins of society. From the middle of the eighteenth century, the elite in the metropolis and beyond opened new charitable endeavors. Philanthropically minded elites sought to champion "social utility" and "an Inclination to promote Publick Good."[24] In London, the elite established foundling and Magdalene hospitals, which took in orphans and unwed mothers. Methodists, too, broadened their charitable activities beyond their own parishioners. Their Strangers' Friend Societies, formed in the 1780s and 1790s, broke new ground by expressly disqualifying fellow Methodists from relief and disavowing proselytism as one of their goals.[25] In the émigrés, these elites found a new set of charitable subjects whose tales of innocence and persecution at the hands of the Revolution endeared them to their benefactors. British philanthropic language was replete with praise for the "worthy and hospitable men" who had been driven from home; they were "unfortunate people" and had every claim upon English "generosity," "hospitality," and the "greatest kindness" and "attention."[26]

Though their language of support was remarkably consistent, the paths by which individual philanthropists came to advocate on behalf of these Catholic refugees were diverse. To some, identification sympathy for the émigré was based on social or family connections. The Earl of Malmesbury (grandfather of the Conservative foreign secretary of the 1850s) received the infant child of a friend who was still trapped in France. Families like those of Lord Dillon and Lord Southwell welcomed foreign relatives.[27] Novelist Frances Burney had a personal connection to the émigrés as well. Through her married sister, Susanna, Burney became acquainted with the refugees living at Juniper Hall, a residence in the Surrey countryside. Living with her sister's family in neighboring Mickleham in 1792–1793, she moved in the same social circle as many of the giants of the emigration, including Germaine de Staël and Charles-Maurice de Talleyrand. For others, compassion was a matter of proximity. Lord Sheffield at Lewes and Lord Dorchester and Sir Thomas Gage at Hastings welcomed the refugees to their estates because so many hundreds arrived on their doorsteps or in their jurisdictions.[28] The same was true for writer Charlotte Smith, whose republicanism did not stop her from opening her home near the southern coast to those who disembarked nearby. Fluent in French, she entertained groups of émigrés in her lodgings for upwards of three months in the winter of 1792–1793. Close contact with the émigrés eventually dampened her enthusiasm for the Revolution. In 1793, she went public in her defense of the exiles in a lengthy poem, "The Emigrants," which deplored the "name/Of Freedom misapplied" and the "lawless Anarchy" of the French Terror. "Unhappy Men," she wrote, "Whate'er your errors, I lament your fate."[29]

These sometimes unlikely activists became personally invested in the émigrés' fates. In April 1793, forty-two-year-old Burney married French army general Alexandre d'Arblay. Charlotte Smith's daughter also fell in love with and married a French aristocrat, Alexandre Marc-Constant de Foville.[30] Close emotional ties did not always translate into familial connections in a strict sense. Edmund Burke, the outspoken critic of the French Revolution from its earliest days, eagerly anticipated the arrival of the French bishops. He had been wrongly convinced (as it would turn out) that they shared his vision for a post-revolutionary France whose stability lay in tradition. Although he would not live to see the end of the exile, Burke made care of refugees one of his major lifeworks, even establishing a school for émigré children. Opened just after the death of his own son, the school became a solace to Burke.[31] He gave admissions priority to those who had lost a father at the hands of the revolutionaries and spoke of the school as "supplying the void in my own family, and being my only comfort."[32]

Compassion for Catholics in distress was at base about seeing beyond nationality to a shared humanity. Yet this shared humanity had in some instances a decided political cast, as it would in the case of Burke's eagerness to draw the French bishops to his dinner table. For Burney too, the politics of her new acquaintances mattered. She was insistent about the liberal sympathies of her friends and distinguished her friends from aristocratic exiles. In a letter to her father, Burney defended Mme. de Staël on the grounds that that although her house had "become the centre of revolutionists before the 10th of August, it was so only for the constitutionalists, who, at that period, were not only members of the then established government, but the decided friends of the king." By contrast, "the aristocrats were then already banished, or wanderers from fear, or concealed and silent from cowardice; and the Jacobins—I need not, after what I have already related, mention how utterly abhorrent to her must have been that fiend-like set."[33]

Despite political differences, it was a shared humanitarianism that would shape the terms in which philanthropists came together to sell the project of refuge to the nation. Notable philanthropists consolidated local support into a campaign that effectively called for national assistance for Catholic men, women, and children. That it would succeed in selling the project of Catholic refuge to the Protestant nation was unlikely at the outset, however. The national campaign, which brought together a broad array of refugee supporters, had to work assiduously to maintain public and official support for these foreigners. To do so, they would have to chart an uneasy course between raising awareness of humanitarian need, mitigating lingering anti-Catholic sentiment, and safeguarding a British nation that to many—including members of the campaign itself—seemed increasingly under political threat from radicals within and outside British borders.

Émigrés and relief workers feared that religious animosity would ultimately trump humanitarian concern among the public at large. This was, after all, the society that had erupted in seven days of violent riots upon news that the government planned to ease restrictions on Catholics. The 1780 Gordon Riots, so named for the man who led the parliamentary campaign against the measure, became an image of chaos that dominated public memory for decades thereafter.[34] Popular anti-Catholicism remained fierce in the 1790s. In the fall of 1792, the same moment at which French priests were reaching British shores, the *Hampshire Chronicle* reprinted an advertisement for a new edition of John Foxe's sixteenth-century *Book of Martyrs* that memorialized instances of Catholic brutality. The advertisement asserted that there was no better book to demonstrate the "absolute duty of every duty of every true protestant to enquire [into] the destructive principles of that abominable persuasion [Catholicism]."[35] Nor did all refugee supporters overlook the refugees' Catholicism. Evangelical moralist Hannah More claimed that "it is not for their popery but their poverty which we solicit." Yet she noted too that "it may be the first step towards their conversion, if we show them the purity of our religion, by the beneficence of our actions."[36]

As far as the government was concerned, the greater difficulty was not religion but whether these "foreigners in distress" were republican Jacobins in disguise. At home, critics of the government had been agitating for parliamentary reform since the middle of the century. Radical Whigs argued for the extension of the vote, drawing on the language of tradition and constitutionalism in their critique of "old corruption." The French Revolution, particularly after its republican turn in 1791, brought to the fore the rhetoric of natural rights.[37] While radical Whigs worked for reform within the existing system, Thomas Paine and English republicans sought to free governance from past precedents.[38] Inspired by Paine and the French Revolution, secret societies like the London Corresponding Society, founded in 1792, sought to spread the new political gospel and to link reform efforts throughout the British Isles. Demonstrations such as one planned for London on November 25, 1792, copied Jacobin iconography, centering in this case on a tree of liberty.[39] Interest in extending the French Revolution cut two ways; the republican National Assembly in France promised "fraternity and assistance to all people who wish to recover their liberty."[40] In Ireland, this promise of assistance against British overlords took practical form. Inspired by French republicanism as well as their anti-British antipathy, members of the newly founded United Irishmen (1791) moved their society increasingly toward French radicalism and, ultimately, an alliance with the French against the British.[41]

For the nation that was moving toward war with revolutionary France, these vulnerabilities caused acute anxiety (figure 1.2). At the Home Office, Dundas pointedly warned local officials about the threat of radicalism from foreign Jacobins. While he was still uncertain of what powers the government could use to expel unwanted foreigners,

1.2 · Isaac Cruikshank (1756?–1811?), *A Peace Offering to the Genius of Liberty and Equality: Dedicated to Those Lovers of French Freedom Who Would Thus Debase Their Country.* Print. London, February 10, 1794, by S. W. Fores. Credit: Courtesy of The Lewis Walpole Library, Yale University. The text above the figure of the French Republic as Medusa reads "Rapine," "Murder," "Famine," "Atheism." The offerings of British "Lovers of French Freedom" include the "Bible," "House of Lords," "the Bank," "India House," and assorted royal and church regalia.

he instructed the civil powers—including county militias—to remain vigilant in quelling disturbances to the peace. As a result, the Pitt Ministry greatly expanded its own powers to counter a threat that would turn out to be exaggerated. By the end of November 1792, institutions of government and finance in London were secured to the hilt. With "the royal proclamation of December 1, the militias of ten counties were called out [although] embodying the militia in this way was illegal," as historian Clive Emsley notes, "except in cases of invasion or insurrection."[42] In Ireland, the Irish colonial government matched their campaign against individual radicals with an attempt to diminish popular support for the still-isolated United Irishmen. The Catholic Relief Act of 1793 aimed to appease Catholics by granting them a limited right to vote—though not the right to sit in the Irish parliament. This ultimately backfired, fueling radical demands for nothing short of complete civic emancipation.[43]

As at the time of the Huguenot flight, these concerns for the security of the state made the refugees' cause a politically exigent one. The administration turned to the French émigrés and a continental model of surveillance to scrutinize the character of the thousands landing on their shores. British officials and the émigrés, the Comité Français in particular, joined in common cause. This alliance brought together members of the Home and Foreign Offices and was "effectively a royalist government in exile," as historian Elizabeth Sparrow has called it.[44] The Comité's connections gave British officials access to intelligence from across Europe and a means of infiltrating gatherings of suspected Jacobins at home.

It was French refugee policeman, Claude Antoine Rey, who helped pen Britain's first bill giving the state authority to vet French refugees and expel those deemed too dangerous to remain.[45] Thanks to émigré assistance, the bill, introduced to Parliament in December 1792, satisfied Dundas's early September inquiries on royal and governmental authorities regarding aliens. While the sovereign could expel individual foreigners from British soil by royal prerogative, Parliament—in times as extraordinary as this—could in passing this bill extend that right into policy. The aliens bill (which became 33 Geo. III, c. 4) would provide the legal teeth for an immense intelligence-gathering effort and give the power of restricting and monitoring movement to local and national authorities.[46] A foreigner's registration in Britain was only short term and had to be renewed with the local justice of the peace every six months. Those suspected of evading the law—whether they were aware of its clauses or not—were subject to arrest and detainment. Upon conviction, they were to be ordered to leave the realm. Some were barred re-entry for life, depending on the severity of their infraction. British subjects would be held accountable too. Shipmasters and landlords were to declare whether they harbored foreigners. Those who did not comply would be subjected to fines that, for shipmasters, could entail forfeiture of their vessel.[47]

The administration's fear of Jacobin influence cast a long shadow over the organization of refugee relief on a national scale. But rather than stymie assistance to the French émigrés, the 1792 Aliens Act gave free rein to officials and philanthropists to help those whom they deemed truly in need. The parliamentary argument on behalf of foreign refugees was, in origin, a rhetorical strategy used by proponents of the Aliens Act. In the House of Commons, Tory MP George Hardinge insisted that the legislation would "pull off" the Jacobins' "mask" and "would catch the emissary or the leveler." The bill would check levelers' urges to "make proselytes here." It also promised to identify a different type of foreigner: the "case of the emigrant and refugee from the desolations and cruelties of Paris." This emigrant, as opposed to the first, "was our friend; he had come to us for shelter and mercy; he had come to us, appealing to a government by law, against a government by the sword." Refugees, even when national security demanded greater regulation, "merited our sympathy," sympathy of which Hardinge hoped the British had given "unequivocal proofs."[48] Hardinge's emphasis on differentiating between foreigners originated at the heights of the Pitt administration. Officials took great pains to ensure that prominent émigrés were not unduly treated as agents of revolution and that those who were not dangerous did not suffer molestation by either British authorities or their new neighbors. Dundas vouched for certain émigrés, writing to local authorities on their behalf, and more generally hoped to check public suspicion where it was unwarranted.[49]

Not surprisingly, Edmund Burke supported the Aliens Act. For Burke, the ministry's insistence on the severity of the situation brought to Parliament the sense of an urgent threat to British security he had long tried to impart and underscored his ideological affinity with those who fled the French Terror. In a December 1792 debate over the bill, Burke redoubled his efforts to convey his fears. He brandished a dagger on the Commons floor, dramatizing the danger now in their midst.

Not all in Parliament were impressed by Burke's melodramatic flourish or by Dundas's insistence that an aliens act was necessary. Those who doubted the extent of the French Jacobin threat were vocal, as the stakes were high. The bill would strip foreigners of their liberties, which, up to that point, had been the same as those of British subjects. Among these liberties were those held dear to the English heart, including habeas corpus and the right to a trial by a jury of one's peers.[50] Yet, as vocal as the opposition was, they never quarreled with the framers' interest in protecting innocent refugees. Though opponents worried about the undue powers the government would accrue in passing the bill, they were careful to espouse their sympathy for the victims of the increasingly violent revolutionary government in France. Radical Whig Charles James Fox decried the bill, claiming that it served only to perpetuate a "spirit of defence." Fox feared that English liberties were under siege and that such scare tactics endangered the chances for political reform. He argued that the government ignored the people's rationality and loyalty to the constitution that made them averse to revolution in the first place.[51] While his objections to the bill were deeply steeped in the politics of the radical opposition, Fox adopted Hardinge's emphasis on the plight of the refugees caught in the midst of the turmoil, turning their situation into a rationale for defeating the legislation. In point of fact, Fox had little love for these particular refugees. The refugees' monarchical politics hardly squared with his radical platform. Yet he admitted that he would "by no means say anything harsh of the emigrants." While he would not support the refugees' return to power in France, "he sympathized with and compassionated the sufferings and misfortunes of those men." For Fox, as for Charlotte Smith, refuge was altogether separate from domestic politics.[52]

The opposition failed to halt the administration's reactionary policy, but the debate cemented an emerging consensus that the French émigrés deserved the government's compassion. Despite their entrenched differences, proponents and opponents of the bill nonetheless agreed upon one thing: the government and the nation bore responsibility for the victims of overseas violence. Their joint interest in the fate of the French Catholic refugees—foreigners they would carefully distinguish from dangerous Jacobins—would pave the way for the national campaign to assist the victims of the French Terror in their midst.

Selling Refuge to the Nation

The Wilmot Committee came to prominence because it effectively married the philanthropic compassion of the elite from across the political spectrum with the Tory Pitt ministry's concern for national security. The logic of charity provision and the concern with screening out Jacobins required that relief providers distinguish deserving refugees from undeserving foreigners. Both further required supporters to remind the nation of the righteousness of the refugees even as public sympathy for their plight waned. In this, the organizational structure of émigré relief was not so different from the national relief campaign launched on behalf of the French Huguenots more than a century before. Yet, in their efforts to assist Catholics, the Wilmot Committee-led national campaign helped to explode the confessional logic for refuge. Effective as it was in uniting the public behind these refugees, their organizational structure exposed the deep tensions in the moral and political underpinnings of refuge present during debates over the aliens bill. The Wilmot Committee and its affiliates deployed the rhetoric of political and humanitarian sympathy, but their method of offering relief increasingly took cues from the Pitt administration's concern for the security of the state as popular support diminished.

Whereas William III nominally rewarded the Huguenots for their service to the Protestant cause, the Wilmot Committee would do so much more explicitly. Members of the French laity received relief only if they served the British state.

The embryonic national campaign gained initial momentum thanks to the efforts of the social and cultural elite; the campaign owed its national prominence, however, to support lent by the Crown. In the spring of 1792, the committee concentrated on raising national awareness and sympathy for their cause. They petitioned the king for his support on April 5, the same day that Hannah More took the message public in an address to the ladies of Great Britain. The committee issued a public advertisement seven days later. They now had the satisfaction to report that "his majesty has been graciously pleased to approve of a collection being made for the relief of these unfortunate persons in the different parishes of this kingdom." The committee had already sent letters to the archbishops and bishops requesting their voluntary participation in a national collection of relief funds, but George III made this request a royal command.[53]

On April 17, 1793, George III wrote a letter to the archbishop of Canterbury indicating that he had been much affected by the representations of the committee for the Relief of the French Clergy. Two days before a national fast day appointed for meditation on the current war with France, the king brought his concern for the welfare of these refugees to the archbishop. The king asked his archbishop to see that "the ministers in each parish do effectually excite their parishioners to a liberal contribution" for the French émigré clergy. To this end, the king requested that all bishops appoint particular Sundays in the coming weeks on which each minister would be made to sermonize on the cause within their parish. A collection would be made at the time of the sermon. Moreover, churchwardens and overseers of the poor were to continue the work into the week, visiting parishioners at their own dwellings to collect subscriptions. The king closed his letter with praise of John Wilmot, to whom the funds would be entrusted. Wilmot and the committee were precisely the "trusty" and "well beloved" individuals whom the nation could deputize for this philanthropic work.[54]

The national campaign also created new refugee supporters who sought to raise funds for the Wilmot Committee themselves. Like the champions of the Huguenots' cause, these philanthropists knew they needed to overcome domestic political divisions, to say nothing of lingering xenophobia, in their attempt to win supporters. Whereas the king's letter openly discussed national security and opposition to the French Revolution, much of the propaganda that ensued tended to take a more moralistic tack. Authors such as Charlotte Smith turned their pens to the refugees' cause, describing their plight and reasons for exile. Some authors, among them Burke, Burney, and Hannah More, also donated the proceeds from publication to the committee. From April 1793 on, so too did many of the ministers who had been asked to preach on the subject. Often "published by request," these sermons were elaborated and printed for a national audience. Again, these sermons did double duty as propaganda and fundraisers. These leading Protestant voices were particularly important in helping to convince doubters that refuge to foreign Catholics was not only safe but also a national and a Christian duty.

Each author explicitly took on the anomaly of an appeal to Protestants on behalf of Catholic clergy. Hannah More appears to have been alone in her mention of conversion. Most commentators worked assiduously to overcome religious rivalry. Burney compared murdered French priests to martyred English Protestants of the sixteenth and seventeenth centuries. She exclaimed: "Let the same generous feeling which would call to life those murdered martyrs [the clergy slain in France], protect their yet existing brethren, and save them, at every risk, and by every exertion, from an end as painful and more lingering; as unnatural, though less violent."[55] The Reverend Samuel Horsley, who addressed Parliament and his own Welsh parishioners on the subject, argued that though "they may differ from us upon certain points of doctrine, discipline, and external rites, [persecuted French priests] are nevertheless our brethren—members of Christ—children of God." They were even "more endeared to us by the example they exhibit of patient suffering for conscience's sake, than estranged by what we deem their errors and corruptions."[56] Reverend William Williams invoked the parable of the Good Samaritan against those who might argue that the refugee clergy "were strangers," "Catholics and Priests," or that "there were more useful charities." Williams's pamphlet argued that withholding charity from strangers ran counter to biblical injunction.[57] That the stranger in question was Catholic was a preposterous objection in "an enlightened age." Their Catholicism was beside the point: "for their faith and worship they must answer unto God."[58]

From the end of April through June and beyond, parishes and the broader reading public throughout the realm heard sermons on the plight of the French refugees. Not all districts responded liberally.

The onset of war with France brought staggering inflation. Economic hardship made it difficult to collect funds not intended for local relief. Especially in rural areas, returns to the committee often included "an apologetic note from the incumbent." One "Huntingdonshire vicar was 'rather ashamed' that, 'after preaching and exhortation' he had so little to send." Others were less apologetic about their parsimony.[59] Radicals were more likely to see the refugee relief efforts as evidence of government's opposition to reform at home and support for the vestiges of the *ancien régime*. As early as September 12, 1792, one Dr. William Maxwell decried efforts to relieve French loyalist refugees. To a crowd assembled outside his London house, he proposed instead a "subscription to support the people of France against their enemies." Although the police quickly dispersed the crowd, Maxwell's address appeared in the *Times*, and radicals issued a similar call in Manchester in the wake of a rumor that some French priests had absconded with French girls.[60]

Overall, the national campaign proved a great success. The critical response to the spate of published sermons was generally favorable. The *Monthly Review*'s coverage of these publications treated them as a subsection in their reviews of religious literature. The journal's editors assumed that there ought to be no reason that the French clergy—Catholics in Britain—should not be provided with refuge. Their reviews of particular sermons opined on the authors' skill at drawing their parishes (and their broader readership) into the national campaign. The editors, for instance, asserted that Reverend George Henry Glasse's "sermon [to his Middlesex parish] is an excellent specimen of that kind of popular harangue which powerfully addresses the passions without suffering itself to transgress the limits prescribed to a correct and classical taste."[61] Their purpose was to praise, not to find fault in, Glasse's sentiment.

Their national campaign of 1793 raised £38,000 in six months. By October 1793, Wilmot's committee received an additional £38,275.[62] Despite its initial success, the committee could not continue its work over time without support from the state. The Treasury contributed from the beginning, but its assistance became all the more critical in subsequent years, as had been the case for Huguenot relief efforts under William and Mary. Together, national and private funds enabled the Wilmot Committee to continue distributing funds to an ever-growing list of recipients. Members of the Wilmot Committee distributed funds to approximately 4,000 French clergy and an increasing number of laypersons: 400 in the fall of 1793 to upwards of 650 in ensuing years. Refugees who did not return to France when Napoleon signed the Concordat with the Pope in 1801 remained on support. Treasury Department affiliates would carry out the work of relief through 1815, when the restoration of the French monarchy made refuge unnecessary.[63]

Assistance from the state had strings attached, even from the start. Dependent on the Treasury for a goodly portion of its revenue, the relief organization's pastoral care reflected the rationales by which its members had sold the project of refuge to the nation. Members of the committee understood their responsibility to ensure that the recipients of national relief were worthy of their care and, more particularly, that they rendered service to the British state at a time of heightened anxiety.

Although vetting French émigrés was not an easy task, it was one for which the committee was particularly well prepared thanks to its experiences with the American War for Independence. The provision of relief to French exiles drew upon the precedent of compensation for Loyalists who had fled the United States in the wake of the American war. Wilmot himself had headed the committee processing Loyalist claims and that work had only just come to a close. The Committee for American Loyalists operated under the assumption that all Loyalists were entitled to some assistance. Although the American war had divided public opinion in Britain, even Fox could not deny that those who had stood by the Crown deserved recompense.[64] Yet not all Loyalists were entitled to equal claims. In 1782, the committee applied a compensation scale set by Parliament. This ranked Loyalists on a finely calibrated scale of sacrifice and devotion to the British cause.[65] The roughly thirteen hundred who fell in the first three classes were considered the most deserving. Those included individuals who had served Great Britain, those who had borne arms, and the "zealous and uniform loyalists." Those who at first had served the Americans—potential opportunists whose allegiances had wavered—were in class six. Persons in more meritorious categories received higher compensation.[66]

With the French émigrés, the British state rewarded those who might assist in the fight against the revolutionary threat. The second Wilmot Committee needed to be even more cautious about questionable loyalties than had the first, however, since the revolution on the Continent was a live threat. Heeding the concerns of the Pitt administration, the committee set out to determine who among the émigrés was deserving of their care. The main work of the committee thus consisted of reviewing testimonials by and about applicants so as to weed out frauds, on the one hand, and Jacobins, on the other.

For priests, the process was relatively straightforward. The bishop knew, or had connections, to most of them already. The committee published an announcement in the London and provincial newspapers requesting that "every French ecclesiastick resident in any part of the country who is in want of relief should address himself by letter to the bishop of St. Pol de Léon." The letter should specify "his late situation in France and the diocese to which he belonged . . . [T]he Bishop having made enquiry sufficient to satisfy him that the ecclesiastick so applying is a proper object of this subscription will be authorized by the committee to administer the necessary relief."[67]

For the laity, the vetting process was much more difficult. The Pitt administration relied heavily upon the Wilmot Committee to examine the loyalty of these aliens. The committee was charged with encouraging commitment in the form of military service. Whether the bishop and the committee were enthusiastic about this demand is not clear, though it was not without precedent. Although the Huguenots had not been required to serve the state in this way, the most honored American Loyalists during the American Revolution were those who bore arms, and there were contemporary examples as well. The British government provided succor for their allies in the fight against France. For example, when the Toulonese could no longer fend off the French army in 1794, the British government acknowledged their effort by providing financial assistance for Toulonese soldiers in their subsequent exile. These men received Treasury pensions through the 1820s.[68]

Nevertheless, there was a good deal of tension over the enlistment bill of 1794 that would enable the state to bring the French émigrés into the British military in their war against France and, soon, against the United Irishmen. For Pitt's administration, the enlistment of all able-bodied French men would solve the problem of an army that was then strapped for manpower. William of Orange had relied on and rewarded the Huguenots who helped to solidify his rule in Britain and on the battlefields in Ireland. The British government at the end of the eighteenth century did the same. Despite this precedent, there was opposition to the bill from across the political spectrum. Refuge, opponents argued, was about compassion and sympathy; pressure to serve the state missed this point. Whigs Philip Francis and Major Thomas Maitland and Tory Lord Mulgrave expressed grave concern over what they termed the "doctrine of retaliation."

Although "replete with horror, bloodshed, and devastation," the doctrine of retaliation was "a principle founded on the law and custom of nations, that any French subject taken in arms against his country, was liable to be hanged."[69] Whig Samuel Whitbread lamented that the refugees would have little choice in the matter: "With the alien bill in one hand, and bounty money in the other, there could exist no doubt of [British] success" in essentially press-ganging refugees into the army. Such soldiers "were sent with a halter about their necks into the field, a situation in which no soldier in the pay of Great Britain should be placed."[70]

Despite major misgivings, the enlistment bill passed into law. As the Wilmot Committee's funds dwindled, there seemed to be little choice in the matter for committee members who had been less convinced that British army required the émigrés' service. During the winter of 1793–1794, the committee had continued to enjoy national enthusiasm for their cause. After their initial charitable returns had been spent, members adopted Frances Burney's scheme of establishing a network of women to raise money from personal acquaintances.[71] By later in the winter, however, the committee relied increasingly on a Treasury grant of £7,880 per month to sustain the 4,008 clergy and 375 laypersons who needed relief.[72] At the height of Robespierre's Reign of Terror in France, those numbers continued to swell while allotted Treasury funds stayed the same. By January 1794, the 375 lay refugees had grown to 450. By the end of the Terror in July 1794, the committee had 629 members of the French laity in its charge and a further 362 awaiting relief.[73] Though Robespierre's executions had ceased, the situation of the émigrés under British auspices deteriorated markedly in the months that followed.

Domestic prices continued to soar and a series of bad harvests further reduced the supply of wheat. As the government tried to restructure relief for its own indigent population, charitable fatigue diminished the sense of national duty that Burney and others had successfully cultivated early in the decade. The challenge of providing long-term refugee support foreshadowed difficulties that activists would encounter in decades to come. Economic fatigue gave vent to fears of a "Catholic menace." What had been a marginal concern over the presence of so many French priests thus became a more dominant anxiety. Officials and elite philanthropists had been somewhat prepared for this conflation of economic and cultural anxieties. The cultural backlash was somewhat easier to manage. Members of the Wilmot Committee urged supporters to ignore public commentary, as Burke had argued from the first; securing the lives of the refugees was more important than pandering to popular prejudice. As concerns grew, philanthropists tried to remove the source of the concern from the public eye, isolating the Catholic clergy by housing 680 priests at the ramshackle King's House at Winchester. Even the most ardent of supporters were thus careful to police the impact of their charges on Protestant society.

The economics of public fatigue were more difficult to manage. Despite initial public enthusiasm for their cause, once-proud French lay émigrés had been reduced to such penury that some were quite literally starving to death. This discovery prompted a response from private philanthropists associated with the Wilmot Committee. Lord and Lady Sheffield organized a visiting society to locate and care for the sick.[74] Under the direction of the Marchioness of Buckingham, the priests made tapestries for the well-heeled classes, and proceeds from their sale were returned to their community. So too were proceeds on embroideries, artificial flowers, and the like sold by other British ladies.[75] While these efforts helped, they alone could not resolve what was already a desperate situation.

Bowing to government demands for additional service to the state, the committee published a call to "all who are capable of bearing arms," insisting "that there is no pretence or excuse for any one of that description who should chuse to continue here dependent on the support of the committee."[76] Able-bodied émigrés formed their own regiments and were deployed to the front lines in the summer of 1795.

The results were disastrous and made a mockery of British claims to be affording dignity in refuge. Just as Whigs Samuel Whitbread and Major Thomas Maitland had feared, the French showed no mercy to captured refugee recruits. Exiles caught taking up arms against their own country were subjected to summary execution. Three thousand six hundred émigrés landed with the British Army in France. Of these, only half escaped the ill-judged battle at Quiberon on June 27, 1795. The 1,000 refugee soldiers who survived the battle fell into Republican hands; of these, 690 were sentenced to death at court martial.[77] Back in Britain, no émigré family was left untouched. A Madame D'Aiguille "went mad upon hearing of the death of her husband . . . [She] left her two children and wandered through the London streets calling his name." A neighbor took in her children as she "was never heard of again."[78] Many families lost their sole breadwinner. Even among the more fortunate 1,800 conscripts who survived, many were maimed and unable to work.

The devastation changed elite attitudes toward refuge. In the wake of Quiberon, the administration's once-dominant idea that there was a quid pro quo between service to the state and relief began to fade. At the time of the Enlistment Bill debate in Parliament, only a minority of speakers had argued that refugees deserved a life of dignity and repose. After Quiberon and into nineteenth century, refuge would be a matter of dignity owed to foreigners as the result of their persecution overseas, not solely a recompense for military—or material—support to their host country.

Unfortunately, this changing rationale for relief did not revive public enthusiasm for supporting the French émigrés. Unable to solicit additional public support for the starving émigrés, the committee was forced to retrench several times, despite the efforts of elite philanthropists to stave off this eventuality. The committee had lowered the stipends given to the clergy as early as 1794. Publicly, at least, these pious souls gladly promised they would cut back on their meat consumption. In 1795–1796, the committee was forced to limit the number of recipients who qualified for aid. Wilmot and the bishop of St. Pol de Léon effected this last reduction. Thereafter, they required that ecclesiastical applicants for relief submit a further certificate verifying that they had indeed been forced to flee France. In 1796, the committee simply disallowed new additions to the list altogether. To be considered a deserving "refugee" under this new regime, a French man or woman had to have no other means of support. No able-bodied man would be considered for relief. Moreover, no man or woman who fled France prior to 1791 would be considered for the lists.[79]

Napoleon's 1801 Concordat with the Pope resolved the committee's financial bind. The clergy were permitted to return to France, and the Wilmot Committee could focus on the needs of the remaining laity. Residual worries about Catholic influence seem to have receded quickly thereafter. While panicky Protestants continued to petition the government about the Catholics in their midst into the 1810s, neither the committee nor the government took heed.

A More "Catholic Humanity"

The public consensus around what Frances Burney had called a national duty to care for the Catholic émigrés did not last long. Nor did it altogether dispel British suspicions of foreign Catholics. The national campaign, however, fundamentally and irrevocably altered the confessional logic that had governed outreach to foreign refugees since the time of the Huguenot diaspora. A Wordsworth poem published in 1822 captured the changing ethos of the time. Wordsworth echoed Charlotte Smith's 1793 "The Emigrants" and took pride in the nation's treatment of the French in the 1790s:

> . . . More welcome to no land
> The fugitives than to the British strand,
> Where priest and layman with the vigilance
> Of true compassion greet them. Creed and test
> Vanish before the unreserved embrace
> Of catholic humanity . . .[80]

Playing on the word *catholic,* Wordsworth emphasized a more universalized religious-cum-national concern for these displaced foreigners, one that sidelined the raisons d'état for refugee relief so central to the in-gathering of foreign Protestants and the French émigrés alike.

Appeals to "catholic humanity" did not mean that refuge would become apolitical. On the contrary, the first modern Aliens Act established an important precedent granting officials the ability to define who presented a danger to the state and who could be called a "deserving refugee." In this, the legacies of the Huguenot and émigré relief continued to shape British refuge after the 1815 Congress of Vienna. Even as the immediate danger of agents provacateurs receded, national concern for foreign refugees continued to stem from a sense of political, as well as moral, affinity with would-be refugees. While a purely strategic relationship with continental refugees had died on the battlefield of Quiberon in 1795, the older military logic of refuge did not disappear until the late 1820s. British military allies such as the Toulonese and the Corsicans from French Wars of the 1790s remained on Treasury pensions. More recent allies were likewise added to the Treasury lists. By the 1820s, however, pensions for military service were receding as a predominant model of refugee relief. Rather than the security of the state, it would be an emergent liberal ideology that brought together Tories, Whigs, and even radicals in advocating refuge for foreign defenders of this new political faith.

TWO

The Consolation of Refuge

The arm which was uplifted to destroy liberty was paralyzed and European liberty was saved. But, Englishmen, your work is not yet complete—the cause of universal liberty is not yet triumphant.

— THOMAS ATTWOOD, 1832

Napoleon's final defeat in 1815 removed an existential threat to Britain's security and centralized dictatorship on the European continent. Nevertheless, as Thomas Attwood, a radical MP for Birmingham, noted, representative governance was far from being a fait accompli in Europe, or even in Britain.[1] Attwood was addressing a public increasingly interested in extending the rule of freedom at home and overseas. What began in the late eighteenth century in abolitionists' quest to end the slave trade became a romantic drive to rescue the peoples of oppressed nations. To many, the power to effect change overseas seemed within Britain's grasp. Britain's commercial networks and her navy crisscrossed the globe, and she occupied a preeminent position at the conference table in Vienna following Napoleon's defeat. Buoyed by the admission of the middle classes into the political nation in 1832, activists increasingly turned their attentions overseas, intent on reshaping the world in their own idealized self-image.

Britain's relative democracy and free press promoted public interest in foreign policy in the modern era.[2] The new, broad-based activism of political liberals had decided limitations, however. Public enthusiasm for intervention often mattered little in the face of official reluctance to intervene. Intervention, the Foreign Office feared, might threaten the international balance of power.[3]

Concerns about the propriety of intruding in another nation's affairs suffused public debates and cabinet correspondence alike. The most committed interventionists aside, commentators tended to admit that direct involvement overseas was not necessarily pragmatic, desirable, or effective. The cause of "universal liberty" which Thomas Attwood espoused on behalf of oppressed Poles did not square with official governmental policy nor with the visions of the more moderate liberal friends of Poland. Conservatives, still concerned for the political hierarchy at home, were even more unenthusiastic about universal liberty.

Nevertheless, this tension over the desirability of intervention was productive. In the space between action and inaction emerged an increasingly robust and standardized humanitarian practice: the practice of providing relief for persecuted foreigners. As this chapter argues, British activists of various political hues turned to the relief of foreign refugees as a means of supporting their cause célèbre at times when furthering that cause through intervention seemed improbable. Expanding efforts to help persecuted foreigners led to two consequences. First, a broadly defined liberal vision produced a more expansive refuge than at the time of the Huguenot diaspora or the French Revolution. The refugees entitled to British assistance now included victims of foreign revolutions as well as revolutionaries themselves, foreign slaves, and persecuted minorities more generally. Far from the mentality of a nation under ideological siege, this new political ethos projected an expansionist vision of Britain's power onto the international stage and made the earlier logic of refuge as a component of national defense increasingly obsolete.

Ironically, the admission that there were limits on the exercise of British power ushered in refuge as a triumphant, nation-defining act of liberal justice and humanitarianism. The traditional Tory and Whig elite embraced the cause of refugee relief, as did many radicals in the name of the British working classes. The power of this resulting humanitarian practice could not be ignored. As Foreign Secretary Malmesbury lamented in the 1850s, for a politician to ignore the fate of refugees was to play with political fire.

The Twin Legacies of the Congress of Vienna

A contemporary observer of Britain in the late eighteenth century might have thought it implausible that anti-revolutionary Britain would in a few decades become a major supporter of revolutionary causes from the Continent. The same observer might just as reasonably have been skeptical that the country with a monopoly on the slave trade would become concerned with the fate not only of its own slaves but also those of other nations. Early campaigns against the international slave trade and continental despotism stemmed from an increasingly proud public appeal for the defense of basic liberties. However, while both movements resulted in a turn to refuge for persecuted foreigners, their paths were distinct, shaped in each case by the diplomatic possibilities of the post-Napoleonic international scene.

Abolitionism was the older of the two campaigns, rooted in more than a century of antislavery sentiment that by the late eighteenth century had become a cohesive movement. After a series of near misses in the 1790s, the abolitionist lobby succeeded in abolishing the British slave trade in an 1807 act of Parliament. It was another thirty years before the British abolished slavery in their West Indian colonies, and it took a century for the practice to die out in the British Empire at large. Despite the piecemeal nature of abolition and emancipation, a grassroots antislavery lobby emerged rapidly. Whereas commentators in the nineteenth century celebrated abolition as providential, historians writing in the Marxist tradition dismissed the role of morality in favor of economic causes, explaining that the British turned from slavery only when it was clear that the practice was becoming less financially viable. While long uncomfortable with the Whiggish story of national destiny, historians now credit morals. The abolitionist campaign required people to rethink the morality of their relationships with others—even at a distance—at a time of rapid social change. Some felt a religious impulse to join the abolitionist cause (figure 2.1). Slavery stymied the spread of Christianity among the enslaved and promoted sin among the free. For others, the point was to encourage individuals to act on fellow-feeling in a society increasingly detached from the moorings of religion. This was the moral work of the Enlightenment and the philosophical work of Adam Smith's 1759 *Theory of Moral Sentiments*. In this ideological constellation, Smith's 1776 *Wealth of Nations* mattered too. New capital networks required moralization. While Caribbean planters fretted about losing out to their competitors when slavery ended, new liberal theorists sought to remake the plantation economy for a laissez-faire world in which laborers as well as goods circulated freely. Abolitionists' pioneering campaign techniques introduced antislavery into homes across the country through sugar boycotts and commemorative Wedgewood china. Together with petitioning campaigns, tactics like these encouraged hundreds of thousands of ordinary Britons—men and women—to connect their actions and those of their nation with the suffering of distant others.[4]

In the eighteenth century, this concern for distant slaves was predominantly about slaves in British colonies. Foreign slaves nevertheless

2.1 · Print from *Poems on the Abolition of the Slave Trade*. R. Bowyer, London, 1809. © The British Library Board, 83.k.10, opposite 19.

sought refuge on British soil throughout this period. Prior to the 1810s, governmental treatment of slaves who crossed international borders mirrored the treatment of non-African refugees. As with the Huguenots, fugitive slaves from Catholic colonies were likely to be welcomed if they claimed Protestant sympathies. The same geopolitics of confession that had made heroes of the French Protestants permitted French slaves to win favor with claims that they had been forced to adopt Catholicism. Refuge in the British Caribbean seems to have depended on the slaves' subsequent conversion to Protestantism.[5] The government drew a similar parallel to non-Africans at the time of the

American War for Independence and the War of 1812. As the government rewarded white Loyalists who served the British cause during the Revolution, so too did it seek to entice slaves to support the British cause in both wars. For this service, Black Loyalists were to receive their liberty at the war's close. Black Loyalists later found themselves in New Brunswick and in the British Caribbean. Black Loyalists from the Revolution also helped to found Sierra Leone in the 1790s. The West African colony was to be a refuge for them and later for Africans liberated from the slave trade.

In the early nineteenth century, refuge as a quid pro quo for service to the British state diminished in the case of Africans at the same time as it did for continental refugees. Activists drew upon an increasingly robust "humanitarian narrative" whose attention to the details of bodily pains "connected the actions of its readers with the suffering of its subjects."[6] As powerful as this new narrative was, however, the forms of refuge pioneered on behalf of the Black Loyalists remained of the utmost importance.

The humanitarian narrative associated with abolitionism depended on detailing the realities of slavery and the slave trade; by contrast, the narrative of concern for continental persecution began with romance. The Greece popularized by Lord Byron was not the impoverished region of the contemporary period but the heroic civilization of the classical age in whose history lay the foundations of Christianity and democracy (figure 2.2). Italy's landscape offered an idealized setting for romantic writers, painters, and tourists.[7] British public opinion enthusiastically endorsed national liberation for both countries. Poland, requiring saving from its three-way partition among Russia, Austria, and Prussia, had a similar allure for the British. Begun in 1832, the Literary Association of the Society of Friends of Poland (LASFP) was quite literally a product of the romantic imagination. Whereas members of the London Greek Committee adopted Byron as the figurehead for their cause, the LASFP was the inspiration of Scottish romantic poet Thomas Campbell. Poland had a certain historical glamor of its own, having boasted greater democracy during the early modern period than Britain. The LASFP hoped to help Poland win back independence and rejoin the path to liberal governance.

The British public viewed the Congress of Vienna (figure 2.3) as an opportunity for their victorious nation to promote liberalism on the Continent while bringing abolitionism to the international stage. Abolition was the easier case to make at the Congress. For one thing, it did not seem immediately threatening to continental rulers

2.2. Luigi Trecourt. *The Poet, Lord George Byron (1788–1824) on the Greek Coastline*. Oil on canvas. 19th Century. © Lessing Archive/British Library Board

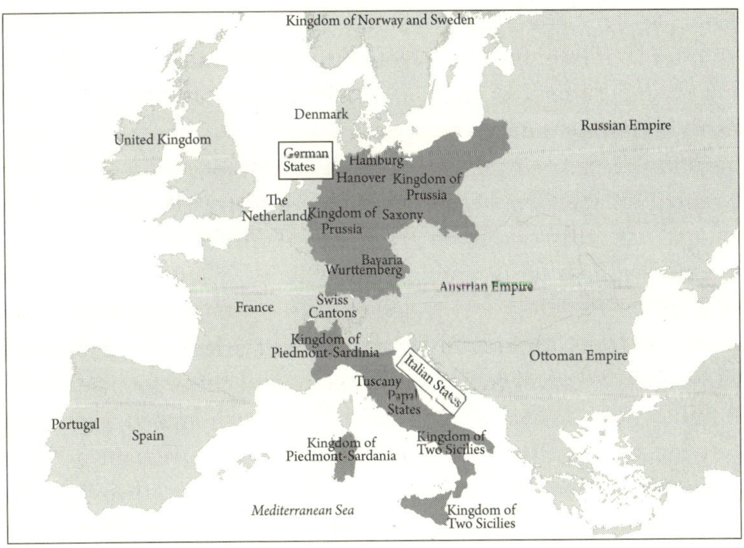

2.3 · Map of Europe at the close of the Congress of Vienna in 1815. Credit: Mathieu Duvall, Imaging and Computing Center, Bates College, Lewiston, Maine. Map based on Lucius Hudson Holt and Alexander Wheeler Chilton, *A Brief History of Europe from 1789–1815, with Maps by William Kelly Harrison* (New York: Macmillan, 1919), 346–347.

concerned mainly with reasserting their authority over would-be radicals at home. Whereas Britain's role on the Continent was contentious, the nation had a well-established role policing the slave trade. The government had assumed responsibility for policing the illegal British slave trade. Since 1807, the Royal Navy helped to enforce the ban on the British slave trade, steering vessels into ports where the Admiralty had established courts to adjudicate cases of suspected trafficking under the British flag. At the Congress of Vienna, the Tory Viscount Castlereagh extended these imperial efforts against the slave trade to the international arena.

The quest for agreements outlawing the slave trade united abolitionist activists with officials who, increasingly attentive to abolitionist sentiment at home, also saw in these treaties the chance to solidify Britain's global power. Even before Napoleon's final defeat, the Foreign Office and abolitionists began to pressure European powers for commitments to end the slave trade. Abolitionist giants William Wilberforce and Thomas Clarkson traveled to Prussia and Russia to obtain support. Castlereagh threatened Spain with the discontinuation of subsidies.[8] These efforts were not immediately successful.[9] They did, however, set the stage for the signing of bilateral treaties in the decades that followed, uniting abolitionists, the public, and the government behind the cause and establishing the tenor for later international negotiations. The British did not have to wait long. Between 1815 and 1843, the Foreign Office brokered agreements outlawing the slave trade with the major Atlantic slave-trading powers: Spain, Portugal, the Netherlands, France, and Brazil after it gained independence from Portugal. These treaties, while imperfect and unevenly adhered to, restricted the trade in human chattel and set deadlines for its elimination under the flags of each of these nations.

Whereas the Congress of Vienna set the stage for bans on the international slave trade it ended in an unequivocal defeat for continental liberalism. The forces of tradition and order triumphed, repressing agitation for constitutional reforms and national sovereignty. While individual statesmen sought to quell dissent within their borders, the Great Powers banded together to suppress revolutionary uprisings, collaboration that would later have disastrous consequences for Polish, Hungarian, and Italian nationalists especially. The British were not spared from the conservative reaction of the 1810s. The Tory government that witnessed the repression of freedoms on the Continent after the Congress simultaneously imposed reactionary measures at home to stymie parliamentary reform meetings and suppress agitation and open rebellion across the Empire.

For a growing cadre of liberal elites interested in foreign affairs, Britain's acquiescence to continental absolutism was tantamount to betrayal. Many of those defeated during the restoration of absolutist regimes across Europe had been erstwhile allies in the Napoleonic Wars. In the titanic struggle with Napoleon, even the Tory government of Britain had supported liberal constitutional parties as viable alternatives to Napoleon-appointed rulers or absolute monarchs. After Napoleon's defeat, however, liberal revolutionaries on the Continent threatened the balance of power across Europe and infringed on British commercial interests. In the Iberian Peninsula, for example, the Tory government spent more than a decade vacillating between neutrality and cautious support for alternatives to Bourbon rule in Europe and in Spanish America. This path became particularly difficult in the face of the European Holy Alliance's attempt to cement conservative rule. In Eastern Europe, the government backed the Ottoman Empire as a critical buffer against Russian territorial ambitions in the region. The British elite supported nationalism within the Ottoman Empire, but official endorsement would have threatened the delicate post-Vienna balance of power.

By the 1820s, acceptance of this status quo seemed increasingly untenable to many British elites. As the repressive measures of the 1810s and early 1820s began to give way to reforms at home, British liberals began to seek reengagement in continental affairs. They considered renewed alliances with the ideologically appealing continental liberals and liberal nationalists. As two members of the Polish Exiles' Friend Society argued in 1833, the British could not escape the consequences of further inaction in the affairs of the Continent: "the Northern barbarians [Austria, Prussia and Russia], who are aiming at the extinction of European liberty and civilization" could "in the end over-run France, and overwhelm England itself—the island-citadel of Constitutional freedom" if left unchecked.[10] British liberals thus began to go beyond romantic sympathy for oppressed peoples to active campaigning on their behalf, quite literally making the foreign struggle synonymous with their fate at home (figure 2.4).

In the two decades following the Congress of Vienna, supporters of Greek and Polish nationalism ardently lobbied for British public and official support. Britain, they argued, was morally obligated to come to the aid of these oppressed foreigners. As a member of LASFP wrote in 1834:

2.4 · Thomas Halliday, artist. Silver Medal of the Alliance between Great Britain and Poland. 1833. Credit: Yale University Art Gallery

> The Poles are without a country, because the nations of Europe have, from first to last, failed greatly in their duty towards them. . . . The civilization of Europe has poorly acquitted itself, in allowing the gallant inhabitants of that country to maintain their desperate struggle without assistance.[11]

For British philhellenes, the geopolitical calculus justifying supporting the Ottoman Empire paled in comparison with the moral imperative to oppose Ottoman repression. Drawing on contemporaries' assumptions about "oriental despotism," British supporters highlighted how greatly Greek Christians suffered under Muslim Ottoman rule, conveniently forgetting that Greek revolutionaries were responsible for the slaughter of Muslims as well. Following news of the massacre of Greeks at Chios in April 1822, a committee of prominent liberal and radical Whigs formed to lobby the public and government on the Greeks' behalf. With Byron as honorary leader (in absentia) the committee's cause had dramatic appeal. The London Greek Committee's membership network swelled to include a veritable who's who of liberal theorists and radical and mainstream Whigs, including David Ricardo, John Cam Hobhouse, John Russell, and Jeremy Bentham. Less famous committee members John

Bowring and Thomas Campbell, a poet, would soon establish LASFP. The committee held protest meetings at London's Guildhall, inviting Foreign Office secretary George Canning and using the high profile affair to raise subscriptions for a Greek loan. The purportedly more liberal Tory George Canning resisted the London Greek lobby's campaign for a long time. But when the diplomatic situation changed in 1826, Canning threw his weight behind the Greeks' cause. While the committee celebrated this change, Canning was still pursuing a diplomatic logic; he now wagered that support for Greece offered Britain a stronger position in the region that would check the Russian agenda in the eastern Mediterranean.[12]

LASFP had a membership whose social profile closely matched the London Greek Committee, but it tended to pursue a more cautious political approach. Its discussions more closely echoed diplomats' worry about the balance of power. Hoping to avoid antagonizing Russia in particular, LASFP members adopted a self-consciously limited platform for overseas intervention. Their journal *Polonia* issued appeals for an end to oppression in terms that were, in comparison to the Greek committee's approach, relatively weak. They reprinted Polish pleas for protection and humane treatment from the Austrian government. While Austria occupied parts of Poland, an "address of the States of Galicia to the Emperor of Austria" appealed for Austrian protection of Poles who had been forced to flee the Russian provinces after czarist offers of amnesty proved hollow.[13] If their calls for Austrian toleration were somewhat weak, members of LASFP hesitated even more to denounce Russia herself. As they highlighted in the pages of their journal, members were wary of accusing all Russians of oppressing the Poles and also worried that condemning the Russian government wholesale would be counterproductive.[14]

Rather than advocate immediate military intervention or revolution, members of the LASFP sought instead to lay the groundwork for later diplomatic work. Like members of the London Greek Committee, they insisted that their nationalist cause ought to be a broad-based British effort. They committed to educating themselves thoroughly on affairs relating to the founding of an independent Poland in order to prepare for the moment when they could call for more direct intervention. The LASFP thus built a reservoir of legal and cultural information on the situation, enabling its members to envision how, in a future free Poland, law and constitution would govern the relations between individual citizens and the government. This approach bore obvious parallels to the way British subjects were then re-envisioning their government. Together with the London Greek Committee, however, the LASFP was pioneering a new sort of public activism in the realm of foreign affairs. As the editors of *Polonia* commented in 1832,

> With the extension of our own national liberties and franchises it is our duty to extend our view over a wider range of human affairs, and to be able to judge for ourselves [. . .] on questions which were hitherto considered to be exclusively the domain of foreign departments, or ministerial and royal congresses.[15]

Through midcentury, continental governments' ongoing attempts to thwart political radicalism and popular nationalism continued to foment political and humanitarian crises, attracting British public interest. While the conservative establishment, still symbolized by Austrian chancellor Prince Klemens von Metternich, clung to its authority, middle-class liberals rallied for free trade, constitutional rule, and a limited franchise. New radical movements increasingly turned to democracy, insisting that only a complete transformation of the relationship between the government and the governed could guarantee the social welfare of the people in the face of rapid economic change. In successive waves, revolution in France inspired unrest across the Continent and set much of its ideological tone. The bourgeois, liberal revolutions of 1830–1831 failed, for the most part (figure 2.5). In 1830, France managed to oust the ultraconservative Charles X in favor of the more trade-friendly Louis Philippe. Belgium won independence from the United Kingdom of the Netherlands. However, even where the middle class managed to carry the day, the workers lost and tension built once more, coming to a head in the late 1840s. After the more socialist-inspired French Revolution of 1848, the continental dominoes fell again in even more rapid succession (figure 2.6). For a few weeks, the more democratic platforms as well as new liberal nationalist regimes seemed to prevail. Yet by 1849, forces of order were once more in charge from east to west.[16]

British reactions to these serial continental crises reflected their diverse ideological persuasions. Conservatives generally deplored the violence wholesale. Liberals and radicals, by contrast, continued to advocate government intervention on behalf of continental nationalists, seeking government support for an independent Poland and a united and independent Italy. They rallied behind the Hungarian cause as well. As in the 1820s, foreign affairs enthusiasts lambasted

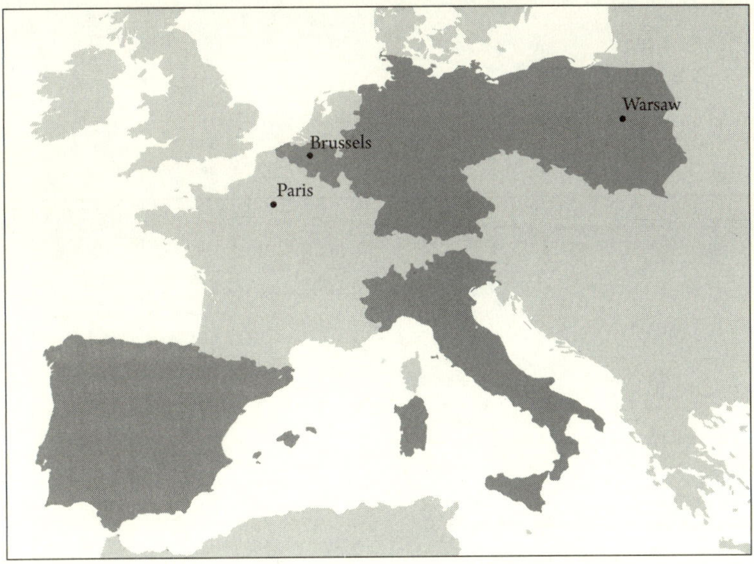

2.5 · Centers of revolutionary unrest in 1830–1831. Credit: Mathieu Duvall, Imaging and Computing Center, Bates College, Lewiston, Maine.

the British government's implicit support for Austrian oppression and derided officials' adherence to the balance of power. Liberals and radicals were less united in their sympathies for continental socialists, however. Anxious about radical agitation closer to home, the mainstream, the liberal public—like conservatives—worried that the banner of democratic reforms could engulf the British Isles in revolution as well. There was some cause for alarm. Chartists admitted that the English of all classes enjoyed relative liberty compared to their European counterparts. Still, undertaking their counterparts' cause was meant to reinvigorate theirs. For a vocal Irish platform within the Chartist movement, this partnership would, Chartists hoped, hone British attention to the plight of Erin as well.[17]

The Turn to Refuge

Refuge as a quid pro quo for service to the British state faded after the battle of Quiberon in 1795 but remained a part of the government's logic through the 1810s. As late as 1828, the Duke of Wellington's Tory administration helped to obtain pensions for Spanish liberals who had fought against Napoleon in the 1810s and were now exiled by the newly restored Bourbon dynasty. Wellington could provide Treasury

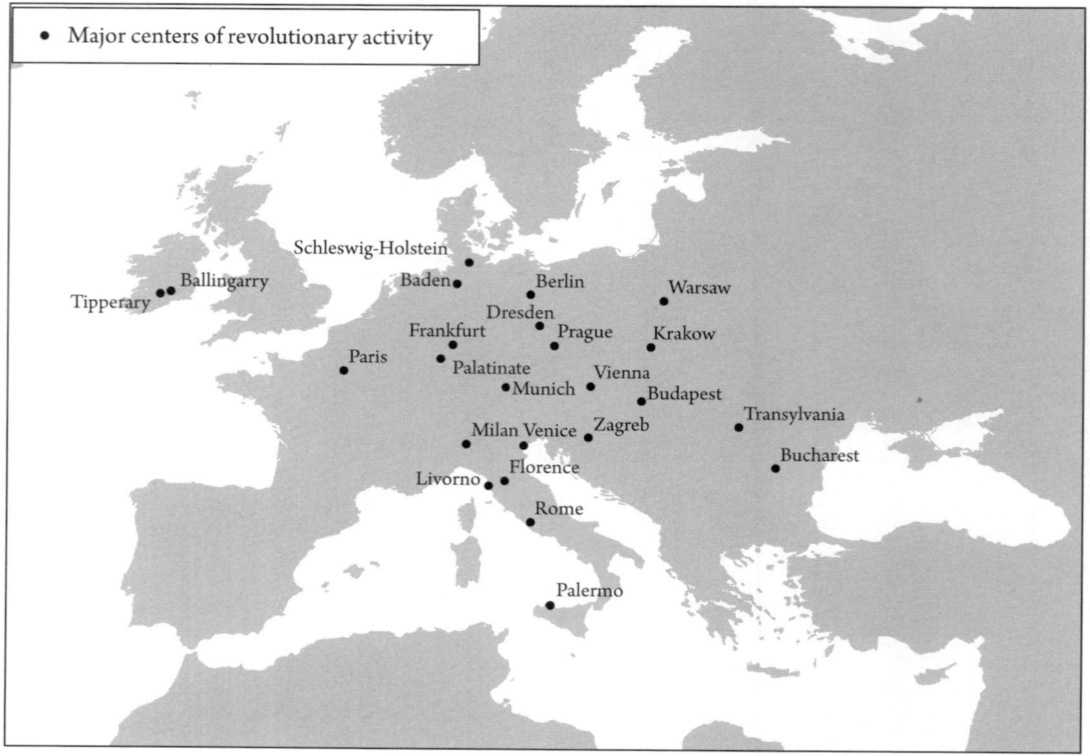

2.6 · Centers of revolutionary unrest in 1848–1851. Credit: Mathieu Duvall, Imaging and Computing Center, Bates College, Lewiston, Maine. Map based on Jonathan Sperber, *The European Revolutions, 1848–1851* (Cambridge: Cambridge University Press, 1994), x–xviii.

assistance to the military exiles of the group. He turned to the public to help civilian exiles who had been forced to flee Spain in the wake of violence following the restoration of the Bourbon monarch as well. His turn to the public was critical in opening up the already-changing ideological rationale for the relief of persecuted foreigners. At the 1828 meeting, John Bowring—famed linguist and advocate of the Greek cause—seconded Wellington's call for relief, noting that refuge ought to extend beyond those who had performed military service. Bowring went further. He argued that the Spanish struggle was not over, that "the seed of liberty had been sown by the British army, and they [the British] were bound to nourish that plant which had been planted, patronized, and encouraged by themselves."[18] For romantic liberals such as Bowring, British responsibility for the spread of freedom had not ended with Napoleon's overthrow. Relief for persecuted foreigners was not about the alliances of the past but shared ideological goals in the present and for the future.

Liberal activists like Bowring would have preferred to see the Bourbons ousted from Spain and constitutional rule adopted. They would have preferred to see Italy and Poland liberated from Austrian, Prussian, and Russian domination as opposed to providing relief for Italian or Polish exiles. So, too, would they have preferred to see the transatlantic slave trade eliminated entirely. Refuge was a consolation prize, an admission—even among the most adamant interventionists—that oppression would not end immediately and that there were limits to British influence on the world stage. Yet those who called for British assistance to persecuted foreigners in the decades following the Congress of Vienna turned refuge into a proud, even nation-defining, act. Campaigns for public assistance to refugees did not follow the older, official logic for refuge. Instead, refuge increasingly reflected the commitments of a self-consciously liberal nation that had shed its earlier sense of embattlement and now offered refuge as a means of promoting liberal freedoms on a global scale. In addition, by the 1830s, refugee campaigns were no longer initiated by government appeals for public charity. Instead, a broad-based, refugee-supporting public began to call on the government to provide assistance. This new approach, remarkably, trumped political divides, becoming a near national consensus. Radicals, the new Liberal Party of the 1850s, and a revamped conservative establishment joined together in celebrating refuge, though their normative visions of governance often remained at odds.

Aware that overseas intervention was difficult, if not impossible, activists in the 1830s began to emphasize how relief for refugees furnished a means of keeping the cause of change alive. This new rationale coincided with the rising number of persecuted foreigners arriving on British soil. The suppression of revolutionary activity in Poland and Italy in 1830–1831 forced patriots to find refuge in supposedly neutral, liberal countries on the Continent. Though there were some Italian refugees in England, most had gone to Switzerland and France. In 1834, however, conditions worsened for these refugees on the Continent. Austria convinced Switzerland to expel these foreigners on the grounds that they were fomenting revolution from exile. Poles and Italians, including Italian nationalist Giuseppe Mazzini, were forced to trek further west. Exiled Poles found shelter in Belgium, France, and Britain. The Italians were less fortunate. Although France had no interest in appeasing Austria, she provided a less than warm welcome to Italian refugees. In 1834, the *Times* reported that Italian refugees had been captured in France, "treated like the most atrocious malefactors, and sent in chains across that extensive country, from Grenoble to Calais, where they were put on board ship, and landed penniless on the British coast!"[19] Within a few years, fear of political dissidence made the July Monarchy less receptive toward refugees more generally.[20]

While the warmth of other nations' welcome to refugees fluctuated with shifting political winds, Britain's relative stability made her the most dependable shelter from continental storms. Britain's lead role in the abolition of slavery also made the Empire a natural destination for people escaping bondage. Responsibility to Africans caught up in the slave trade was the direct result of anti-slave-trade treaties. Banning the trade in the Atlantic world did not, of course, end it immediately. The trade continued illegally, since smuggled slaves could be sold in open and legal colonial markets throughout the Americas (including the British West Indies through 1833). Seeking legal teeth to enforce its international treaties, the British government would make this ongoing trade the subject of diplomatic correspondence and a flurry of bilateral treaties that licensed the Royal Navy to search and seize suspicious vessels and established courts of mixed commission—courts that included judges from both signing powers—to adjudicate cases of suspected trafficking.

From the 1810s to the 1860s, the Royal Navy and the courts policed the illegal slave trade in the Atlantic world. The naval squadron ushered captured vessels into the closest of several port cities with mixed commission courts: Rio de Janeiro, Havana, Freetown (also the seat of the

Admiralty Court in Sierra Leone), and Cape Town. Africans found on slave ships were kept on board the ship during the trial. If the slaver was not condemned under one of the treaties, then the ship's captain was allowed to proceed to his original destination. If the court determined that the vessel was subject to one of the extant treaties outlawing the slave trade, the ship and its cargo were seized and the bounty awarded as a prize to the capturing squadron. In principle, the trade-ban treaties required governments in the jurisdiction where captured vessels were tried to safeguard the Africans on board.[21] If the ship was condemned, captive Africans were to be freed. As the treaty with Portugal read:

> And as to the Slaves [of a condemned vessel], they shall receive from the Mixed Commission a certificate of Emancipation, and shall be delivered over to the Government on whose Territory the Commission which shall have so judged them shall be established, to be employed as Servants or Free Labourers. Each of the two Governments binds itself to guarantee the Liberty of these Individuals as shall be respectively consigned to it.[22]

The new humanitarian law thus required the signing powers to provide refuge for liberated Africans. As the British incurred increasing responsibilities for foreigners in need of refuge, officials turned to the public for assistance once more. The Admiralty and Colonial Office sought assistance from missionaries—the Anglican Church Missionary Society (CMS) in particular—to attend to the pastoral care of Africans liberated from the slave trade.

Escaped foreign slaves, like liberated Africans, found harbor on British soil. Once slavery became illegal in British Canada and in the Caribbean in the 1830s, American refugee slaves sought their freedom by fleeing to British territory when they could. American slaves' flight to British Canada accelerated in the wake of the US Fugitive Slave Act of 1850, which made it illegal to harbor runaway slaves in the free states of the North. Britain's role as enforcer of a network of bilateral treaties outlawing the slave trade gave her further responsibilities to victims of illegal trafficking. The treaties outlawing the slave trade required signing powers to shelter "recaptured" slaves, as they were called, but included no details on how signing powers—especially those whose economies continued to rely on slave labor—were to guarantee the freedom of those liberated from the illegal trade. Wary abolitionists observed that Africans allegedly "liberated" in other countries' jurisdictions often disappeared into the slave population. The same could be said about fugitive slaves in the British Caribbean prior to emancipation in 1838. However, the British had grappled with the question of how to protect slaves needing refuge before. By the 1810s, Sierra Leone had become the default refuge for illegally trafficked Africans. Abolitionists consequently pressed the government to take custody of Africans rescued from captured ships, liberated in the slave hub of Spanish Havana, or emancipated in British colonies. By the end of the 1840s, the British government had assumed responsibility for tens of thousands of liberated Africans.[23]

As the nineteenth century progressed, British soil thus became the preeminent destination for persecuted foreigners, black and white. Advocates of the Polish cause—members of the LASFP in particular—had led the way in turning a concern for the fate of liberty on the Continent into support for refugees in the 1830s. Originally, the LASFP had little to do with the provision of refugee relief; it instead emphasized learning about Polish history in preparation for future independence. There was no discussion of refugees in the group's constitution. Though early issues of its journal *Polonia* discussed the dire plight of exiles, they did so to draw attention to the cause, not to advocate refuge. By 1834, this changed. Henceforward, refugees provided a practical means for the LASFP and its supporters to demonstrate love for the Polish people and support for their nationalist cause. The LASFP called upon "Englishmen of wealth and rank" to "come forward, if you wish to assist the Polish cause." The situation of the society and its would-be donors was unique, argued the LASFP. Activists had the chance to advocate "the spotless cause of Poland" and also "to solace her exiled youths and patriots here, as well as abroad, with such assistance as the very slender means we have to command will permit."[24] As Polish exiles were chased across Europe in search of safe harbor, the LASFP took responsibility for their care.

By the mid-1830s, the LASFP, affiliated societies, and the press worked assiduously to turn what was essentially a consolation prize for more enthusiastic interventionists into a point of national pride. The British media attributed the nation's kinder treatment of refugees to its superiority in humanitarian sentiment and governance. As the *Times* claimed in July 1834, news of secondary persecution on the Continent—this time by allegedly liberal nation states—provoked consternation from the British press. The *Times* was outraged that the French did not allow their Italian "prisoners" any choice about their place of banishment. The newspaper also expressed dismay that the French would use Britain as though it were a French penal colony. Concerned Britons who had supported European revolutions in 1830–1831 became providers of refuge when liberal revolutionaries had nowhere else to turn.[25]

Members of the LASFP argued that Britain's failure to aid these continental exiles would be a national disgrace. They called on the government to assist them in this humanitarian act. Even the bourgeois French king, Louis Philippe, though he had expelled Italian revolutionaries from France, had approved an annual grant for Polish relief, as the LASFP pointed out as early as 1833.[26]

Members of Parliament repeated the LASFP's arguments and loudly expressed sympathy with the exiled patriots, many of whose estates in Poland were being confiscated by the Russian czar. Despite this high-minded rhetoric, parliamentary support turned out to be rather stingy. The Treasury's relief funds had to be renewed each year, and the annual £10,000 sum ultimately granted to refugee Poles was inadequate for their needs. The LASFP thus maintained its campaign for official support, continuing to point out that the Treasury grant paled in comparison to Louis Philippe's pensions, which were worth twelve times as much. At Victoria's coronation, the *Times* celebrated the public's magnanimous donations for Polish relief, but opined that "such an act of bounty [on the part of Parliament] would come with peculiar grace at this time of national rejoicing, and would surely be gratifying to the feelings of the illustrious personage [Victoria] in whose honour our capital is now filled with unusual splendor."[27] In the event, Parliament did not rise to the poetic occasion, merely renewing the parsimonious yearly grant. As a consequence, private involvement in refugee relief would be indispensable.

As it turned out, the Polish exiles were comparatively fortunate, being the only refugee group to receive governmental assistance of this kind. Nevertheless, a growing number of societies followed the LASFP model by adopting a dual commitment to liberal reforms overseas and relief for foreign refugees. Assisting refugees became a concrete way to demonstrate support for liberal reform on a global scale. Among these groups were the Democratic Friends of Poland, the Fund for European Freedom, and the Garibaldi Fund, in addition to existing organizations like the British and Foreign Anti-Slavery Society (BFASS) and missionaries of various denominations that added refugee relief to their charitable repertoire.

The tactic of aiding refugees enjoyed spontaneous success among diverse liberal organizations. But not all concerned activists accepted this practice without question. In the wake of the American Fugitive Slave Act, for instance, most British abolitionist groups turned their attention to the resettlement of the thousands of needy refugees in Canada. The Bristol and Clifton ladies' branch of the BFASS considered this to be insufficiently proactive, however, and confronted the group's national leadership.[28] The ladies of this local branch lamented that there was relatively little being done that was "truly" antislavery. Having applied to the BFASS for instructions, they found the suggestions to be "so vague and unsatisfactory, that with the exception of occasionally contributing to the support of schools and other institutions for the emancipated negroes and free coloured people (which objects, though philanthropic, are not *anti-slavery*)" that they "could find no occupation beyond that of collecting funds." Irked at the BFASS's seeming unwillingness to strike at the root cause of persecution, the Bristol and Clifton Ladies' Anti-Slavery Society seceded from their parent organization. To justify the break, the association's 1851 report declared that no one could

> flatter himself that by subscribing to the Colonization Society . . . or by aiding a "vigilance committee" in the questionable kindness of encouraging slaves to escape . . . or by charity to the freed slaves in Canada . . . he is doing anything to enlighten the conscience of the American people, or rouse the slaveholder to the guilt of his position.[29]

In their future activities, the Bristol women preferred to reach out to the American societies and send funds for more radical antislavery efforts intended to revolutionize American morality itself.

The Clifton and Bristol Ladies' Anti-Slavery Society was an exception, however, and even their representatives had to admit the appropriateness of broad support for refugee slaves. Despite their vitriolic attack on refugee-centered work, the ladies' society admitted that assisting refugees constituted action of at least some worth. The society still reprinted portions of a letter from a Reverend Young on the resettlement of fugitives in Canada, which he pronounced to be the "most effectual means for us in this country to aid in the abolition of slavery."[30]

What is remarkable about the turn to refuge is that, like the abolitionist movement to which many refugee relief workers belonged, it represented individuals from all social and political backgrounds. Historians of the 1790s have highlighted the role of the elite in providing refuge for French émigrés. Historians examining midcentury continental revolutionaries highlight the support of British radicals, many of whom they show to be Nonconformists and atheists.[31] Both perspectives understate the diversity of relief personnel.

British political and cultural elites, critical in the earlier period, remained prominent in the provision of refuge, repeatedly coming to the assistance of continental exiles, American refugee slaves, and liberated Africans. As had been the case during the refugee crisis attending the French Revolution, elite activists' exceptionally wide networks of personal acquaintance often gave them prior familiarity with prominent continental exiles. For example, prior acquaintance made the Marchioness of Landsdown the logical patroness for Hungarian patriot Theresa Pulszky. Mme. Pulszky sought out her friend upon her arrival in London in 1850 and later paid fulsome tribute in her memoirs to her friend's support. Lord Dudley Coutts Stuart, the longest-serving member of the LASFP and the foremost refugee spokesperson in Parliament, was the nephew of Sir Francis Burdett, who had helped to organize a private relief committee for the Spanish exiles in the 1820s. Burdett's daughter Angela was a close friend of none other than Louis Napoleon during his pre-1848 exile in England. As the Baroness Burdett Coutts, she succeeded (and exceeded) her father's and cousin's philanthropic efforts, assisting refugees from slavery, from continental revolutions (both revolutionaries and their victims alike), and from the Ottoman Empire. She continued her charitable activities until her death in 1906.

As in the 1790s, the membership lists of relief organizations show strange political bedfellows making common cause. Stuart was a middle-of-the-road member of the rising Liberal Party; Burdett, a radical Whig; and his daughter, a conservative rumored to have attracted the affections of both Louis Napoleon and Wellington.[32] The 1859 Neapolitan Exile Fund is another case in point. Conservative Anglican Lord Shaftesbury was vice president and chairman of the committee. His board included political antagonists such as liberal Peelite John Russell; ex-Tory and anti-Peelite Viscount Palmerston; and a rising star of the Liberal Party, William Ewart Gladstone.[33]

Though the social elite remained vitally important to British private relief initiatives, the middle and working classes became increasingly involved as well, drawn into refugee relief less through personal connections to friends on the Continent than through increasing familiarity with refugee causes or friendships with foreigners already in exile. They tended to be political liberals or radicals of various shades, and many were Protestant dissenters who supported continental causes out a belief in liberal progress.[34] Radical artisan William Linton and middle-class positivist Frederick Harrison, for example, became acquainted with foreign refugees in their midst. Linton met Giuseppe Mazzini in early 1844 and later in the decade turned to helping other European revolutionaries. Harrison, who had been tutored by European exiles in his youth, supported French communist refugees in the early 1870s.[35] Middle-class abolitionists and missionaries undertook the cause of foreign slaves as an outgrowth of their antislavery activities. Their growing concern for American fugitive slaves in the late 1840s and 1850s was something of a relief from daunting practicalities of assisting British ex-slaves in the Caribbean.[36]

For conservatives and the nascent Liberal Party, refuge was reflective of a Britain they saw as championing enlightened governance. Radicals, by contrast, turned to refuge as an additional avenue for addressing pressing political concerns at home as well as overseas. As early as the 1810s, populist politicians in and out of Parliament connected Castlereagh's support for continental oppressors with domestic attempts to quash reform. By the 1840s, at the height of Chartist campaigns for democratic reform, radicals speaking on behalf of the working masses embraced the cause of foreign refugees as well. They formed associations modeled on the LASFP in order to establish connections with continental socialists. Foremost among these were Linton's People's International League and the Democratic Friends of Poland. Although even the most anti-establishment Chartist would admit that Britain was more liberal than her continental neighbors, prominent Chartists—Ernest Jones, in particular—used the refugees' experience at the hands of both foreign and British oppressers to decry the remnants of authoritarian rule at home. Jones linked Austria's repression of refugees with the British state and society's oppression of the working classes. Advertisements for subscriptions in the radical newspapers emphasized this point. An article in the *Star of Freedom* put a radical twist on the "sacred duty" to "relieve and protect refugees." "Sacred" duties need not be religious in origin; the *Star of Freedom* argued that they could be grounded in "justice and fraternity," forces just as weighty and sublime.[37] Jones took this message further before a crowd gathered to support refugees in December 1850. He warned that the refugees arriving in England would be disappointed by the absence of the much-vaunted liberties they had been led to expect. "In England," he explained, they could meet in the open air, provided the police did not interrupt them; they could utter what they thought fit, provided they feared not imprisonment; they had a free press, but it would not report them. . . . The law did not respect persons, but it had a great respect for purses; and, whilst they were insulted with charity, they were denied justice. . . . He trusted the time would soon come when these exiles could return to their own free country, and leave us enjoying the reality, and not the mockery of freedom (hear, hear).[38]

Jones had reason for his cynicism about British liberalism, since he had recently been a political prisoner. Yet he was equally relentless in his criticism of the British working classes. For Jones, British democracy was "a mean, servile, and crouching thing. Ever since the time of the Puritans, it had been craven and selfish." Jones "hoped to god that those gallant exiles would prove the leaven that would infuse the true spirit of Democracy throughout the whole of their ranks."[39] In subsequent years, few radical meetings convened without a token refugee on the platform. This helped certify the international character of their cause and signified the need to act now, so that others would not be martyred in the fight against oppression.

In the short term, radical support for continental refugees yielded no discernible political payoffs for the Chartist cause, though historians have long scoured the record for such evidence. Officials and more mainstream refugee supporters bristled at radical support for refugees. A short-lived aliens act, passed in the midst of the 1848 European revolutions, readied the government to expel foreigners deemed too likely to combine forces with domestic radicals. In fact, there were few grounds for this official anxiety. Refugees like Hungarian nationalist Lajos Kossuth were leery of associating too closely with controversial political radicals. Even democratic Polish and French refugees were hesitant to draw attention to the parallels between their causes and that of British political prisoners (much to the chagrin of radical politician and Irish nationalist Fergus O'Connor). Too close an association with British radicals would have cost refugees much-needed mainstream support.[40] Home Office spies further allayed concerns that refugees might foment violence in Britain and the new aliens act lapsed in 1849 without having been put to use.[41]

The cautious liberals of the LASFP worried that radical support for foreign refugees would undercut public support for the LASFP's more moderate stance. The rise of democratic parties and, later, socialist and communist revolutionaries also alarmed LASFP members. Liberal romantics in the mid-1840s feared that democratic revolutions on the Continent would go beyond simply ousting foreign oppressors to indulge in dangerous and violent experiments. Members of the LASFP immediately distanced their society from the revolutionary agitation they assumed to be taking place in the democratic circles in Britain itself. In 1846, the LASFP's report reiterated an argument set out by Polish exile Prince Czartoryski in 1836: that those still languishing under despotic rule in Russian, Austrian, or Prussian Poland "might submit to a thousand humiliations . . . for they dare not, by taking up arms, expose themselves to the severe and just reproach, of having steeped their country in blood and covered it with scaffolds, without a sufficient and reasonable chance of success."[42] The 1846 report endorsed a wait-and-see approach. Following the failed uprising in Galicia and the formation of Linton's International League in 1846, the society attempted to disown Polish extremists among the refugees. They did so in the 1846 report by first denying that Poles, "in general," were "addicted to violent doctrines or extreme opinions." The report insisted that "the declamations of some of the Refugees, at popular assemblies in France and England, must not be taken for the voice of the people." While it was "natural that men, suffering from the evils of despotism, should be disposed to rush into the opposite extreme," these were not the men who have "played any leading part in Poland." Those who have not "upon reflection become converted to more temperate views," the LASFP argued, "have been discovered to be nothing else but Russian agents in disguise."[43] In contrast to such recklessness, the LASFP endorsed the approach recommended by Czartoryski: patient waiting.

There was little basis for the LASFP concern initially. For members of William Linton's International League, common cause with the refugees for the time being meant fraternal assistance and verbal support. Starting in the early 1850s, however, British radicals grew increasingly convinced that the time for action was at hand and started to get actively involved in continental insurrections. Chartist George Julian Harney hoped that the public would support a Polish legion in the Crimean War. Although these hopes were disappointed, middle-class radicals did in fact support Garibaldi's Italian nationalist army. The Garibaldi Fund, founded in 1856 under the auspices of regular refugee supporters George Holyoake, James Stansfeld, William Ashurst, and R. H. Crawford, among others, provided arms to Italian soldiers. The fund raised an incredible £30,000 in four years, a sum that Chartists claimed came from their working-class base.[44] In addition to financing campaigns, middle-class men (and a handful of women) enlisted in the army of national liberation, as Byron had at the time of the Greek Wars. Jessie Mario White famously followed Mazzini to Italy and was imprisoned alongside other revolutionaries. Joseph Cowen, William Shaen, and W. E. Adams formed their own society of friends of Poland, this one with a more democratic bent than the LASFP. Like the Garibaldi Fund, this committee finally managed to raise funds for what would be the last Polish insurrection in the 1880s.[45]

While mainstream refugee supporters fretted over radical interventionism, the government strove to curb such activities. As Lord Palmerston had warned, he would not tolerate plotting on British shores. Refugees, he declared, "were bound to abstain from courses calculated to give umbrage to foreign governments, and to disturb the internal tranquility of any foreign country."[46] In the 1840s, the British government forwarded Mazzini's correspondence to the Austrian government. In the 1850s, the British government relayed Home Office spy John Sanders's reports about the French refugees on Jersey in the British Channel Islands to the French ambassador, Count Walewski (who had himself been active in the Polish nationalist cause). Even though Sanders did not believe the refugees posed a threat to Napoleon III's regime, the Home Office continued to apprise Walewski of the refugees' every move. British radicals were not immune. Italian Felice Orsini's attempted assassination of the French emperor in 1858 drew renewed attention to British radical interventionism, and the government brought Chartist publisher Edward Truelove to trial for publishing *Tyrannicide,* which the prosecution claimed encouraged the attack.[47]

Such cases did not play well before the British public. Rather than exposing unseemly radical support for foreign refugees, they tended to have the effect of drawing the nation together behind the cause of refuge writ large, since they were construed as a slight on British freedoms and the sanctity of British refuge. Beyond Chartists' parliamentary reform platform, their campaign for refugees thus had a tremendous impact on the national stage. As John Belchem has argued in his account of support for Polish and Hungarian democrats in the north of England, radicals' campaigns for refugees brought their voices into a discourse of national enterprise—that of refuge in the name of the British nation—and made them participants in the national political conversation.[48]

The Power of Public Opinion

In December 1854, nine months after Britain declared war on Russia, Richard Cobden questioned the motives behind Britain's entry into the Crimean War. The Liberal MP emphasized how naïve ordinary Britons had been about the causes of the war. The British public believed, among other false rationales, that the government declared war on behalf of oppressed nationalities in the East who were threatened by Russian aggression. Cobden demanded "whether the ground on which the public impression is founded—that we are going to war to aid the Poles, Hungarians, Moldavians, or Wallachians—has not been entirely delusive." For Cobden, the answer was yes. Cobden was less certain, however, whether such a premise for war—if genuine—would be acceptable. Though ardently antiwar, he admitted "that were it likely to advance the cause of liberty, of constitutional freedom, and national independence, it would be a great inducement to me to acquiesce in the war, or, at all events, I should see in it something like a compensation for the multiplied evils which attend a state of war."[49]

Cobden's observation and his own admission underscored a profound shift in British responses to foreign refugees. In the sixty-five years since the outbreak of the French Revolution, British sympathies for persecuted foreigners had expanded dramatically, as had their sense of national responsibility to come to the aid of the oppressed whenever and wherever possible. This sense of duty was no longer about rewarding service to the British state, but about liberal freedoms.

The public force of refugee support was so deeply entrenched that a politician would suffer should it become generally known that he had failed to help foreign refugees. Tory foreign minister George Canning grasped this public enthusiasm, carefully presenting himself as sympathetic to the Greek cause and emphasizing the importance of recognizing public sentiment in his diplomatic correspondence. A British minister needed to tread carefully so as not to be accused of delivering up a refugee. In 1825, Canning conveyed the political importance of appearing solicitous of refugees to the French Prince de Polinaque in correspondence on the question of French slaves who escaped to the British Caribbean colonies. The French prince was irate over Britain's unwillingness to extradite slaves. Though he expressed sympathy, Canning told the prince that nothing would allow him to give up the refugee slaves. Whatever Canning's personal feelings on the subject were, he explained that not even "the power given [to the colonial governor] by the [colonial] alien acts" enabled the "delivery of the person to punishment or slavery, in the colony from whence he may have fled." The public in Britain would simply not tolerate the expulsion of a refugee.[50]

Canning's awareness of the political costs of ignoring public political morality was prescient. Within three years, the Duke of Wellington—who had earlier cultivated popular support for Spanish refugees—discovered the wisdom of Canning's intuition. Concerned for British neutrality, Wellington promised the Portuguese government that he would disperse a contingent of revolutionary exiles from port cities and separate exiled military leaders from their soldiers.[51] To the public, Wellington's attempt to maintain British neutrality in the eyes of Portuguese allies was an insult. At the time, the Portuguese refugees were being fêted at elite balls and bazaars held in their honor. Writing to the *Times* in December of 1828, H. Woolcombe demanded recourse on behalf of all Englishmen. He explained that "the Portuguese refugees had thrown themselves upon the hospitality of the inhabitants, and it was a duty to receive them well, as it was the duty of every Englishman to support all who were friends of constitutional liberty."[52]

Wellington weathered media outrage over the treatment of Portuguese refugees, but public passions on the subject of refuge persisted. The 1844 letter-opening affair infuriated mainstream British opinion but also particularly elicited the interest of British radicals. Public outrage forced Parliament to investigate accusations that Mazzini's letters had been passed from the Home Office to the Austrian government. William Linton and William Lovett led the charge against Home Office secretary James Graham, linking Graham's breach of Mazzini's privacy with the defeat of the nationalist Bandiera brothers immediately upon their June 1844 arrival in Naples. The brothers might not have met so ignominious an end, Mazzini's supporters raged, if the Foreign Office had not interfered. Joseph Cowen, then a student at Edinburgh, was just one of a whole new generation of radicals initiated by the scandal into political protest and a lifelong interest in the lives of foreign refugees.[53] Mazzini and Kossuth kept the public memory of this outrage alive. Their Fund for European Freedom, which raised money for refugees in exile, issued certificates highlighting sacrifices made in the cause of liberty (figure 2.7). The signed prints bore "an emblematical engraving of a battle of the flags of Hungaria and Italia, with figures weaping [*sic*] for the fallen: a tomb inscribed with the names of Bandiera [. . . and other martyrs]: a war horse without a rider."[54]

2.7 · Certificate received upon subscribing to the Shilling Subscription for European Freedom, a fund organized by George Jacob Holyoake. The print boasts the (printed) signatures Giuseppe Mazzini and Lajos Kossuth.

A decade later, the power of public sentiment about refugees had its most spectacular demonstration by making and then unmaking Palmerston's Liberal administration. Palmerston and the new Liberal Party rose in popularity in the early 1850s, thanks to the former foreign secretary's assistance to Hungarian refugees in the wake of their failed nationalist revolution. Palmerston's activities not only won him middle-class support but also brought important backing from Chartists, who had been particularly hostile to Palmerstonian Liberalism and who hoped that their association with continental exiles would further the radical cause at home.[55] Palmerston's willingness to bring public opinion into foreign policy decisions and to use force to make those opinions felt around the world gave new weight to refugee supporters' campaigns.

Yet within the decade, in 1858, Palmerston's apparent abandonment of foreign refugees caused his downfall. In the aftermath of Orsini's attempted assassination of Napoleon III, Palmerston brought a conspiracy-to-murder bill before Parliament. Although the bill targeted British radicals as well as foreigners in Britain, it would have placed restrictions on asylum for foreign nationals. Like the Aliens Act of 1793, it would have enabled authorities to observe foreigners and extradite those deemed dangerous revolutionaries either by British authorities or by their foreign allies. The bill and the trial of Dr. Simon Bernard, who purportedly helped Orsini plan the attack on the French emperor, provoked a vitriolic public backlash. Chartist protesters accused officials of abandoning essential English freedoms and liberties.[56] As Mazzini highlighted in a letter written more for the British public than for Napoleon (to whom it was addressed), the French usurper had been "an exile in England," where he had "incessantly plotted against a constitutional king, to whom you had pledged your honour to conspire no more and you finally organized an armed descent on the shores of France." That he could demand British assistance now would be, in the mind of an Englishman, to

> desert the old traditions of an individual liberty, which has proved a blessing to our land, by enacting measures implying, if they are to be enforced at all, a wholesale system of espionage, secret police doings and arbitrary interpretations? Why should we abandon our honest, clear precise method of legal definitions, and resort to those vague formulas of excitation and instigation?[57]

Mazzini's open letter captured British uneasiness with the conspiracy-to-murder bill. The bill would require liberal Britain, so proud of its tradition of refuge, to renege on this practice at the request of foreigners.

Public debate over the bill came to a head in the trial of Dr. Simon Bernard. His attorney, Edwin James, drew a flattering contrast between the English jury's prudence and respect for the rights of asylum seekers and French hysteria:

> Tell him [Napoleon III] that on this spot your predecessors have resisted the arbitrary power of the crown, backed by the influence of crown-serving and time-serving judges. Tell him that under every difficulty and danger your predecessors have secured the political liberties of the people. Tell him that the verdicts of English juries are founded on the eternal and immutable principles of justice.[58]

The jury found Bernard not guilty, and the court declared that an alien could not be indicted under current law if the only evidence of that crime came from abroad.[59] The verdict discredited the conspiracy-to-murder bill, which failed in its next reading in Parliament. The bill's collapse brought Palmerston's administration down with it. In the public's mind, the administration had betrayed its own ideals.

In just over sixty years, refuge had become a defining national commitment to an expansionist liberal ethos. Individuals and groups came to refugee support for a variety of reasons, from a radical vision of "universal liberty" to a sense of religious duty, with many more diffuse humanitarian motives in between. The common campaign for refugee support brought all these diverse impulses together. The moral power of liberal humanitarianism in the face of foreign oppression was such that British radicals tried to use their advocacy of refugees to consolidate their own respectability within mainstream public opinion. Of course, this powerful popular sentiment could only crystallize around a core set of narratives and organizational practices, to whose development the next chapter will turn.

THREE

Telling Stories, Taking Action

In October 1851, newspaper presses hummed with excitement, preparing their readers for the arrival of Hungarian leader Lajos Kossuth (figures 3.1 and 3.2). The Hungarian Revolution had ended, the constitution-based Hungarian Diet forced to disband and its army dissolving before advancing Austrian and Russian armies. Britons were sure that Hungarian exiles deserved better than near-imprisonment in the Ottoman Sultan, where they had been driven by the Austrians in 1849. In Parliament, Lord Dudley Coutts Stuart celebrated Palmerston's instrumental role in negotiating the release of the Hungarian refugees from the Ottoman Empire.[1] British diplomats had overseen Turkish efforts to relieve the Hungarian exiles and keep Austrian demands for extradition at bay for nearly two years. Finally released in 1851, these Hungarian freedom fighters and their Polish sympathizers made their way to British Malta and onward in search of more secure shelter.

With the band of soldiers set to arrive in Britain that fall, Coutts Stuart, Quaker publisher Charles Gilpin, and liberal non-interventionist Richard Cobden "prepared to act as trustees of the Kossuth fund." Chartists George Reynolds, Fergus O'Connor, "and other disreputable partisans" sought to "claim the great constitutional hero as one of themselves." In Southampton, reporters noted townspeople preparing to meet Kossuth and his compatriots upon their landing. In London, Gilpin "gained high honor in moving that the Common Council should give him a congratulatory address in open court—a proposition [that] carried almost unanimously." London's Marylebone vestry adopted a similar address. Bath and Birmingham were "astir" with preparations as well.[2]

RECEPTION OF KOSSUTH, ON BOARD THE "MADRID" STEAMER, AT SOUTHAMPTON.

3.1 · Kossuth's arrival in Southampton, England, on October 23, 1850. *Authentic Life of Louis Kossuth, Governor of Hungary: His Progress from His Childhood to His Overthrow by the Combined Armies of Austria and Russia. With a Full Report of the Speeches Delivered in England, at Southampton, Winchester, London, Manchester, and Birmingham. To which is Added, His Address to the People of the United States of America* (London: Bradbury and Evans, 1851), 30.

M. KOSSUTH ADDRESSING THE PEOPLE AT COPENHAGEN-HOUSE.

3.2 · M. Kossuth addressing the people at Copenhagen-House [London]. Print, *Authentic Life of Louis Kossuth*, page 71. A crowd of twelve thousand working-men was said to have marched with banners from Russell Square to hear Kossuth speak (*Authentic Life*, 70).

Few refugees were greeted in this manner. More often than not, persecuted foreigners arrived to the welcome of their fellow refugees or countrymen only. Russian Alexander Herzen wrote of London that there was "no town in the world which is more adapted for training one away from people and training one into solitude." The "opaline fog" mirrored his mood, he recalled gloomily. This sort of commentary on English hospitality was common among refugee writers. Fictional characters, too, echoed these sentiments as foreign-born authors commented on the impenetrable and the imposing character of the "Englishman's castle."[3] Each home was designed as though the inhabitants expected Louis Napoleon to mount a siege, German author Max Schlesinger wrote in 1853. Schlesinger's characters found friends among the English. Even so, his Englishmen approached foreigners with condescension. One English character "thank[ed] God in his morning's prayers, that he has not been created a foreigner."[4]

Yet, the enthusiastic coverage of the Hungarians' arrival was hardly unique. By the time of the Hungarians' arrival, the image of the down-on-his-luck romantic hero had become a standard figure in Victorian culture. Refugees and their supporters propagated dramatic narratives of persecution in the local and national press. Celebrated fugitives—black and white—toured the British Isles, recounting their tales to rapt audiences at public meetings that were restaged in newspaper stories for audiences across the country. Scholars of the nineteenth century have documented the organization of relief for one group or another of foreign refugees but have not reconstructed the broader cultural pattern these particular cases form when placed together. As this chapter highlights, narratives about refugees, while replete with details of specific struggles, bore remarkable similarities to one another. The manly refugee and his victimized family deserved British esteem and assistance. While down on his luck, the heroic refugee still possessed courage, liberal principles, and a strong sense of honor and justice. This narrative genre, which was propagated by refugees and their supporters alike, taught British audiences who refugees were and how to treat them. By midcentury, stories about the heroic refugee made sympathetic responses to refugees a British cultural norm, one upon which activists relied to raise funds for refugee relief. Admittedly, charitable funds were never sufficient, and activists and philanthropists grappled constantly with the difficulty of integrating foreign refugees and providing long-term relief. Nevertheless, these rhetorical acts were critical in giving shape to a broader humanitarian norm. Through these narratives the British established what became the classic concept of refuge for persecuted foreigners—one robust enough to include foreigners of all political, social, religious, and racial backgrounds.

Refugee Narrative: The Anatomy of a Genre

In Charles Dickens's 1859 novel *A Tale of Two Cities*, the rescue of persecuted foreigners took place in an atmosphere of tense secrecy. Jarvis Lorry explains to Lucy Manette when telling her how he assisted in her father's escape from prison:

> Better not to mention the subject, anywhere or in any way, and to remove him—for a while at all events—out of France. Even I, safe as an Englishman, [...] avoid all naming of the matter. I carry about me, not a scrap of writing openly referring to it. This is a secret service altogether. My credentials, and memoranda, are all comprehended in the one line, "Recalled to Life"; [*sic*] which may mean anything.[5]

For real-life refugee supporters, the effort to rescue foreign refugees from persecution overseas was anything but stealthy. It was a noisy, nation-defining affair. Refugee supporters—both private philanthropists and public officials—relied on protest meetings and media coverage. Nevertheless, the way in which Dickens's novel romanticized British rescue captured several essential features of a newly robust narrative genre that helped British audiences identify persecuted foreigners and sympathize with their plight.

A Tale of Two Cities joined countless other tales that found heroism in the flight of persecuted foreigners. These narratives coalesced into a distinctive genre by the 1840s and 1850s. This genre helped anchor the definition of the refugee. Like all powerful human narratives, the refugee genre contained a standardized set of events coupled with appropriate ethical judgments. The genre helped rule persecuted foreigners in or out of the category itself. Refugee stories thus had a powerful impact not only on those who heard or read them but also on those about whom they were told.

The standardized refugee narrative developed out of two areas in which tales of persecution had gained a foothold in eighteenth-century British culture: as a convention of eighteenth-century philanthropy and as a literary theme. The narrative of refugee suffering dovetailed with a broader rise in middle- and upper-class philanthropy. Within the expanded philanthropic milieu of the eighteenth century, refugee narratives resembled begging letters. These letters, in which the hopeful supplicant laid out his or her claims on public or private charity, were published in newspapers and presented to charities. As historian Donna Andrew argues, eighteenth-century authors of begging letters described "their dire circumstances, and in so doing, creating a compelling narrative in which both neediness and deservingness played equal roles." Though most letters were ostensibly addressed to local elites, they were often broadcast widely.[6] (Even if elites did most of the philanthropic giving, wider public knowledge of supplicants' dramatic tales helped garner welcome public recognition of donors' generosity.) For foreigners, there were few other ways to seek relief. Sometimes ineligible for parish relief and hoping to avoid the degrading stigma associated with the institution, destitute foreigners tried to show that their virtue entitled them to assistance beyond that provided to ordinary paupers.[7] Like the authors of begging letters, refugees set out to win the hearts of their potential benefactors with tales of virtuous woe.

Begging letters differed from the refugee narratives in that they emphasized the personal plight of their authors. The point was to show how the writer's plight was more heart wrenching than that of other paupers. The refugee narrative, by contrast, demonstrated the similarity of the foreigner to his or her British hosts and also to other refugees. Nothing would be more pitiful and intriguing to the middle- and upper-class humanitarian than innocents of similar circumstances who had been brought low by fortune. Their innocence could reach epic proportions in their supporters' tales. Identifying herself as the "Author of *Evelina* and *Cecilia*," Burney penned a florid appeal comparing the suffering of the French clergy to England's Protestant martyrs of the sixteenth and seventeenth centuries. Not only were these Catholics worthy charitable subjects, they were comparable to British Protestants' most stalwart and long-suffering ancestors.

Moreover, refugee narratives, in stark contrast to begging letters, made individual stories representative of the larger social ill of persecution. An 1825 article in the *Times*, for instance, detailed the distress of a single Spanish family, the family of "a gentleman (a distinguished officer)" whose wife had aged prematurely with the "mental agony" and "fatigue" of exile, as she worked herself to the bone to maintain her family. The article, which aimed to solicit funds, went on to detail the family's harrowing escape from Spain. The officer's wife and children had been thrown into the dungeon and made their escape only by a timely ruse.[8] Donors were asked to support a community of similar families. The "distinguished officer" in question was a "constitutional Spaniard" who had made himself "obnoxious" to "Ferdinand's monks." But other "constitutional Spaniards" faced similar tribulations. As the author of this article noted, "it is not a solitary example of the privations endured by this portion of our helpless fellow-creatures: we could name 50: we will mention one."[9]

Because refugee narratives moved between an individual's story and a larger context of persecution, they were able to extend across the particular characteristics of their protagonists. Supporters of the Spanish refugees also collected funds for Italian and Portuguese refugees. Advertisements and public meetings grouped these refugees together, highlighting the way in which the trials of one group could stand in for the trials of others. The ethical extensibility of these narratives ultimately enabled them to reach across racial and religious boundaries, since the moral characteristics of their protagonists arose from their struggle against persecution rather than their initial group membership.

Refugee narratives could be found in a variety of settings. Since the Terror of the 1790s, exile had been a pronounced literary trope. Novelists and relief organizers had used these stories about the woes of oppression and the sorrows of exile to solicit subscriptions on émigrés' behalf, as had Charlotte Smith at the time of the French Revolution. By the mid-nineteenth century, these tales were quite common. Refugee narratives were written by English-speaking, elite refugees; by educated fugitive slaves; by relief campaigners who spoke on behalf of larger groups of refugees of all classes; by journalists who repeated these tales; and by famous authors, such as William Wordsworth, Ann Raikes Harding, and Frances Trollope, who drew upon the popularity of refugees' stories in their writing. These tales of persecution were printed in the form of novels and memoirs, and in relief committee reports. In news periodicals, these tales came in the form of advertisements, reprints of meeting proceedings, and articles (foreign and domestic) describing the movement of refugees. The genre, then, was robust enough to work orally or in print, in multiple publication venues, and in fiction or nonfiction. The genre gave audiences a familiar template through which to understand the diverse particularities of new refugee stories.

One can parse out four constitutive elements of the refugee narrative. The first two involve the refugees' personal traits. First, refugee stories highlighted their protagonists' innocence. Refugees were in no way responsible for their plight, and their opposition to their governments stemmed from pure motives. The second element formed a counterpoint to the first, ensuring readers that their innocence was not passivity. In the classic narrative, refugees were courageous and determined. Refugee narratives hinged on an adventure-packed tale of escape while hinting at the coming difficulties of life in exile. Despite trying circumstances, the refugee was bent on continuing his or her battle against oppression and, simultaneously, was a model liberal individual willing to work hard to earn his or her keep. The final pair of characteristics of the refugee narrative focuses on the refugees' larger social context. The third element emphasized the continuing tragedy facing those left behind. Finally, refugee narratives highlighted and welcomed British support. Some featured heroic British intervention on the refugees' behalf, while others emphasized the comforts of British hospitality after fugitives had found safe harbor on British territory.

1. A Clear Conscience: A sine qua non of any refugee narrative was to prove that the exile was fleeing for good reason. The exile had to face a truly intolerable situation at home. European revolutionaries faced prison or death for their opposition to a repressive government or were routed on the field of battle. Roman liberals fled to British Malta when the Pope, backed by French forces, returned to the city in 1849. British diplomats helped Hungarian troops to safety when Austria ended its bid for independent, parliamentary government the same year. Fugitive slaves were typically depicted as facing more than the quotidian trials of servitude. They also tended to face some traumatic hardship such as separation from a family member or targeted abuse by a vicious master. Harriet Beecher Stowe's fictional George and Eliza Harris fled in part because they had been separated. In real life, American slave Tom Wilson likewise fled a cruel master after having been separated from his wife and children. Unlike the Harris family, the Wilsons were never reunited.[10]

In contrast with the fugitive from justice, the refugee was not a murderer or a thief but innocent and pure of purpose. When those lines blurred, as in Frances Trollope's 1832 adventure *The Refugee in America*, the point of the refugee narrative was to carefully exculpate the refugee from blame. Trollope's story cleared the Earl of Darcy from a false charge of murder and showed the true villain to have been the cause of young Darcy's flight.[11]

Refugee supporters ensured that the objects of their charity were deserving individuals. Aristocrats and famous revolutionaries might need little introduction, but where this was not the case, British philanthropists arranged for prominent leaders of exile groups to vouch for the character of rank-and-file members. American antislavery campaigners offered testimonials about the fugitives they forwarded to England after the 1850 passage of the Fugitive Slave Act. Fugitive slave couple William and Ellen Craft, for example, had the backing of the Massachusetts Anti-Slavery Society.[12]

The chaos of revolutionary upheavals made it especially necessary for refugees and their friends to explain clearly what roles exiles had played in the events overseas. The authors of refugee narratives guided their readers through a complicated skein of revolutions, counterrevolutions, military coups, and political betrayals. This careful contextualization lent the exile credibility. Within months of her arrival in Britain, for example, Hungarian patriot Mme. Theresa Pulszky published a narrative that intertwined her personal history with the history of her homeland. She detailed her proximity to the revolution, the danger of her situation, and her flight with her children into the mountains and across Europe.[13]

Some refugees had compromising biographical elements to parry in their public presentation of self. In some cases, these testimonials were hotly disputed. For instance, the Hungarian general Artúr Görgey, who had assumed leadership of Hungary and its army following Kossuth's exile, faced charges of treason for his surrender to a Russian and Austrian army in 1849. Görgey used his 1852 *My Life and Acts in Hungary in the Years 1848–1849* to combat these accusations. His memoirs were immediately countered in a publication that once more denounced him to an English audience.[14]

Like Görgey, the Italian refugee Luigi Bianchi had to make a special effort to prove his innocence to the British public. Bianchi had been a Catholic priest, which implicated him in the corrupt anti-liberal intrigues of the papacy. He managed this potentially discrediting past in his 1859 *Incidents in the Life of an Italian: Priest—Soldier—Refugee* by recounting his forced induction into the priesthood by his family at a young age. From his insider's perspective, he wrote, he came fully to understand Catholic corruption, and at last joined the nationalist cause when papal reforms turned out to be little more than a façade.[15] Bianchi capped his redemption narrative by retelling how his British hosts helped him convert to Protestantism.

Görgey and Bianchi were correct in thinking that their public image mattered a great deal. Other foreigners who did not manage to cast their overseas activities in a positive light suffered for it. For instance, the Austrian general Julius Jacob von Haynau, known to British audiences as the "Austrian butcher" for his ruthless flogging of women and children, got a rude reception at the hands of a working-class mob, which turned the lash on him.[16] Haynau's treatment reflected the degree to which the public had acquainted itself with refugee-related events abroad by the middle of the nineteenth century. A half-century earlier, the Marquis de Lafayette, whose role in the American Revolution did not endear him to the British public, got away with just a heckling while in exile in Britain in the 1790s.

2. Fortitude and the liberal individual: Refugee narratives emphasized their protagonists' personal courage in flight and their firm adherence to their causes. In cases where refugees were not revolutionary leaders being hosted in middle- and upper-class circles, they also evinced a solidly bourgeois work ethic, whatever their actual class backgrounds.

Refugee narratives lingered on the harrowing details of their protagonists' flight. Following the passage of the Fugitive Slave Act, British newspapers reported on the escape of dozens of American slaves. Stories would often first be told locally, upon the fugitive's arrival, and would be repeated nationally within days. For example, the *Times* republished the *Liverpool Albion*'s story detailing Tom Wilson's brutal treatment at the hands of his master (Wilson was burned with a red hot iron and attacked by dogs), his separation from his wife and family, and his escape through alligator-infested swamps. Wilson was lucky enough to be smuggled aboard a ship bound for Liverpool by a few black sailors.[17] Favorite stories, like that of the Crafts, would become so well known that they hardly needed more than a sentence of introduction in coverage of their public appearances. Ellen Craft had disguised herself as a white gentleman and traveled openly to Massachusetts with her husband, William, who was dressed as her slave.[18] European revolutionaries, too, had dramatic and courageous escape narratives. Giuseppe Garibaldi's long trek—with the Austrians, French, and Spanish hot on his heels—was well known and would become the backdrop of Mrs. C. G. Hamilton's 1857 novel, *The Exiles of Italy*. Several chapters in her novel would begin with biblical quotes, dramatizing the mythic proportions of her heroes' exile.[19]

Valiant refugees did not give up the fight once safe on British soil. They continued to oppose their home government; some even ventured back, risking re-imprisonment or death rather than abandon their country. Dickens's French refugee Charles Darnay returned to France to help an old family dependent out of prison in *A Tale of Two Cities* (1859). Mrs. Hamilton's fictional protagonist, Belmonte, could not endure the idleness of exile and returned to battle. In a fit of romantic torment, Belmonte took leave of his English love: "To leave Clara, and to leave her thus, was to turn from the star that had arisen on his dark horizon." But, he could only imagine staying with her "if ever" he saw his "own fair Italy freed from the tyrant's power."[20]

When offered pardon or amnesty by their former persecutors, the classic refugee—real and fictional—refused. Belmonte viewed his pardon as an embarrassment. Gabriel, a Russian exile in Alfred Godwine's 1857 *The Refugee, A Novel Founded on Phrenological Observations,* rebuked the insincerity of the Great Powers' offers of amnesty to his fellow refugees. Gabriel himself refused the czar's offer of a personal pardon and explained that, in accepting a pardon, exiles "may themselves have to forget the wrong done to them by the rashness which characterized the decrees and steps of the late Emperor."[21] British admirers valued this steadfastness just as much when manifested in real life by the great exiles—Mazzini, Kossuth, and Garibaldi. Like the fictional Belmonte, Kossuth lived out his life as an exile, refusing to debase himself by accepting Austrian amnesty. He did so at great personal cost, missing his last opportunity to receive his mother's "benediction on my tempest-tossed head."[22]

Archetypal rank-and-file refugees demonstrated their personal fortitude in another important way. They proved themselves willing to work hard while in exile, humbling themselves if they had been members of the social elite or proving their assiduity in honest labor if they were former slaves. Refugees like the Spanish families of the 1820s fell significantly in class status as they tried to eke out a living away from home. The typical narrative depicted such people as bearing their suffering stoically. They lived on diminished means while trying their best to earn an honest and industrious living. In this sense, refugees were both like and unlike the poor in the language of social welfare of the day. While their heroic struggles overseas set them apart from other charitable subjects, refugees' industriousness further assured would-be sponsors that they were "deserving" of assistance. As hard workers, they were unlikely to become dependent on poor relief in or outside of the iconic Victorian workhouse.

Relief committees reported extensively on efforts of refugees and their supporters to find employment. Praising the 1851 Hungarian and Polish arrivals, James Spurr commended the refugee under his management. Spurr claimed that he was "thankful—not servile—I know him to be industrious, sober, and so far honest, and have every confidence of a continuation of these virtues." Spurr reflected further in a letter to fellow-sympathizer Joseph Cowen that "some of your friends may say—aye but who is this man that thus gives character to the Alien Stranger." In response, Spurr asked for whom was it more natural to give "every satisfaction as to character for veracity if necessary" than a local man who was also "a citizen of the world."[23]

In the cases of fugitive slaves, the need to demonstrate a bourgeois work ethic was particularly pressing. Defenders of slavery had long argued that Africans were "naturally" lazy and needed to be forced to work; abolitionists urgently needed to prove that slaves, once freed, were capable of working to earn their keep. Chronicles of runaways to the British Isles often ended with a description either of the type of work the ex-slave could undertake or with the observation that the ex-slave had already found employment or a patron. The Ladies' Society to Aid Fugitives from Slavery, for example, reported happily on their placement of these refugees in gainful employment particularly suited to their skills.[24]

Personal agency was critical to the refugee narrative. In cases where it was lacking, persecuted foreigners might not even qualify as genuine refugees. This was the crucial distinction that divided fugitive slaves from Africans liberated from the slave trade. While both were central to abolitionists' efforts, only the former fit the refugee narrative. Even philanthropists' stories of liberated Africans lacked this element of individual valor and fortitude. Commentators depicted those liberated from the slave trade as a largely undifferentiated crowd; while appropriately grateful for being freed from slave ships, they could never become heroes of their own story. That role instead fell to British naval officers or missionaries. The few exceptions feature liberated Africans as individuals only once the missionaries had raised them to a new level of "civilization." Even then, the liberated Africans figured not as courageous freedom fighters but as sidekicks who helped to staff schools in Sierra Leone and otherwise aid missionaries in their work.[25] Liberated Africans were never referred to using the term *refugee*, although Sierra Leone would offer a model for overseas British refuge. By contrast, fugitive slaves were seen to have a will of their own and so could more plausibly be cast as classically liberal subjects and thus bona fide refugees. The case of liberated Africans thus illustrates the power of stories to create symbolic distinctions with very practical consequences.

3. Symptoms of a larger ill: Stories about refugees took pains to describe the ongoing character of the crises that had driven their protagonists into exile. On one level, of course, refugee narratives were basically stories with a happy ending: the protagonist ended up

making his or her way to freedom. Tales of refuge always counterbalanced this note of relief, however, by emphasizing that the brutal persecution that had originally set the plot in motion did not end with the protagonist's personal safety. These stories continuously reminded readers that others still suffered overseas. Refugees themselves spoke of fallen comrades, family members left behind, and their oppressed countrymen in general. This trope of innocents left behind was perhaps most explicit in the case of fugitive slaves. Few slave narratives omitted the pain of family separation and an acute consciousness of loved ones who still felt the sting of the slaver's lash.

European exiles sounded similar notes of dismay about their loved ones back home. The French refugees exiled on Jersey in the Channel Islands after Louis Napoleon's December 1851 coup d'état lamented their powerlessness to protect their families from the new emperor's vengeance. Their newspaper, *l'Homme,* claimed that Napoleon was hungry for additional martyrs. He knew, they said, that countless mothers and sisters were dying of starvation because their husbands, sons, and brothers were unable to provide for them while in exile. These innocents would perish while "guarding the dignity of those absent."[26]

As this example suggests, there was a decidedly gendered note in this element of the typical refugee narrative. The nature of the contests on the Continent meant that the vast majority of revolutionary exiles were men—and soldiers.[27] They left behind their less mobile dependents: women, children, or aging parents. The Polish, French, and Hungarian refugees made it clear that their escape was an exception and that great violence continued to be visited on their families. Kossuth bemoaned his inability to return to the Continent to visit his dying mother.[28] The plight of the women left behind by refugees could appeal particularly to the sympathies of female refugee supporters. One Polish exile wrote to Harriet Beecher Stowe from Glasgow, begging her "to pray now and then for the poor Polish mothers. . . . A mother yourself, you have given comfort to other mothers. . . . [T]hough letters from their children do not always reach Polish mothers, your book is accessible to them, and gives them the conviction that their offspring, far as they are from them, are still within reach of maternal feelings."[29]

Refugee narratives of successful escapes often included heart-rending subplots in which comrades or loved ones failed in their flight. For instance, Garibaldi's escape story included the death of his fearless but weakened wife (figure 3.3). Mrs. C. G. Hamilton's novel

3.3 · *Giuseppe Garibaldi with his Dying Wife Anita, 1849.* Italian Unification (Risorgimento), Italy, 19th century. © De Agostini/The British Library Board (11406585)

about Italy dwelled on the sorrow of this loss but also highlighted Garibaldi's countless fallen comrades whose flights ended with imprisonment or summary execution. Hamilton's fictional Brunetti holds his dying child while imprisoned with a small band of fleeing patriots. When asked if his head hurts, the son replies, "Yes . . . but it will soon be well. . . . Heaven is nearer than England. . . . [W]hen you go to England I shall go there and rest. May I not, dear father? I am so weary."[30] Newspapers featured the tragic tales of slaves captured or killed en route to freedom. As the *Times* reported shortly after the passing of the American Fugitive Slave Act, one family was cornered on a ferry, almost to the Canadian shore. "In his desperation," the article detailed, the husband "seized his razor, and, drawing it forcibly across his throat jumped into the canal. His wife, with their child in her arms, leaped after him; all determined to die rather than again come under the slaveholder's power." The parents were plucked from the water and returned to slavery, but the child drowned.[31] Such stories reminded readers that the fortunate refugees who arrived safely on British shores were but a fraction of those affected.

4. The British to the Rescue Refugee narratives highlighted the role of British assistance and refuge in ending an exile's horrible ordeal. British audiences for these stories could take pride in their communities' gifts of freedom, financial support, and emotional sympathy for refugees. The dénouement of refugee narratives thus provided their audiences with a glow of satisfaction and, not least, implicit instructions on how to become involved in the story.

When telling their own stories, refugees did their best to convey their emotional dependence on their hosts' sympathies. The Hungarian patriot Theresa Pulszky ended her escape memoir with a lament about her loneliness and isolation in London and dedicated the book to her hostess, the Marchioness of Landsdown, who had taken the first steps to comforting her. The heroic Kossuth described his painful separation from his dying mother and sought from his readers the maternal comfort that she could not now provide.[32]

This basic narrative theme of British succor came in several variants. One version highlighted British eagerness to help before refugees had even arrived. Some newspaper reports tracked the movement of refugees as they struggled to find safe haven, as did an article detailing the Italians' forced march through France in the 1830s. Coverage of refugee affairs prior to their arrival in British territory was meant to generate excitement and encourage preparations for their landing. Local philanthropists thus planned a ball and announced a subscription in the lead-up to the arrival of the Polish-Hungarian contingent in Liverpool. The *Daily News* reported, "Many men of the highest local influence and commercial standing have interested themselves on behalf of the refugees. . . . [J]udging by the preparations which we witnessed at the Emigrant's home [a facility for foreign travelers] in Moorfields . . . we cannot doubt that these poor fellows will have just cause to be grateful for English hospitality."[33]

An even more dramatic variation on the theme of British assistance showed Britons actively involved in rescuing exiles on the Continent. Italian exile Luigi Bianchi emphasized the role of a helpful diplomat from the British consulate in Rome who sheltered him for two days

while securing a passport for Bianchi to travel to British Malta.[34] Once ultimately settled in Edinburgh, Bianchi lionized his British helpers:

> My mind finds most light in consolation in reflecting on the delicate traits of benevolence of which I have been the object, and among the English more than any other people. I have always found the English without ostentation, but full of generosity, and render thanks to the divine goodness for placing me among those who could sympathize with me. . . . May God bestow on all my friends ample returns . . . for the good they did me was dictated by a pure and simple Christian spirit.[35]

Fiction romanticized real life. In Dickens's *A Tale of Two Cities,* Charles Darnay escapes the guillotine thanks to the ruse of Sidney Carton, Darnay's English rival for the heroine's affections. Carton disguises himself as Darnay and actually goes to the guillotine in his stead. In Mrs. Hamilton's novel, Belmonte's English friends, the ancient aristocratic De Vere family, rush to his side after his imprisonment in Rome, ultimately convincing the Roman authorities to release him.[36]

Bianchi's story illustrates a final variant in depictions of British assistance: the refugee's absorption into British society. Bianchi converted from Catholicism with the guidance of his British helpers and advisers. Novelists tended to signify the refugee's social incorporation into English life by having him marry into his benefactor's family. Belmonte, for example, marries Clara De Vere. Anglicization could also be completed in the following generation, when an exile's child, usually a daughter, married an English spouse. The essentially Anglicized Lucy Manette marries Darnay after his initial rescue at the outset of Dickens's novel.[37] Still, as their narratives reminded their audience, refugees never forgot the misfortunes that had propelled them to British shores, and they longed for a means to return to a liberated homeland.

From Moral Outrage to Organized Relief

In nineteenth-century Britain, public initiatives to provide refugee relief grew out of expanding concern for persecution overseas.

A mutually reinforcing cycle of protest meetings and press coverage introduced geographically, politically, and socially diverse Britons to refugee politics. This mobilization was aimed primarily at making a political and a moral statement against the perpetrators of a humanitarian crisis, be it ongoing slavery, the American Fugitive Slave Bill, or a disastrous revolution on the Continent. Only secondarily did supporters form committees to organize relief for refugees arriving on British territory. This transition from moral outrage to practical support was not seamless. Nonetheless, public remonstrance was the crucial catalyst for creating relief organizations. The emergence of an increasingly standardized refugee narrative provided activists with a powerful, if idealized, template for lobbying on these foreigners' behalf. In each case, the refugee narrative proved a powerful tool for building and promoting what was fast becoming a core moral consensus about how to treat foreigners who fit the refugee mold.

The timing of these waves of public sympathy and outrage was often linked to the arrival of prominent exiles or refugee supporters. For instance, in late 1850, the national press celebrated the arrival from Boston of William and Ellen Craft and reported on their speaking engagements as they toured England. Kossuth's disembarkation in 1851 fueled a spate of media attention to continental exiles. And following the publication of *Uncle Tom's Cabin* and Harriet Beecher Stowe's 1853 visit to England, the level of public antislavery activity increased dramatically.

Meetings to protest barbarities overseas were held largely, but not exclusively, in port cities. Southampton, London, and Liverpool were common landing places for the refugees, as was Bristol to a lesser extent. But meetings also mushroomed up along the tour routes of prominent exiles, particularly in Manchester, Newcastle, Hull, and Birmingham, each of which would become important refugee support centers in the course of the nineteenth century. Public meetings in these cities typically took place in suitably august venues. In London, for instance, sympathizers were welcomed in places such as the lord mayor's Mansion House; the Duke of Sutherland's Stafford House; and Exeter Hall, a gathering place for voluntary societies of all sorts.

The press played a key role in the cycle of public mobilization against overseas injustices. Outrage over the American Fugitive Slave Act began primarily in the press. News articles and editorials lambasted America's adherence to the slave system, on the one hand, and the slavish obedience of Northerners to the new law, on the other. These sentiments appeared in newspapers across the country and across political lines. In the case of continental outrages, the reaction was similar but tended to be followed more immediately by public meetings in which the sympathetic could express their indignation together. These meetings themselves became fodder for press coverage. Some specialty publications, like the BFASS house organ, the *Anti-Slavery Reporter*, diligently printed the minutes of each of the organization's general committee meetings. But even ordinary metropolitan, provincial, and radical newspapers reported frequently on the proceedings of protest meetings.

Wherever they were held, protest meetings featured local notables. Sometimes these notables were important humanitarian activists and organizers in their own right. Others seem mainly to have symbolized the respectability and gravitas of the meeting; this in turn attracted press coverage. London meetings in particular read like a social who's who, bringing in a crowd similar to the aristocratic endeavors of the Committee for the Relief of the French Catholic Clergy and Laity. In addition to the lord mayor and members of the aristocracy, the Anglican hierarchy—particularly the archbishop of London—and the commercial classes became actively involved.[38] To some degree, of course, local notables themselves received an affirmation of their moral and social status when they presided over these portentous public occasions. It was natural, then, for activists on the fringes of polite society to attempt similar rituals of protest in order to assert their own legitimacy. From the middle of the 1840s, for instance, Chartist leaders organized parallel meetings at places such as the artisan-based City Mechanic's Institute or the John Street Institution. These radicals ensured that establishment voices would not monopolize the responsibility (and prestige) of rallying against persecution and aiding refugees.[39]

The point of these meetings and their press coverage was to provide an oral platform for the refugee narrative already endemic in the press. Each meeting included a narration of the history of the crimes overseas and tales of persecution. If refugees were already in the country, they told their stories personally or were featured prominently at the meeting, standing on the platform as their histories were recounted. These personal narratives included a recitation of the evils inherent in autocratic rule, whether it was the oppression of absolute rulers, of slavery, or of foreign rule. The tales highlighted the personal experience of the exile at the hands of the foreign oppressors, the injustices they faced, their courage, and their flight into exile. Kossuth, Mazzini, and fugitive slaves William Wells Brown and William and Ellen Craft toured the country as veritable celebrities. Lesser-known refugees were sought after as well; in telling their stories, many of these men and women included tales of their absent leaders.

Next, meeting attendees expressed British revulsion at the foreign governments' crimes, often resolving to communicate their outrage to the British government. The London city government at Guildhall, for instance, addressed letters to the Foreign Office, requesting that Palmerston do all in his power to secure the safety of the Hungarian refugees. One resolution, carried unanimously by the lord mayor, aldermen, and Commons on May 22, 1851, expressed how "earnestly [the Court of Common Council] hopes that Lord Palmerston may deem it consistent with his duty to interpose his friendly offices with the Government of the Sublime Porte to promote the liberation of the illustrious captives."[40] The local authorities of the Borough of Finsbury did the same. Antislavery advocates likewise continued to address their memorials to the ministry, as they had since the founding of the BFASS in 1839. Upon the passage of the Fugitive Slave Act, BFASS protest meetings expressed particularly righteous ire at the United States's inability to follow through on its self-proclaimed mission to champion liberty. One meeting of the BFASS aimed particularly taunting barbs at American hypocrisy:

> How extraordinary that the men of the United States should be such resolute sticklers for the rigid observance of mere law! Where would the States have been but for deliberate and organized resistance to law? Have the Americans forgotten the opposition made by their fathers to the famous stamp act?[41]

At the close of the century, the Mansion House would go so far as to directly petition persecuting governments. Though they rarely received an encouraging response, the lord mayor and eminent Londoners addressed letters of remonstrance to the czar himself, begging that he treat the Jews more humanely.[42]

In raising awareness of foreign crises, organizers used these meetings and their publicity to generate short-term relief for newly arrived refugees. Invited speakers were welcomed into the houses of local notables and members of philanthropic societies. Organizers concluded meetings by collecting subscriptions. Activists collected funds for two purposes: to assist refugees directly, even in anticipation of their arrival, and to promote the refugees' cause. These purposes were often indistinguishable. Mazzini and Kossuth asked potential subscribers to contribute to their Shilling Subscription for European Freedom expressly to benefit their cause, but the proceeds were ultimately turned over for the relief of continental refugees themselves.[43]

Even in overtly refugee-oriented subscription advertisements, most of the space with was filled with information about the crisis overseas rather than the needs of the refugees.

Members of the social and cultural elite remained prominent advertisers of relief funds, and newspapermen—often themselves a part of refugee support societies—worked tirelessly to promote the funds across the country. The BFASS and the American and Canadian antislavery societies joined forces to testify to the character and integrity of fugitive slaves and assure potential donors that their efforts were indeed worthwhile. Charles Dickens, Francis Newman (brother of Cardinal Newman), and Lord Dudley Coutts Stuart sat on the board for the Italian Refugees Fund (1849), along with Richard Cobden and William Makepeace Thackeray. The Italian fund used Dickens's liberal *Daily News* as a mouthpiece for relief organization. These well-known members of the refugee board each took turn addressing the audience via the *Daily News*.

The most recognized refugee supporter at midcentury, Coutts Stuart also attended meetings across the country. At a meeting in Newcastle, he inaugurated a subscription for the Hungarians as early as November 1849, almost as soon as the nationalists had been defeated. Sitting on the platform with Coutts Stuart, the mayor opened the proceedings, announcing that it was quite an honor to have the "opportunity of giving assent to this great cause, side by side with a man whose name had become illustrious through the civilized world as the friend of the exile and the hero."[44]

As a logical extension of the activities of European refugee supporters, agitation on behalf of American fugitive slaves also drew on an emerging cadre of experts on refugee affairs. In this manner, relief workers among radicals and elites alike developed more flexible, more expansive views of their own charitable endeavors, adapting expertise gained in one refugee crisis to the next. Nonconformist William Ashurst, a member of the Society of Friends of Italy, wrote under a pseudonym for the American antislavery newspaper *The Liberator*. Lord Shaftesbury, who would draw a favorable contrast between Harriet Beecher Stowe's character Topsy and English working-class children in ragged schools, was active with both Neapolitan exiles and American fugitive slaves. Baroness Burdett Coutts similarly provided charity to both liberated Africans and continental revolutionaries before her attentions turned to Muslims in the Ottoman Empire.

The public's sympathies overlapped as well. Crowds gathered to hear fugitive slaves and continental exiles on tour, and newspapers that reported on European exiles did not hesitate to condemn the American Fugitive Slave Act. British journalists themselves promoted the connection between these two refugee groups. Charles Gilpin brought both causes to light in his capacity as editor of the main Quaker journal, *The Friend*. He also published the memoirs of the ill-fated Hungarian Baroness von Beck. The BFASS's *Anti-Slavery Reporter* celebrated the 1846 insurrection in Galicia (Austrian Poland), likening the condition of the Galician serfs to that of American slaves.[45] Radical journalists including Chartists George Julian Harney, George Holyoake, W. E. Adams, and William Linton denounced American despotism and reprinted escape narratives.[46]

Whereas the press reported the proceedings of refugee support meetings and subscription lists nationally, most collections were made locally. Organizers solicited subscriptions by reaching out to neighbors. Members of the Society of Friends of Italy, for example, received membership cards. They also received a card (presumably certifying their right to collect funds) listing the society's objectives and providing talking points for the campaign.[47]

Elite supporters held balls to raise funds.[48] At bazaars, especially popular through the 1820s, they sold refugee artwork, a legacy of the 1790s, when aristocrats bought and sold émigré handicrafts. Britain's "humble" relied on concerts and lectures, rather than balls and bazaars, to bring supporters together.[49] Nonetheless, working-class donors still received tokens for their support. Contributors to the radical Subscription for European Freedom received cards in return. George Holyoake, editor of the journal *The Reasoner* did not "doubt [that the card, "large and handsome enough for framing," would] adorn many a cottage mantelshelf throughout our land" (see figure 2.7).[50]

The money raised by each refugee group was generally handed over to its leader, who would then disburse it to rank-and-file refugees. This procedure allowed exiled leaders to use their familiarity with their compatriots to help distinguish between real and fake refugees.[51] American fugitive slaves tended to arrive individually in the British Isles and would receive direct support from members of the BFASS and concerned philanthropists. If they were returning to larger fugitive settlements in Canada, these individual slaves left Britain with funds and supplies for their new communities. When no such representatives made their way to the British Isles, British committees forwarded money and clothes to community leaders in North America.[52]

Supporters helped more directly when possible. Prominent refugees were welcomed into British homes. Over the years, Joseph Cowen alone entertained Louis Blanc, Mazzini, Garibaldi, and even (it was rumored) Irish Fenians and continental anarchists in his Newcastle home. For the rank and file, local hotel owners pitched in, as they had during the French Revolution. In Newcastle, a Mr. Johnson offered rooms in his Temperance Hotel for the Polish and Hungarian exiles. Liverpool, a major port city, was already equipped for Irish and English transmigrants; temporary shelters for these emigrants were turned over to the refugees for a short time.

Inevitably, the ubiquity and power of refugee narratives attracted opportunists who calculated that they could tell an eloquent story without having experienced persecution first hand. By the late 1840s, philanthropists were becoming concerned about fraudulent claims to refugee status. In May 1846, the London Mendicity Society uncovered a case that threatened to make the society's name into an unfortunate play on words. The society's begging letter department launched an investigation into dubious claims by several applicants. Styling themselves "Russian refugees," these letter writers asserted that they had been "resident in Persia, but being of the Christian faith, they were so cruelly persecuted that they were obliged to fly." Having left "their wives and families behind them," "the prayer of their petition [was] to raise a sum of money to redeem their families from bondage."[53] Eventually, the investigator and foreign consul determined that these supplicants were not Russian at all, but Polish. It seemed likely that they were not even refugees but professional beggars who earned a living poaching from one set of refugee relief funds after the other. *The Refugee Circular,* a Chartist newsletter for the supporters of Polish-Hungarian exiles in the 1850s, cautioned readers about similar impersonators presenting themselves as refugees in towns throughout the north of England. The BFASS warned of imposters from America such as Reuben Nixon, who used his familiarity with British adaptations of *Uncle Tom's Cabin* and with other escape narratives to obtain funds from an eager abolitionist public.[54]

Refugee aid societies sought to counter this epidemic of freeloading by institutionalizing checks on the authenticity of refugee claims. The editors of the *Refugee Circular* advised donors to send subscriptions to their central committees, not directly to the *soi-disant* refugees themselves.[55] Similarly, a notice in the *Temperance Chronicle* regarding fugitive slaves suggested: "All collections made on their behalf should be forwarded to some person in Great Britain or Ireland who is willing to act as trustee, and whose name will guarantee that no more than the sum required shall be solicited."[56] These organizations relied on trustworthy informants from the relevant refugee community in their efforts to verify claims and even distribute funds. In the case of American fugitive slaves, who were less likely to know one another than, say, the soldiers in Kossuth's army, British philanthropists were forced to turn to American newspapers and antislavery societies for assistance whenever possible.

Unfortunately, exiles could not always be identified satisfactorily. The known presence of foreign spies, like beggars in disguise, complicated matters immensely. Growing political divisions between exile groups after 1848 made it increasingly difficult to rely on one exile to vouch for another. The case of the Baroness von Beck offered concerned refugee supporters a case in point of the growing difficulty of vetting refugee tales.

Like Mme. Pulszky, Wilhelmina Racidula—who presented herself as the Baroness von Beck—sought to publish her memoirs immediately upon arrival in Great Britain in 1850. As had so many other refugees from Austrian oppression, she detailed her treatment at the hands of her Austrian overlords and her escape, as well as her very favorable impressions of the British constitution as an expression of "Anglo-Saxon genius."[57] An unknown member of the Hungarian bid for independence, the Baroness von Beck highlighted her connection to Kossuth. It was a connection that she would use to her advantage again upon her arrival in Birmingham in 1851. There she solicited financial backing for a second memoir but was quickly arrested for fraud; more specifically, she was accused—on questionable grounds—of being an Austrian spy. Racidula was imprisoned while awaiting trial, and her papers (still with her host) promptly disappeared. The poor "baroness" "died of broken heart" before her case could be heard.[58]

Wilhelmina Racidula's death caused a great sensation. Her accusers maintained that she was beyond doubt a spy and not even a baroness. In local and national newspapers, they derided sympathy for her as evidence of "flunkeyism, and a maudlin sentimentality." Such sentimentality denigrated the real heroism of Hungarian patriots, they claimed. Her supporters detected class snobbery in these accusations: did it matter, after all, whether she was an aristocratic baroness or not? Her supporters further argued that the disappearance of her papers was evidence that von Beck herself had fallen victim to Austrian spies. Each side awaited confirmation from the Hungarian leaders and from Kossuth about the veracity of her tale. In the end, her identity remained uncertain.

The case of the so-called Baroness von Beck highlighted the damaging consequences of a protracted debate over a self-professed refugee's identity. To her opponents, the case represented the problems inherent in a refugee narrative that was too readily retold to too great effect by frauds. Yet, it also suggests that by the early 1850s the media was saturated with widely recognizable tales of persecution and the public was expected to react according to a set of standard procedures in aiding the foreign refugees in their midst. The standardization of public and private responses to real refugees made failure to meet these expectations cause for outrage. For Chartists, in particular, the death of the Baroness von Beck was horrifying precisely because it was the result of just such a lapse in protocol.

High-profile cases of potential fraud, like that of von Beck, were rare. At least in the short term, the questionable character of a few refugees did not compromise public enthusiasm for exiles as a group. Aid societies policed fraud, and there was little question that genuine refugees deserved all the support listeners could afford.

Rhetorical Power and Practical Shortcoming

To paraphrase the seventeenth-century French moralist, La Rochefoucauld, fraud was a tribute of sorts to the power of the liberal refugee narrative.[59] Its hold over British sentiment in the mid-nineteenth century was impressive indeed and could lead them to override even their racial prejudices. Harriet Beecher Stowe understood this well and used the heroic figure of the liberal revolutionary refugee to win readers' hearts over to her dark-skinned protagonist, George Harris (figure 3.4). As the fleeing slave confronts his pursuers in *Uncle Tom's Cabin* (1852), Stowe breaks into the narrative with the following reflection:

> If he had only been a Hungarian youth, now bravely defending in some mountain fastness the retreat of fugitives escaping from Austria into America, this would have been sublime heroism; but as it was a youth of African descent, defending the retreat of fugitives through America into Canada, of course we are too well instructed and patriotic to see any heroism in it. . . . When despairing

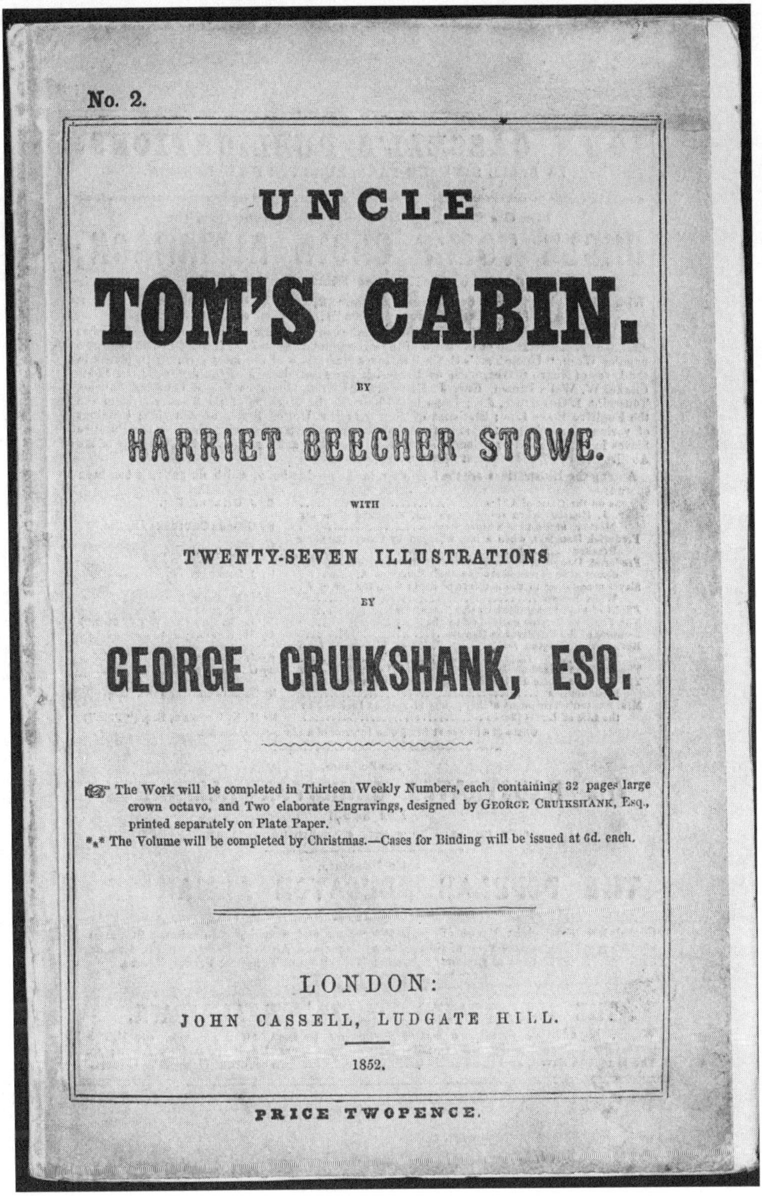

No. 2.

UNCLE

TOM'S CABIN.

BY

HARRIET BEECHER STOWE.

WITH

TWENTY-SEVEN ILLUSTRATIONS

BY

GEORGE CRUIKSHANK, ESQ.

☞ The Work will be completed in Thirteen Weekly Numbers, each containing 32 pages large crown octavo, and Two elaborate Engravings, designed by GEORGE CRUIKSHANK, Esq., printed separately on Plate Paper.

*** The Volume will be completed by Christmas.—Cases for Binding will be issued at 6d. each.

LONDON:

JOHN CASSELL, LUDGATE HILL.

1852.

PRICE TWOPENCE.

3.4 · Title wrapper of *Uncle Tom's Cabin*. No. 2. Serialized version. London: John Cassell. Credit: Courtesy of the Bowdoin College Library, Brunswick, Maine.

> Hungarian fugitives make their way, against all the search-warrants and authorities of their lawful government, to America, press and political cabinet ring with applause and welcome. When despairing African fugitives do the same thing,—it is—what *is* it?[60]

Stowe's parallel between American fugitive slaves and European patriots was meant to shock her readers. She demanded that they celebrate her black heroes as much as they lionized those icons who battled oppression in continental Europe.

In Britain, where *Uncle Tom's Cabin* sold a million copies within months, Stowe's point hit home.[61] By the early 1850s, British culture was saturated with stories, real and fictive, of escape from oppression. Assistance to refugees involved more than simply opposing tyrants and helping their victims; Britain's newly vigorous liberal ideology provided the empathetic humanitarianism of refugee narratives with a strong agentic backbone. Canonical refugee narratives implicitly recognized assertive and independent-minded freedom fighters—good liberal subjects—among the oppressed.

American refugee slaves thus embodied liberal ideals then gaining traction within British culture. Like Stowe, British refugee supporters were confident of the link between European revolutionaries and fugitive slaves from America, and they bridled when others failed to recognize the connection. Like Giuseppe Mazzini, George Harris had faced the fire of his pursuers. As had Theresa Pulszky, Eliza Harris had been separated from her husband and forced to flee with her children. Like continental exiles fleeing to England, American fugitive slaves bound for Canada found comfort in the homes of British subjects.

Harnessed to increasingly standardized routines for gathering assistance, refugee stories enabled activists to mobilize resources to follow through on their commitment to persecuted foreigners regardless of class or racial background. In so doing, refugee supporters modeled liberal freedoms and philanthropic generosity. In contrast to autocratic rule on the Continent, Britain enjoyed constitutional freedoms. In contrast to America's racial despotism, *all* Britons—even blacks after 1838—were freeborn. Public pride in the relative freedoms of British society was palpable enough to make refuge for persecuted foreigners a touchstone liberal-cum-national act. For the moment, the moral triumph of rescuing the persecuted obscured the all-too-real social tensions refugees faced in exile. Among the refugees, many became Anglophiles. French exile Alphonse Esquiros professed to have found in England "incarnated in the manners, laws, and public life that liberty which was pursued in France through so many struggles and has not yet been attained." Resolute socialists too saw much to praise in English society. French socialist Martin Nadaud found friends among workers and gentlemen, and even Simon Bernard extolled British justice after his 1858 acquittal in the Orsini Affair.[62]

Not all refugees were so enthralled with British society. French radical Alexandre-Auguste Ledru Rollin did not endear himself to anyone when, three months after his arrival, he penned his *De la Décadence de l'Angleterre*. Even less irascible foreigners could be provoked into serious critiques of British society. Herzen, like many observers from state-dominated societies, admired the liberties embedded in British institutions but found public opinion to be unexpectedly oppressive. He described as a peculiar sort of "torture-chamber; your neighbor, your butcher, your tailor, family, club, parish, keep you under supervision." For Schlesinger, it was English class snobbery that made a mockery of the freedom of movement. So internalized was Englishmen's "fear of 'losing caste'" that London "admits not even of one single circle of free and general sociability!" Friedrich Engels, author of *The Working Class in England* (1845), saw the costs of class stratification as even more pervasive and crippling.

Refugees understood the unseemly side of urban life all too well. The metropolitan police reported in 1854 that of the approximately two thousand refugees in London, two-thirds were impoverished. For many a refugee unable to find employment, prison or the insane asylum became a last recourse.[63] Activists and the public at large could overlook these harsher realities at the height of a refugee crisis, when refuge was a cause célèbre in the press. The refugee narrative and the burst of public attention and generosity it occasioned suited the needs of newly arrived refugees well. However, it was less well suited to the challenge of caring for refugees in the longer term, when heroic stories became yesterday's news and the daily challenge of making a new life in a strange land took the place of extraordinary and dramatic circumstances.

FOUR

Taking Refuge in Empire

In 1823, London, says Count Pecchio, was peopled with exiles of every kind and country; presidents of republics, and generals of armies; the widow of the negro king Christopher . . , and the dethroned Emperor of Mexico, met together in one spot, the Elysium, or, as a satirist would say, the Botany Bay of illustrious men, and would-be heroes. It was a sort of magic vision, worthy of Merlin himself . . . "The fashionables took a delight in exhibiting a new 'lion,' which is the name given in England to any person of celebrity who is invited to an evening party, to be shown as the wonder of the day to two or three hundred persons, squeezed together like anchovies in a barrel . . . How soon did this curiosity pass away! The exiles, lions and all, were speedily buried in oblivion. There is no tomb so vast as London, which swallows up the most illustrious names for ever: it has an omnivorous maw. The celebrity of a man in London blazes and vanishes away like a firework: there is a great noise, numberless invitations, endless flattery and exaggeration, for a few days, and then an eternal silence."

— *GENTLEMAN'S MAGAZINE* REVIEW OF *SEMI-SERIOUS OBSERVATIONS OF AN ITALIAN EXILE, DURING HIS RESIDENCE IN ENGLAND* (1823)

By the middle of the nineteenth century, the British were well versed in refugee affairs. A coherent narrative instructed the public in how to recognize and respond to persecuted foreigners. Yet, there was a practical problem at the core of their template for refuge. British responses to refugee crises were built on sensation. As Italian exile Count Pecchio wryly noted, once a particular crisis was old news, refugees were in danger of being forgotten entirely.

Few relief societies, formed in the moment of crisis, were prepared for the *longue durée* of exile. What would happen to the refugees when the crowds dispersed? When the powerful narrative that obscured differences of class, race, and religion found new heroes to lionize? When refugees began to look more like paupers than independent freedom fighters? Or when they found work at the alleged expense of native-born Britons? There were few cases where refugees could be repatriated before relief coffers were depleted.[1] Impoverishment could follow quickly for those who were not poor already. Writing in 1853, Chartist George Julian Harney deplored this dark reality. Harney noted that foreign refugees were free to come to the Britain, once there, they were "free to starve."[2]

The prospect of integrating large and diverse groups of foreigners into British society on a more permanent basis was daunting from the start. As time passed, popular commentaries on refugee affairs became suffused with the very politics of class, race, and religion that was set aside in the excitement of the initial turn to refuge. Given these difficulties, why did philanthropists and public commentators remain optimistic about the prospects of British refuge? Why did the emerging humanitarian norm take root, let alone become a nation-defining pursuit?

Despite the difficulty of maintaining enthusiasm for charitable drives, the public accepted that British refuge was likely to last a long time. The public did so because it counted on philanthropists' and officials' ability to find refuge for the persecuted somewhere—at home, in the Empire, or under the British aegis overseas—without straining the social fabric. The chapter examines how relief workers helped refugees, whom they had taken such care to distinguish from run-of-the-mill immigrants, to become just that. To succeed, the refugees would have to prove to be the paragons of liberal virtue so celebrated in the refugee narrative. They would have to be—or become—hardworking, sober, morally righteous individuals. Moreover, they would have to show this in a way that did not test the patience of their host society.

Scholars of British-refugee relations in the nineteenth century have rarely looked beyond the reception of persecuted foreigners in the British Isles. On the few occasions when they glance further afield, they tend to question whether the transmigration of homeless foreigners to the Empire and further overseas should be called "refuge."[3] Certainly the quality of overseas exile could be questioned, just as refuge in Britain rarely lived up to the standards set in the refugee narrative. But the role of transmigration in refuge provision should not be discounted. Short of being able to return refugees to their homes, was not refuge somewhere—especially under the aegis of the British flag—preferable to persecution? Public commentators, activists, and officials believed so. Indeed, it was the very existence of overseas outlets that provided Britain with the physical space for what was fast becoming an expansive national moral commitment. Without the ability to offer long-term refuge elsewhere, the British would not have come to advocate refuge as a universal humanitarian norm.

After the Crowds Dispersed

Concern over how long-term refuge might challenge the fabric of British society became a defining feature of British-refugee relations once the immediate fanfare subsided. "The refugee" was becoming a potentially universal category—applicable to any foreigner who faced persecution overseas. But this broad humanitarian sentiment did not alter the fact that British society, though increasingly wealthy in aggregate, had limited resources for its own poor, let alone for foreign refugees. Over the *longue durée*, anxiety over scarce resources developed along the lines of broader social divides. In the case of the French émigrés, religious concerns were paramount. For other refugee groups, the dominant concern was racial, political, socioeconomic, or a mixture of all three. Thus, the prospect of long-term refugee resettlement exposed the very foreignness of these exiles that the refugee narrative was supposed to transcend.

National relief for French Catholics in Protestant Britain exploded the earlier confessional model for refuge. Yet sympathy with the French émigrés in the 1790s could not entirely overcome religious tensions. Even commentators who supported the refugees' cause expressed concern. In 1796, for example, the *Monthly Review*, long an advocate for the French Catholic clergy, responded to anxieties voiced by Thomas Mathias, a "concerned Anglican." Mathias had asserted that the national charity lavished on the priests—a sum of £200,000—was excessive. In return for this charity, Mathias claimed, Protestants were being subjected to Catholic subversion of the Protestant social fabric. Mathias backed his claims with reproductions of letters demonstrating local concerns about "popishness," dating from 1745 forward, from areas that were then leaders in the relief campaign, including Winchester and Oxford.[4] The *Monthly Review* editors responded forcefully to Mathias's publication, but they did not dismiss his concerns entirely. They conceded that Mathias's complaints that "the [Pitt] Ministry, the Bishops of Durham and Winchester, and the University of Oxford" were sending poor Protestant children to the priests for Catholic education were "at least very plausible grounds of alarm." The editors "strongly call[ed] on the parties implicated for a satisfactory explanation."[5]

The editors of the *Monthly Review* were not alone. Thanks to the vigilance of the bishop of St. Pol de Léon, only one French priest was caught in the act and ultimately expelled under the purview of the 1793 Aliens Act, which gave the Home Office the power to investigate and expel suspected *agents-provocateurs*.[6] More worried about political disaffection, the Home Office did not prioritize cases of proselytizing. Nevertheless, anxious individuals called on the government to protect their families against the Catholic presence. In 1805, for instance, the Home Office's new Aliens Office received an alert that a French priest who had been invited into an Anglican household managed to convert the mother and daughter.

The complaint ensued from a domestic quarrel over whether the husband/father had the right to remove the daughter from her mother. As late as 1820, a Caroline Barrett of Portsmouth wrote to Lord Sidmouth about the insidious activities of refugees intimately connected with her own family. Barrett hoped that the Home Office would employ her for her knowledge or at least permit an interview with the secretary. The Home Office seems to have politely declined Mrs. Barrett's kind offer.[7]

Local religious anxieties extended beyond the more obvious Protestant-Catholic divide to ongoing debates about the place of Protestant Nonconformity. The 1689 Act of Toleration had introduced a degree of freedom of conscience for non-Anglicans. But England, and Great Britain after the Act of Union with Scotland in 1707, was still an Anglican state and remained so through the 1820s. Even continental Protestants were pressured to support the Church of England. The cautious James II forced French Huguenot churches to conform to Anglican liturgy as a gesture to potential political enemies at a time of great tension over the monarch's religion. The Protestant monarchs who succeeded James also required that foreign Protestant churches conform if they wished to receive national charitable assistance.

Anglican distrust for Nonconformity found its way into public discussions of the Catholic émigrés in the 1790s as well. Supporters of the French émigrés had a way of interspersing their praise for these refugees with invectives against Protestant Nonconformity, a rhetorical tactic that irritated its targets. For instance, Welsh Unitarian David Jones lambasted the Anglican bishop Samuel Horsley for the way in which he argued for the émigrés' cause in the 1790s. Jones rejected Horsley's assumption that dissenters, having supported the initial 1789 Revolution, must be "abettors of everything that has since happened in that country." Horsley might have spoken with that "elevation for which humanity appears one great brotherhood."[8] Yet, by Jones's reading, Horsley accused Nonconformists of being opponents of order and property—not to mention treacherous atheists.[9] In Jones's estimation, Horsley's intolerant tone threatened to jeopardize the country's already tenuous social peace.

Religious anxieties diminished greatly in the nineteenth century, though they would re-emerge in a different fashion with the arrival of Jewish refugees after 1880. Nevertheless, worries about refugees' impact on the social fabric continued to simmer, even among refugee supporters. Members of the mainstream liberal LASFP watched with alarm as democratic and socialist exiles joined the growing number of Polish refugees in Britain in the 1840s and 1850s. The new influx of Poles could not be adequately maintained by the parliamentary grant that had supported Polish refugees since the mid-1830s. At only £10,000 per annum, the grant provided just enough for the initial pensioners and was now woefully inadequate.[10]

Polish refugee supporters had their hands full simply defending their existing grant. In the House of Lords, the Conservative MP Lord Eglington complained that the Poles used more of the funds allotted to refugees than any one other group and that the majority of this generous grant paid for medical services to treat "diseases . . . such as he would not name in their Lordships' House; and for the cure of which it would ill become this nation to contribute."[11] Eglington's arch accusation of sexual immorality provoked an immediate rebuff. Nonetheless, it was clear that government support of refugees was conditional on respectable conduct. Refugees needed to maintain the high moral stature they had earned by sacrificing themselves for conscience's sake. Although Eglington's allegations did not stick, they must have reminded refugees that they were under their hosts' strict scrutiny.

Refugee morals were a middle-class and elite preoccupation. The public at large was more concerned that refugees might compete economically with native-born Britons. Native-born workers had rioted against Huguenot weavers in the seventeenth century. Such resentment did not dissipate entirely over time. Economic difficulties in the 1830s hit the domestic textile industry particularly hard and exacerbated the long-standing antagonism between British workers and now-British descendants of the Huguenot diaspora. In this context, working-class radicals argued that Huguenot industry had only served to deepen economic oppression.[12] More generally, critical commentators lamented the extent to which elite philanthropists prioritized "refugee scamps" over the needy at home. One writer for the Tory newspaper *The Age* chastised eager philanthropists thus in 1834: "We perceive that a meeting has been held in the City to get up a Ball, the proceeds of the tickets to be distributed amongst 'the poor Poles.' This is too bad. 'Charity (the proverb says) begins at home.'"[13] Three years later, when there seemed to be no slackening of national enthusiasm for foreign refugees despite increasing distress among the British working classes, a writer at *The Age* lashed out at refugee supporters once more, describing such support as "the sickening monomania which infects our aristocracy touching these Poles, and their indifference to the sufferings of British artisans, who toil for their decoration and comfort."[14]

Given this backlash, it is not surprising that refugees took strides to minimize potential criticisms and to protect their communities. The luckiest were those who married into English families or who had wealthy friends in and outside of the refugee community who could continue to support them once popular fanfare subsided. For example, Friedrich Engels bankrolled several members of the German exile community, including the entire Marx family. Proximity to foreign communities could also make the transition to life in Britain more manageable. Through the eighteenth century, foreign Protestant churches not only welcomed the fleeing Huguenots, but they also dispersed the so-called royal bounty, making proximity essential for the receipt of funds. More generally, cosmopolitan neighborhoods such as Spitalfields in London's East End, Soho, and Central London writ large meant that refugees from Huguenots to Jews to Bangladeshis in the twentieth century found compatriots among whom they could settle. Even continental anarchists found safe harbor there, much to the British public's chagrin. Wealthier members of these communities tried to support their less fortunate brethren. Like affluent refugees throughout Britain, Johanna and Gottfried Kinkel received a steady stream of begging letters from impoverished Europeans.[15] Mazzini established a school to aid Italian immigrants in 1841. More established Jews supported the Poor Jews' Temporary Shelter in the East End, an organization that would exist in different incarnations from the early 1880s through the mid-twentieth century. The French community on the Channel Island of Jersey did what it could to draw foreign revolutionaries out of their isolation on the island and across Britain through their newspaper *L'Homme*.[16]

While refugees attempted to assist their own, British activists also strove to mitigate social tensions associated with the long-term resettlement of refugee groups. They tried to enable refugees to become self-sufficient members of the community and thereby live up to the descriptions of ascetic hard work so highly praised in the refugee narrative. Activists also insisted on the similarity of refugees to native Britons. The more akin the refugee seemed to the British observer in social, political, or simply basic emotional outlook, the more sympathy he or she would accrue. In practical terms, refugees and refugee supporters believed that self-conscious efforts to conform to British expectations would ease the social tensions consequent on longer periods of exile.

The government similarly made assimilation a point of their assistance to larger refugee groups. Officials hoped to help Huguenot merchants integrate into their new homes in the seventeenth century. The effort was part of the state's interest in bolstering England's commercial competitiveness against the then-dominant Dutch. Existing British policies did not make it easy for foreigners to attain subject status; without it, transmitting "real" property from one generation to the next was impossible. Moreover, aliens were subject to double taxation.[17] Charles II promised to have a general act of naturalization passed in Parliament. No general act passed. But Charles II and James II offered letters of patent to facilitate applications for denizen status on an individual basis.[18] By 1688, 5,659 of the roughly 50,000 Huguenots had become denizens, a status by which—akin to the modern status of permanent resident—foreigners were afforded property rights, though they remained subject to additional taxation.[19] In addition to the emblematic silk weavers who settled in Spitalfields, whole communities of tanners, maritime traders, linen manufacturers, and lace and cloth makers fled to towns across England and Ireland, bringing their trades with them. In 1709, forty years after discussions regarding naturalization had begun, Parliament finally passed a general act for Huguenot naturalization. The act did not make naturalization automatic or free; refugees would have to opt in and pay a fee.

Despite the government's best intentions, only 333 Huguenots took advantage of the act in its first ten years on the books.[20] Apart from wealthier Huguenots, few refugees were interested in naturalization. Most were more concerned with getting their next meal than with protecting wealth and merchant interests. Moreover, most refugees preferred to believe that they would someday return to a home freed from persecution. Even if they had the wealth to make naturalization a possibility, most refugees would not have undertaken what was thus a pessimistic action.

More generally, refugees relied on activists to assist them. Although few relief committees planned on providing long-term support, those that did helped smaller groups of refugees to find jobs. Affiliates of the Wilmot Committee in the 1790s—female notables especially—helped French priests make and sell tapestries from their isolated home in Winchester, while a similar set of philanthropists organized bazaars and sold artwork to help Portuguese,

Spanish, and Italian exiles in the 1820s. Elite and even middle-class families employed refugees as tutors for their children and helped refugee women to find jobs in domestic service. The Baroness Angela Burdett Coutts made transforming exiles into good liberal subjects something of a religious endeavor, akin to the missionary fervor associated with the project of "civilizing" African subjects. A great friend of Conservatives Shaftesbury and Wellington, as well as Louis Napoleon, the baroness reached out to the French communist exiles as well, though she did not support their cause. Directing her missionary work through the Reverend T. Marzials, an Anglo-Huguenot himself, Burdett Coutts separated a group of communist refugees from their fellow exiles and provided them with religious education and work—twin paths to salvation so far as their benefactress was concerned.[21]

Preferential employment for foreign refugees might have fueled working-class anxieties about competition, but Chartists, in their efforts to appropriate a share of the moral glory of supporting refugees, painted it as a point of working-class pride. When officials and the more elite LASFP prepared to resettle abroad the contingent of Polish and Hungarian democrats who arrived in 1851, Chartists throughout the country established their own charitable endeavor with the aim of enabling them to settle more permanently in Britain. The short-lived Chartist *Refugee Circular* exclaimed that it "devolves legitimately upon the working classes, in Liverpool and throughout the country, to discharge that duty towards these homeless and friendless exiles, that should have been performed by the representatives of English power and authority." Chartist plans for refugee settlement would live up to previous examples of British liberality and hospitality, they argued.[22] Chartist organizers hoped that these refugees and their cause would become emblematic of the common democratic struggle and would help to create a network of like-minded, international-thinking British subjects. Because Chartist refugee supporters subscribed to the broader idea that refuge for persecuted foreigners had to enable the individuals in question to become self-sufficient, hardworking, and sober members of liberal society, they bore the burden of proving that such integration was possible in the over-saturated job market of the time.

The Chartists' plan coupled a model of assistance by subscription with an effort to parcel refugees out in smaller, more manageable groups. Rather than pay into a general collection, subscribers—or a group of subscribers—were to sponsor a specified refugee, paying for his living expenses directly.[23] In a letter to the Chartist newspaper *Northern Star* in March 1851, radical artisan William Linton reminded his audience that this would not be a "life-burden." If Chartists could "divide themselves into relief committees of twenty men, each committee undertaking to *guarantee the support of one man*, the work is done. 20 x 232 is 4640." Linton calculated, "There are 4,640 Chartists; not one of whom ought to shrink from even the sacrifice of *sixpence a week to save his brother from starvation*." The small fund would enable the refugees to avoid starvation while they learned English. Once they had learned English, they would find gainful employment.[24]

William Costine and James Spurr's Liverpool Polish and Hungarian Refugee Committee put parts of Linton's scheme to use. Whereas Linton's efforts did not require refugees to live near their sponsors, the Liverpool committee sent its refugees in groups to hosts throughout the country, particularly in the north. Willing hosts invited only the number of refugees they could afford. The committee's broad network—connected by the radical press and the *Refugee Circular*—enabled branch associations to learn of the scheme and keep tabs on its progress. Linton treated relief as an emergency tactic only, but branches of the Liverpool committee were instructed to help provide housing, English lessons, and willing employers.

In Northern England especially, Costine and Spurr's plan took root thanks to the region's increasingly cosmopolitan population and the efforts of radical republican Joseph Cowen. The radical press never commented on other foreigners in the region, but it celebrated the native welcome given to foreign refugees when Cowen and a group of "zealous friends of liberty and humanity" invited a contingent of twelve Polish refugees to Newcastle. (As many as ninety were assembled for a meeting in Newcastle before being sent to nearby towns.) The *Newcastle Chronicle* noted that the welcoming party was "crowded to excess, hundreds unable to obtain admission." It would be "necessary," explained the editors, "to hold another meeting or soiree at a future time." Among those who led the meeting were the same town notables who had supported further emigration to America.[25] Taking its cues from the Liverpool committee and from Linton's scheme, the Newcastle refugee committee organized parties of twenty or thirty individuals to take the charge of one of the twelve refugees, each group raising funds and finding employment for their designated refugee. The committee also helped to organize soirees, inform Newcastle residents of the situation, and elicit residents' sympathy and financial support.[26]

The Liverpool committee and its network seem to have fared well overall. Like Newcastle, the branch association in Sheffield welcomed thirty-one refugees, of whom eight went to Glasgow, fourteen to Leeds, and nineteen remained in Liverpool. Among other towns, Hull, Northampton, Royton, and Dundee took roughly two apiece. In this manner, the joint effort absorbed the 219 exiles.[27] Refugee supporters emphasized their success: of the twelve refugees brought to Newcastle, nine were employed by July. One, for instance, worked as a moulder at a factory. Another moved slightly out of Newcastle for employment at a North Shields magnesia works.[28] Testimonials spoke very highly of the refugees. Invariably, they were upstanding, sober, and dedicated workers. Whatever their class of origin, the refugees were said to appreciate the work they received and generally to reflect well on the "friends of liberty and humanity" who had enabled them to remain in the country.

Having won the battle to provide both political and social succor, radical circles throughout the north of England, in Newcastle especially, continued to welcome foreign refugees. Refugees appeared on stage at radical political meetings throughout the 1850s and beyond. Moreover, the campaign redoubled radicals' investment in larger-scale campaigns for refugees. Even though they scored no discernable wins for their own political platform, British radicals came to the defense of a national right to refuge time and time again. Both the radical press and speakers at local radical meetings held up this assistance to refugees as evidence of working-class generosity, even as the refugees themselves assimilated and disappeared from the historical record.

The Chartists' pioneering model remains a familiar method of relief to the present day. Unfortunately, little is known about what happened to many of these refugees over time. Several rose to prominence in Newcastle and Gateshead, but what absorption in British towns meant for the majority of the refugees is a mystery.[29] After celebratory remarks on their employment and behavior in the first years of their placement, they disappeared from official records. In areas like South Shields, the refugees blended readily into the tapestry of global Britain, becoming almost indistinguishable in a composite population that included internal migrants and foreign laborers in addition to fugitives from persecution overseas.

The Overseas Outlet

The very existence of external outlets for refuge—both in and outside of the British Empire—gave force to refuge as a rapidly expanding humanitarian act. Without it, British activists and officials could never have found the resources or the popular will to provide refuge for so many. Overseas resettlement of refugees was similar to emigration schemes for British subjects, the number of which was on the rise by the middle of the nineteenth century. Overseas resettlement in both cases provided a multipurpose social safety valve. Especially when resettled at the outposts of the British Empire, new colonial subjects supported imperial growth. Black Loyalists and liberated Africans helped to settle areas considered too unhealthy for the European constitution. More broadly, refugees helped to expand agricultural and trade ventures as well as British liberal and religious ideals—or at least that was the goal. Refuge thus became a project for missionaries, naval officers, and civil servants across the globe.

In the eighteenth century, the transmigration of foreigners was a relatively standard way for groups of refugees to achieve self-sufficiency over time. Overseas refuge was generally reserved for groups like the Black Loyalists, who seemed different from middle-class white Britons. Ethnicity was not the sole determining feature; religious and class differences also factored into the mix, as did the refugees' own sense of where their exile community could best resettle. Although welcomed in Britain, many Huguenots and white Loyalists, for example, also sought out opportunities elsewhere in the British Empire.

Whereas Huguenot transmigrants chose an overseas alternative, Lutheran Salzburgers and Palatines who fled Catholic persecution were less fortunate. These poor Protestants seemed to lack the craft skills that made the Huguenots desirable immigrants. Consequently, they were pushed to the American colonies.[30] Similar anxieties were all the more apparent in the case of Black Loyalists fleeing the American War for Independence, fugitive slaves, and Africans liberated from the slave trade. In each of these cases, race divided the foreigners from their British protectors. There was little serious consideration of giving Africans liberated from the slave trade a home in Britain. Even Black Loyalists—fewer in number and more familiar with life in the British Empire—found it difficult to resettle in British Nova Scotia in the wake of the American War. There declining conditions in the 1790s forced many to the brink of starvation, making these ex-slaves eager to seek out alternative solutions.[31] In 1791, abolitionists Thomas Clarkson, Granville Sharp, and William Wilberforce established the Sierra Leone Company, opening an alternative that many of the black refugees in British Nova Scotia welcomed readily. They set out for West Africa in 1792, along with Zachary Macaulay as governor of the fledgling colony. There they would be joined by free blacks then living in Britain. Together, they founded the colony that would become the go-to refuge for Africans liberated from the slave trade and Black Loyalists who fled the United States in the wake of the War of 1812.

In the 1790s, the French émigré priests were likewise encouraged to relocate to Quebec, where they would tend to the Acadian population under British rule. Lord Landsdown had advocated a migration to Canada at the time of the second reading of the Aliens Bill in late 1792. His Majesty, Landsdown pointed out, could grant lands in Western Canada to the refugees if they should be refused repatriation.[32] After all, Canada already had a French Catholic population that the British inherited in the Treaty of Paris of 1763. When the Wilmot Committee made its initial appeal to the public, it likewise mentioned the possible removal of the refugees to Canada, with the caveat that such a move would not be feasible for several months.[33] As the crisis persisted, French priests seriously considered moving to Quebec, but few ended up following through on the offer.[34]

In the nineteenth century, the scale of international refugee resettlement under British aegis expanded with the growth of imperial power and the swelling number of foreigners seeking British refuge. By the 1850s, approximately five to seven thousand refugees resided in Great Britain,[35] but a far greater number sought sanctuary across the British Empire. An unknown number hoped to gain access to the British Ionian Islands in the course of the Greek War for Independence in the 1820s. By the late 1840s and early 1850s, hundreds of continental exiles—Italians especially—sought shelter in British port at Malta, and dozens of French and assorted other European revolutionaries made their homes on the small island of Jersey in the Channel Islands. Fifty thousand American fugitive slaves lived in British Canada as of 1851, having followed paths blazed by Black Loyalists in the eighteenth

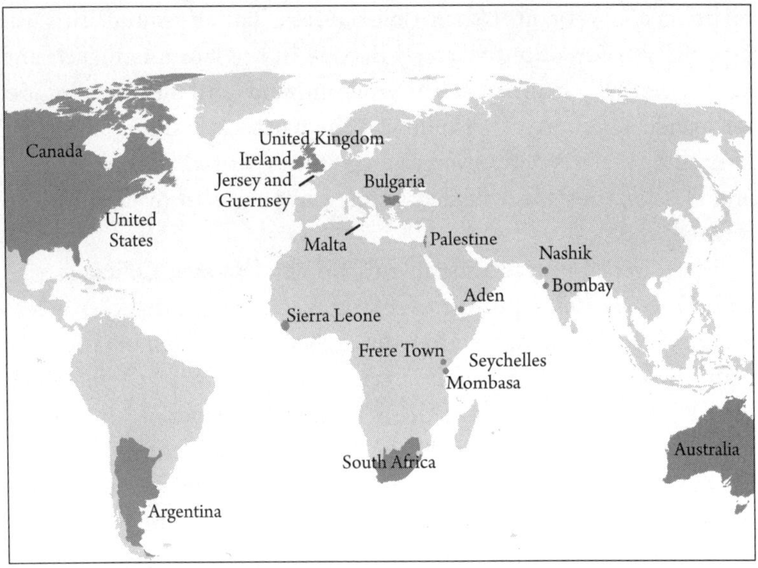

4.1. British-supported places of refuge, c. 1700–1940. Credit: Mathieu Duvall, Imaging and Computing Center, Bates College, Lewiston, Maine. (Note: for convenience, this map reflects place names from 1940.)

century. Another sixty-five thousand liberated Africans—those caught up in the illegal slave traffic—were resettled in British Sierra Leone and, later, in British-run outposts across East Africa, on the Arabian Peninsula, and in British India. Toward the century's close, famine refugees from the Princely States in South Asia sought the questionable relief offered by the British Raj, and in Latin America, officials wrestled with revolutionaries who hoped to find protection from their pursuers in British ships and embassies.[36]

British overseas refuge extended far beyond the bounds of formal empire, both through diplomatic intervention and philanthropic outreach (figure 4.1). In the 1790s, one member of the Wilmot Committee suggested that the British try to convince Holland to take in more refugees in order to relieve Britain of the "excess" population.[37] By the 1850s, Palmerston's Foreign Office famously helped convince the Ottoman Sultan to protect Kossuth's defeated army from Austrian attempts to pursue them in Asia Minor. The Foreign Office similarly supported the Swiss when they came under pressure from their neighbors for harboring revolutionary exiles.[38] Philanthropists were equally dependent on diplomatic endeavors when they provided refuge outside British territory. Often, they relied on civil servants to help dole out relief on the ground. This was especially true in Southeastern Europe in the late nineteenth and early twentieth centuries. The predominant philanthropic model for overseas refugee relief followed the patterns of imperial refuge. Even after the loss of the American colonies, British philanthropists and missionaries spearheaded public campaigns to resettle foreign refugees there.

There were two variants on this imperial model. Officials tried absorbing smaller contingents of refugees into existing overseas settlements. For example, after the arrival of the "democratic" and "working-class" Polish and Hungarian refugees in 1851, officials in Liverpool tried to convince them to move to America. Through a translator, Liverpool administrator and local social reformer Edward Rushton informed each group that "those who had proved themselves the best friends of Poland were desirous to avert the worst calamities of exile—the dependence on other people for subsistence."[39] In this country, Rushton continued:

> Our own people find it difficult to obtain even the means of supporting life; and in their [the refugees'] case the difficulty would be augmented by their ignorance of the language of the country. . . . [H]e knew that his countrymen would cheerfully give them employment if they had the means, but they had not.[40]

In point of fact, Liverpool regularly witnessed the influx of Irish in numbers much greater than those of the Hungarian and Polish contingent that spring. Life for the Irish was far from easy in the England, but the economy absorbed these immigrants. Nonetheless, officials and members of the LASFP argued that an inability to speak English prohibited the new refugees from being integrated into the local economy.[41] In an attempt to reward those who accepted the offer, the government promised further aid to those who would leave immediately. Most of the Hungarian exiles at Liverpool accepted the offer of assisted passage to America at once. The Poles did not—a choice that meant they would have to fend for themselves, as more radical newspapers were quick to note. Nevertheless, the model was considered quite a success. When another shipload of Polish and Hungarian refugees arrived at Southampton in June 1851, the mayor wrote to Parliament asking what funds might be expected to help defray the costs of the refugees' maintenance. According to the *Daily News*, Prime Minister

John Russell authorized funding on the spot. As with the refugees in Liverpool, the funding came with conditions. Governmental funding was "to be limited to those refugees who were willing to go to America." The mayor of Southampton began arranging for a ship to America immediately.[42]

The second model of overseas resettlement required the creation of entirely new communities. Sierra Leone provided the most spectacular example, becoming a colony in the process. This model began as something of an afterthought of the campaign against the slave trade. After the Congress of Vienna, the government set up vice admiralty and mixed commission courts to adjudicate vessels caught in the now-illegal trade. A special branch of the Colonial Office, the Liberated Africans Department, oversaw the ships' human cargo while cases were in court. If the Africans were freed by court order, the Department turned them over to missionaries. It was through this partnership, a consequence of bilateral treaties outlawing the slave trade, that missionaries and officials pioneered what became standard methods of training homeless foreigners in the ways of independent living.

The settlement of liberated Africans was as central to the growth of the missionary project as it was to abolitionism. As historian Elizabeth Elbourne argues in her work on Southern Africa, missionaries made the "civilizing" work of empire a popular endeavor and ultimately a national one in the nineteenth century. They hoped to demonstrate the salubrious effects of religious and practical instruction on liberated Africans. As Elbourne notes, this work helped justify Britain's expanding global role in metropolitan eyes. The project had a pragmatic side as well. Productive settlements would bolster the British Empire and trade interests in the region. The popularity of this missionary work at home in turn raised the funds necessary to further expand fieldwork overseas.[43]

Founded in the 1790s, Sierra Leone was at the vanguard of overseas missionary work by Anglican and Nonconformist organizations alike (figure 4.2). The colony, while led by the Anglican Church Missionary Society (CMS), was divided into two missionary zones. Wesleyan Methodists took charge of pastoral care for liberated Africans who remained in Freetown, while the CMS organized care in agricultural settlements that they established in the countryside on land grants received from the government. These settlements were to become hubs for production and for spiritual and practical training centered

4.2 · "Free-Town, Sierra Leone," Rev. John Leighton Wilson, *Western Africa: Its History, Conditions, and Prospects* (New York: Harper and Brothers, 1856), 418.

on the local church. Adults received allotments of land on which they were to build their own dwellings and cultivate crops to sustain their families. The parish would care for widows and their children, as well as the large orphan population. Missionaries tried to prepare the children in their care to become leaders of village life—model Christians as well as experts in practical trades and farming. In order to fund these activities, the CMS raised money from supporters in London and even offered to name young pupils after their more substantial donors.[44]

As the CMS London headquarters stipulated, missionaries hoped to establish a "native machinery" by which Sierra Leone could be maintained. On the one hand, an African elite was a necessity given the number of missionaries and colonial officials who succumbed to disease, a far greater problem in West Africa than in Southern Africa. On the other hand, enabling liberated Africans to run their villages would further prove the antislavery movement's point that Africans were capable of becoming independent and productive liberal subjects. "Being thus relieved," missionaries would be able to "devote their energies . . . to making missionary tours, with native missionaries, into the interior of Africa," an endeavor aimed at establishing trade and religious ties with local rulers further afield.[45]

Missionaries celebrated Sierra Leone as a triumph on both counts. Novelist Mary Martha Sherwood celebrated her protagonist

Dazee's resettlement in his adopted home of Sierra Leone. In the 1821 *Dazee, or the Recaptured Negro,* Dazee finds long-term sanctuary in the British colony, where he was brought upon being liberated from the illegal slave trade. Dazee settles in well, becoming a zealous convert to Christianity and excelling in the missionaries' schools. However, he is heartsick over the loss of his mother. When he establishes his own small homestead, he resolves "to build [for his mother] a hut at one end of his garden, which should exactly resemble the little dwelling in his native village." Dazee passes years in Sierra Leone looking for his mother on every slave vessel brought to court. When he is about to give up hope, she arrives. Although her arrival brings Dazee immense joy and comfort, he realizes that he has much changed himself. His reconstructed family life must be Christian. Dazee thus works tirelessly to convert his mother. After two years, he sees his mother baptized at last.[46] For liberated Africans—the not-quite-heroic refugees of the refugee narrative—Dazee's trajectory highlights the best outcome possible in the eyes of pious abolitionists: development into a full-fledged liberal subject under benevolent British tutelage.

The CMS's greatest success story followed a trajectory similar to that of Mrs. Sherwood's protagonist. As the tale was retold triumphantly for metropolitan audiences, Samuel Crowther, an African from the Yoruba territory, had been captured by slavers as a young boy and brought to Sierra Leone in the mid-1820s. Crowther embraced Christianity and went on to be ordained in London. Accompanying the Anglican Reverend Townsend on a mission into Yoruba country in the 1840s, he chanced to find his long-lost mother and two sisters. Crowther did not remain with his family. Rather, he continued to serve in the Anglican Church, becoming the first African bishop in 1864.[47] While not every liberated African could become as illustrious a figure, British philanthropists made good-faith efforts to create a welcoming new home for the tens of thousands of Africans resettled in Sierra Leone. An 1841 order, for instance, required the Liberated African Department to provide the newly liberated with "the particular kind of food that they used in their own countries."

One anonymous observer was confident enough about the success of Sierra Leone to poke fun at the colony's neighboring Liberia, the less fortunate parallel American enterprise. In contrast to Liberia, she wrote, Sierra Leone enjoyed the rule of law. Under the colonial and Christian aegis, the liberated Africans thrived, while those in Liberia had to contend with the less than stable apparatus of self-government. The writer went on to describe the airs Liberian women assumed, the inability of Liberian men to keep their families together, and the general ills of the Liberian climate.[48]

Sierra Leone became the model for resettling American fugitive slaves as well as religious and ethnic minorities from across continental Europe. Foremost among the exporters of the Sierra Leone model were the missionaries themselves, who were quite explicit in their intentions to replicate this successful model for refuge around the world. In this manner, the CMS sought to reproduce the West African endeavor in India. A Mr. and Mrs. Isenberg of the CMS established the African Asylum in Nashik, India, in 1860. Essentially an orphanage and industrial school in one, the Asylum provided training for African children recaptured from the Eastern slave trade. Although their numbers were small, the graduates of the new enterprise were celebrated for their work ethic and their loyalty to the British. One can imagine that this loyalty was particularly welcome to British onlookers shaken by the 1857 Sepoy Rebellion in India. Quite a few of the Nashik graduates became engineers in the construction of the Indian railways.

When the attention of the efforts against the slave trade turned east in the 1870s, Colonial Office officials, members of the Admiralty, missionaries, and official emissaries worked together once more to establish smaller-scale asylums on the model of Sierra Leone in Aden, Mombassa, and the Seychelles. Graduates from the African Asylum in India helped in the founding of these new societies. Their professed loyalty to their British champions became legendary as one group of the Nashik graduates trekked back into Africa with explorer and missionary David Livingstone. When Livingstone died on that ill-fated venture, a group of Africans accompanied his body back to England in 1873, an act much celebrated in the metropolitan press. Livingstone's wish had been to return with these British-trained Africans to their homeland. He and Sir Henry Bartle Frere, a diplomat and staunch antislavery advocate, believed that nothing short of an undertaking on the scale of Sierra Leone in East Africa was required in order to provide adequate shelter to these homeless Africans. CMS-raised graduates of the African Asylum at Nashik founded the eponymous Frere Town in what would shortly become the British East Africa Protectorate (modern-day Kenya). Surrounded by slave-owning neighbors, the small settlement was constantly threatened from the outside. Liberated African William Jones, from the African Asylum in India, valiantly defended the mission's inhabitants—predominantly runaway slaves—from their African and Arab masters.[49]

The model entailing the creation of small refugee settlements de novo in colonial outposts was applied outside of Africa as well, though the similarity to Sierra Leone was not a conscious one on the part of either refugees or British activists. For example, a Canadian application of this model enabled American fugitive slaves and Russian Mennonites to find homes away from their persecutors. Abolitionists and missionaries—especially the Congregationalists, Baptists, and Quakers—aided the fugitive slaves, and the Quakers took an active interest in the resettlement of the Mennonites, fellow pacifists fleeing Russian military conscription. Officials initially housed many of the refugee slaves in empty barracks. Hundreds found relief, and later employment, in larger Canadian cities, especially Toronto.[50] Permanent resettlement plans, however, usually envisaged plots of land clustered around a village, as did black settlements at Dawn, Elgin, and Wilberforce. Both ex-slaves and the Mennonites thus founded outposts on the frontiers of the Canadian West, where philanthropists and the refugees alike believed they would become more independent and self-supporting than in the increasingly crowded towns in the east.

For the Mennonites, the isolation of the frontier dovetailed well with the community's quest for religious freedom—a quest that later took them to Mexico and British Honduras. For American fugitive slaves, by contrast, removal to new settlements on the frontier was less a choice than a last resort in the face of mounting racial tensions in northern cities in the United States and Canada. In both cases, however, British missionaries celebrated the refugees' endeavors, sending funds and agricultural supplies to the communities to assist their new ventures and to relieve them of temporary distress as they awaited the first fruits of their labor.[51]

The village model of refugee resettlement promised to be a tool for resolving difficult humanitarian and diplomatic situations beyond North America. For example, the Great Powers' establishment of an autonomous Bulgaria as a new homeland for the persecuted Christians of the Ottoman Empire made the remaining Muslims in the territory into a minority population. Diplomatic efforts focused on guaranteeing civil rights to this new minority, but one British businessman proposed a solution that was at once the outgrowth of more than a century of refugee resettlement and a forerunner of twentieth-century population transfer schemes. Charles Hanson, who had business ties in the Ottoman Empire, suggested that the

British incorporate a group—like the Sierra Leone or East India Companies—that would move Bulgarian Muslims to lands that the company purchased from the Ottoman rulers. There, under British aegis, the refugees would turn wastelands into profitable agricultural developments.[52]

Hanson's scheme never gained momentum, but other activists turned to the Ottoman Empire to resettle ethnic minorities on a smaller scale. Philanthropists established refuges for Eastern European Jews in and around Jerusalem, then a part of the Ottoman world. British notables such as former diplomat Joseph Finn and his wife, Elizabeth Anne Finn, provided critical support for the Committee of the Society for the Relief of Persecuted Jews, also called the Syrian Colonization Fund, and the Anglo-Jewish community eagerly reported on the progress of communities established there. Christian groups also focused on resettlement in the Ottoman Empire, often seeking to convert Jews in the process, which raised hackles in the Anglo-Jewish community and with the Ottoman authorities. Members of the Foreign Office were hesitant to assist in these endeavors, fearful that involvement would strain British-Ottoman relations. They looked askance at requests for assistance, perhaps because of these groups' tendencies to claim extensive protections the government offered to British subjects and Britain-based organizations overseas.[53]

Despite this early reluctance, officials in London became directly involved with calls for a Jewish homeland by the 1890s. In keeping with their earlier efforts in Sierra Leone and East Africa, the government looked for a proper place of asylum for Jews under direct or indirect British protection. The proposed solution was to give Jewish settlers the British colony of Uganda. Officials, including Joseph Chamberlain and a young Winston Churchill at the Colonial Office, believed Uganda to be in need of a settler population. Given the scarcity of interested Englishmen and women, Jewish Territorialists (the term then used for those who, in contrast to Zionists, advocated for a Jewish homeland outside of Palestine) seemed to these officials to be ideally suited for the task. Russian Zionists did not welcome the 1903 proposal. Nonetheless,

Anglo-Jewish author and leading Territorialist Israel Zangwill believed that it was essential to relieve pressures on asylum in Britain proper.[54] Zionists turned down the Uganda offer in 1905, but that refusal did not end the role of British imperial power in the quest for a Jewish place of refuge.

International organizations continued their own efforts to resettle refugee Jews from Central and Eastern Europe in the manner pioneered by British missionaries and philanthropists. Beginning in the 1890s, German-Jewish Baron Maurice de Hirsch's Argentinian settlements employed the agricultural village model for Jewish refugees. Hirsch and the Jewish Colonization Association (JCA) planned similar settlements in Canada as well. By 1900, the JCA had resettled almost five thousand Jews in Argentina alone.[55] Moreover, leaders of both the English and continental Jewish communities and League of Nations officials counted on the ability of the British Empire to absorb foreign refugees when Latin American governments warned that they would not admit additional refugees. The 1917 Balfour Declaration, by which the British government declared its intent to make Palestine a Jewish homeland, was as much a logical extension of a long-standing imperial model for refuge as it was an outgrowth of late nineteenth-century Zionism. As National Labour politician R. D. Denman emphasized in response to the growing refugee crisis in the 1930s, refuge was the raison d'être of the League's blessing for the Palestine Mandate in the first place.[56]

When Jewish refuge in Palestine seemed to be failing because of mounting Arab-Jewish violence, officials and international philanthropists continued to seek out alternatives in the British Empire. Through the 1930s and 1940s, the British government considered resettling refugees in British Guiana, British Honduras, Tanganyika, and Cyprus, among other locations. While the schemes were eventually dismissed, they received serious Colonial Office and international study. US president Franklin D. Roosevelt sponsored further investigations in conjunction with the conference he called at Evian, Switzerland, on refugees from the Third Reich, and later as part of a top-secret project that broadly considered global migration schemes.[57]

The fact that this overseas model of settlement remained so entrenched should be somewhat surprising. Internationally supported refuge in the colonial Empire ran contrary to rising anti-imperial sentiments among many of the same humanitarian activists by the interwar era. Moreover, activists and British officials continued to count on resettlement schemes of this sort despite mounting evidence that many imperial refuges, including the much-celebrated Sierra Leone, did not provide persecuted foreigners with security.

Practically, Sierra Leone was a disaster—one that should have diminished British pride in refuge provision. Instead of the rosy picture missionaries depicted, the reality was that few liberated Africans raised in this system ever found their families again, let alone followed in the idealized footsteps of Dazee or Reverend Crowther. Even the 1841 Colonial Office order to provide familiar food to the liberated Africans was essentially a dead letter. As early as the 1820s, officials, civil servants, abolitionists, and missionaries questioned whether the missionary-run settlements in Sierra Leone offered a viable refuge for homeless Africans. Europeans living in Sierra Leone were especially prone to disease. While this made liberated Africans more desirable as settlers, it also meant that the colony's managers died in great numbers. The issue of missionaries' and officials' deaths was what first drew critical scrutiny to the Sierra Leone project. In this context of perpetual change, neither trade nor agriculture was thriving. More alarmingly, without constant vigilance, liberated Africans often disappeared from missionary-run villages, presumably because they were stolen into slavery once more.[58]

Faced with this brutal reality, philanthropists explored alternatives. Officials weighed whether to abandon Sierra Leone for what they hoped would be the healthier location of Fernando Po (contemporary Bioko), a British island further south along the West African coast. Missionaries and abolitionists increasingly pinned their hopes on using Sierra Leone less as a model of settlement than as a base for missionary drives deeper into the African continent. With government backing, they sent an antislavery expedition up the Niger River in 1841. The endeavor was at once an imperial venture and an aggressive move against oppressive forces, namely, slavery and "heathen" religions.[59] The Niger expedition aimed to strike evil at the source, but it also eschewed more pressing and complicated concerns about how to manage the hundreds of Africans still freed by the court at Freetown each year. As it became increasingly difficult for Sierra Leone to absorb incoming ex-slaves, the Liberated African Department permitted more and more of them to be conscripted into military service or forwarded to the West Indies as indentured laborers. The latter policy had the effect of attracting an unlikely group of new supporters to the policy of halting the slave trade: West Indian planters.[60] Indentured labor had been heralded as a necessary stepping-stone toward free society. Indeed, Africans liberated in Sierra Leone were themselves frequently indentured. Nevertheless, the concession to the planters seemed even at the time to be an egregious violation of the political point of refuge. The BFASS protested this turn of events. Nevertheless, this practice became general policy by the mid-1840s.

Given what they saw, missionaries on the ground in Sierra Leone could easily have turned away from their work with liberated Africans, discouraged by the challenges of fulfilling their "civilizing project." They would not have been alone. Historian Catherine Hall contends that in the West Indies, abolitionists found it increasingly difficult to argue that liberated slaves could be quickly transformed into model subjects in the Victorian liberal mold. In Southern Africa too, as Elizabeth Elbourne notes, tensions in the Kat River Missionary Station—like Sierra Leone, a home for liberated Africans—dampened missionary and official enthusiasm.[61] It is notable that missionaries, abolitionists, and public commentators did not curtail their concern for foreigners in need of refuge, whether black or white. Perhaps this continuity can be attributed in part to morally clarifying public outrage at the American Fugitive Slave Act. Whatever the case, the Sierra Leone model for overseas refuge remained largely the same. Moreover, later in the century, the public and activists were still recalling celebratory accounts of Sierra Leone in the 1820s and 1830s.

"Far from the Madding Crowd"

The fact that Sierra Leone continued to offer an example of how useful the resources of the Empire were for maintaining the moral momentum of the refugee narrative is somewhat strange. Yet, this is precisely the path that philanthropists and officials followed in the decades to come. The new generation of British refuge providers self-consciously patterned their initiatives after the West African utopia, illusory though it was. Did these proud refuge providers simply fail to notice that Sierra Leone was, in fact, not so much a triumph as a tragic example of resettlement gone awry? Whatever the case may have been, Sierra Leone was spun by missionaries as a success story, one that turned liberated Africans, a group that did not comfortably fit the liberal refugee narrative, into good liberal subjects.

Writing from Freetown, Sierra Leone, under the pen name Mary Church, an anonymous English missionary captured the religious fervor with which the CMS directed its efforts. In an 1833 letter, Church noted that CMS spokesman, the Reverend Haensel, chose a sermon that seemed particularly appropriate. In order to describe the scene around him, Haensel "took for his text, the cities of refuge commanded for the Israelites,"[62] comparing them to Sierra Leone's missionary-run villages. Upon hearing this sermon, Church reflected that

> Sierra Leone is in my opinion, a place very much calculated to excite devotion, for it must be impossible to have constantly before your eyes, a people raised as these are from the lowest state of barbarism, to the exercise of most of the social virtues, by means of religion, and not to feel the unspeakable mercy of the author of it.[63]

This was not just a place of asylum where the inhabitants would be protected from the ravages of the slave trade. Rather, Church highlighted, it was a mission of salvation. Church saw evidence of the effectiveness of British refuge in the missionaries' schools, in labor and commerce, and in the refugees' gratitude for the benevolence showered upon them.

Reports like that of the pseudonymous Mary Church were propaganda. The friends of the Sierra Leone mission used her voice to redeem their project, justifying it as a success that would satisfy the ultimate authority on refuge—the Bible. Church's depiction of a happy city of refuge was intended to bolster a project that by the 1830s many believed to be flailing.[64]

These accounts must have been comforting for metropolitan audiences who were eager to believe that overseas refuge offered a viable outlet for humanitarian activism. Keenly aware that British society could not accommodate large groups of persecuted foreigners for the *longue durée*, officials, philanthropists, and the public at large assumed that the Empire could. This assumption was not always justified, and many homeless foreigners languished in the outposts of the Empire. The sad truth, of course, was that they did so largely out of sight of the general public. As a result, the refugee narrative and the solutions it envisaged were not undermined by inconvenient realities. Refuge thus became—and remained—a powerful nation- and empire-defining act, so compelling that the government threatened to intervene in local colonial affairs when refuge was on the line.

FIVE

Colonial Refuge in the Metropolitan Eye

It is our bounded duty not to embroil the King's Government by yielding to any *supposed humanity upon light and slender evidence of danger* to the Parties.

— SIR FREDERICK ADAM, BRITISH LORD HIGH COMMISSIONER OF THE IONIAN ISLANDS, 1825

Using language that prefigured later asylum policies, the British Lord High Commissioner of the Ionian Islands instructed his staff when to admit foreigners fleeing violence in the eastern Mediterranean. Whether Muslim or Greek, women and children could receive asylum in British territory when they flew "from *immediate danger*," in which they ran "*the risk of being butchered*." The High Commissioner admitted that "*where that imminent danger exists, humanity cannot be sacrificed to any consideration of policy*."[1] Armed men presented a different case, however. While "humanity" might urge otherwise, these foreigners were not to be admitted onto British soil. They presented too great a threat to British neutrality, a risk the British were unwilling to take the outset of the Greek rebellion against their Ottoman overlords in the 1820s.[2]

The situation was repeated in the western Mediterranean a decade later. In 1830, acting governor of Gibraltar General George Don promised Spanish authorities and the Colonial Office alike that British officials took every precaution to ensure the security of the Spanish Crown, then under threat from liberal revolutionaries who sought to replace the Bourbon line. Don's measures were insufficient. In January 1831, refugees and a motley crew of British supporters nearly set sail from the port without detection. Fearing another attempted exploit, Spanish authorities suspended communications with Gibraltar until all refugees had been removed. Don complained about how presumptuous it was for the Spanish to threaten their British allies in this manner. Nevertheless, with the blessing of the Colonial Office, he complied with the Spanish Crown's demands. By May, 118 refugees had been removed from Gibraltar and dispersed to British Malta or to the French port at Algiers. These refugees could continue thence to destinations of their own choosing with expenses paid by officials in Gibraltar. Reassured of their security, Spanish authorities recommenced communication with their British neighbors.[3]

Metropolitan commentators would have protested vehemently had they known of these abridgements of the promise of refuge to persecuted foreigners. These official responses to refugees in the Mediterranean violated two assumptions increasingly central to the cultural notion that refuge was a moral-cum-national British duty. First, refuge was a fail-safe means of aiding foreigners when intervention was impossible. Second, this moral responsibility extended to all outposts of the Empire.

If activists and public commentators had closely examined the official record, they would have realized that these assumptions were not always true. Yet, perhaps because they were unaware of these earlier challenges to imperial asylum, the metropolitan public was all the more outraged when two high-profile cases at midcentury made it painfully clear that the reception of foreign refugees was far from guaranteed across the British world. Local authorities turned away refugees from Malta during the Italian revolutions of 1848–1849. This was the first such instance that came to the attention of the metropolitan media. Then, in the winter of 1860–1861, it appeared that administrators and the local judiciary in Canada would render refugee slaves to the United States.

This chapter examines the moral outcry and its aftermath in these two cases. Supporters rallied to the refugees' defense. Activists demanded that the imperial government install on all British soil the same protections refugees enjoyed at home. Doing this risked straining already tense relationships between central and colonial authorities within the Empire and jeopardized friendly international ties that the government had assiduously cultivated.

Perhaps surprisingly, the imperial government took heed of the public outcry in both cases. Refusing to provide a staging ground for revolutionaries, as British authorities had in the Ionian Sea and Gibraltar, was one thing, but refusing refuge was another. Officials in Britain recognized the distinction. Parliament and the Queen's legal council investigated the conduct of authorities on Malta and then in Canada. The liberal Empire needed to live up to its humanitarian responsibilities. Indeed, as far as refugee supporters were concerned, such responsibilities would be what helped to make the Empire liberal in the first place.[4]

The Italian Refugees and a Rogue Governor on Malta

Malta offered the closest neutral territory for those fleeing from revolutions and counterrevolutions in Italy. Fifty-eight miles from Sicily, the British island had provided a distinctly cosmopolitan refuge since the 1830s (figure 5.1). Having once been ruled by Sicily, Malta's upper classes spoke Italian long after the island was captured from the French during the Napoleonic Wars and made a Crown colony. The number of refugees who settled in Malta is not precisely known. Each shipload of refugees who fled in the wake of the 1848–1849 revolutions brought between fifty and three hundred additional persons, though not all necessarily disembarked.[5] Local authorities were troubled less by the number of refugees who sought safe harbor than by their political complexion.

While a logical place for refuge, Malta seemed ill-equipped to harbor those who had fought (and lost) in the various Italian revolutions. Malta had experienced political turmoil since the 1830s, the root cause of which was a deep divide over reforms to the colonial constitution. As it stood into the 1840s, the constitution provided no representation for the local population and required all administrative orders to be submitted to London for review.[6] Amenable to some liberal reforms,

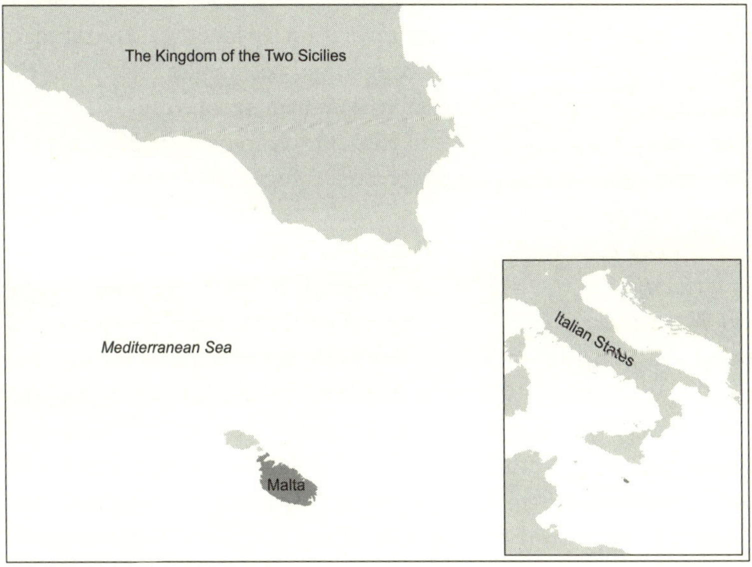

5.1 · Map of Malta. Credit: Mathieu Duvall, Imaging and Computing Center, Bates College, Lewiston, Maine.

the Colonial Office and local Anglo-Maltese authorities hoped to steer a path that mirrored changes in governance in the British Isles. In the 1830s, this meant allowing for greater freedom of the press. In the 1840s, the aim was to provide some representation of the Maltese in the local council.

The greatest challenge to reform in both moments, however, was appeasing contending factions within Maltese society. Colonial authorities needed to navigate between local radicals demanding more inclusive reforms and conservative Catholics who feared both radicalism and the encroachment of Protestant rule. Anxious about the influence of revolutionary agitation across the Mediterranean, Colonial Secretary Earl Grey renewed attempts at limited reform in the late 1840s.[7] In 1847, he sent Irishman Richard More O'Ferrall to take charge of Malta. O'Ferrall would be the first Roman Catholic and first civil (as opposed to military) governor, a combination that Grey must have seen as a peace offering to both conservatives and liberals (if not radicals) on the island.[8]

It was in the midst of these reform attempts that Italian refugees sought refuge on Malta. In each instance, their arrival threatened to exacerbate preexisting tensions at a delicate time of change.

In the 1830s, the arrival of the first anti-papal Italian refugees compounded the Church's fears that its traditional hold over society would be undermined.[9] Newly instituted freedom of the press certainly enabled the circulation of revolutionary ideology. The refugees established revolutionary newspapers, and within just a few years, the island became a center for Italian nationalism, second only to London. Enraged by these developments, the Church and elite families repeatedly demanded that these "dangerous" refugees be expelled lest they radicalize the island's youth.

Officials took heed and in 1843, the Queen's Council issued an order clarifying the right of the governor in Malta to expel foreigners. Nevertheless, Malta not only retained its revolutionary newspapers but also became a point of departure for nationalist invasions of the Italian Peninsula. It was there that the Bandiera brothers planned their ill-fated attack on the Kingdom of the Two Sicilies (Sicily and Naples) in 1844. In the course of the 1848–1849 revolutions, Malta once more became the first port of call for many on the run. As the refugee community thrived, so too did the likelihood that they would precipitate a political showdown between Maltese conservatives led by the Catholic Church, radical revolutionary sympathizers, and the British colonial authorities.

In the wake of the uprisings in 1848, the refugees were conservatives, including many religious men with whom Catholic conservatives identified. When the fortunes of the revolutions changed, the refugees changed too. By 1849, they were Roman, Neapolitan, or Sicilian revolutionaries and supporters of the peninsula-wide revolutions. The Neapolitans and Sicilians fled from the Kingdom of the Two Sicilies when the Bourbon king defeated insurrections in both areas. The Roman refugees fled the return of the Pope backed by the French military. As before, these revolutionaries were more likely to receive warm Anglo-Maltese support, while their opposition to papal power alarmed the Maltese Church.

Careful not to alienate this powerful constituency, Governor O'Ferrall approached the Foreign Office in May of 1849, begging officials to stop refugees from making Malta their destination. Using the port as a point for transmigration was one thing, but the governor did not believe Malta would survive continued migration onto the island. In a letter to Grey, O'Ferrall demanded whether "Malta is to be the refuge of the outcasts of all adjoining countries." He feared the prospect of having within the fortifications of Malta "men of desperate fortunes" who could have a "corrupting influence" "on the minds of young men, and that the best disposed may be corrupted." O'Ferrall hated to use the "power of expulsion," a power he said was "very liable to abuse," but he could not let the influx continue.[10]

In the ensuing months, O'Ferrall made two significant changes to previous practices. He invoked an 1818 set of Maltese police instructions that distinguished between dangerous and non-dangerous foreigners. On the authority of this order, O'Ferrall held that foreigners could remain on Malta only if they reported themselves to the authorities. Upon reporting themselves (or being reported by the captain of their vessel), the foreigners were to give assurance (through a respectable third party) of their good character and that they would not become dependent on the government for their welfare. If a foreigner did not meet these criteria, he or she was liable to be removed.[11] In effect, the governor of Malta had in his hands the equivalent of an aliens act, one that was more severe in criteria than either the 1848 or the 1793 acts in Britain.

Second, O'Ferrall asked the superintendent of quarantine and marine police to hold all refugees on board ship. The only individuals allowed landing were those who fit the authorities' criteria of the deserving or those in need of extraordinary medical attention. The ships that arrived after May 1849 thus remained in the port. Maltese authorities ensured that the passengers had supplies, but they were detained until they could be transferred to a second ship bound for their final destination. As before, most refugees were en route to Britain or the United States and continued there without further concern.

Yet, O'Ferrall's policies elicited grave concern on Malta and from London. The first cause for concern was the case of Neapolitan "deserters"—soldiers, Bourbon officials claimed, who had deserted their army during the insurrection. Upon their arrival at Malta, O'Ferrall refused to admit them onto the island, concerned that they were "not the type to follow the law." He instead secured them passage to Algiers in June of 1849. But they were not accepted in Algiers either, and the ship of refugees sailed around the Mediterranean for weeks in search of safe harbor. They returned to Malta in early August. O'Ferrall was at a loss. He attempted to secure *in writing* that they would not be punished if he returned them to Naples. Unsuccessful in this request for amnesty, he kept them uneasily on Malta while Palmerston tried his hand with the Neapolitan government, again to no avail.[12]

The precarious situation of those who sought refuge on Malta might not have come to the metropolitan public's attention if it had not been for the refusal of asylum to nationalist refugees who fled the counterrevolution in Rome. One of these, the Italian nationalist writer Christine Trivulce, princess of Belgiojoso (near Milan) wrote Palmerston to express her outrage. She had "rel[ied] fully on the justice of the English and on my own character" but had been refused. She was ultimately admitted, but could not secure the safety of the others on board. The princess was convinced that such a barbarous act could not have taken place with the full knowledge of the English Cabinet, as the "English humanity and justice are too well known to the whole world."[13] It would not be long before the matter circulated around Westminster and reached public ears.

For a metropolitan public that was still leery of Catholics in positions of authority, the Irish Catholic governor needed to account for his actions. The metropolitan press painted O'Ferrall as a rogue who ignored a particularly British moral imperative to provide shelter for persecuted foreigners. From August of 1849 through the spring of 1850, news that refugees were refused landing on Malta wrought sharp criticism. Those who were permitted to land, the British discovered, were often allowed into the port only long enough to be herded from one vessel to another. Worse yet, many were turned away outright, according to a September 8 report in the *Morning Chronicle*.[14]

Metropolitan criticism focused on the dreadful condition of the ships, lamenting the disrespectful treatment of wounded heroes. The refugees ought to be provided with better succor, supporters argued. Instead, they were simply left to bleed. Outrage transcended political division. The conservative *Morning Chronicle* and the liberal *Daily News* reported the same abuses. The *Daily News* went further in its attacks. O'Ferrall's treatment of Roman liberals was especially appalling. Without guarantee that they could pay for their onward passage to Britain, the newspaper reported, O'Ferrall did not allow Roman liberals to land at all.[15] The newspaper's editors noted the colonial government's apparent preference for Jesuit refugees, who had been allowed to land on the island in 1847. The editors decried this act as evidence of O'Ferrall's papal sympathies. The *Belfast News-Letter* followed suit. The Catholic Maltese population, led by an Irish Catholic governor, was making a mockery of British liberalism.[16]

Parliament responded to the accusations immediately. Members of both the Commons and the Lords questioned the Colonial Office about the legality and propriety of O'Ferrall's actions. Conservative MP Monckton Milnes asked the undersecretary for the state of the colonies, Mr. Hawes, whether the refugees "whose bravery had undoubtedly excited the admiration of the civilized world" had been denied permission to land in Malta. If this were true, the implications were dire, Milnes continued. He posed the alternative to Hawes. If British Malta did not shelter persecuted foreigners, he wondered if the Colonial Office was ready to endorse this "want of hospitality" elsewhere in the Empire as well. Hawes retorted that the colony simply could not accommodate so many refugees. Unsatisfied with this response, Scottish radical MP Joseph Hume pointed out that "even the report of such a transaction was disgraceful of the country."[17]

Facing public and parliamentary ire, the Colonial Office investigated the colonial governor in turn. It is unclear from the archives whether the Colonial Office officially recalled Governor O'Ferrall during the inquiry. That fall, O'Ferrall ceded his responsibilities temporarily, and he and his family returned to Britain. In September, the *Daily News* asserted that O'Ferrall had been recalled and reprimanded by the imperial government, and had promptly resigned his post. The conservative, Anglo-Maltese *Malta Times* denied allegations of the reprimand but not the temporary recall. The paper's editors also pointed out that O'Ferrall had not in fact resigned his post, prompting the metropolitan newspapers to print corrections. Whatever his treatment while in London, the governor and his family returned to

Malta at the end of October to celebrations on a great "scale of magnificence," according to the *Malta Times*, which remained staunchly loyal to the governor. In addition to chastising the metropolitan press for its ignorant meddling, the newspaper defended O'Ferrall and the authorities' efforts to rid the island of agents provocateurs.[18]

Governor O'Ferrall continued to justify himself to the imperial government long after his return to Malta. He railed against metropolitan intrusion and argued that a pan-imperial policy of asylum was dangerous. Through the winter of 1850, he took pains to show the Colonial Office and Parliament that his government was responsive to the refugees' physical needs. To refute accusations of neglect, he highlighted deliveries of medicines, food, and supplies while refugees remained in the harbor on board ship. The death of one Neapolitan deserter, Ferdinando di Bartolomeo, he argued, occurred despite the expert attention his officers provided. Indeed, Her Majesty's attendants went to great lengths to save refugees, O'Ferrall explained, hazarding personal exposure to dangerous diseases while assisting Bartolomeo and others like him.[19] O'Ferrall also cited public health concerns as a reason to contain incoming refugees. With an outbreak of cholera already ravaging the island, space for quarantine was scarce, he claimed. The best place for the quarantine was often on board the refugees' ships.[20]

The bulk of his correspondence attended to the political threat, however. O'Ferrall argued that the local population shared his concern about these foreigners' nefarious political aims. To this end, he forwarded a letter from the archbishop in his correspondence with the Colonial Office. According to the archbishop, "the corruption of manners and the immoralities generated in these islands by the contact of inhabitants with persons, who at various periods repaired hither from Italy" now "sow amongst the youth the wicked ideas wherewith their minds are unfortunately filled." The archbishop demanded that "Your Excellency refuse an asylum to [such] beings."[21] Appended to the archbishop's letter was a petition to the local government reiterating these same points and bearing the signatures of 210 loyal Maltese.[22]

While no barriers could bar the entry of foreign refugees to the British Isles, the Colonial Office enabled the governor general of Malta to regulate entry in direct response to local pressures of space, public health, and political intolerance. Grey's instructions did forbid the colonial governor from "prevent[ing] the landing in Malta of persons who may seek refuge there from political troubles in any of the countries bordering on the Mediterranean." The colonial secretary provided a significant caveat, however. Grey accepted the argument of local authorities that Malta could not afford asylum to foreign refugees in all cases, despite public opinion at home.

Grey's instructions did less to regulate the influx of foreigners to Malta than to provide local authorities with the means of keeping tabs on dangerous foreigners. Refugees could land only if they were "in a situation to comply with the law of the island, which requires that before strangers are allowed to land they shall have security against becoming a burden upon its resources from their inability to maintain themselves."[23] Grey further attended to the safety of the colony, indicating that the governor ought to dictate where the refugees lived in the hopes of keeping them from such strategic sites as the fortifications in the capital. Finally, he gave O'Ferrall the ability to "order the removal from the island of every foreigner who shall be proved to have abused its hospitality" and in instances where "offense is given to friendly powers, by its [Malta's] being allowed to become a place from whence plots may be carried on against the existing government of any state in amity with Great Britain."[24]

The *Malta Times* editors interpreted this final point as a moral statement that revolutionary refugees were dangerous individuals, not valiant victims. Addressing the refugees, the editors also admitted that they had a right to asylum on Malta. Refugees could "remain in peace and security, provided you are so inclined." The editors aired their skepticism on this last count, stating that "many of you owe your very means of subsistence to the families of that country, which you have deceived, by betraying its confidence, and endeavouring to cause riot and bloodshed."[25] Reporting that the colonial government had actually instructed three such refugees to quit the island in March 1850, the editors of the *Malta Times* wondered at anyone who could possibly "feel for these ungrateful men." To feel for these refugees "would be to participate in their crimes towards their own country, as well as in their base ingratitude to the flag that protects them."[26]

Grey's grant to Malta of the right to vet foreigners and regulate their activity was similar to measures that the home government had allowed itself in the first British Aliens Act of 1793, passed during a period of great national peril. On the other hand, this set of restrictions far exceeded any permitted in the home islands during the nineteenth century.[27] Far from Britain and surrounded by revolution, the government on Malta indeed felt itself to be under siege.

The metropolitan furor died down. There would be more sensational causes to undertake, among them the plight of American fugitive slave John Anderson. Who was more in need, more deserving of British refuge, than the persecuted foreign slave? No local exigency could cost Anderson—at the crossroads of two nation-defining British traditions—his sanctuary on British soil. Or could it?

The Fugitive Anderson, International Morality, and Local Pride

While an enthusiastic metropolitan public celebrated Canada as an "ark of freedom," abolitionists and fugitive slaves alike feared for the sanctity of refuge in the North American colony. Raiding by American slave catchers had long threatened those slaves who reached Canada. These forays into British territory were all the more troubling in light of repeated requests by the US government to sanction the pursuit of runaway slaves on Canadian soil. The British government in Canada had consistently refused such requests since they had commenced in the 1810s, but had never resolved the issue definitively, thus increasing abolitionists' fears. The Executive Council in Lower Canada issued a general order in 1829 that no fugitive slave should be remanded to America unless "his offense would have made him liable to arrest by the laws of Canada." This loophole was troubling, however. What if the slave stole a horse or committed some other crime en route? Could he or she be extradited? An 1833 ruling in Upper Canada explicitly gave the governor-in-council the right to refuse extradition on a case-by-case basis. But there was no guarantee that compassion for the refugee slave would rule the day.[28]

When Britain and America signed the Webster-Ashburton Treaty in 1842, the issue became all the more pointed. The treaty resolved border disputes between the United States and the Canadian Territories, most prominently trade issues and the western border in a period of expansion across the continent. Article Ten of the treaty, however, bore directly on fugitives. It set out an extradition agreement under which an individual who committed one of a number of felonies—recognized as such by both British and American law—could be extradited to face prosecution in his or her home country.

In Britain, the BFASS protested the agreement vehemently, highlighting its implications for fugitive slaves. British laws no longer allowed slavery, so simply running away from a master was not an extraditable offense. Indeed, the 1836 abolition of slavery in Canada brought with it a sizeable increase in the number of American slaves who sought refuge there. The treaty protected fugitives from slavery but provided no guidance on what would happen if a slave committed theft—or murder—en route to freedom. BFASS protests yielded little. Foreign secretary Aberdeen acknowledged the treaty's silence on this score but insisted that it was not the government's intention to jeopardize these refugee slaves. Officials would prevent the extradition of slaves if necessary, he promised.[29]

While abolitionists nervously took Aberdeen at his word, his assurances meant little with regard to the affairs of British Canada by 1860. In the years since 1842, the jurisdiction of Canadian affairs had begun to devolve away from central imperial oversight and onto independent local institutions. While Britain still controlled Canada's foreign policies (and would through the 1920s), local institutions were increasingly in charge of domestic affairs. This meant that though Canada remained a colonial dependency, it maintained a separate legislature to which the colonial governor—and the imperial Parliament—deferred. The only power Britain maintained in Canadian governance was over the colonial governor directly. Although antislavery sentiment also ran high in Canada, abolitionists did not know how newly independent Canadian courts would rule if presented with the question of extraditing an American slave. Such a question fell in between the domestic responsibilities of Canadian institutions and the international ones of the imperial power. With the American Fugitive Slave Bill in full operation and more than fifty thousand American fugitives living in British Canada, a test case seemed inevitable.[30] Nearly two decades after the treaty was signed, abolitionists had the test case they had been anticipating.

John Anderson had been a slave in Missouri until 1853 (figure 5.2). Separated from his family, Anderson had just been sold to a master who refused to allow him to see them again.[31] Rather than submit, Anderson took flight, first bidding his wife and children goodbye (figure 5.3). En route to Canada, Anderson was stopped by Seneca Diggs, a local Missouri man who was suspicious of Anderson's claim to be on an errand for his master. When Diggs attempted to recapture Anderson, Anderson reportedly stabbed him and managed to escape. Diggs died shortly thereafter. Under a false name, Anderson established himself as a freeman outside Toronto, where he lived unmolested for years. In 1860, Anderson confessed the murder to a man he thought to be his friend. That friend informed local authorities and Anderson was imprisoned. No witnesses appeared against him and Anderson was released. Within days, however, a Detroit police officer—and slave catcher—swore that Anderson was guilty

5.2 · Portrait of John Anderson from Harper Twelvetrees, *The Story of the Life of John Anderson, Fugitive Slave* (London: William Tweedle, 1863). © *The British Library Board, 10881.aaa.2, frontispiece.*

of the murder of Diggs. Pursuing his case, the slave catcher secured the help of authorities in Missouri and of the US secretary of state, who demanded Anderson's extradition in October 1860.[32] Could Anderson be extradited? Murder was extraditable; escape from slavery was not.

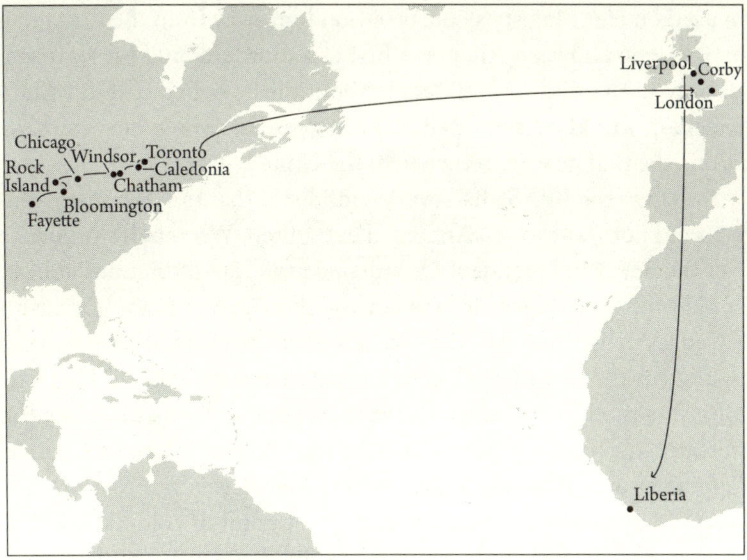

5.3 · John Anderson's Journey, 1850–1862. Credit: Mathieu Duvall, Imaging and Computing Center, Bates College, Lewiston, Maine. Map based on the account from Harper Twelvetrees, *Life of John Anderson*.

The Canadian press took a great deal of interest in Anderson's case from the start, reporting daily. Reporters "compar[ed] Anderson to Garibaldi, to a ravished negro maid seeking to escape from her abductor, and to the manly symbol of all Africa."[33] Despite the outcry, the justices of the Canadian Court of the Queen's Bench ruled against Anderson by a vote of two to one. Then the matter became one of imperial concern and a sensation in metropolitan Britain. Canadian and British abolitionists argued that if London did not step in, Anderson would be sent to his death.

The Canadian court's decision to extradite Anderson produced a massive public response in Canada and in Great Britain. In Toronto, the meeting convened to protest "the danger to the cause of humanity and liberty which would result from the rendition to the US of the fugitive Anderson." The meeting was reportedly the "largest the city had seen."[34] In Britain, antislavery advocates went to work immediately, collecting funds for Anderson's defense through advertisements in the Sunday newspapers.[35] At last, the BFASS had their test case juxtaposing international and moral obligations.

Technically, Anderson's case would be appealed to the Canadian appellate court, not to London. However, abolitionist demands focused on Her Majesty's courts in London, away from the Canadian justices who had seen Anderson first as a murderer and his slave status only as an unimportant detail. Abolitionists hoped that in Britain Anderson would be acquitted and safeguarded from what would be certain death if he were returned to the United States.

Although the BFASS had every confidence that the British government did not want to see Anderson extradited, Whitehall's influence over the newly independent Canadian courts was ambiguous at best. Could Whitehall intervene in the case without jeopardizing good faith in Canadian institutions? The Queen's Bench in Westminster was the highest court of appeal in England. Did it extend to Canada? Had new power invested in Canadian institutions gone so far as to negate the Westminster court's ultimate jurisdiction? English barrister Thomas Tapping wrote in the *Law Magazine and Law Review* of February 1861 that the question was "the most important point of colonial law that has occurred within modern times."[36] Canadian law journals echoed Tapping, emphasizing concern for the independence of the Canadian institutions at the same time as they felt for the imprisoned fugitive slave. As British officials nervously watched the Canadian courts, they wondered whether the imperial government could risk the offense they would cause in trying Anderson's case in London.

Abolitionists and the British press were confident that Whitehall would intercede. The BFASS took its case to Parliament and, after many failed attempts, brought their protest before the administration. In Parliament, Edwin James, the same barrister who had successfully argued on behalf of French refugee Simon Bernard in 1858, undertook Anderson's case. Confident that moral right would win in the end, the *Times* opined:

> That we, who look with such scorn upon the little State of Saxony for delivering up a Hungarian nobleman who had trusted to her hospitality, should, in our strength and our grandeur, deliver up a wretched slave who had run for our soil as to the ark of freedom, may be argued as logical necessity in a court of law, but is an obvious impossibility as a fact.[37]

The Ministry seemed genuinely amazed that they were forced to confront this test case at all. Lord Lyons, the British envoy in Washington, lambasted the United States for obscuring critical details in the extradition request. US secretary of state General Cass had failed to mention that the escaped "felon" was a slave. Had he known, Lyons implied, he would have viewed Anderson as a refugee from unjust governance instead.[38] Once initial steps had been taken to return Anderson, however, the request could not be dismissed. The administration at Whitehall demanded that Canadian authorities consider carefully the implications of their planned action. The Duke of Newcastle, secretary of state for the colonies, implored Canadian authorities to consult with the Colonial Office before executing the extradition order, insisting that the interpretation of the Webster-Ashburton Treaty was in jeopardy. Newcastle was himself convinced that extradition in this case ran counter to its terms. With a decided note of disappointment in the Canadian proceedings, Newcastle argued that the Canadian courts did not, in fact, have the diplomatic power to make this sort of determination. He admitted that the power to extradite Anderson could well be in the hands of the governor.[39] This was preferable. The governor was at least subject to imperial oversight. Buying time, Whitehall corresponded with the United States, hoping that impatient American diplomats would appreciate transparency.

Communication with the United States was, however, secondary to imperial interest in seeing the decision of the Canadian court reversed and Anderson freed from jail. BFASS secretary L. A. Chamerovzow at last managed to convince the government to consider issuing a writ of habeas corpus to bring Anderson before metropolitan courts. Whitehall, if it could claim jurisdiction, might override the decision by the Canadian Court of Queen's Bench.

Still, it was difficult to foresee the consequences for Canadian-British relations of such a display of imperial power. Newcastle's assertions aside, the government debated whether it could, or should, circumvent the authority of the Canadian courts and issue a writ of habeas corpus. Some officials deferred to the authority of the Canadian courts, determining that the imperial government had no right to intervene. This argument struck most as odd because Canada was not yet independent, even though devolution had begun. Still, it underscored the seriousness with which the imperial government viewed Canada's sovereignty in these matters.

It also made the pro-removal case rather cut and dried. Edwin James argued that Canada was still a colony and "the Court had as much right to issue this prerogative writ into Canada, as a position of the British crown, as into the Isle of Wight or Yorkshire." This right had been used in case after case, as "these writs had gone to Calais, when a possession of the British crown, and also to Ireland, and he should contend that Canada stood in precisely the same position, as a possession of the British crown."[40]

The Westminster court issued the writ of habeas corpus on November 23, 1860. Lord Chief Justice Cockburn's ruling was careful to recognize the propriety with which the Canadian court system had acted. He praised the devolution of authority to Canada and acknowledged that the writ "may be felt to be inconsistent with that higher degree of colonial independence, both legislative and judicial, which has happily been carried into effect in modern times." He assured those affected by his decision that "we are quite sensible" that they might feel it as an offense. The fact remained, he continued, that, "the legislature has not gone so far as to expressly abrogate any jurisdiction which the courts in Westminster Hall might possess with reference to the issuing of a writ of *habeas corpus* to any of HM's dominions."[41] Citing opinions from Coke in the seventeenth century through Mansfield in the eighteenth, Cockburn held that "nothing short of legislative enactment, depriving this court of such a jurisdiction, would warrant us in omitting to carry it into effect, where we are called upon to do so for the protection of the personal liberty of the subject," though that subject was in fact a foreigner.[42]

Despite Cockburn's confidence, legal scholars outside the Queen's Bench argued that the matter was not so straightforward. Thomas Tapping maintained that Cockburn had ignored fundamental changes in colonial case law that had curtailed Westminster's ability to intervene, if indeed they had ever possessed such jurisdiction over the colonial courts. Tapping disputed that the justices could hear cases from any territory beyond England, Wales, and Berwick-on-Tweed (a disputed area at the Scottish border). Only those three areas had been specified in the court's seventeenth-century patents from the reign of Charles II (31 Car. II. c. 2). Indeed, Tapping explained that the justices "have so constantly refused (except where specially authorized by statute) to accept jurisdiction over a local action arising, or crime committed out of England, that the jurisdiction of the court is [still] practically and actually coextensive with its judges' patents."[43]

Even if the justices had expanded their jurisdiction, Tapping continued, the recent establishment of a separate judiciary made Canada wholly independent, invested with every power to hear cases and appeals without deference to Westminster (22 Vict. c. 10 section 3). To deny this, as the Westminster court did by issuing the writ of habeas corpus for Anderson, was tantamount to withdrawing Canada's independence. Leaving his strict study of the law behind,

Tapping concluded with a dire prognostication. He asserted that a "dangerous and alarming precedent has been established, which sooner or later may be made the stepping-stone for further encroachments, and may ultimately lead to a collision between the judicatures . . . to end, probably, with a second declaration of American independence."[44] The *Upper Canada Law Journal* was less dire in its assessment of Canada-Britain relations. Nonetheless, the editors explained that "men of all politics . . . pronounced the act of the English court both high-handed and unfounded. Birth was given to a feeling of resistance, which will not in all probability slumber till the assumed jurisdiction of the English court is tested and defeated on national grounds."[45]

As it turned out, the writ of habeas corpus was never executed. On February 1, 1861, Chief Justice Draper issued a writ for Anderson to be remanded to his higher Court of Common Pleas in Canada. On February 16, Draper issued a decision that reversed the initial ruling. Anderson was free.

As far as the *Toronto Globe* was concerned, Draper's writ was issued as a direct counter to the writ issued in England. Writing to Newcastle in early February, Sir William Fenwick Williams, commander-in-chief of the British army in Canada, forwarded the newspaper's unofficial take on the matter from February 2, fourteen days before Draper's decision was handed down. The *Globe* assured readers, "We think there is now every ground for the assurance that Anderson is safe." Moreover, the *Globe* was convinced that the chief justice would do all in his power to get Anderson "a speedy discharge, without the trouble and cost being incurred of sending him to England."[46] Within two weeks the *Globe*'s hunch proved correct.

The superior court's reversal hinged on a technicality—the warrant used to detain Anderson had not specified a charge of murder. Under the Webster-Ashburton Treaty and the Consolidated Statutes of Canada (May 1849, chap. 89), the Canadian government could properly detain and hear evidence against an American felon accused of murder. Draper held that in the Anderson case there had been no accusation of murder: the warrant specified only that "he did willfully, maliciously, and feloniously stab and kill one Seneca T. P. Diggs." The word *kill* did not make it possible to treat the charge as "assault with intent to murder"—the necessary charge for the case to be considered. Draper admitted that such burden did not necessarily rest on the warrant, as it would on an indictment. Nonetheless, the wording of the initial complaint—even in the warrant—was of particular importance in this case, a case in which not all felonious acts could be heard by the Canadian courts under the operation of the Webster-Ashburton Treaty.[47]

On both sides of the Atlantic, the concerned public was elated. The sigh of relief was perhaps greater with regard to Canadian independence than to abolitionist sentiment. Shortly after the February 16 ruling, the *Globe* admitted general uneasiness over the possibility of ceding jurisdiction. A *Globe* article argued:

> The peculiarity of this case of Anderson would have justified a great stretch of authority that tended to save the unfortunate man from the vengeance of his enemies; but it would be neither convenient nor consistent with the independence of the Canadian people that English judges should have the power to ignore our courts, and issue their writs to our sheriffs and jailers as if we had no provincial judges.[48]

The threat of intervention had led the Canadian court to rule in a manner consonant with public sentiment. That ruling, however, was not a broad win for a right to refuge. Draper had dismissed the defense's attempts to throw the case out on jurisdictional grounds; thus, fugitive slaves were presumptively subject to trial for acts committed during flight. Even Anderson's safety remained uncertain. The decision did not bar US authorities from making another attempt to extradite Anderson, this time adhering to the technicalities required under the Webster-Ashburton Treaty. Rather than tempt fate, Anderson fled to England shortly after his liberation.[49]

The Limits of Imperial Refuge

For the metropolitan public, refugee supporters would remember the cases of John Anderson and the Italians on Malta as moral victories. The story of the Italians' treatment on Malta lived on in cultural memory as a public shaming of those who treated refugees improperly. Safe in Britain, Luigi Bianchi could celebrate the grandeur of British refuge ten years later. "By the laws of England," he explained, "I had a perfect right to take up my residence on English soil, which Malta, as an English possession, must be considered." Bianchi's memoirs demonized the "inflexible" O'Ferrall, whom he blamed for his expulsion.[50] Though the affair was long in the past, the charge continued to galvanize sympathetic support for refugees more generally.

Metropolitan abolitionists welcomed Anderson with open arms. After being freed from a Toronto jail in February of 1861, Anderson sailed for England at the urging (and the expense) of the BFASS. Anderson did not record his thoughts on his time in England; his narrative was written from the perspective of his British champions. Only his evocative retelling of his time in slavery and his eloquent words of thanks to his friends were included. In typical fashion for a celebrity refugee, he was welcomed by a mass public meeting led by London notables. His triumph was the British abolitionists' triumph. After a tour around England, Anderson was slated to become the pupil of a London clergyman under whose care Anderson was to be molded into an ideal sober, hard-working, and self-supporting liberal individual. His six years of independent life in Canada between his escape and his capture were set at naught, and Anderson was expected to "[devote] himself exclusively to learning, to enable him to transact the ordinary business of life creditably."[51]

Anderson did not take readily to this tutelage, however. He was apparently too distracted by the sights and sounds of London and was promptly transferred to the countryside to concentrate on his studies. After a year's residence there, Anderson's hosts held discussions about where to settle him permanently. Again, from the sound of it, Anderson did not have much of a voice in the deliberations. The abolition society decided to pay for Anderson's passage to Liberia, the small nation in West Africa founded and run by his fellow American ex-slaves. There, Anderson was to become a landed proprietor, making use of his agricultural experience in the American South. His British friends had no doubt that Anderson would succeed and become a leader of the young Liberia and an inspiration for his race as a whole.[52] Anderson's time in Africa was short, as it turned out: he died within a few years of his arrival. Having shipped Anderson to Africa with great pomp and circumstance, British abolitionists closed their story of Anderson's triumphant rescue. They idealized Anderson the iconic refugee slave and promptly forgot Anderson the man.

These triumphs—questionable though they might seem to more modern sensibilities—were typical for British refuge at its height, as imperious in its moral demands on the refugees as it was on their British hosts. The crises demonstrated the vitality of refuge in the political and cultural repertoire. The political will to maintain British refuge was so powerful that it threatened to trump colonial policies that stood in its way. Refuge was not a legally encoded right, but normative claims for refugees seemed to approach the status of natural rights.

Nevertheless, there were stirrings of something else in these refugee crises at midcentury, a realization, partial though it was, that refuge would not always be tenable. Colonial exigencies increasingly demanded that metropolitan officials and activists bear in mind the constraints on imperial resources and colonial willingness to provide refuge. Powerful sentiments of outrage and moral responsibility might claim attention from the radical fringes to the heights of the imperial government. Nevertheless, officials and activists alike would have to admit—as officials in Gibraltar and the Ionian Islands had known for years—that circumstances could make refuge for persecuted foreigners impossible.

Threats to refuge on Malta and in Canada did not end in the strong commitment to open asylum and policy reform sought by the public. While public memory offered an alternate history, the fact remained that refugees could not be harbored if doing so meant endangering the local peace or further straining imperial-colonial relations. On Malta, refugees had to refrain from revolutionary activities while in exile, or else seek shelter elsewhere. In Canada, Anderson was freed on a technicality, and those involved refused to set the wide precedent abolitionists had long desired. In each location, metropolitan and local authorities were fortunate. The outbreak of the American Civil War two months after the verdict in Anderson's case made setting a precedent unnecessary, at least for this corner of the British world. Italian nationalists' successful bid for unification in the 1860s also ended the need for these freedom fighters to seek refuge elsewhere.

At midcentury, refugees who could not find shelter in one corner of the Empire could—like Anderson or the Italian nationalists—find asylum further afield. By the century's close, this would not necessarily be the case. This turn of events would have considerable ramifications for the British moral-cum-national responsibility toward persecuted foreigners worldwide. The quest for a legal language of right expressing the moral imperative to provide refuge would become all the more pressing.

PART II

A National Tradition or a Universal Right? Refuge and the Law

SIX

Heroes, Villains, and the Parameters of Political Asylum

Popular novelist Mrs. C. G. Hamilton examined the annexation of Scotland in her 1857 *Exiles of Italy*. In the novel, several of her English characters engage in lively conversation with Italian refugees about whether the Austrian occupation of northern Italy can be compared with English rule of Scotland. Mr. Mowbray assures the others that the comparison is inapt, but he admits that Scotland had revolutionary heroes akin to the Italian refugees who aspire to a unified and sovereign Italy. The "spirit of [Scottish] patriotism took refuge in one man," the fourteenth-century William Wallace, whose valor Mowbray cannot deny. With Wallace's bid for independence safely in the past, even the English can see romance in his daring acts. Mrs. Hamilton's novel thus endorses revolutionaries' bids for independence in the 1850s, just as Mr. Mowbray celebrates Scotland's early nationalists. At the same time, Hamilton recognized a broader ethical concern. In the novel, Mr. Lyndsay responds to Mowbray's praise for Wallace with a lament: If revolutionaries fail, "they are stigmatized as rebels and disloyal, and banned for disturbing the peace of mankind."[1] Lyndsay thus admits that the difference between dangerous criminals—traitors—and patriots can be a matter of perspective.

Changes in the international scene in the late 1860s and 1870s forced the British to pose the questions implicit in Lyndsay's lament. Many beloved refugees of the nineteenth century had blood on their hands: John Anderson had killed a man on his way to freedom, and Garibaldi and Kossuth had both led revolutionary armies (figure 6.1). So what was the difference between foreign refugees and criminals? Was it simply a matter of sympathy for the fugitive's cause? Sympathy was a matter of perspective (figure 6.2). Even foreign refugees began to

6.1 · "Garibaldi the Liberator," *Punch, or the London Charivari* 39 (June 16, 1860): 243. Credit: Courtesy of the Bowdoin College Library, Brunswick, Maine

seem less deserving of sympathy when the comparison between political contests overseas and political contests on British soil became more palpable in the last third of the nineteenth century.

The matter came to the fore after 1865 in debates over the language of a new extradition act designed to establish a template for Britain's bilateral treaties. Legal experts and parliamentary Liberals hoped that the new law would succeed where the reigning Webster-Ashburton Treaty

6.2 · "The Fenian Guy Fawkes," *Punch, or the London Charivari* 53 (December 28, 1867): 263. Credit: Courtesy of the Bowdoin College Library, Brunswick, Maine.

with the United States had failed. They sought to include a clause making the political offender—or refugee—exempt from extradition demands for the first time. The language of the resulting 1870 Extradition Act was a triumph for a normative standard that had become intrinsic to Britain's international identity since 1815. Yet the campaign to codify a right to refuge in national and international law encountered challenges immediately. What would happen when Britain sought to bring a fugitive traitor to justice? Could the nation that provided refuge for foreigners ask for the extradition of a British national?

These concerns were not new, but they became particularly acute due to the changing tenor of radical politics in the era. This chapter examines public and official attempts to refine the right to asylum first articulated in the 1870 Extradition Act against the backdrop of an increasingly violent Irish nationalist movement, on the one hand, and the advent of continental communism and anarchism on the other (figures 6.3 and 6.4). Together, these new revolutionary forces put pressure on the 1870 exemption clause. After all, proponents of these new creeds did not simply target undemocratic governance. Their propensity toward "propaganda by deed"—revolution by way of dynamite and assassination—endangered civil society as well. For the next thirty years, British officials and activists would face accusations of hypocrisy, accept new insecurities, and become more cautious in their support for foreign revolutionaries.

This chapter tracks the contentious interplay between formal law, popular politics, and humanitarian norms. It takes extradition out of the context of high political and legal history, and shows the public and government being forced to confront the terms of their own moral claims in their quest to encode refuge in law. They questioned for the first time whether their proud support for refugees was too inclusive and whether refuge should be considered a legal right. In the process, British politicians and legal experts realized that the mechanisms of the law introduced a new formal logic into the once diffuse and morally charged category of the refugee.[2]

1870: The Liberal Triumph

The 1870 Extradition Act (33 & 34 Vict. c. 52) was a triumph for British commitment to protect foreigners from political prosecution overseas. Parliament wrote and passed the act in the wake of renewed international interest in extradition treaties as a means of bringing fugitive criminals to justice. Such treaties were increasingly important given the ease with which criminals could escape across national borders via train and across oceans via steamship. The act targeted murderers and those—including frauds and thieves more generally—whose crimes were against property. The act also offered the first explicit exemption for refugees. Section 3.1 stated: "A fugitive criminal shall

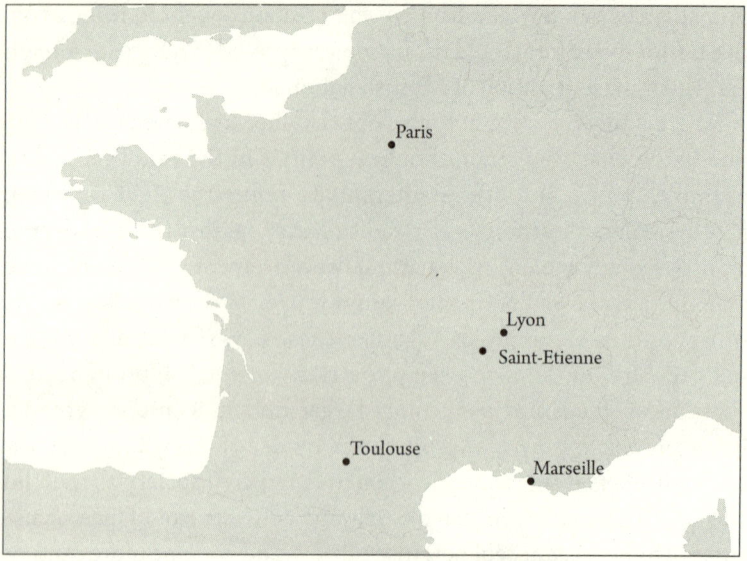

6.3 · Communist Uprisings, 1871. Credit: Mathieu Duvall, Imaging and Computing Center, Bates College, Lewiston, Maine. Map based on Encyclopædia Britannica Online, s. v. "Commune of Paris" (updated July 2014), http://www.britannica.com/EBchecked/topic/443691/Commune-of-Paris.

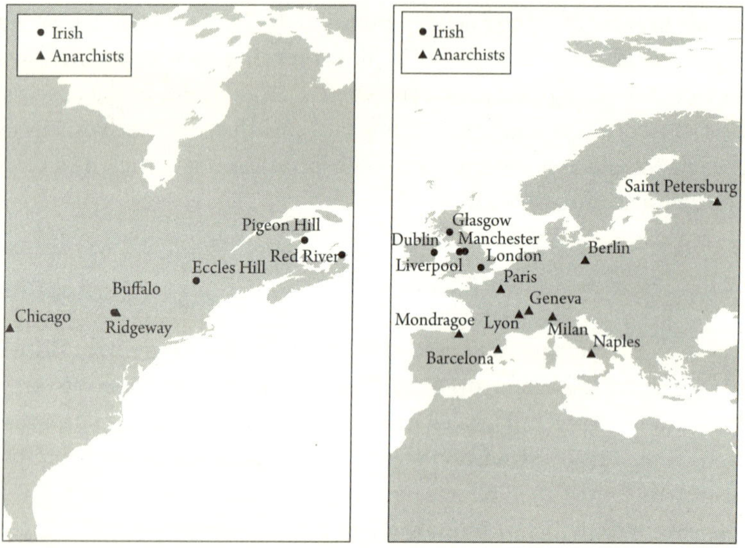

6.4 · Major attacks committed by anarchists and by the Irish Fenian Brotherhood, c. 1865–1905. Credit: Mathieu Duvall, Imaging and Computing Center, Bates College, Lewiston, Maine. Map based on the work of Richard Bach Jensen, *The Battle Against Anarchist Terrorism: an International History, 1878–1934* (Cambridge: Cambridge University Press).

not be surrendered if the offense in respect of which his surrender is demanded is one of a political character." But why, after so many years of providing refuge, did the British feel it necessary for the "political refugee" to appear in law?

There was British precedent for the bilateral extradition treaties that became so popular in the latter decades of the century. The British had two prior treaties: the 1842 Webster-Ashburton Treaty with the United States and an 1843 treaty with France. Neither exempted political offenders. The absence of clear directives regarding fugitive slaves, for instance, challenged British asylum practice under the Webster-Ashburton Treaty. Although British officials never intended the treaty to be used to surrender fugitive slaves, Anderson's case threatened to undercut that assumption. Louis Napoleon's 1851 coup d'état likewise made the silence of the French treaty on that score problematic. A new convention written and presented by Lord Malmesbury in 1852 would have provided a remedy. Clause Seven of the proposed convention specified that "political offenders" be exempt from extradition. The terms would have been groundbreaking, but the bill never passed Parliament and was eventually dropped.[3]

By the 1860s, the question of whether to renew the 1843 French extradition treaty came before Parliament.[4] In point of fact, the treaty, though several times invoked by France, had never been put into operation. In considering its renewal, Liberals and Conservatives weighed the benefits of an act that placed trust in a foreign legal and political system.[5] Despite their doubts, members of both parties agreed that a well-formulated extradition agreement was desirable: no one wanted to see "real criminals" evade justice. The time to act was now, the 1843 French treaty having lapsed in the late 1860s as the British studied whether and how to renew it.

Liberals' main concern was that any treaty must take the vicissitudes of French politics into account. Any treaty with the mercurial French would have to uphold the principle that all political offenders—whether foreign or not—deserved protection from local political vengeance. They were reluctant to abrogate Britain's ability to vet the evidence used against the foreigners whose extradition had been demanded. Trusting French governments in this matter seemed dangerous enough.[6] For John Stuart Mill, the point was more universal. British officials were as likely as the French to be blinded by momentary or local politics. As Mill declared before Parliament: "The great majority of people, especially people in power, are ready to believe almost anything against their political enemies, especially those who have said or published things tending to excite disapprobation of their conduct."[7] Mill believed that British political judgment deserved oversight as much as Louis Napoleon's did.

Other Liberals agreed with Mill's universalism; yet for MPs like William McCullagh Torrens, the point was less about an abstract right than a sacred British tradition. Against the French treaty, McCullagh Torrens quoted a letter from Frenchman (and former refugee) Louis Blanc, who lamented: "To pass the present Bill would be, to a certain extent, to make the right of asylum a snare; to forge a weapon not unlikely to be used against innocent persons, and to incur the accusation of having surrendered to a foreign despotic power the dignity of a free nation." While Blanc called asylum a right, McCullagh Torrens saw refuge in different terms. He "looked upon the maintenance of the present law as part of the national religion, and any abandonment of it as a violation of the most sacred of our national traditions."[8]

Rather than rely on foreign officials whose judgment was suspect, Liberal Sir Francis Goldsmid recommended that any new extradition treaty include a clause for the protection of political offenders. Conservatives foresaw difficulties in the wording of such an exemption, but they too were amenable to considering such a clause.[9] The House of Commons appointed a select committee to study the issue in 1867–1868. The committee's recommendations were reflected in the language of the extradition bill proposed two years later and in the finalized 1870 act itself (33 & 34 Vict. c. 52). This legislation in turn would provide the framework for the more than thirty extradition treaties the British signed between 1870 and World War I.

The act, passed under the auspices of Gladstone's Liberal administration, enshrined the right of the "political offender" to asylum for the first time. Section 3.1 outlined the exemption for "political offenses" and provided a safeguard against foreign governments' claims that an extradition request was *not* political. Rather than rely on the evidence presented by a foreign government, the act allowed the fugitive the right to instigate examination on his or her behalf. Demands for extradition would be dropped if the fugitive "prove[d] to the satisfaction of the police magistrate or the court before whom he is brought on *habeas corpus*, or to the secretary of state, that the requisition for his surrender has in fact been made with a view to try or punish him for an offense of a political character."[10]

There was another first in the 1870 act. The "political offender" could be either a foreigner or a British national or a colonial subject.[11] The act thereby recognized refuge as an international right. Irish nationalists had as much right to asylum in America or in France as the continental revolutionary enjoyed in Britain. The act assumed that America and France could also refuse extradition for these "political offenders." This codified right to asylum thus was a triumph for a capacious liberalism, one that recognized that though Britain might have been exceptional, its subjects might require protection against unjust justice. This was a particularly remarkable triumph given that it passed in the wake of ongoing Irish Fenian raids on Canada. Despite concerns for their security, the British refused to narrow the definition of the "political offender" they now exempted in law. The foreign and the domestic "political offender" now existed within a single framework in foreign policy.

The act did not remain unchallenged for long. The formal terms of the law captured the ambition of normative claims about refugees to date, but it did not reflect growing public skepticism of foreign exiles. The continued radicalization of Irish nationalism, as well as the rise of communism and anarchism on the Continent after 1870, thus tested the act's broad exemption to the breaking point.

Into a Single Frame

A June 1871 issue of London's *Penny Illustrated* satirized an encounter between supporters of French communist refugees and supporters of Irish Fenianism on Clerkenwell Green in Central London. The meeting's purpose was to sympathize with the communists, but the article focused on an altercation between the chair of the meeting and an Irishman in the audience. The chair denounced the French government. French ministers, he declared, wrought bloodthirsty vengeance on the Communards after the fall of the Paris Commune the previous month. To this, the Irishman shouted: "That is a lie, Johnson, and you know it; you would all be as bloodthirsty if you dare." A "great uproar" ensued. Although the chair, Mr. Johnson, tried to quiet the heckler, he succeeded only in getting more Irishmen involved. Another Irishman condemned British support for the French communists. He shouted, "The Irish Fenians were gentlemen compared with the Communists! . . . [T]he Fenians committed no robberies (cheers) nor would they hold with such robbers as the Communists (groans and cheers)."[12]

The fight over the relative merits of continental communists and Irish Fenians was meant to be darkly amusing for the *Penny Illustrated* audience. Public support for the Paris Communards was tentative at best. Since the first news of the Commune that March, tales of assassination, robbery, and arson abounded in the British press. The public ultimately supported Communard refugees, but that support was cautious and quiet.[13] Indeed, the June 11, 1871, rally was one of only a few held on communists' behalf, and it took place only after news of Versailles's brutal reprisals reached Britain.

Despite the Irishmen's assertions, Fenians were hardly "gentleman" either. The Fenian Brotherhood was a new, more violent group of Irish nationalists, increasingly popular in Ireland and in America, where they raised funds for their cause. By 1871, they were known for their bombings and military raids in Ireland, Britain, and Canada. Their violence in Britain seemed particularly egregious. In bids to free their comrades, Fenians attacked a police wagon in Manchester and a prison in Clerkenwell in 1867. The British response to the "Manchester Outrages" in particular was decisive: three of the conspirators were executed. But the two men freed from the prison wagon in the attack fled. They were later known to have resumed their agitation in America, safe from the reach of the British police.

Few commentators had previously linked celebrated continental refugees with Irish nationalists. This was not for want of links between the two. British political radicals and Irish nationalists had long fled to France or America to escape trial at home. Moreover, many of these "offenders" had comrades in Britain who befriended foreign refugees and supported their causes, becoming proponents of the right of asylum in the process.[14] Still, it was hardly politic for activists to compare their government's treatment of "political offenders" with the plight of noble liberal freedom fighters on the Continent. Scenes like that portrayed in the *Penny Illustrated* were rare before 1870. In the context of formalizing extradition protections for political offenders, however, both the existence of British political prisoners and the frightening radicalism of contemporary continental revolutionaries made these linkages unavoidable.

The question of how to respond to the new breeds of revolutionary weighed heavily on the public conscience from the spring of 1871 onward. In the wake of the Paris Commune, the mainstream and conservative media fretted that the French communists might find ready allies among the disaffected working classes and Irish nationalists. Even progressive journalists like W. R. Greg denounced the French Communards as "desperadoes" and worried that communism's international scope would soon bring similar destruction to Britain. Greg fretted that "the lazy, loafing, intermittent labourer likes nothing better" than to make trouble: "the call of arms will always be obeyed most readily and in greatest numbers by the most dangerous classes, and by the most dangerous of every class."[15] Greg also underscored the connection between the Communards and Irish nationalists. Similarly, the *Liverpool Mercury* reported in early June that a "number of persons who were identified with the Fenian movement in London, Liverpool, Manchester and Dublin took their departure some time ago for France."[16]

Radicals did what they could to calm such fears and distance themselves from continental communism. Positivist Frederick Harrison, for example, assisted Communard refugees but assured the public that he "was not, as has been assumed or insinuated, the unhesitating apologist of its [the Commune's] acts. Believing as I do communism in all its forms to be a dangerous dream, I unhesitatingly condemned all that was communistic in the movement."[17] Mainstream commentators remained on heightened alert, however, and their anxieties redoubled with the advent of continental anarchism in the later 1870s.[18]

Continental pressures ensured that British officials, activists, and the public at large were well aware of the implications of their exemption for political offenders. Though untouched by revolutionary continental communism, Britain would not be isolated from the anarchists' "propaganda by deed" for long.[19] Bismarck's banishment of German Socialists in 1878 brought prominent socialist-anarchists to England, where they established newspapers and held meetings, as had other foreign refugee groups. With anarchism came a redoubled revolutionary interest in the use of dynamite, a weapon previously employed by Irish Fenians and Russian Nihilists.[20] Even if the Irish and anarchists did not make common cause, their similar tactics seemed to put civil society at greater and greater risk.[21]

In this context, continental rulers campaigned for British extradition of political offenders. In 1871, the French foreign minister thundered that communists were "beyond the pale of civilization, outside of any right to refuge. [They were] demonic murderers, [guilty of] infernal burnings, sacrilege and looting [which] cried to heaven for vengeance."[22] The Russians pressed their case as well, the March 1881 assassination of Czar Alexander II making them the fiercest advocates of international collaboration against anarchism. Although all of the conspirators in Alexander's assassination were killed or captured shortly after they struck, the Russian state considered the larger network of anarchists to be culpable, since they had committed "incitement" to murder. Alexander III believed that these far-flung "co-conspirators" remained a danger to the state, and Russia called for an extradition league to pursue political offenders.

Even if the British wanted to extradite these more loathsome revolutionaries, they had to contend with their commitments in the 1870 Extradition Act. Were arson, assassination, and robbery—crimes that targeted the social order—political crimes? Where should they draw the line? The British would not be alone if they decided to refuse asylum to these new breeds of violent revolutionaries. In the wake of the Commune, Belgium went so far as to order Victor Hugo, then a resident of Brussels, out of the country for writing a letter in support of his countrymen.[23] By 1876, the Belgian government took additional steps to enable the extradition of suspected assassins. Officials proclaimed that any attack on a sovereign or the sovereign's family disqualified a perpetrator for asylum. In April 1881, the German Reichstag concurred, calling for extradition treaties to pursue all political offenders.

Uncertain what these changes meant for Britain, commentators and officials searched for a concerted response to the extradition requests they now anticipated from European powers, beginning with the French. Opponents of a right to asylum sought a test case to help the government narrow Britain's open-door policy. The home secretary, for example, recommended that a "notorious 'scoundrel'" like Frenchman Félix Pyat (who had libeled the queen in 1855) be brought to trial to demonstrate to the public how unlikeable refugees were.

Radical Charles Dilke and fellow MPs Whalley, Mundella, White, and (Jacob) Bright, by contrast, had begun to organize what they hoped would be a broad-based defense of asylum in late May 1871.[24] Their campaign was unnecessary, as it turned out. Gladstone—though he too distanced himself from the Communards and their radical supporters—committed Britain to the right of asylum. In advance of anticipated French demands, Gladstone determined that complying with extradition requests was simply impossible under existing law.[25]

Ultimately, the British press sided with the administration and the refugees for two reasons. First, few public commentators could deny that this new breed of revolutionaries had a political creed upon which its adherents acted. W. R. Greg acknowledged that one "could detect 'some distinct political theory' in the commune and could urge the extension of the right of asylum to the fugitive Communards."[26] Secondly, these foreign trials would surely be politically charged, and even more violent offenders seemed to deserve better than such questionable justice. This sentiment was strengthened in the wake of the Commune's collapse. News that the French government had indiscriminately killed thirty thousand Parisian men and women in the final days of the Commune dispelled any British doubts that these particular foreigners deserved to be called genuine refugees.[27] Official French trials that fall only confirmed the impression that yesterday's persecutors were now themselves victims of disproportionate political vengeance. They were convicted, journalists reported, for crimes that were concocted. A *Times* correspondent described with horror the death sentences given to four women accused of being *pétroleuses.* By many accounts, he explained, these alleged female arsonists were figments of the inflamed French imagination.[28]

Perhaps sensing this turn of opinion in Britain, the French government never requested the extradition of Communard refugees. If they were disappointed, the French authorities quickly resolved to make the most of this situation and use Britain as a makeshift prison for political offenders. Much to the chagrin of British officials and commentators, the French government assisted additional communists to British shores.[29]

Anarchism more severely tested the boundaries of what constituted a political offense. Still, the public could not deny that the actions of anarchists were based on political ideology. In response to the assassination of Alexander II in March 1881, the Home Office brought two counts of libel and ten counts of conspiracy to murder against German Johann Most's anarchist newspaper, the *Freiheit.* Most's London-based newspaper, which circulated throughout the Continent, was said to have played a key role in promoting anarchists' assassination campaigns. Indeed, just after Alexander's death, Most published an article that "threatened in no uncertain language," the *Times* explained, "all rulers 'from Washington to Constantinople,' with a fate like that of Alexander II."[30] Johann Most was found guilty and sentenced to sixteen months in prison with hard labor. Though Most was not in danger of extradition, the trial provoked public dismay at the government's attack on political expression. The trial appeared to be an infringement on the freedom of the press and evidence of the reach of continental powers into domestic British affairs (a point the home secretary tried to deny). The majority of commentators judged that, though the refugees in question were an unsympathetic lot, Britain was meant to be more liberal than her continental neighbors, just as the classic refugee narrative had long asserted.[31]

Such comparisons between liberal Britain and the despotic Continent proved critical in the public mind. It is unclear whether Russia or the other continental rulers approached the British state to change her extradition policies in the wake of the 1881 assassination of the Russian Czar. Members of both Houses of Parliament were nonetheless well aware of continental calls for collaboration and confronted the administration to demand if this had indeed taken place. The Earl of Granville flatly denied the charge in May 1881.[32] Yet, Russian interest in an extradition treaty—if not made in the spring of 1881—had been hinted at during the previous year and, in the wake of the assassination, the Cabinet weighed such a treaty negotiation closely. Gladstone's administration knew that signing such a treaty with Russia would be politically impossible, no matter how horrified Victoria had been at the thought that conspirators would be safe in England if they had managed to escape Russia.[33]

In this respect, Johann Most's 1881 trial offered a means of buffering foreigners from overseas vengeance and protecting British asylum. As jury members themselves remarked, Most's trial and sentencing in British courts was merciful. The alternative was surrendering him to foreign authorities, thus yielding to continental demands for a new British extradition policy. The mainstream British public might have been glad to see anarchists brought to justice, but they meant to uphold British justice.[34]

Despite having succeeded in their efforts to maintain the political offender exemption, activists were hesitant as to how to receive these foreigners. The refugees needed to be provided with relief; few could overlook their poverty. Supporters were less certain of how to obtain relief when sympathy for refugees was thin at best. Traditional, large-scale protest meetings on the refugees' behalf seemed impossible. Notables could hardly endorse relief organizations if sponsorship meant tacit acceptance of noxious political convictions.

British ambivalence did not mean an end to older models for relief. Rallies, standard between 1820 and 1860, persisted among more radical refugee supporters. Working-class rallies like the Central London meeting depicted in the *Penny Illustrated* were rare but did take place. Supporters within British radical communities organized important relief schemes. Frederick Harrison established the largest operation, collecting funds and finding employment for more than a hundred French men and women and collecting subscriptions from private individuals ranging from the "M.P. [who] sends £100" to "an old housekeeper [who] sends £5."[35] As was typical, most refugees ended up sheltering in cosmopolitan Central London, though some found employment throughout the country through Harrison's efforts. As in previous periods, these refugees became prominent participants in the radical ecosystem. Anarchists established newspapers in London and held meetings. Socialist exiles distributed Marx's account of the Commune, *The Civil War in France*, as propaganda for the International Working Men's Association.[36]

Mainstream charitable collections increasingly distanced themselves from political propaganda. In the wake of the Commune, politicians often contributed to relief funds so that the refugees would not starve, but they did so privately and quietly. Harrison did not advertise their names, as had been the norm for relief subscription lists in prior crises. Moreover, long-standing refugee supporters adopted strategies used for liberated Africans across the Empire but rarely seen in Britain proper. The Conservative Baroness Burdett Coutts offered a model of relief that treated these refugees as barbarous foreigners in need of civilization. Through the Anglo-Huguenot Reverend T. Marzial, she funded a project to rehabilitate forty of the most hardened French communists—those whom the French police had dumped on English shores. Providing them with room and board in 1872, Marzial separated this group from their comrades and provided them with clean clothes and "a stock of bibles and other 'good books.' "[37]

The Marzial/Coutts program was an isolated scheme and one about which few details are known. Nevertheless, it emphasizes the break from earlier practices. Revolutionary refugees were no longer held up as paragons of civic and moral virtue, as Mazzini, Garibaldi, and Kossuth had been for their middle- and upper-class supporters. Nor was it assumed that refugees would be dedicated, sober workers, as Chartists had portrayed the 1851 Polish-Hungarian contingent. Instead, exiles were treated as essentially different and potentially undesirable. As with the liberated Africans resettled at the outposts of Empire, the point of refuge was to provide moral guidance and a sober, Christian structure to daily life—a stark contrast, so it was believed, to these foreigners' habits.

The violence of "propaganda by deed" further dampened British enthusiasm for refugees. Yet, the newly codified right of refuge for political offenders came under greater scrutiny only when the Irish nationalist violence struck home. Then—and only then—would public outrage be sufficient to prompt officials to attempt to narrow the 1870 exemption clause. Between 1882 and 1885, the Irish Republican Brotherhood renewed their campaign of dynamite attacks, targeting prominent politicians and the public at large. They were not anarchists. But few could ignore that these nationalists' tactics and their targets were one and the same.[38]

It was the assassination of two British officials—the chief secretary for Ireland, Lord Frederick Cavendish, and his permanent undersecretary, Thomas Henry Burke—in Phoenix Park, Dublin, on May 6, 1882, that made changing Britain's foreign policy regarding "political offenders" politically feasible (figure 6.5). The murders exposed imminent threats to British security that the country had been spared, for the most part, since the 1860s. In response, Parliament passed the Explosive Substances Act in 1883 to enable the police to capture would-be assailants. Changes in domestic law were not enough, however. Those directly responsible for the assassinations were captured within British territory. As with the assassination of Alexander II, the network of conspirators was considered to be much larger. Just a year after the British rejected international offers to collaborate on extradition, officials sought the rendition of conspirators from overseas. The attempt to bring five main fugitives to justice failed utterly. In the early spring of 1883, the men believed to be the main conspirators behind murders (Frank Byrne, Patrick Tynan, John Walsh, P. J. Sheridan, and John McCafferty) were tracked to France and America. Requests for their extradition from either country proved fruitless. French newspapers, in particular, denounced the attempt, running an "anti-British campaign, reminiscing on the themes of ancient Franco-Irish friendship and Britain's refusal to extradite the communard refugees of 1871."[39]

Britain was rebuked. America became to Britain what Britain had been to the Continent: a refuge for political "desperadoes." The British could do little but shrug their shoulders at "American sentimentalism," as many termed it.[40] Cavendish's brother, the Duke of Devonshire, switched political allegiances over the matter. Once a friend of Gladstone's and a proponent of Irish Home Rule, he became the leader of the Liberal Unionists.[41]

Though these particular offenders were lost, officials knew that there would likely be more who would make America their refuge. Gladstone's administration and the mainstream public were equally eager to pursue a new treaty with the United States to permit the extradition of Irish nationalists guilty of "propaganda by deed." The legal community began to press this cause in professional journals and in the mainstream press. Legal scholar E. L de Hart came to the conclusion that the 1870 Act had to be amended to reflect a hierarchy

6.5 · "On the Trail [for the Phoenix Park Murderers]," *Punch, or the London Charivari* 84, (February 24, 1883): 91. Credit: Courtesy of the Bowdoin College Library, Brunswick, Maine.

of political crime, insisting that "political motive is not in itself a sufficient reason for protecting the criminal."[42] The London *Times* used the Phoenix Park murderers to demonstrate how despicable "political offenses" could be and demanded whether it was right that the "authors of the crime escaped absolutely without punishment, because, forsooth, their offense partook of the nature of a political crime." They might be "political offenders, because the motive of their offense was political, but they were vulgar murderers, notwithstanding." The 1886 article insisted:

> In short, the principle which prompts us to extend the aegis of protection over purely political offenders, over men with whom we may from time to time sympathize warmly, is noble in theory; but practical men are beginning to doubt whether the balance of convenience does not lie with the arguments of those who contend that every state is capable of dealing with its own subjects and ought to receive every help in so doing.[43]

Even the radical *Reynolds's Newspaper* reported with interest the discovery of the Phoenix Park conspirators and attempts to bring them to trial in the 1880s and 1890s. In this case, at least, *Reynolds*'s editors subscribed to a belief that the murderers—and assassins more generally—were not covered by the exemption for political offenders. However, they understood the challenge of arguing this case internationally better than their more mainstream counterparts. Extradition of the Phoenix Park murderers would only work if it could be argued that the conspirators were not political actors and that they had no connections with organized Irish nationalist groups. *Reynolds*'s editors were proud that they would have to argue the case in this manner, for, they explained, it meant that "the lesson that we have taught the world as to the extradition of political criminals has happily been well learned by others."[44]

Had British opinion changed within a single year simply because of an attack at home? Perhaps. Yet even though mainstream and radical press were both willing to narrow the political offender exemption, they remained quick to advocate on behalf of foreigners—even anarchists—who were mistreated overseas. In this vein, anarchist victims of the Spanish atrocities in 1896–1897 elicited avid metropolitan interest. The Spanish military's unduly harsh treatment of Cuban revolutionaries had already been in the news.[45] In London, concerned onlookers organized a protest committee and held public meetings to call attention to the government's response to the bombing of a Barcelona church in June 1896. Sympathizers did not excuse those responsible for killing eleven people in the attack. They argued, however, that the government's pattern of retaliation was disproportionate to the perceived threat: it amounted to a "new Inquisition."

Rather than seek out the real perpetrators, the Spanish used the event to round up "more than four hundred" "dangerous" individuals, from members of working-class associations to republicans and socialists, as well as anarchists. Their methods of inquiry fell "very little short of torture," the London committee argued, and differed little from those used by the Spanish in Cuba and the Philippines.[46]

Was this solicitude for foreign political offenders hypocritical when compared to Britain's attempts to extradite Irish nationalists taking asylum in America? By the 1880s, America and France in particular were leveling just this sort of accusation. Regardless of how one parses this moral question, there is considerable historical interest in examining the British attempt to square the circle: to preserve asylum for foreign refugees while denying asylum overseas for Fenian assassins. The logic they used reveals much about contemporary conceptions of what made justice, in fact, just.

The Quest for a Language of Right

In 1883, jurist and diplomat Sir John Rose lamented that the government had not already refined the political offender exemption clause. Rose argued that there had been a "time when we were neither open to the imputation of panic, nor to the charge of asking other nations to stretch their previous systems to some special case in which we were immediately concerned."[47] The changes they set out to make in the wake of the Phoenix Park murders, Rose feared, would no longer be seen to reflect "sober judgment." There had in fact been opportunities for "reasoned suggestions" that Rose believed should have been seized before 1883. In 1868 and 1878, two separate committees had convened to discuss international extradition law. Each made recommendations about whether to exempt crimes considered to be "political" and what exactly constituted "political crime" in the first place. But Parliament delayed action until after the Phoenix Park murders. The Harcourt Bill of 1885 refined the broad "political" exemption of the 1870 act in a manner meant to tack between American liberalism and continental reactionary conservatism.

The first commission to tackle extradition law was an 1868 House of Commons select committee called while the 1866 French extradition treaty was still on the table. The second was a royal commission of appointees drawn from the legal establishment in 1878.[48] Whereas the first commission established the terms of the exemption clause, the second commission set out to revise those terms. Unhappy with the broad scope of the 1870 definition at a time when anarchism was clearly on the rise, Benjamin Disraeli's Tory administration called the royal commission to deliberate on the question of the political offense exemption clause. Despite the space of a decade between them, both commissions explored whether an attempt on the person of a sovereign ought to be considered a political act and whether a political offender could be considered for asylum if his or her violent act was not committed during a period of open insurrection.

Despite their similar briefs, the ethos of each committee differed greatly. The 1868 House of Commons select committee heard testimony that Britain was as unlikely to be granted a request for a Fenian who had, for instance, killed bystanders while freeing his comrades as Britain was to surrender a Mazzini, Kossuth, or Garibaldi.[49] The commission hoped to remedy this situation. Fenians' actions, Mill argued, were not those of political insurgents. But pinpointing a definition of political offenses that included "good" insurgents and ruled out "bad" ones proved more difficult than it seemed.[50] London's chief police magistrate T. Henry suggested linking political exemptions to open civil war while disavowing assassination attempts. He explained that the killing of a police officer, for instance, might be political if part of an uprising, but not if it took place in an isolated alleyway.[51] In this respect, Garibaldi and Kossuth, for example, were still "legitimate" refugees.

In the end, the committee decided against making the definition of political offense explicit. They suggested only that assassination—or attempted assassination—should not be a political crime. Ultimately, Parliament passed the 1870 Extradition Act without refining the scope of the political offender category. In 1876, lawyer E. S. Roscoe celebrated this failure as a matter of liberal triumph and a sign that Britain had moved past her own political insecurities and had definitively distinguished herself from continental despots.[52] Within two years, however, that open liberalism seemed too dangerous for even a modernized, relatively democratic nation to maintain.

The 1878 royal commission issued more specific recommendations. Whereas the 1868 committee had admitted that Fenian offenders would not be brought to justice, the 1878 royal commission insisted that violent "propaganda by deed" was not a properly political act. The commissioners highlighted conspiracies to assassinate sovereign rulers as especially beyond the pale. Moreover, the commission held that someone who set fire to a prison at the "risk of burning all those within the prison" could not possibly deserve to be exempted from extradition demands. They admitted that the motive might have been political, but motive alone could not exonerate such indiscriminate acts. Commissioners warned that "these are crimes in respect of which—though the motive was a political one—we cannot think that any immunity should be afforded."[53]

The royal commission report stated, "We would ... decline to recognize the suggestion of a political motive as a ground on which a magistrate or judge should refuse a demand for the surrender of a person accused of what (in the absence of such motive) would be an ordinary crime." Assassination and arson were thus extraditable. The only exceptions would be for acts committed "during a time of civil war or open insurrection," as such acts, whether or not they are "justified or excused by circumstances," at least "take place openly, in the face of day."[54] By these guidelines, the Communards would still have been considered genuine political refugees entitled to asylum, though the renowned fugitive slave John Anderson would have been extraditable. (The commission did not note this latter fact; perhaps they had forgotten about it or perhaps they reasoned that the United States's abolition of slavery now made such cases moot.)

The commissioners further recommended specific procedures to be adopted under any new extradition act. First and foremost, they insisted that Britain must never sign an extradition treaty with a nation whose judicial system did not merit confidence.[55] Second, British magistrates were to play prominent roles in agreeing to the extradition of a particular offender. As the commissioners detailed, magistrates would study the facts of the case to determine whether the supposed crime was a crime under British law. Furthermore, accused persons had every right to make their case before the British magistrate if they could provide evidence that they would be tried for a political or local offense despite their home government's claims to the contrary. Only after a British magistrate had been satisfied that the crime was not political could a foreigner be remanded to face trial overseas.[56]

To many, the commission's recommendations made a good deal of sense and provided a roadmap for the reforms officials had sought since the passing of the 1870 Extradition Act. In a moment of relative calm, however, Parliament lacked the political urgency necessary to turn these suggestions into law. The commission's suggestions were thus left untouched. For four years, it seemed that few were willing to undertake the unsavory task of refining the broad political offenses clause. That would change in 1882.

The Phoenix Park murders brought this period of procrastination to an end. The flight of suspected Fenian conspirators across the Atlantic prompted Gladstone's Liberal government to train its attention on drafting a template for an extradition treaty with the United States. The primary goal in this endeavor was to narrow the scope of the political offender exemption to bring the Fenian leadership within their reach. This would, of course, leave American fugitives vulnerable to similar extradition demands, a point with which the British had once been distinctly uncomfortable. After the abolition of slavery in the United States, however, the situation had changed; the British tended to trust American justice, even in cases where there might have been a political motivation for the crime. As proponents of extradition law reform had pointed out as early as 1866, if John Wilkes Booth had somehow escaped to English soil, British authorities would surely have returned him to the United States for trial. If they were not careful to define political offense, the likes of Booth—the loathed assassin of a much-loved president—would be safe.

The challenge in drafting new extradition language was that faith in the American judiciary was not enough. Any resulting British law would provide the go-to language for treaties with continental powers as well as with the United States. British officials and the public at large would have to be comfortable with a definition of political offense that could work in a variety of contexts.

It was home secretary (and member of the 1878 commission) Sir William Harcourt who offered what seemed to the British to be the best compromise. Harcourt's 1885 draft treaty considered neither arson nor dynamite murders nor assassination "political." In this respect, he adopted the recommendations of the 1878 committee, but with a key change. In view of the daunting fact that almost any act targeting a public official could be styled as politically motivated, Harcourt stipulated that any crime punishable under British law was prima facie not political, "unless . . . connected with an existing condition of open warfare or insurrection."[57]

This language preserved a right to asylum for those who simply articulated distasteful political ideas. Freedom of speech and right to political opinion—cornerstones of modern liberal rule—were thus safe.[58] However, Harcourt's emphasis on an open state of war or insurrection ruled out Fenian violence, and any conspiracy to engage in open insurrection would also be deemed criminal.

After all this careful legal parsing, British officials were sorely disappointed. American negotiators rejected the proposal immediately and the broad parameters of the political offense clause remained unaltered in the 1890 Anglo-US extradition treaty. The popularity of Irish nationalism in the States made it as politically unfeasible to extradite these revolutionaries as it had earlier been for the British to contemplate returning fugitive slaves to America.

As Sir John Rose might have predicted, distance from Phoenix Park diminished the urgency with which the public clamored for change to the political offender clause. Not even the anarchist bombing at Greenwich Park in February 1895 shook the public's growing faith in their own police system as superior to a formal extradition agreement that might infringe on political asylum.[59] Matters might have been different had French anarchist Martial Bourdin managed to do anything other than blow himself up in Greenwich Park. As it was, however, Salisbury's Conservative administration (1895–1902) understood public commitment to refuge to be a sad fact, one that handicapped the administration's foreign policy. Officials attempted one last revision of the law that year. The press's response was definitive: even those willing to try passing a new extradition act declared that the political exemption must be protected.[60]

A Spectacular Failure? The Power of a Moral Category

William Torrens, a member of both committees on extradition law, had anticipated the viewpoint that ultimately prevailed. Torrens penned a dissent to the 1878 commission's recommendation that the government narrow the definition of "political offenses." He urged that "Parliament cannot affect ignorance of the disparity of foreign laws, and the repugnance to our own of the principles on which criminal justice is frequently administered under them." Only by upholding the 1870 act's broad exemption could the British guard "the presumption of innocence which we regard as fundamental" and which "is not acknowledged in several of the greatest States of Europe."[61] To Torrens, the right to refuge for the political offender was the hallmark of modern liberalism—a sign that a nation had shed her insecurities and committed herself to the notion that everyone deserved just justice.

Despite dwindling British enthusiasm for a broad right of asylum, the irony is that the country's failure to incorporate a narrower definition of political offenses in international law helped to guarantee the very triumph of modern liberalism that Torrens—along with John Stuart Mill, E. S. Roscoe, and others—had envisioned from the start. Britain's failed attempts to rewrite her own language on political offenders became prominent on the international stage thanks to several controversies involving extradition to the Continent.

The 1890 case of Angelo Castioni and the 1894 case of Théodule Meunier, whose extradition from Britain had been requested by the Swiss and French governments, respectively, established contemporary precedents around the distinction between political action and criminalized terrorism.[62] Whereas officials had not succeeded in introducing detailed procedures in formal law, the judges of the Queen's Bench succeeded in instituting the narrower definition of "political" at the heart of the failed Harcourt extradition bill. In the wake of their ruling for Castioni and against Meunier, "political offenses" in British common law would be limited to those committed at a time of open insurrection only.

At the behest of the Swiss government, Angelo Castioni was arrested on October 3, 1890, at his London residence on the charge of having murdered Luigi Rossi. Castioni had shot and killed the Swiss state councilor the previous month in Ticino, Switzerland. Taken before the magistrates at Bow Street, Castioni was held for extradition.[63] Castioni's case was brought before the Queen's Bench for review in early November 1890. His lawyer Charles Russell demonstrated that the murder was a part of a revolutionary upheaval in the Swiss canton and that Castioni did not target Rossi for assassination or bear him private ill-will. The murder was part of a political uprising in which an "armed multitude" faced the local gendarmerie at the Ticino government house.[64] Castioni was thus a "political offender" and exempt from extradition according to the 1870 act. Justices Denman, Hawkins, and Stephen agreed. Whereas the lawyers for the Swiss side tried to represent Castioni as a man who took advantage of a moment of upheaval to commit murder, Justice Denman found that "it appears perfectly plainly from the evidence that this man Castioni was a person who had been taking part in that movement [political upheaval] at a much earlier stage."[65] Castioni was discharged.

The judges made Castioni's case an opportunity to further specify a definition for "insurrection," however. Offenses, they held, could only be political if there was an "open insurrection," but what did this mean? Castioni's lawyer, Russell, had argued that the political should include "any offense committed in the course of a furthering of civil war, insurrection, or political commotion." As legal historian Christopher Pyle explains, this would have sanctioned refuge for "rioters of almost every stripe." Instead, the judges emphasized that timing alone did not make for a political offense. More than happening at a time of "organized" revolution, the act would have to be "done in furtherance of, done with the intention of assistance, as a sort of overt act in the course of acting in a political matter, a political rising, or a dispute between two parties in the State as to which is to have the government in its hands."[66]

Anarchists' "propaganda by deed" seemed to be ruled out by this narrowed definition of insurrection. Mainstream commentators did not consider anarchist "dynamitards" to be members of organized politics. The Queen's Bench indeed used this specification from the Castioni case as a common-law precedent four years later. Whereas Castioni's action had taken place as a part of open insurrection by these standards, the same could not be said about Théodule Meunier's bombing campaign in France.

In March 1892, Meunier, it was charged, attempted murder by throwing a bomb into the Loban Barracks. A month later, he was believed to have thrown a bomb into the Parisian Café Véry, killing two people.[67] Using the justices' language from Castioni's case, the prosecution held that because "the prisoner did not belong to a party having a form of government of its own or which sought to impose a form of government upon another party" he could not be considered a "political offender." Anarchism more generally, Justice Cave held, "is the enemy apparently of all Government, and its operations are not directed primarily against the Government but only incidentally, and secondarily against the members of the political body." Rather they "are directed primarily against the members of the general body, the citizens, and apparently only casually against the Government or governing body."[68] As an anarchist, Meunier was thus extradited and would stand trial in France the following month.

For British commentators across the political spectrum, the Castioni decision was a triumph. Having condemned Castioni's initial incarceration, Tory and radical newspapers alike celebrated his liberation as evidence that it was "'the desire of the English people' that rebels 'should not be surrendered to their victorious opponents.'"[69]

The fact that jurists refined the political offender category in case law as opposed to formal treaty was significant. It dispensed with the thornier question of with whom the British could sign extradition treaties and ensured that British officials could vet each case thoroughly before turning the fugitive in question over to his or her home government for trial. British case law set international precedent that America and the international community would adopt in ensuing years: it offered not only a means of defining political offenders but a means of identifying a new category of criminal—the modern terrorist.[70]

International pressure to narrow the political offender exemption in international agreements did not immediately diminish, however. Despite the new common-law precedents, continental powers urged the British government to sign formal international accords against anarchists. This urging only increased with ongoing dynamite campaigns on the Continent and the assassination of Austrian Empress Elisabeth in September 1898. Though Salisbury could not afford to take part directly in the Rome Anti-Anarchist Conference in 1898, the Conservative administration sent delegates to report on the proceedings.[71] These diplomats found themselves in the familiar position of schooling continental neighbors on the staunch liberalism of the British public on this issue.[72] From the outset of the proceedings, the delegates explained carefully their continued refusal to sign any international accords that resulted from the conference meetings. On the one hand, their explanations offer clear evidence that the British distrusted the extent to which continental powers would seek to police not just criminal action but political opinion.[73] Salisbury directed diplomat Sir Philip Currie to stick to principle, underscoring that Britain would not compromise "so long as no evidence exists of criminal intent, or to our assenting to expel persons on any grounds from this country, or to interfere with the liberty of the press, unless a charge of incitement to crime can be made and sustained."[74]

On the other hand, British delegates did not play into international concerns that the British did not intend to bring "criminals" to justice. Currie and his negotiating partner, Home Office permanent undersecretary Sir Kenelm Digby, explained that a foreigner who assassinated a sovereign would be subject to extradition. The assassination of a sovereign, Currie highlighted, would not be automatically viewed as political, though other countries considered it so. Digby further explained that his government accepted that "political crime" excluded assassination and included any "crime of violence" only if it were committed "in furtherance of existing civil war or existing open insurrection."[75]

The British government never signed the conventions of the Rome conference, though officials continued to ruminate about the matter through the turn of the century. Instead, they promised only to increase attention to the activities of foreigners in their midst and to continue relaying information from the Home Office to nervous foreign powers. As Digby insisted, they would rely on their own judiciary system to differentiate between political and nonpolitical offenses; this they would do on a case-by-case basis as they had with Castioni and Meunier.[76]

Metropolitan press coverage of the Rome Anti-Anarchist Conference's proceedings was minimal. But Salisbury seems to have read the public accurately, demonstrating the degree to which even the Conservative government had internalized the liberal consensus on this matter. The government was likely extrapolating from public interest in the cases of the Spanish anarchists and the Paris Communards. The few press reports issued on the Rome conference congratulated the administration for assuring that the tradition of asylum would be protected.[77]

Legal Rights and a New Tale of Caution

Despite diminished sympathies for new breeds of revolutionaries, the public remained steadfastly supportive of asylum for persecuted foreigners. In the wake of Fenian, communist, and anarchist "propaganda by deed," this was increasingly a commitment to a more abstract language of right. The legal exemption of political offenders from extradition was a momentous development for British refuge at home and on the international stage. Yet, in many respects, it concealed a shift in British enthusiasm for foreign refugees.

Literary critic and popular novelist Edward Dutton Cook captured this mood of increasing world-weariness in his last novel, *Doubleday's Children*. The novel, serialized in 1876–1877 in Dickens's widely sold journal *All the Year Round* and later published in at least two separate printed editions, grappled with generational differences in British sympathy for foreign revolutionaries. Set in late 1840s London, the novel projects contemporaries' fears of refugee violence onto the past, using different characters to ventriloquize the range of responses available to those who come in contact with foreign refugees in their midst.

Raised in cosmopolitan Central London, the three Doubleday orphans are surrounded by refugee supporters. Their deceased father's closest friend, Mr. Grisdale, is a radical who has romanticized refugees his entire life. Each Doubleday child—Nicholas, Basil, and Doris—has to grapple with this romance and come to his or her own conclusions about how much sympathy refugees deserve. Their responses range from disdain for foreigners (Nicholas), to modulated support for their causes but not their tactics (Basil), to unreflective empathy for their misery (Doris). It is Basil's voice of caution that carries the author's implicit endorsement. Basil is a moral-force Chartist who is as hesitant in his views of continental "conspirators" as he is of physical-force Chartism. He warns Doris, who has befriended a French exile (Paul Riel), that the Frenchman is a conspirator plotting against the French king. Basil admits that Riel might not be "directly chargeable," but "there is a certain line of conduct which seems to lead to assassination, or to nowhere." He adds that fighting for "liberty" is the refugee's term; "we will call it tyrannicide."[78]

Doris, whose blind sympathy represents the naïveté of unqualified support for refugees, marries Paul despite Basil's advice. Thenceforward, the Doubledays face the reality of having a French conspirator in the family. Nicholas despises Riel and attempts to shun his sister, but he has his own troubling passion for the daughter of a Spanish refugee. Basil fears for his sister but cares for the impoverished couple. Doris is initially defiant. She resists Basil's warning of refugees' violent tendencies. She retorts that "it is sufficient for me that M. Riel is a refugee . . . surely he is well deserving of our sympathy and our assistance, if, indeed, we can assist him." No sooner is Doris married, however, than she comes to understand what being an exile means. She recoils at the thought that her husband is more devoted to his country than to her. In an echo of Basil's words, Doris realizes that her spouse is committed to "what we plain English prefer to call murder." Upon Paul's inevitable return to France, Doris cannot but see his self-professed "duty" as a mistaken calling. Though desperately in love with him, she wonders whether she ought to pray for his safe return. "Can I pray," she asks Basil, "that he may return a murderer?"[79]

Cook's cautionary tale of the consequences of welcoming a foreign refugee into the heart of a British family captured the changing ethos of the time. Although far from a rejection of refuge wholesale, *Doubleday's Children* offered a strong corrective to the heroic refugee narrative that had long shaped the default British response to foreign refugees. Whereas the classic refugee narrative celebrated refugees' heroic opposition to oppression overseas, the new plotline identified refugees as potential villains. Even if they were not yet "directly chargeable" with specific crimes, exiles were not worthy of unconditional support. Outright sentimentalism, which Cook depicted as a typically feminine weakness in the character of Doris Doubleday, made studied reflection impossible and threatened the fabric of British society. Welcoming an exile into the British home had been the consolation prize at the heart of the classic refugee narrative when exiles could not return to a home freed of persecution. Here, by contrast, Doris's marriage to Paul Riel tears the British family apart. Not only is her refugee husband unable to support her and so fails the independent liberal ideal, but he also abandons her for his beloved France.

Perhaps fortunately for Doris, Paul dies of wounds he sustains while ousting King Louis Philippe. He is a revolutionary hero, but redeems himself (and Doris) by repenting of his violent means before he dies. Author Joseph Conrad would not be so forgiving in his more famous rendition of this new plotline thirty years later in *The Secret Agent.* In Conrad, the questionable heroics of Paul Riel gave way to images of unfathomable violence associated with dynamite and assassination. For Conrad, the Paul Riels of the world were less likely to leave their wives than to entrap their British families in their machinations, as does Verloc's brother-in-law, who becomes the unsuspecting player in an anarchist plot and its only victim.

Whereas a previous generation organized welcome meetings and rallied behind revolutionary refugees' causes, British charitable relief for refugees now became a quieter affair. Within Britain, the cause promoted and celebrated was the institution of asylum itself as a humanitarian, liberal practice. More ambivalent toward revolutionaries, the diverse cadre of metropolitan refugee supporters looked further afield. Increasingly, their charitable objects were refugees across the globe. They found the valor that seemed to be missing among continental dissidents in more distant persecuted foreigners. Rather than looking for revolutionaries, they looked increasingly for victims. They were learning to prefer the feminized helpless innocent to the iconically masculine freedom fighter.

SEVEN

The Limits of Imperial Humanitarianism

It is the early 1870s. A British man-of-war sails near the coast of Zanzibar, East Africa. The sailors eye each passing vessel, ready to pounce at signs of illegal slave traffic. A small Arab dhow filled with Africans catches their attention. One African jumps overboard and swims to the British ship. The sailors pull the man to safety. The Arab master is irate. He demands that the captain return his slave. The captain hesitates. The slave, he discovers, was not illegally traded according to Britain's treaties with the sultan of Zanzibar. The slave was not freshly captured from the interior of Africa, nor was he being transported outside of the sultan's territories. He is the Arab's domestic slave. He works along the coastline at one of the pearl fisheries, to which the dhow was in transit. He is a fugitive from legal slavery.

Is the slave a refugee? Should the British provide him with asylum? If the captain returns the slave, he has violated a sacred British tradition of refuge—an act that will earn him the ire of the metropolitan public. If he does not return the slave, he risks offending the Arab master and the sultan, to whose good will the anti-slave-trade squadron owes its right to patrol in these waters. What can he do?

Official fears that foreign slaves would ask for refuge in this manner were real. Individual slaves working in coastal pearl fisheries had asked for assistance before.[1] As far as the Admiralty was concerned, the proximity of the squadron and legal slave laborers made it only a matter of time before droves of slaves escaped in the hopes of receiving asylum from British officials. In addition to being a diplomatic nightmare, this scenario also exposed a practical difficulty. Fugitives could not be provided asylum on board a British vessel permanently. Where would the Admiralty put them? This was not a concern specific to the care of runaway slaves. The fugitive slave question became the focal point of the larger concern for sheltering Africans liberated from the illegal slave trade in the Indian Ocean region. Sierra Leone and the Caribbean had provided destinations for liberated foreign slaves in the Western Hemisphere, but the British did not then have a colonial foothold in East Africa. The small-scale African asylums in the region seemed woefully unequal to the task. Officials worried that providing asylum required colonial expansion, a cost the imperial government was not necessarily willing to shoulder.

This chapter examines British responses to the Admiralty's three fugitive slave circulars of July 1875–August 1876. The circulars were Admiralty instructions for Her Majesty's ships regarding the admission of fugitive—or runaway—slaves. The first circular of July 1875 limited the admission of foreign slaves so that no fugitive who escaped from legal slavery could be considered a refugee. When the metropolitan public learned of these instructions, the public outcry was tremendous. As concerned commentators rightly worried, the circulars occasioned the first referendum on the costs of open asylum and the lengths to which the British were willing to assert their global authority to this end. Protecting fugitive slaves remained difficult through the turn of the century, even after the Imperial British East Africa Company (IBECA) took control of the region in 1888. From 1875, however, concern for the diplomatic and financial costs of continued refuge altered the way in which officials were to apply the refugee category to foreigners. To the astonishment of the metropolitan public, a royal commission tasked with studying the issue argued that a whole group of people—foreign slaves—could be excluded from the humanitarian category because officials feared they could not afford refuge.

Their claim spelled the beginning of the end of imperial refuge; it challenged the broad moral-cum-national responsibility toward persecuted foreigners in the teeth of public opposition. Proponents of the circulars used international legal norms to restrain moral demands where previously officials had used the nation's might to recast those norms. To justify their departure from a proud tradition of refuge, proponents questioned openly whether British refuge was viable, and whether the slaves were not even better off at home than in poorly run British refuges. This language was tainted with racial prejudices regarding the possibility of "civilizing" liberated Africans. Their utilitarian argument could have been made earlier about refuge in Sierra Leone. Debuted in the late nineteenth century, however, the critique of British refuge drew force from the language of humanitarianism itself, mirroring growing concerns about the nature of indentured labor. In so doing, it offered a harshly realist rejoinder to the moral politics of refuge, highlighting its dependence on British capacities to provide meaningful relief. It was an argument that, within years, was reprised in the face of rising Jewish migration to London's East End.[2]

New Harbors of Refuge

The British had signed antislavery treaties with East African rulers as early as 1820. But the international Indian Ocean slave trade only became the focal point for the navy after the Atlantic trade was declared dead in the 1860s. As with the Atlantic trade, a byproduct of policing the trade was the creation of a body of homeless Africans—those released from the illegal trade. Although the need to provide for these foreigners was not new, the prospect of sheltering an untold number of fugitive slaves, in addition to thousands of liberated Africans, terrified officials. Not only would the offer of asylum to fugitive slaves offend the sultan, it threatened to put more pressure on asylums for liberated Africans than the British could bear.

As in the Atlantic, the responsibility to protect liberated Africans fell, by treaty stipulation, to the British. Until there was no slavery in the Indian Ocean, the British would have to locate safe havens where the liberty of illegally trafficked slaves could be secured. The Admiralty brought captured slave dhows to courts in their colonial territories at Aden (in modern Yemen on the Arabian Peninsula), the Cape Colony, South Africa, or Bombay. Here the slaves would be freed, and shelter and employment of some sort provided. These asylums became inadequate, however, since the source of the slave traffic was near Lake Nyasa, southwest of Dar es Salaam, in the interior of Africa (now Malawi). In 1866, the British established a Vice Admiralty court in Zanzibar to be closer to the source (figure 7.1).[3] Five years later, Sir Henry Bartle Frere, member of the India Council and former governor of Bombay, offered an alternate solution to the challenges of patrolling the Indian Ocean trade. He suggested a new treaty with the sultan of Zanzibar. In addition to targeting the slave market, the treaty would restrict the legal transport of slaves to routes via Dar es Salaam and Zanzibar, making Zanzibar's 350-mile coastline more manageable for the squadron to patrol.[4]

These improvements created a new problem, however. Without a colony in or near East Africa, where were the British to take Africans liberated at Zanzibar? The problem was not insignificant. Estimates presented to Parliament in 1871 showed that the navy caught fewer than 7 percent of the slaves trafficked illegally.[5] If the squadron became more effective, how would officials manage the thousands of additional Africans who would then be in their charge?[6] The Admiralty could still transport liberated Africans to Aden, the Cape, and Bombay. But officials considered all three places too inconvenient. Could the liberated

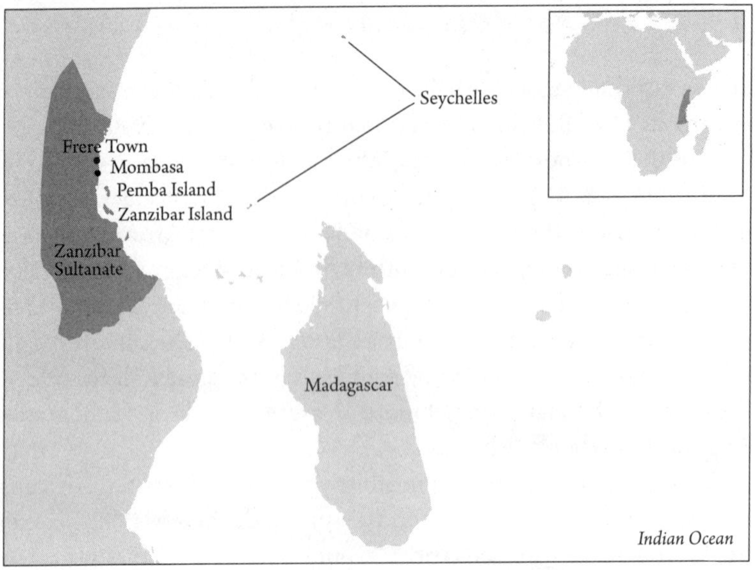

7.1 · Area in question as part of the fugitive slave circular debacle of 1875–1876. Credit: Mathieu Duvall, Imaging and Computing Center, Bates College, Lewiston, Maine.

Africans stay in Zanzibar, under the sultan's watch? Diplomats considered this in the early 1870s. But, cautious not to disturb the sultan's legal domestic slavery, officials did not stress this option in the 1860s.[7] Moreover, abolitionists feared that the freed slaves could easily be re-enslaved if left so close to the domestic slave market. Prior experience with liberated Africans would have indicated that this was a likely occurrence. In Cuba, where slavery had been legal, countless liberated Africans disappeared into the slave-based economy.

So where were the British to shelter liberated Africans? Missionaries had offered to shoulder the expense of asylum. The CMS, in particular, sought to extend its system of African asylums and industrial schools into the region. By the late 1860s, the CMS spoke enthusiastically about establishing villages in and around East Africa as they had in Sierra Leone in the 1810s–1840s. In anticipation of this work, they had even purchased land in the British Seychelles, just north of Madagascar, and eyed additional acquisitions on the mainland within the sultan's domain.[8]

The cost of ending the trade weighed heavily on those involved. Despite the CMS's offer to open new asylums, the government began to scrutinize its own financial commitments. In a confidential memorandum to Gladstone, the Treasury balked at the expense of renewed abolitionism in the East. The squadron's cruisers already cost £130,000 annually, the memorandum stressed, and the maintenance of liberated Africans £15,400.[9] The memorandum's author considered it inappropriate that such costs should fall to Britain alone. He asked whether "we [should] constitute ourselves alone the naval police of the world, or can we hope for effectual cooperation from other European powers, or from America? Experience has hitherto proved the contrary." "The consequence of any such attempt," he continued, "would probably be that we should have to bind ourselves to keep up large squadrons . . . and we should find ourselves encumbered with greater expense and greater responsibility than ever."[10]

Fiscal concern thus became subsumed into a larger debate over how Britain ought to wield its international clout in the region. The conservative memorandum writer shrank from using imperial power to police the slave trade, and the Treasury followed suit. Financial costs aside, the author argued that further treaty negotiations with the sultan threatened to result in a de facto expansion of empire. He asked with a note of bewilderment if "the Imperial Government [was] prepared to reduce their [the sultan's and Arab chiefs'] territories to the condition of the protected states of India, or to go even further, and absolutely annex them."[11] The implication was that they were not prepared to do so.

Not all officials were so opposed to this extension of a moral empire. Nor were they certain that abolitionism would result in the extension of formal empire that the memorandum writer feared.[12] Parliament examined the draft treaty and the role the British proposed to take in East Africa prior to Frere's departure. An 1871 House of Commons select committee enthusiastically supported the abolitionist endeavor and gave Frere carte blanche. The committee recommended that the British throw the full weight of "all legitimate means" available behind the abolition of the trade in the region.[13]

Gladstone's administration, however, took the Treasury's concerns to heart and restructured Britain's treaty commitments prior to Frere's departure. The administration took the unprecedented step of altering Britain's commitment to liberated Africans. The resulting 1873 treaty and Slave Trade Consolidation Act that codified the treaty reflected Treasury and diplomatic uneasiness with the costs of refuge. Rather than provide for liberated slaves on British soil, as had become standard practice since the 1824 Slave Trade Act, this act specified (Article III) that the "Sultan [not the British] engages to protect, to the utmost of his power, all liberated slaves, and to punish severely any attempt to molest them or reduce them again to slavery." This act did not mean that the British would abandon the project of protecting liberated Africans—not all slavers were captured in or near the sultan's territories. Nevertheless, the practice of leaving the ex-slaves' liberty to the sultan so as to spare the Treasury left liberated slaves vulnerable to abduction by domestic slavers.[14]

After the British created the court at Zanzibar in 1866, they faced two problems. On the one hand, they had to grapple with a several-fold increase in the number of slaves being rescued from the illegal slave trade if the naval squadron in the region proved to be as effective as officials anticipated. On the other hand, the increased British presence in the region threatened to destabilize legal domestic slavery. It became all too probable that legal slaves would flee en masse to a nearby naval squadron that was tasked with an expressly antislavery mission. In 1875, this nightmare scenario provoked action from the Admiralty, which had firsthand experience with the difficulties of providing for liberated Africans in the region. They knew they could not afford to provide asylum for a whole population of would-be refugees.

Although there was a great deal of official and metropolitan discussion about how to provide refuge for freed slaves, there was no public discussion of what to do about fugitive slaves in East Africa.[15] The nightmare situation the Admiralty anticipated in East Africa was most akin to cases in which legal slaves fled to British consular houses outside the British Empire. In these situations, as on board British men-of-war, British agents could not keep the foreigners in their care permanently. These islands of extraterritorial English jurisdiction had to take local custom into account. In practice, most of the fugitive slaves were returned to their masters. But if this was the unwritten protocol, why did the Admiralty feel the need to impose formal instructions on squadron officers off the East African coast?

In short, British officials on the ground feared that the popularity of liberating slaves—an act that promised much media attention at home, to say nothing of the prize associated with each capture—would impair sailors' judgment in the moment. A former British consular agent at Zanzibar, Henry Adrian Churchill, provided the case in point. In his testimony before the 1871 House select committee, Churchill told of a scene outside the window at his house in Zanzibar. A group of eager British sailors had pounced upon a supposed slave vessel. The slave dhow's captain carried papers indicating that these slaves were being legally transported. However, from Churchill's position on land, it looked unlikely that the British sailors would let the prize capture go so easily. Churchill intervened to defuse the tense situation. As one of the very few British operatives in the region, Churchill was certain that, had this incident not occurred right outside his window, the matter might have ended quite differently.[16]

Churchill's example pinpointed the difficulty in regulating the distinction between legal and illegal slavery, especially where eager British sailors disliked having to watch the legal slavery that surrounded them. Though this could have happened anywhere along the coast, Churchill's worry was local: that slaves working on the shoreline, particularly in the pearl fisheries, would take advantage of their proximity to British ships anchored in the sultan of Zanzibar's territorial waters. Working in the water, slave laborers might swim to British ships in great numbers if they knew—as increasingly they did—that British officials promised slaves their freedom.[17]

Should droves of *legal* domestic slaves seek asylum on British ships, it was not too difficult to imagine that chaos would ensue. The flight of legal slaves en masse would devastate the pearl fishery industry, enrage the sultan and his subjects, and inundate the British with more ex-slaves than it could handle.

It was in this context that the Admiralty issued the first circular on July 31, 1875. The exact origins of the circular, its author, and why it was issued when it was are unknown. Nonetheless, its sweeping terms offered what seemed to many to be an unaccountable check on when and where the British could provide refuge to fugitive slaves.

The first fugitive slave circular divided asylum into two categories: asylum in the territorial waters of foreign nations and asylum on the high seas. In territorial waters, naval officers were to return a slave to his or her master unless it could be proved that he or she had been enslaved contrary to existing treaties outlawing the slave trade. Only if a slave had been illegally traded would British officers be allowed to offer asylum. On the high seas, officers would have to take any fugitive on board and provide asylum if that slave was in imminent peril (e.g., risk of drowning). However, the instructions stipulated that the slave would need to be returned to the master if a request was made when the British vessel entered the territorial waters from which the slave had fled. There was only one caveat in these instructions. The circular specified that officers ought to "exercise their discretion [when returning slaves to their masters] in endeavoring, according to the circumstances of each case, to obtain an assurance that the slaves will not be treated with undue severity."[18] The circular gave no indication of how such an assurance could be enforced.

The Admiralty issued the July 31 circular when Parliament was out of session. No one in Britain took note until that fall, when someone at the Admiralty leaked the circular to the metropolitan press. The response was deafening.

By October 1875, the British press from London to the provinces responded vociferously. This reaction was somewhat at odds with metropolitan responses to refugees more generally. Sympathy for refugees was at an all-time low in the wake of the Paris Commune. Experts were then in the process of determining how to refine the terms of the 1870 Extradition Act to distinguish between deserving refugees and violent criminals—a distinction that seemed impossible to make. Eager for a clearer moral victory, the public embraced the issue of the fugitive slave circular, reviving traditional moral protest on behalf of slaves and foreign refugees at once. From the end of September 1875, abolitionists, local government councils, and private associations organized protest meetings on the refugee question on a scale not seen since the early 1860s.

Metropolitan Reaction: A Humanitarian Norm in the Balance

Most commentators agreed that the circular flouted Britain's humanitarian traditions and kowtowed to an institution against which she had long fought. The protests allowed the abolitionist public, which opposed the 1873 Slave Trade Act, the chance to focus their anger. It incited such a strong reaction because the public had long assumed that fugitive slaves were refugees. But while commentators were unanimously appalled at what seemed like undue deference to slave-holding powers, few agreed on the scope of Britain's international rights and obligations in the region. Could the British follow humanitarian imperatives wherever they led? In the winter of 1875–1876, the argument increasingly became a partisan one, with liberals taking the lead against the circular. By February 1876, the Tory government responded, beginning a systematic examination of the public's assumptions about the nature and scope of refuge.

Although the circular itself came as a surprise, news of it reached a metropolitan public that was ready to rally around the refugee slave's cause once more. Whereas few had openly supported the French Communards in their exile four years before, slaves were Britain's most celebrated refugees. More than continental refugees, fugitive slaves were liberal Britain's refugees, the nexus of equally long national traditions of abolitionism and asylum for persecuted foreigners. Prominent abolitionists had been harnessing public interest in liberated Africans for the last five years. The circular would give them—and the public at large—a focal point for outrage at the Treasury and consular retrenchment in the East.

British abolitionists had been skeptical about the strength of the government's commitment to ending slavery in the East. After the 1873 Slave Trade Consolidation Act ended the government's obligation to care for liberated Africans, Missionary groups—the CMS especially—continued to press for the expansion of African asylums in the Indian Ocean region and close to Zanzibar in particular. They condemned the government's retrenchment in no uncertain terms. But the CMS also looked ahead, working with Frere to solicit public funds for African asylums. By 1874, the CMS was in possession of land on the Seychelles and the promise of £1,000 from the Baroness Angelina Burdett Coutts for the establishment of an African asylum on the East African mainland.[19]

Until 1875, the scope of CMS public antislavery meetings had been limited; the British public had never been very concerned with the condition of liberated Africans. Tales of British captains in hot pursuit of illegal slavers were more dramatic and satisfying than the ongoing task of "civilizing" the liberated Africans in their care. Public outrage in the fall and winter of 1875–1876 became as widespread as it did because abolitionists focused their concern for liberated Africans in the East on the celebrated figure of the fugitive or refugee slave.

The circular became the talk of newspapers in London and in the provinces (figures 7.2 and 7.3). By January, prominent local organizations held meetings across Britain to discuss the circular and make their opinion heard. As with refugee meetings in the past, the proceedings of each were reprinted in the local and national press. Thus, the London *Times* printed fifty-four articles about the circular between January and February 1876. In January alone, the *Times* reported on seventeen separate meetings in town halls and other public venues across the country.[20]

The outcry was a testament to the power of the refugee question in moral politics. This was not new. In this particular crisis, however, three points came to the fore. First, the British assumed that slaves were just as entitled as political offenders to be included in the refugee category. Second, the British had the sovereign right to provide

7.2 · "Flag of Freedom," *Punch, or the London Charivari* 69 (October 2, 1875): 131.
Credit: Courtesy of the Bowdoin College Library, Brunswick, Maine.

refuge on British soil anywhere in the world. Third, this right, associated with British soil, extended to British ships. As English soil, British ships maintained the same right to provide asylum as mainland England. If these three assumptions were correct, then the circular was not only unjust, it compromised Britain's interests as a sovereign nation.

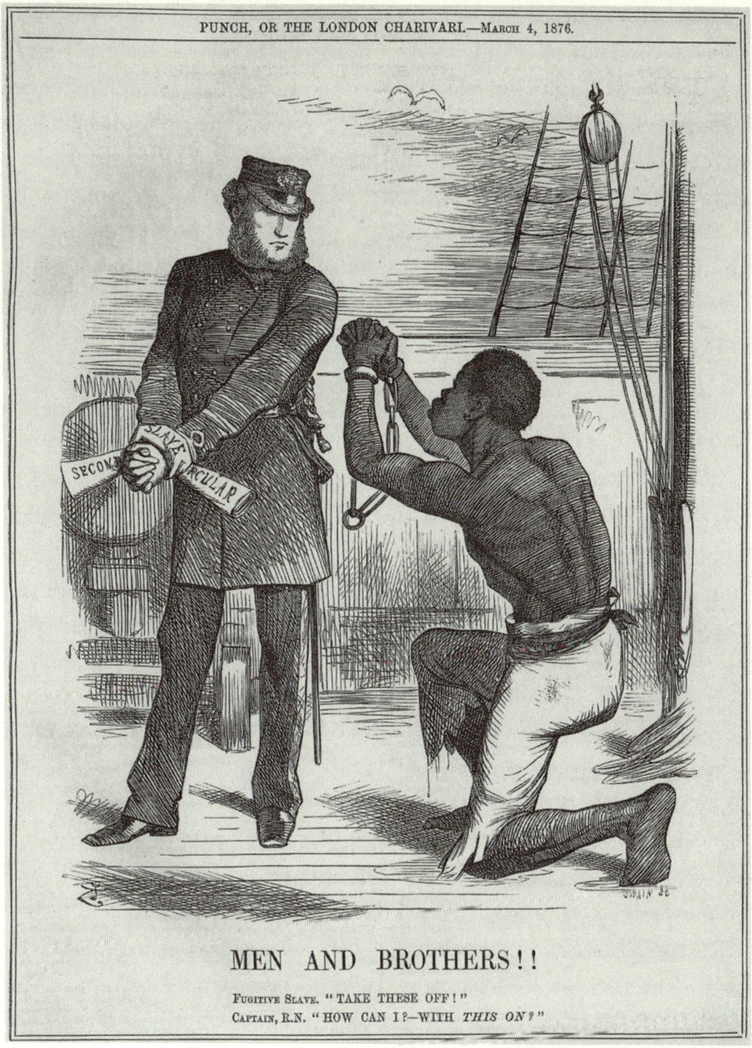

7.3 · "Men and Brothers," *Punch, or the London Charivari* 70 (March 4, 1876): 79. Credit: Courtesy of the Bowdoin College Library, Brunswick, Maine.

It was this last point about sovereign rights that united the public against the July circular. Legal scholars and politicians, Tory and Liberal alike, condemned the Admiralty's instruction that slaves rescued on the high seas would have to be returned to their masters when the ship returned to that foreign port. The command, legal scholars argued, violated recognized international law. The public tried out a variety of analogies and characterizations of the Admiralty's circular.

Notables denounced it as either an intentional slight to British and international law or as "slipshod nonsense," "a crime and a great blunder." Radical Joseph Cowen's *Newcastle Chronicle* proclaimed that even "Jefferson Davis himself did not dare to dispute the right of the bondman to liberty, if once fairly under the British flag." The Admiralty's dictate, the *Chronicle* continued, was like a Russian *Ukase*, not worthy of the country whose courts had, since the days of Somersett, upheld the rights of the slave to liberty.[21] This "obscure" document might have simply warned officers not to encourage slaves to run to British ships, MP Sir Henry James suggested in the *Times*. James argued that the circular instead appeared to surrender the recognized sovereignty of British soil itself, to say nothing of compromising Lord Mansfield's 1772 ruling that forbade slavery on English ground.[22]

Antislavery tradition aside, the legal community was amazed at this disregard for British law on board men-of-war. A Cambridge legal scholar, styling himself "Historicus," believed the circular was more than an unfortunate "blunder." He found that the Admiralty pitted itself against international law. National vessels were "domestic soil" on which the laws of England applied. This was fact, he claimed, on the high seas and in territorial waters.[23] "You may shut the door of your own house against a man," Historicus explained, "or turn him out if he comes in without your leave." "But," he continued "if you admit him you cannot while he is there deal with him contrary to [English] law." Slavery was not recognized in the laws of England. So an officer on a British vessel could not lawfully return a foreign slave to his or her master.

Historicus was correct that English laws presided over her vessels on the high seas. Legal theorists on international and maritime matters agreed that no one state could claim jurisdiction on the high seas. A ship on the high seas fell under the jurisdiction of the laws of the nation whose flag the ship flew.[24] Tories, then in power, tried to downplay Historicus's argument and the widespread outrage against the circular's interpretation of rights on the high seas. They tended to view the circular as simply a "mistake," a muddling of international law that anyone could have made.[25]

In the face of forceful objections and a weak defense, Disraeli's administration suspended the circular in early November. In December, the administration withdrew it and formally issued a second. Unlike the "hastily" constructed first circular, the December circular granted that a British man-of-war was—in point of international law—English soil, even in foreign waters. The major achievement of the second circular was thus that it recognized that a slave who gained asylum on board a British ship on the high seas was free. While the slave could not remain on the vessel permanently, he or she could only be removed from its shelter in territorial waters if the receiving nation guaranteed the ex-slave's liberty. However, the circular did not support the same procedure if the slave reached the ship in foreign territorial waters. Here, local custom trumped British jurisdiction. The circular proclaimed in a didactic tone that "you are bound by the comity of nations . . . not to allow [the ship] to become a shelter for those who would be chargeable with a violation of the law of the place." Fugitive slaves could only be taken on board if their lives were in danger, and then only until the imminent danger had passed.

The new circular appeased Conservatives who had been concerned with British sovereignty on the high seas. The return of slaves to their masters in territorial waters seemed less offensive. Proponents liked the respect the new circular displayed for the "comity of nations," the technical term in international legal theory for the recognition of local custom. Emissaries of foreign governments (ships and ambassadors alike) had generally been accorded immunity from local jurisdiction. But this practice was not without reciprocal expectations, as Swiss jurist Emerich de Vattel argued in the mid-eighteenth century. The emissary, he explained, "needs to conform to the customs and laws of the country in all his external actions, so far as they are unconnected with the object of his mission and character."[26] It was time, proponents of the second circular argued, that naval officers had instructions to ensure that they acted accordingly.

A firestorm ensued. Public meetings, begun that fall, took place with greater regularity. At each, notables lambasted the administration's support for the second circular, declaring the instructions nothing less than a reversal of British moral norms and a disgrace to her international power. Opponents underscored that the officials missed the basic fact that slaves were the same as political refugees and Britain could never do too much for either.

At a large February 14 meeting at Exeter Hall (London), covered by newspapers across the country, Liberal MP Henry Fawcett summarized the matter succinctly. He demanded rhetorically: "Where was the man who in the face of his countrymen would declare that England had done too much in giving freedom to slaves—that we had gone too far in offering an asylum to political refugees?" Fawcett echoed what had become, by February 1876, the dominant Liberal position with regards to "countries with local laws so opposed to our institutions." He claimed that the British could not simply defer to the comity of nations, since "we cannot give them any recognition [that] constitute [*sic*] exceptions which we should leave to the experience and judgment of individual commanders."[27] Lawyer Arthur Cohen

seconded Fawcett's avowal that the refugee slave and the political refugee were part of one category when he outlined the same position in greater detail a few weeks later:

> It is important to remember that there is a class of persons who stand in exactly the same position as fugitive slaves—namely, political refugees. They, too, have violated the laws of their own country but they have done nothing which our law recognizes as criminal; and if our officers were instructed to treat fugitive slaves in the same manner as political refugees, no principle of international law would be violated while England would support the sacred principle of human freedom in the manner in which the country is resolved it shall be upheld.[28]

Criticisms took on a sharply partisan cast that winter at a key moment in Disraeli and Gladstone's contest for control of the government. In this vein, one letter to the *Newcastle Chronicle*'s editor denounced the Tories' false antislavery sentiment, citing their defense of Jamaica's Governor General Eyre ten years prior.[29] For another writer, this was the very "nature of Toryism to favour privileges and to oppose freedom." Whereas the circular had been a "cabinet issue," it had become for the Tory government a point of principle and they had "decided to stand or fall by it."[30]

Liberals carried the public sentiment of outdoor meetings to Parliament. Their intent was to demonstrate the force of popular opinion against the administration's attempt to draw "a direct difference between the treatment of fugitive slaves and political refugees," as one MP called it.[31] MP Evelyn Ashley declared that "all that was wanted was that slaves should be treated on just the same footing as political refugees . . . and he, for one, should rejoice that it was a Conservative majority in this House" that would prove the matter beyond party squabbles, and safe-guard "our consistency and reputation as an anti-slavery Power."[32]

Tories insisted that public outrage against the circular was blindly sentimental, just as public support for the dangerous continental communists had been four years before. But Conservatives keenly pointed out that the problem was larger than party politics. When the Liberal opposition decried the Tory's pro-slavery circular, Disraeli's government unearthed Gladstone's embarrassingly similar instructions from 1871. Tory C. E. Cawley found comparable instructions from Liberals dating to the 1860s.[33]

For the public at large, the finer points of legal and political argument meant little. A man described as a "working man" identified the issue clearly at the February 15 Exeter Hall meeting. As the *Liverpool Mercury* reported, the man said

> he knew nothing of international law, but if it supported slavery the sooner it was "knocked on the head" the better. What this remark lacks in polish is amply compensated for in force. . . . Slave-holding states, who cannot understand the extreme sensitiveness of Englishmen on this subject, may perhaps feel surprised that we should speak so lightly of the obligations which rest upon our ships whilst in their ports. But they may be sure that, whatever the risk and whatever the cost, the people of this country will insist that the deck of a British ship shall never be made into debatable ground when the question of slavery is involved.[34]

As far as the public was concerned, to accept the circular would be more of a reversal of antislavery precedent than the British could bear.

Therein lay the difficulty. As the editors of the Society of Friends' journal wrote, "We suspect it will be found extremely difficult to reduce to writing any directions that shall at once do justice to the anti-slavery feeling of the British nation, and be also just to those countries in which slavery exists."[35] At an impasse, Disraeli turned to a royal commission—modern politicians' classic expedient when confronted with a political conundrum too difficult to solve.

The Royal Commission: An Inquiry into a Right of Asylum

On February 14, 1876, Disraeli appointed a royal commission to examine if the British were contravening international law or custom by providing refuge in territorial waters. As with the inquiry into extradition laws, the point was to determine if asylum was always possible. In extradition law, any limit placed on asylum was a matter of bilateral agreement at most. Here, by contrast, the unsavory task was to determine whether the British could ever intercede in the international realm on behalf of these particular foreigners.

One *Punch* cartoonist lampooned Disraeli's motivation in appointing the commission. The cartoonist explained that Disraeli's decision was an "extinguisher trick" and depicted Disraeli whisking a ball labeled "the Second Fugitive Slave Circular" under a hat labeled "Royal Commission" (figure 7.4).[36] The assumption was that, by handing the decision to a commission, he would receive a response in keeping with cautious diplomatic concerns. If this were the case, Disraeli

7.4 · "The Extinguisher Trick," *Punch, or the London Charivari* 70 (February 19, 1876): 59. Credit: Courtesy of the Bowdoin College Library, Brunswick, Maine.

sorely miscalculated how best to achieve his desired result. The eleven appointed commissioners were eminent jurists and international theorists, all well established in their careers on the bench, as theorists, or as colonial administrators.[37] They were not uniformly proponents of international legal systems, however. Nor were they uniformly pro- or anti-imperialist, and so had different positions on the exercise of British global power. They ended up issuing three contradictory opinions on the extent to which the British could and ought to intervene in foreign affairs in order to provide refuge. Commissioners attempted to minimize the differences between their varied opinions. H. C. Rothery claimed that these differences were simply theoretical. Yet, these "merely" theoretical differences highlighted opposing views of global affairs and the role that each commissioner hoped to see Britain establish as an international model. Opinions on this score ranged from the moralist-cum-imperialist to the realpolitik model of the more conservative diplomat.

The commission's primary task was to determine whether or not the British could—or should—accept refugees on board her ships in foreign territorial waters. More than a question of international law and courtesy, the commission was a referendum on the scope of the refugee category. The commissioners were evaluating the metropolitan assumption that all foreign slaves could be refugees, as well as a deeper claim: whether political refugees were, in point of law, entitled to British asylum either.

The task entailed more than an examination of legal precedent; it demanded a thorough investigation of the circumstances in the Indian Ocean region, particularly around Zanzibar. The commissioners did not limit themselves to the study of the reception of refugees. They heard testimony on the living conditions of liberated slaves in East Africa and in British-run refuges and pulled relevant Colonial Office and Admiralty files relating to liberated Africans in Sierra Leone between the 1820s and 1840s.

The commissioners began with a survey of domestic, international, and foreign protocols regarding the reception of fugitive slaves. Nowhere among the treaties outlawing the slave trade could they find rules pertaining to the reception of fugitive (as opposed to illegally trafficked) slaves. Their survey of foreign protocols uncovered a range of responses to fugitive slaves. The United States, Germany, and Italy would not surrender a slave who sought asylum on board a national vessel. Portugal and the Netherlands would. Russia and France reserved discretionary power to the officers in cases of distress, though Russia generally prohibited strangers from coming on board in the first place.[38] On this spectrum, British officers, like all but the Portuguese and Dutch, had been given discretionary power.

The absence of a single protocol for asylum in territorial waters made the decision before the commission a profound one. The commissioners' response would set precedent for how Britain would act as a global power, either following the suggestions of international legal theory or pursuing her own course.

This was not an easy decision to make, especially since politicians and legal scholars were divided on the utility and desirability of international law from the start. International law was an inherently amorphous concept, since there was no international tribunal to enforce it. Rather than a legal code, international law derived from the sometimes religious, sometimes secular "natural law" theory. In practice, states abided by its norms according to an accumulation of common practice, any breach of the "law" being subject only to the opprobrium of other states. The British had been central in driving international standardization through individual treaties. Nonetheless, British theorists and diplomats remained hesitant to bind the Empire to international convention even as it became the subject of scholarly investigation and theorization.[39]

Broadly speaking, the commission divided into two camps: those who believed that discretionary power ought to remain with British officials and those who opted for imposing limits in the interest of preserving a comity between nations. What is surprising about this division is how unpredictably the differences were aligned. Political affiliation was not a reliable indicator of opinion; James Fitzjames Stephen—whose empiricism defied political categorization—ultimately sided with the Conservative Lord Chief Justice Cockburn.[40] Nor was association with the Admiralty a reliable indicator of opinion, since Phillimore and Rothery, both with legal experience working for the Admiralty, took opposing views.

Commissioners who took the first tack held that because a British ship was English soil its officers had no need to adhere to local law. Maintaining courteous relations with host countries was admittedly desirable, but the British ought to be at the vanguard of international morality, not complying with a law as distasteful as slavery.

Sir George Campbell held the most radical views on this score, echoing Liberal arguments against the circular. Campbell believed that Britain was morally obligated to side with the slave, not the master or the slave state. Since no international law or treaty required the contrary, Campbell hoped to see Britain "advance with the times" alongside "all the most civilized and powerful nations." He held that the "time has come when this country may fairly say, 'we will under no circumstances aid in the enforcement of slavery,—we will have nothing to do with this nefarious and accursed thing.' " Campbell argued that he would go so far as to "prohibit" officers from surrendering slaves who had received asylum.[41]

Phillimore, Bernard, and Maine echoed Campbell's claim that it was high time that international law unequivocally denounce slavery. In their statement for the commission, they argued that international law "is not stationary" and "admits of progressive improvement" that "varies with the progress of opinion and the growth of usage."[42]

Whereas international law was flexible and capable of progress, British law was unambiguous. Phillimore, Bernard, and Maine argued that British officers could not legally return a slave to his or her master once that slave had been admitted to British refuge because English law did not recognize slavery. In this, fugitive slaves were exactly like political refugees. In both cases, the foreigners in question had violated only local laws. Her Majesty's government would be remiss in instructing its officers to uphold these laws where English law reigned.[43]

Archibald, Thesiger, Holland, Stephen, Rothery, and Cockburn did not agree that Britain could, in good faith, keep fugitive slaves on board British ships in territorial waters. In their statements, this group—the majority of the commissioners—sought to correct the legal assumptions made by their peers and by the public at large. Members of this group agreed that fugitive slaves were not necessarily the same as political refugees. Moreover, even when slaves could be considered refugees, this group argued that such categorization did not necessarily allow the British to provide asylum. The British could not ignore local customs in the territorial waters of foreign states; respect for local laws compelled the return of slaves and of political refugees in some, if not all, instances.

Contrary to public opinion, Cockburn and Stephen argued that the British could not help fugitive slaves as they helped political refugees because doing so would help slaves evade local justice. Unlike the political refugee, who fled the suspension of justice, the fugitive slave's flight was a "breach of the local law committed by the slave in withdrawing himself from the possession of his master, in derogation of the rights which the law gives to the latter."[44] Cockburn extended the analogy between the slave and the fugitive criminal. Whereas a British officer could protect a refugee, Cockburn was not "prepared to assent" to actions by which "within the waters of a foreign state, the law of that state shall be powerless to arrest the criminal and bring him to justice."[45]

In his statement, Stephen was more understanding of how outrageous it would sound to a British audience. But he was no less exacting. Though slavery might be abhorrent, he was not ready to allow the British to ignore the local rights of the slave master. He cited the expense the British had undertaken to compensate slave owners in the 1830s as proof that there was precedent even in antislavery British law for slavery as a legitimate property right.[46] If Britain did not return the slave, Stephen continued, the action would be an act not of a neutral or allied power but of an imperial power. It would be akin to an act of war.

From this point, Cockburn's and Stephen's statements diverged based on the degree to which each felt the comity of nations to be absolute. Stephen avoided claiming that asylum should never be allowed. While he hoped the British would not so disrespect their hosts in territorial waters, he allowed for an imposition of British norms. However, he insisted, "If it is done it should be done openly and avowedly as an act of power, as an invasion on moral grounds of the sovereignty of independent nations."[47] In this, Stephen might have more readily agreed with Phillimore et al. However, as a commissioner with the task of determining the legality of refuge for fugitive slaves, he did "not see how it [could] be justified as an exercise of a legal or quasi-legal right."[48]

By contrast, Cockburn was more absolute. He called extraterritoriality—the notion that British ships were English territory in foreign waters—a "fanciful appellation."[49] For Cockburn, this had grave implications for fugitive slaves and for political refugees. He argued that there was actually no basis in international law for asylum for either group. The revolutions in the nineteenth century had made asylum on board British vessels seem to be a standard practice. But it was only the frequency of such extraordinary circumstances that made the practice appear routine.[50] Consequently, the British could talk of no legal right to provide asylum in the territorial waters of a foreign state.

The final report of the commissioners was a strange combination of these divergent opinions. Campbell's populist outlook was excluded, and Campbell refused to sign the joint report. The ten others recommended that ship captains retain the right to vet would-be refugees, as

Maine et al. had hoped. However, the report was not a simple victory for open refuge. The tone of the Conservative commissioners permeated the report, making it a strange mixture of arguments that left the decisions to individual officers yet missed no opportunity to check officers' enthusiasm for exercising this right.

The final report dwelled on the character of Eastern slavery. The commissioners did so in order to paint a picture that contradicted metropolitan belief in the utter obnoxiousness of slavery and the universal appropriateness of flight from bondage. The commissioners reaffirmed Britain's commitment to end slavery eventually. But they emphasized the difference between Arab slavery and the more oppressive system of bondage in the Americas. There, perhaps flight was justified. In the Indian Ocean region, by contrast, slavery was relatively benign. Slaves thus had little need to flee in the first place.[51] The British would only make a decent situation worse by interference, according to what commissioners had heard. Any rumor that the British "navy would liberate all fugitive slaves" would "irritate the Arabian masters, and induce them to regard their domestic slaves with suspicion and distrust, and possibly to treat them with severity."[52]

Nonetheless, there needed to be criteria by which individual officers judged whether or not a slave deserved to be considered a refugee and provided with asylum. Two recommendations stood out. First, commissioners held that the officer should keep the slave on board only if, in doing so, he was protecting the slave from something other than slavery itself (e.g., cruel treatment). Only in this situation did the commissioners liken the slave to a persecuted refugee, who fled the hot-blooded vengeance of his master, just as the refugee fled the mob. The second criterion was particularly vague. Commissioners asked that the officers consider what was best for the slave when weighing whether or not to provide asylum.[53]

These criteria challenged dearly held public assumptions about runaway slaves. Previously, the fugitive who could tell an effective tale of persecution had met the first barrier to becoming a refugee. It could no longer be assumed—as the public had long done—that a slave had such a tale of persecution to tell simply by virtue of being a slave. Furthermore, concern that refuge might not be better for the slave/would-be refugee was a major break in the refugee narrative that called into question the practical possibility of creating a viable, liberal asylum. If refuge was not viable, ought it to be continued? For the first time, the royal commission weighed this alternative seriously.

In Search of the Way Forward: Refugee Relief in a "New World"

The metropolitan public assumed that freedom was self-evidently more humane than slavery. Was this true? For the fugitive slave commissioners, inclusion in the refugee category depended on whether or not a slave would actually find a "better" life in British refuge than he or she had at home. Could the British adequately care for an untold number of ex-slaves when resources—diplomatic and financial—were so scarce?

The commissioners (Campbell excepted) were not certain. Their doubt rested on concern over the scale of the endeavor, a point that had caused anxiety since at least 1871. Whereas that anxiety had initially been about financial resources, the commission turned the Treasury's point into a broader one about the socioeconomic viability of African asylums. The asylums, commissioners worried, already struggled to produce ideal hard-working, liberal subjects. There had been previous discontent with the "progress" of liberated Africans in West Africa. But the commissioners offered the first systematic study of whether the poor quality of refuge was itself a reason to refuse asylum in the first place. How could relief workers possibly manage when the number of ex-slaves in need of resettlement skyrocketed?

In their quest to systematize asylum policy, the commissioners examined the past and future viability of British refuge. There was a liberal humanitarian element in this line of inquiry, a real concern that the life that the liberated and fugitive slaves were promised in British asylum was little better than slavery by another name. At a time when metropolitan philanthropists had begun to decry coolie labor across the Empire, the commissioners wondered whether the forced indenture of freed slaves in these asylums was really an improvement for ex-slaves.[54] There was a darker side to the commissioners' concerns as well. For the first time, the character of the would-be refugee—long assumed to have been heroic and independent minded—was called into question. This was the first real appearance of racist claims in the debate over the "refugee question": the commission discarded the image of the refugee whose valor was previously emblematic of liberal ideology in favor of a view of liberated Africans as chronically in need of supervision in order to become "civilized subjects."

Thus far, the project seemed to be failing. The evidence before the commission emphasized the miserable conditions in which the British had long maintained their liberated African charges. For instance, the neglect of the liberated Africans in Aden was well known, as the Reverend Edward Steere told the Anglican Church Congress in 1871. Only half survived their first year there. Those who did survive were kept in prison until some employer at Bombay took "them off its hands as apprentices." Whereas the government pays "£5 a-head to the sailors for every slave taken out of a slave dhow," Steere lamented, "when he is landed, the English government grudges to spend five-pence for his welfare."[55]

The initial settlements on the Seychelles in the late 1860s did not seem to fare much better. By most reports, conditions on the Seychelles had improved under CMS supervision after 1871. Nonetheless, the general picture before the commission was one in which liberated slaves fell "into the hands of French Creoles," in whose employ they fared worse than they had in slavery, according to Captain Sullivan.[56] Bartle Frere agreed, stating that "they come into a system of compulsory labour, and there is very little power of looking after them" despite the best intentions of the missionaries. Worse was what happened to young women; Frere insisted that "unless some pains are taken with them they are very apt to go wrong."[57]

Officials and missionaries reported that bringing liberated Africans to the Seychelles was tantamount to forcing them into exile. Frere testified that there were "very proper ordinances on the subject of their treatment, and there is a good climate" northeast of Madagascar. Nevertheless, "it is far from their own homes; they look upon it as great banishment."[58] Captain Sullivan further emphasized how much "worse off" the slaves were when "taken and liberated and sent to the Seychelles."[59]

Though disposed to question the "success" of the civilizing endeavor to date, commissioners had to consider how to continue colonial asylums for liberated Africans. After all, they recommended that officers maintain the right to admit refugee slaves who would then need resettlement. Furthermore, despite the dismal reality of refuge, slaves might be so tempted by the prospect of liberation that they would continue to seek asylum despite its harrowing reality. Officials and missionaries recognized that they would have to provide constant supervision for their charges, a cost that the government and missionaries would have to shoulder as they did in Sierra Leone.[60] Commissioners thus noted that "in all these cases it would appear that some plan of compulsory labour for a limited period, at regulated wages, is the only mode of providing for the liberated slaves."[61] They made this pronouncement begrudgingly, knowing how difficult it would be to enforce this "free" labor and how the liberated African's "condition must in great measure depend on the character of the master to whom he has been temporarily assigned."[62]

The character of the ex-slave mattered equally, and it was with this in mind that commissioners recommended that naval officers study each slave whom they considered admitting on board. Through interpreters, the officers should explain to the would-be refugee slaves that, "although released from slavery, they cannot live in idleness."[63] Commissioners assumed that only slaves who had been truly poorly treated by their masters would flee from their homes. The interpreter, it was thought, would easily detect well-treated slaves who were of dubious character and intended to evade work altogether.

If refuge was simply a second exile in which the inhabitants struggled to become liberal subjects, could the British in good conscience continue this practice? Arab domestic slavery might be more benign than British refuge. Those who testified at the hearings agreed that if the British were to continue to provide refuge to fugitives, further territorial acquisition on the mainland, closer to the Africans' home, would be necessary. Loath to recommend imperial oversight in the region, which risked great animosity from the Arab elite, commissioners gathered information about how the British could provide a better quality of life for foreign slaves not by allowing them to cross international borders but by collaborating with the sultan to secure relief for them under his jurisdiction. Obtaining the sultan's protection of these individuals was in keeping with diplomatic caution and portended shifts in the relief of persecuted foreigners that characterized humanitarian aid well into the twentieth century.

Yet, it was far from clear to commissioners what precisely was entailed in this alliance. Officials' opinions differed on this score, ranging from encouraging legal abolition as the British did in India to expanding private British refuges within the sultan's domains.

Frere wished he could convince the sultan to set aside territory for a local depot where liberated slaves, as well as fugitives, could live freely. In a document appended to the commission's report, Frere outlined a course by which the British could encourage the sultan to declare "Mombaza to be free soil." As the British had done in India, the sultan would warn his courts throughout his territory "not [to] exercise their authority to support slavery" but "simply [to] ignore it." The result, Frere claimed, would be only to separate slaves from cruel masters, without upsetting much of the status quo.[64] Frere assumed that most slaves would not flee, but those who did would have been treated exceptionally poorly and hence would be entitled to refuge. The escaped slaves would become internal refugees, never leaving the sultan's soil and, therefore, not depriving him of his population.

Putting this into effect would require diplomatic leverage, however, and was not likely to gain the sultan's favor, let alone that of local slave masters. It had been difficult enough to secure the new slave trade treaty several years earlier. Instead, refuge within the sultan's purview could mean one of two other plans.

The commission emphasized the possibility of Arab employers taking charge of the fugitive and liberated slaves. Rather than transporting them to British soil, ex-slaves could be set to work on the sultan's plantation, for example. Frere explained that the sultan was already employing liberated Africans as wage laborers and could take more.[65] Diplomatically, this solution seemed congenial to the sultan's immediate economic interests. The commissioners had heard evidence suggesting that there was a need for labor of this sort within the sultan's territory and that the liberated Africans already working there were indeed paid for their labor.[66]

The other possibility was to promote new philanthropic asylums on the sultan's land. Such projects were already underway. Although most liberated Africans were forwarded to the Seychelles by the mid-1870s, the CMS also owned a piece of land just inland from Mombasa on the coast, north of Zanzibar. Frere Town, as it was called, had been established in 1874. The crucial difference for British officials and CMS missionaries was that Frere Town was on the African mainland and it was not a British dependency but a privately owned property under Islamic law and the sultan's watch.

There was a thin line, however, between private British asylums in the sultan's domains and the extension of British imperial authority. When the 1871 select committee asked Frere how the sultan could guarantee the freedom of ex-slaves, Frere explained that it would be by the sultan's power. But was the sultan's power sufficient given the number of routine northern Arab slave raids into his territories? To this, Frere admitted that ultimately "British power" would help to bolster him and protect the refuges.

Proponents of expansion lambasted the half-hearted protection that these schemes would provide. CMS secretary Edward Hutchinson feared that it would be a mistake to support "a *quasi* free settlement under the Sultan's flag and rule, instead of a real one in British territory for the reception of the free slaves." His arguments revealed how little the public knew about British involvement in East

Africa. Hutchinson likened the options as a choice between creating a Liberia or a Sierra Leone as America and Britain had done in West Africa decades earlier. Willfully blind to the difficulties liberated Africans had experienced in Sierra Leone, Hutchinson explained that "the colony of Liberia has lately been passing through scenes of anarchy and confusion for want of good government, contrasted with which the peace and prosperity of Sierra Leone stand out as a testimony to the wisdom and forethought of its protectors."[67]

In policy terms, commissioners' evaluation of asylum conditions amounted to a test of the much-despised 1873 slave trade treaty that had eliminated Britain's legal obligation to care for liberated Africans. Commissioners kept returning to basic skepticism that large-scale refuge was viable for the immediate need of so many would-be refugees. Despite their stern warnings, commissioners were divided on the implications of their investigation for the future of British involvement with fugitive slaves, whether or not they were to be refugees under direct British rule. Ultimately, commissioners did not subscribe to a single type of trusteeship, either direct British rule or Arab oversight, for fugitive and liberated slaves. Still, through its deliberation on fugitive slaves and Eastern slavery more broadly, the commission exposed the range of moral and practical challenges inherent in expanding refuge for humanity's sake.

The Fugitive Slave Question in the History of Imperial Refuge

The commission published its final report in June 1876, and the government sanctioned the third fugitive slave circular in August of that year. This final circular mirrored the commissioners' indecision. Its tone conveyed doubt as to whether officers should provide asylum at all. In the end, it tried to strike a balance between respecting local laws and relying on a British naval commander's judgment. It held that "it is not intended, nor is it possible, to lay down any precise or general rule as to the cases in which you ought to receive a fugitive slave on board your ship." Nonetheless, the instructions continued, "you are as to this to be guided by considerations of humanity . . . whether your ship is on the high seas or within the territorial waters . . . but in the latter case you ought, at the same time, to avoid conduct which may appear to be in breach of international comity and good faith."[68]

Officials thus attempted to encode their reluctance to refuge in policy. From a modern perspective, it seems ironic that opponents of open refuge looked to law as a means of narrowing Britain's humanitarian commitments, given law's present-day role in safeguarding human rights. Yet, as in the case of the "political offender" in extradition law, the strictures of a broad moral norm made it difficult to find a legal mechanism capable of identifying legitimate refugees among asylum seekers. Neither the commission nor the third circular solved the problem at hand.

Nonetheless, the crisis of 1875–1876 allowed for a focused study of concerns entailed in the provision of refuge both to fugitive slaves and Africans liberated from the slave trade.

These concerns became more pronounced when the IBECA gave Britain a stronger foothold in the region. The rapid increase in the number of fugitives in British refuges, Frere Town especially, nearly provoked armed conflict between refugees and the local population. By the later 1880s, IBECA director George Mackenzie had to defuse the situation by securing the official manumission of the fugitives in CMS refuge. With "no personal investment" in the endeavor, however, Mackenzie forced the CMS to end its intake of fugitive slaves.[69]

From time to time, the metropolitan press covered the triumphant escape of a fugitive slave to British soil in East Africa. More generally, however, the public forgot about the fugitive slave circulars and the distinct problem of the refugee slave. The Admiralty issued its third circular without much public reaction or commentary from the metropolitan press. There had been some interest in the commission's final report, but no public demonstrations as had taken place at town hall meetings the previous winter. Perhaps commissioners had succeeded in communicating the difficulties inherent in a policy of open asylum. More likely, the Bulgarian atrocities—the massacre of Bulgarian Christians in the Ottoman Empire—deflected attention from the circular at an opportune moment. News of these atrocities reached the metropolitan public within weeks of the commission's report and the final circular. If there was doubt that slavery was tantamount to persecution, there was no doubt in the public mind that the massacre of Christian minorities was persecution. Bulgaria offered a more satisfying outlet for interventionism, one on which Gladstone capitalized in the months that followed.[70]

The fugitive slave question never regained the metropolitan attention that it commanded in 1875–1876. Nonetheless, the same concern for scarce resources caused a much wider retrenchment of relief efforts on behalf of refugees in the decades to come. The Empire no longer had the capacity to assist in the migration of whole populations of persecuted foreigners. The contest over resources changed the refugee narrative itself. The narrative of valor and liberal individualism clashed with the reality of ex-slaves' continued economic dependency in the Indian Ocean region. The narrative changed irrevocably as the British grappled with how to provide for those with claims on their hospitality. The national and imperial provision of refuge would narrow considerably. In the wake of Eastern European pogroms of the 1880s–1900s, even activists were forced to limit the number of people to whom the category could apply.

EIGHT

Hardening the Humanitarian Heart

By 1893, Parliament and public commentators were hotly debating whether Britain would have to restrict immigration. The nation's famous open-border policy had been a hallmark of liberalism in the nineteenth century. Increasingly, however, the island seemed incapable of absorbing the number of impoverished Eastern European Jews entering the country. Anti-alien ideologues deplored the conditions which this unrestricted immigration foisted on the local population. Conservative commentators and trade unionists alike complained that Jewish competition, particularly in London's East End, undercut wages and degraded housing conditions. Governmental inquiries found that the actual scale of immigration was "infinitesimal" compared with the population as a whole.[1] Nevertheless, as arch-Conservative MP James Lowther informed Parliament that year, public opinion was already exercised in the matter.[2] By 1893, living conditions in the East End had been part of a twenty-year-long debate about housing prices, urban squalor, and moral reform. In the midst of worker strikes and a growing trade union movement, the immigration debate became a proxy for deeply felt anxieties about the state of the Victorian economy.[3] Whereas the politics of class divided Britons from one another, anti-alien sentiment, later accompanied by the jingoistic fervor of the Second Anglo-Boer War, seemed to unite them.

Parliament's response to this outpouring of xenophobia ran into a thorny distinction. Among the immigrants whose entry Parliament planned to restrict were refugees whom the British were morally bound to protect. Even the most adamant proponents of restriction never denied that refugees ought to be permitted asylum. But how were authorities to know who was who? Liberal A. J. Mundella, president of the Board of Trade and the son of Italian refugees, pointed out the contradiction in restrictionist arguments:

> [Keir Hardie] was very strong for some measure; but when the question was put to him, would he prevent political refugees from coming into the country? he said, "Certainly not"—or persons who left their country because of religious persecution? and again the hon. Gentleman replied, "Certainly not." If these are excluded, what is there left to be dealt with?[4]

Scholars of immigration to Britain interpret this late nineteenth-century moment as the first awakening of British interest in foreigners. They argue that the influx of Eastern European Jews and the attendant rise of anti-Semitism brought the issue of border policies to the fore for the first time. In painting this portrait of British xenophobia, they tend to collapse refugees and immigrants into a single category. Even if they recognize refugees as a distinct category, they dismiss the distinction as meaningless at this historical moment. The distinction was indeed under attack. Nevertheless, the 1905 Aliens Act—the culmination of more than twenty years of debate over whether to restrict immigration—was not a sudden departure in British political culture but reflected a deep national commitment to maintaining a distinction between persecuted foreigners and run-of-the-mill migrants.[5]

This chapter examines responses to the situation of Eastern European Jews in the context of more than a century of refugee relief. The aliens debates of the 1890s and early 1900s took the shape they did precisely because philanthropists and officials had to grapple with the fact that old models for long-term refugee relief were proving more difficult to carry out. Previously, popular xenophobia had been held at bay by the practice of sending refugees abroad. The possibilities for refuge overseas seemed to diminish after 1880, however. This meant that, for the first time, there were fewer safety valves for the social tensions provoked by this small but highly visible and concentrated group. The prospect of receiving an untold number of Eastern European Jews, made all the poorer in their flight, forced the British to reckon with the scope of what had become a broad normative injunction to protect refugees. The situation exposed both the power of normative claims on behalf of the persecuted as well as the material foundations that had made those claims possible for much of the nineteenth century. Far from negating the distinction between refugees and immigrants,

8.1 · Anti-Jewish violence, 1880–1906. Of the more than two hundred pogroms in the region during this period, outrages in these centers claimed the most lives during this period. Credit: Mathieu Duvall, Imaging and Computing Center, Bates College, Lewiston, Maine. Map based on John Klier (2010), "Pogroms," *YIVO Encyclopedia of Jews in Eastern Europe*, http://www.yivoencyclopedia.org/article.aspx/Pogroms.

however, the crisis forced officials and philanthropists within and outside of the Anglo-Jewish community to encode their concern for bona fide refugees in law.

An Old Model Rejuvenated

By the end of the nineteenth century, British concern for persecuted foreigners was under intense pressure quite apart from the influx of East European Jews. The depredations of anarchists and Irish Fenians and the challenges of providing for fugitive slaves in the Indian Ocean region dampened public enthusiasm for these humanitarian subjects. That a proud tradition of refuge would end at the dawn of the twentieth century was not a foregone conclusion at the time, however. On the contrary, a new era of international collaboration helped to reinvigorate British outreach to persecuted foreigners. The immediate occasion for this shift was the end of the Crimean War in 1856. The war pitted Britain, France, and the Ottoman Empire against Russia. The allies aimed to check Russian territorial ambitions in Ottoman lands, and the Russians claimed to be protecting their Orthodox brethren. To the Western allies, this was not an entirely spurious rationale. At the time of the war and in ensuing decades, an anxious British public worried alternately about Ottoman treatment of Christians and Russian aggression. And indeed, the war—together with subsequent British intervention in the region—produced two new models of relief for persecuted groups: one among states and one among private philanthropists of different nations.

On the level of state responsibilities, the war ended with the allies pledging to protect minorities, Russia's claims to this role having been forfeited in the Treaty of Paris of that year. This meant, in part, the creation of new spheres of influence. The same treaty sanctioned the creation of Romania as a new, predominantly Christian nation from Ottoman territory. The Great Powers wrote protections for minorities into the constitution of the new state, requiring the Romanian government to uphold the civic rights of all parties. Under this agreement, Romanian Jews were to become citizens. The victors pressed the Ottoman Empire to follow suit. In an edict of the same year, the Ottomans formally recognized and promised to protect their minorities. This pattern of concerted international influence would continue, providing the basic template for minorities' protection used under the League of Nations.[6]

Unfortunately, international insistence on civic rights did not ensure that minorities would be spared persecution. It did, however, mean that British diplomats incurred a shared international responsibility to monitor the situation and to pressure offending governments when persecution occurred. Indeed, when the Ottomans broke their promises in the 1876 "Bulgarian atrocities," Russians and then other Europeans intervened in the region once more. The Great Powers were thus able to use international norms to legitimize intervention. Their solution, in this case, was in keeping with the longer history of British imperial refuge. Instead of easing tensions within the Ottoman Empire, the Great Powers established Bulgaria as an independent Christian nation, a refuge for the persecuted to call home. While this solution protected Christians, it did little to aid Jews or Muslims in the area, the latter becoming the subject of secondary schemes for international refuge along a similar imperial model.

The Crimean War also brought together philanthropists across national lines in efforts to stave off the sorts of humanitarian disasters witnessed in the conflict. This second development—epitomized in the 1864 signing of the Geneva Convention and establishment of the International Red Cross—aimed to protect soldiers in war and to guarantee the neutrality of civilians who came to their aid. For British philanthropists, involvement in international charitable networks like the Red Cross breathed new life into work that had at times lost sight of its international ties. British missionaries and abolitionist groups had long worked in tandem with sister societies overseas. London-based church organizations had traditionally employed foreigners in the field. This sort of international cooperation had been subsumed, however, in the turn to imperial discourse in the early nineteenth century. The pendulum began to swing in the other direction at the century's close.[7]

Although not about refugee relief per se, this revived internationalism facilitated new efforts to protect persecuted foreigners. The Society of Friends established the War Victims' Fund in the next major European conflict—the Franco-Prussian War of 1870–71. The fund aided soldiers as well as those fleeing in the wake of Prussian advances. Later in the decade, long-time refugee supporter Angela Burdett Coutts forged new alliances with American and German female philanthropists and diplomats through the Turkish Compassionate Fund. Formed in the wake of the 1876–1878 war with Russia, the group provided shelter, food, and employment for those forced to flee their homes, a monumental effort that would be celebrated at the 1893 World's Fair in Chicago.[8] It was in this context too that members of the Anglo-Jewish elite broadened their charitable efforts to involve greater collaboration with officials and coreligionists elsewhere in the world, connections that would prove indispensable when it came to orchestrating relief and transmigration in the wake of Eastern European pogroms.

Within Britain, international alliances buoyed enthusiasm for rescuing the persecuted of all faiths. Indeed, at a time when many questioned the politics of revolutionary refugees, few could deny the moral imperative to help these innocent victims of religious persecution. The media attention given to diplomatic and philanthropic work ensured that a new generation of would-be refugee supporters learned to recognize and condemn the mistreatment of religious and ethnic minorities. In the early 1870s, for instance, the British press was quick to call out the Romanian government for mistreating its Jewish population despite the provisions of the 1856 Treaty of Paris. Romanian officials had enacted laws that made it difficult for Jews to become full citizens and barred them from specific professions. Anti-Jewish violence became endemic, and Romanian officials blamed popular movements for the outrages and did little to curb them. International pressure yielded temporary results, but Romanian authorities lapsed as soon as the outcry abated.[9] The pattern recurred in Russia in 1881 and 1882 when anti-Jewish violence spiked as the result of the assassination of Alexander II, an act for which Jewish nihilists were blamed (figure 8.1). In the wake of pogroms, the Russian government issued a series of restrictions on the Jews. The May Laws of 1882 forced Jews to leave towns smaller than ten thousand in Russia's Pale of Settlement, the area of western Russia to which Jews had been periodically expelled since the eighteenth century. Further restrictions followed on Jewish access to higher education and the professions. By 1891, Jews were expelled from Moscow and forced into overcrowded towns in the Pale.[10]

The British reaction to the persecution of Romanian and later Russian Jews followed older models of outrage and relief organization. The British response typically began with media coverage of the crisis and public rallies in support of the oppressed. These meetings were not just local affairs; newspaper coverage brought them to national attention. As in the past, attendees at each meeting resolved that outrages against the Jews were a "disgrace to modern civilization" and that "justice demands the relief and indemnity of those who have suffered," including the "equality of civil rights." They further resolved that the government ought to be prevailed upon to promote these ends.[11] Thus, meetings in the 1870s, 1880s, and 1890s followed a set pattern.

In 1872, the lord mayor of London held a meeting to protest the outbreaks of violence against Jews. Prominent members of the Anglo-Jewish elite, including Lord Nathaniel Rothschild, were present in force, but the meetings were conceived as British—not Jewish—affairs. As in previous cases, the meeting called upon local notables, among them long-time refugee supporter Lord Shaftesbury serving as chair, several prominent MPs, and high-ranking Anglican officials.[12] Within days of the meeting, Shaftesbury led a deputation to the administration to demand that the government join in the protest.

A decade later, activists would remember the 1872 protests as a model to be emulated in Britain's protest of the Russian May Laws of 1882.[13] Once more, the Mansion House meeting drew heavily on religious figures and notables known for their vocal opposition to the treatment of Bulgarian Christians in 1876. Attendees then took their turn to adopt resolutions condemning violence against the Jews and expressing hope that Gladstone's administration would exercise a "friendly influence with the Russian Government" to bring these incidents to an end.[14] Reporting on the atrocities permeated the press. The *Times* of London reported on the Southern Russian pogroms with such alacrity that they were forced to retract some of their statements when official accounts showed the violence to have been less devastating than initially believed.[15]

By 1891, attempts to influence Russia became all the more insistent. The leader of the parliamentary opposition, William Gladstone, lent further weight to domestic protest by publishing an open letter to Samuel Montagu deploring Russian actions and urging further investigation of the situation facing Russian Jews.[16] Following a protest meeting at Guildhall London, two "representative Englishmen," the Earl of Meath and Sir Albert Rollit, traveled from London to Russia to deliver the Guildhall petition of that year. The editors of the *Jewish Chronicle* hopefully predicted that this petition "from the citizens of the greatest city in the world, craving justice and mercy for the Jewish subjects of the czar, would of itself have been a weapon of such enormous moral force as to be well-nigh irresistible."[17]

By the 1880s and 1890s, activists had perhaps more reason to believe that their demands for intervention would be received favorably, given Gladstone's vocal support for Bulgarian Christians and, later, the Armenians. International agreements helped too. Since 1856, the Great Powers' interest in minorities in the Ottoman Empire provided a basis for future action, even if much of their involvement in the region stemmed less from humanitarian concerns than from the demands of the balance of power.

While not groundless, then, these hopes were highly optimistic. It was even less likely that the Foreign Office would take the greater step of intervening in the internal affairs of the Russian Empire. Britain simply did not have the diplomatic clout with Russia that it had over the Ottomans. The two nations were frequently at war, competing as they did for influence in Central Asia as well as in southeastern Europe more generally. This would change in the early twentieth century, when they began negotiating a possible alliance against the growing German threat. Even then, however, Foreign Office critiques of Russian policy would have seemed imprudent at a time of delicate talks.[18]

Speakers at meetings decrying Russian pogroms hoped to persuade officials that intervention was necessary, but like activists in the past, they generated funds for refugee relief instead. The final resolution of the 1882 Mansion House meeting established a fund for Russian Jewish refugees that would remain the primary vehicle for relief to Jewish refugees through the turn of the century. The conveners raised over £100,000 at the meeting. Thereafter, notable attendees formed a committee to oversee the distribution of the new fund. The resulting Mansion House Russo-Jewish Refugee Committee joined forces with the Anglo-Jewish Association to create the Conjoint Mansion House Fund (MHF), which set to work immediately. They dispatched £500 to relieve Russian Jews who had fled to the border town of Brody, Austria, in the wake of the pogroms.[19] MHF monies also helped Jewish refugees migrate elsewhere and relieved those who ultimately arrived on British soil. By the winter of 1883, MHF had assisted 1,591 cases or 2,749 refugees arriving in Britain proper.[20]

The influx of destitute Russian Jewish refugees to England—particularly to London's East End—was quite noticeable in the wake of the 1881–1882 pogroms and May Laws. Still, the majority of these foreigners used England only as a stopping ground for transmigration. As refuge providers had come to expect, asylum within Britain was but one form of British refuge. Most Eastern European Jews were keen to press onward to America. Those who could pay their own passage did; many benefited from the assistance of local branches of the Anglo-Jewish Association, along with other smaller philanthropic organizations. Of the 2,749 Russian and Polish Jews who entered Britain in 1882, for example, only 489 remained by the end of that year, the vast majority having voluntarily migrated onward. Of those who departed, 616 men, 188 women, and 278 children continued to the United States, and 11 men, 3 women, and 5 children went to Canada.[21]

Along with continental and North American organizations, the MHF helped transmigrants move elsewhere. To facilitate this process, the MHF supplied provisions, defrayed transportation costs, and solicited further support from long-time refugee supporters like Burdett Coutts to fund agricultural training and schools for children where they resettled.[22] Within Britain, Jewish communities and officials at port cities provided temporary housing. In Liverpool, for example, the local branch of the Anglo-Jewish Association used MHF resources to secure a building large enough to house four hundred persons at once. They attended to the sanitary conditions of the building and furnished food, clothing, and desks at which refugees could write letters that the committee forwarded free of charge. By July 1882, they had already shepherded 6,274 Jews to America alone.[23]

Yet the work of the MHF and its affiliates was far from complete. While they made similar efforts in 1891, their successes were becoming harder to celebrate as rising tensions over foreigners' presence made the arrival of refugees increasingly an occasion for alarm. The mode of relief remained the same, but the public sentiments that greeted them changed dramatically.

A Model Pushed to its Limits

An estimated twenty thousand of the Jews who fled Russia in 1881–1882 alighted in the town of Brody at the eastern edge of the Austro-Hungarian Empire. Many refugees would remain there for weeks in makeshift shelters. As they waited, the refugees depleted most of their resources. Anglo-Jewish activists feared these conditions from the start, believing that the refugees' increasing poverty and misery would accustom even the able-bodied to dependence on charity.[24] In an attempt to impose greater cleanliness and order, the Russo-Jewish Fund committee asked the India Office to send an ex-Indian civil servant to attend to the conditions at Brody. The MHF hoped that such an individual, with experience gathered from the recent Indian Famine, would command much authority in the East and be able to maintain camp morale.[25] By July 1882, philanthropists had managed to provide for the Jews at Brody. Most were sent on to other destinations, via Hamburg and Britain to the Americas and to British Dominions. Three thousand of those who remained in Brody—those deemed unable to work—were returned to Russia, where philanthropists believed they would now be safe.[26] The immediate crisis caused by the pogroms and the promulgation of the Russian May Laws was thus at an end.

Despite this relative success, the Brody moment had lasting ramifications for refugee relief worldwide. Anticipating future expulsions, the governments of countries of immigration—particularly America and the British dominions—began to close their doors to certain categories of migrants. New York moved to restrict immigration in June of 1882. Nine years later, the US federal government barred "undesirable" aliens on a national basis, a decision that—while aimed to restrict Chinese immigration—had immediate ramifications for Eastern European Jews as well. To settle in the United States, prospective migrants would have to be "promising" immigrants, able to support themselves as artisans or agriculturalists. The British dominions followed suit. The Canadian government enabled the governor general to bar destitute migrants in 1886, and Australia and South Africa followed in the 1890s. South Africa went so far as to force a ship carrying Jewish refugees back to Britain in 1903.[27]

Neither America nor Canada ever closed their doors entirely to Eastern European Jews. Nevertheless, the conditions they placed on transmigration, together with the threat of complete closure, plagued British philanthropists. Immigration officials obliged the MHF committee and its affiliates to distinguish which refugees were ideal candidates for self-reliant resettlement elsewhere. Their task was complicated by the requirement that immigrants to the United States be artisans or farmers. This meant that fewer Jews could resettle in urban areas like New York. Schemes to make refugees into agriculturalists assumed a capacity for hard physical labor in the fields, as Moritz Ellinger of the New York Hebrew Emigrants' Society emphasized. Those who did not fit this description, he argued, "the aged and helpless[,] should remain in Europe at least until those on whom their care depends have been successfully established in their new homes."[28]

If Anglo-Jewish philanthropists were to continue to send Jews to America, they would have to rework their expectations for the refugees who remained behind. As early as 1882, they admitted that selective transmigration would mean that "those too old or too weakly, or deemed otherwise unfit for emigration, are kept here—a permanent burden on the Jewish community; but the most capable are sent to America at the sole cost of the mansion house fund" (figure 8.2)[29] The MHF committee, then grappling with the refugees who remained at Brody, wrote that the misery of camp life reduced these refugees to despair. The MHF assumed that this remainder, demoralized by their experiences, would never again be fit for emigration or capable of self-sustaining labor. Unlike refugee relief organizations in the past, the MHF would not be able to disband; the charity would have to operate more permanently.

In Britain, the reaction to the restrictions of other countries was immediate. Anticipating a backlash against Jews in Britain, the Anglo-Jewish community sent a representative to Washington, DC, in June 1882 in an attempt to convince the American government to accept more migrants.[30] By 1890, officials began to monitor the apparently increasing number of foreigners who remained in Britain, unable to move elsewhere. The government revived the lapsed 1836 Aliens Act, which required shipmasters to count the numbers of foreigners upon arrival and to report their points of

8.2 · Russian Jews being examined by a doctor before emigration from Liverpool to the United States. Wood engraving from *The Graphic*, November 21, 1891, p. 597. Wellcome Library no. 38324i. Credit: Courtesy of the Wellcome Library, London.

origin. Though the Board of Trade thus had a tally of how many arrived, the number of foreigners leaving Britain was less easy to calculate. The MHF could provide some figures, but doubt over the accuracy of these numbers emboldened proponents of immigration restriction, becoming a favorite complaint of theirs through the turn of the century.

Uncertainty about the numbers of refugees accumulating within Britain fueled the search for overseas outlets. Several surprising public figures known for their anti-Semitism joined this endeavor. Journalist Arnold White traveled to Russia in an attempt to persuade the czar to slow the pace of the Jewish expulsions. Writer W. H. Wilkins became an unexpected proponent of new settlements overseas. In his 1892 *Alien Invasion*, this Conservative advocate of immigration restriction argued that "there are many practical ways in which we can show our sympathy with the persecuted Russian Jews if we wish to do so, notably by combining to divert the stream of immigration from our now densely populated little island." The more practical approach, he explained, was to help "the would-be immigrants to move on to some new land beyond the seas."[31]

British philanthropies, as well as the international Jewish Colonization Association, continued to seek out alternatives in the Ottoman Empire and in South America, while Israel Zangwill's Jewish Territorial Organization contemplated establishing Zion in British East Africa.[32] Though these destinations offered alternatives to America and the white settler colonies of the British Empire, none of them seemed adequate to the need. At the turn of the century, the fate of Baron de Hirsch's settlements in Argentina rested on settlers who many thought would fail to adapt to agricultural life and who, ignorant of the local language, seemed likely to be cheated by the native inhabitants. Small-scale settlements in the Middle East seemed vulnerable as well. Though philanthropists and Zionists continued to forward settlers to the region, the Ottoman government began to check the immigration of Jewish families in the 1890s. Tension between the Ottomans and Jews embroiled the Foreign Office in debate over whether and how to protect those who traveled to the region on British passports or as part of charitable schemes organized by British subjects.[33]

Without large-scale overseas outlets, the number of Jews who remained in the United Kingdom grew. This accumulation of foreigners could not have happened at a worse time. The situation in the last decades of the nineteenth century was one of seeming economic crisis. British preeminence appeared to be in peril. The depression of the 1870s had passed, but industrial growth decelerated; the nation that had dominated the first industrial revolution now seemed vulnerable to competition, especially from rapidly industrializing Germany and America. These more generalized economic fears intensified the debate around the effect of the global economy on ordinary Britons, a concern that socialists and conservatives alike began to exploit.

Though a small group relative to the overall population, foreign Jews in the East End were visible to a degree that fueled protectionist impulse that became particularly powerful at the height of the Second Anglo-Boer War (1899–1902). Public opinion in the East End became stridently anti-alien immigrant, anti-Semitic, and even anti-refugee. These threads of opinion were often so deeply entangled with one another that together they threatened the sanctified place of the persecuted in British culture. More or less explicitly anti-Semitic anti-alienism took three concrete forms in the 1890s and 1900s: concern over social welfare and public order, fear about unfair labor competition and the social effects of capitalism more generally, and anxiety over the apparent degeneration of the British race.[34]

Conservatives as well as social reformers demonized Jewish foreigners by portraying them as being as far from independent liberal subjects as possible. Wilkins and White equated Jews with increasingly negatively perceived foreign socialists and anarchists—those proponents of the "vilest of political sentiments." White went so far as to assert that the only "dangerous" form of socialism in London was "either alien or Semitic."[35] Major William Evans-Gordon staked his career as MP for the East End district of Stepney on the need to end alien immigration, citing the "fact" that, although relatively few Jews were in English poor houses, 39 percent of incoming Jews in 1901 found themselves in the books of the Jewish Board of Guardians. This figure was meant to inspire fear that Jews might soon wind up in the workhouses as well.[36] Looking beyond the "statistics," socialist Beatrice Potter (later Potter Webb) held Jews responsible for degrading the quality of life for all laborers, since "they lacked pride and any definite standard of life" and "were able to live at a level Englishmen could not."[37] White employed the same dehumanizing language that would be used against Boer families during the Second Anglo-Boer War: foreign Jews had "a scanty regard for cleanliness" and "nearly approach the conditions of animal life."[38]

Proponents of restriction argued that Jewish labor competition was exacerbated by Jewish management practices. The Jewish capitalist now stood not only for the boom-and-bust of the stock exchange but also for the dreaded competition of the sweatshop. Sweatshop owners were reputed to undercut native-English East End boot and textile industries especially effectively. They did this by using cheaper alien labor and working their laborers around the clock, even on Sundays, a claim that seemed to furnish further evidence of the "Jewishness" of sweatshops for the more anti-Semitic of the anti-alien commentators.[39]

The Boer War brought the Jews-as-ultra-capitalists accusation to the fore, with critics blaming Jews for the war itself. Liberal war critic J. A. Hobson first made this claim in his 1902 *Imperialism: A Study*. Hobson accused Jewish financiers of dragging the British government into the war. He claimed that "the business capital of every State" is "controlled, so far as Europe is concerned, chiefly by men of a single and peculiar race."[40] British finance was no different, according to Hobson, and only this Jewish financial interest in South Africa brought the British into conflict with the Dutch Afrikaners. Though not on its face an argument against Jewish immigration, Hobson's diatribe against Jewish interests undercut British sympathies for foreign Jews.

The point was also a popular one for the trade unionists, who tended to favor immigrant restriction in order to check labor competition.[41]

Such were the opinions of the most vocal commentators toward destitute Jews and Jewish capitalists by the turn of the century. In popular culture, Jews seemed to be the quintessential vampires, preying on society like Dracula in Bram Stoker's 1897 novel, or the all-too-real Jack the Ripper, who some believed to be Jewish.[42] Though pointed anti-Semitism was a minority opinion in politics, it dominated the 1903 Aliens Commission.[43] The Anglo-Jewish elite feared that this would be the case and that Jews more generally would become a target of animosity in England. Consequently, Anglo-Jewish charity focused on shouldering the costs of relief almost entirely within the Anglo-Jewish community, and helping their coreligionists assimilate into British society as best as possible. Despite these efforts, "the Jewish Question" became an existential crisis. The proud metropolitan public that had so readily overridden barriers to refuge in the Empire was forced to reckon with the limits of their nation-defining humanitarian practice.

Bona Fide Refugees

> If these men and women are political exiles and religious refugees, and we, in England, are bound in conscience, in faith, and in fealty to the splendid tradition of our freedom and our power, to give them protection, safety and home, then let us do it, as in the sight of God, with some thoughtfulness, some wisdom, and some care.[44]

The Reverend Reaney's 1892 essay appeared in Arnold White's anti-Semitic, anti-alien volume. At the end of a century of British imperial refuge, even Reaney and the harshest critics of Jewish immigration paid homage to the humanitarian imperative to provide refuge. In 1899, Arnold White proposed a restriction bill that, "without in any way impairing the protection and asylum hitherto accorded to political and religious refugees from other countries, . . . prohibit[s] the coming into this realm of such alien, unskilled, diseased or incapable paupers as are likely to become a public or private charge."[45] Evans-Gordon, too, insisted that he was "as unwilling as any man to deny the right of asylum to a political refugee." "But," he continued, "there is a great difference between that and admitting the professional criminal, or leaving unregulated an immigration *en masse* which is ousting our people from their homes and steadily building up a ghetto."[46] Therein lay the heart of the problem. As A. J. Mundella had pointed out to Parliament in 1893, how could the British both close their doors to Eastern European Jews and maintain a right of entry for the persecuted? Were not these new immigrants also refugees?

What the interlocutors in this debate did not recognize fully was that critical elements of the refugee narrative had been changing since the 1870s. The classic refugee narrative valorized the fight, lauding refugees who did battle for their freedom. Refugees became particularly deserving of sympathy because they were forced to leave behind families—wives, children, parents—who continued to suffer under the weight of oppression at home. After the 1870s, it was this more passive group of foreigners who gained central stage, while revolutionaries—who never disappeared from the genre entirely—became less prominent.

The change was both necessary in a changing global political context and, at the time, convenient for many British sympathizers. Rising ethnic nationalism and religious persecution were making refugees out of broader swaths of the population than ever before. Quite simply, the demography of the refugees themselves was changing. Eventually, the sheer scale of potential mass migration would limit the sympathies of host nations. For the time, however, the new set of refugees actually helped British activists solicit interest in helping the persecuted at a time when the public and officials were increasingly wary of new breeds of violent revolutionaries who were sometimes willing to target civilians. The pure victimhood of these new refugees was something of a relief when contrasted with these disturbingly bloodthirsty radicals. As a consequence, the iconic refugee changed from a liberal freedom fighter to the helpless woman, child, or aged person—a prototype of the refugee that remains with us today.[47]

Jewish victims of Russian oppression ought to have fit the evolving image of refugees as helpless innocents rather than fighters. However, limited avenues for transmigration and the attendant rise of anti-alien sentiment dampened sympathies for these refugees at the gates. The result was a discussion of refugees that attempted to exclude the Jews in their midst, even though the difficulty of this exemption would become clear when pressed.

In addition, commentators began to focus on persecuted Christians, even though the classic refugee narrative had long transcended religious, as well as race and class, differences. Armenian and Bulgarian Christians began to take center stage in British relief efforts, their situation becoming a cause-célèbre following massacres

8.3 · New icons of persecution. Armenian refugees (not dated). Bain News Service. LC-B2-4490-10[P&P]. Credit: Courtesy of the Library of Congress, Washington, DC.

in the 1890s (figure 8.3). The Huguenots also enjoyed a revival as refugees, if only in fond retrospect. Their history and the degree to which they were able to blend into English life made them seem the ideal sort of refugee settler.

Renewed emphasis on Christian refugees was the product of two developments, one pragmatic, the other more about the politics of assimilation. Pragmatically, it offered a means of allocating scarce resources at a time when the international Jewish community seemed capable of caring for its own. The Society of Friends offered a case in point. Though they were then expanding their relief efforts in general, Quakers were undecided as to whether to intervene on behalf of refugee Jews. Their journal, *The Friend*, was almost entirely silent on the Jewish Question, a silence that was conspicuous in the wake of the 1881–1882 pogroms and those of the early 1890s. Instead of discussing the plight of the Jews, the editors focused on Christian minorities, especially the Russian Stundists who were pacifist dissenters like the Quakers. When discussions of Jewish persecution and the first aliens bill saturated the press, prominent Quaker George Cadbury—of Cadbury Chocolates and an important Birmingham-area social reformer—focused on the Stundists in an eager search for an appropriate philanthropic outlet.[48]

It would be "cowardly," Cadbury exclaimed, if the British Quakers did not do the same for their own [near] "coreligionists," the Stundists, as Jews did for their foreign brethren.[49] Cadbury's coreligionists were apparently uncomfortable with his suggestion that they help fellow dissenters exclusively, since they did not follow up his conversational gambit. Aiding one's nearest brethren was one thing; it was another thing to refuse pointedly to aid visibly distressed non-Christian refugees.

The trend of focusing on Christians was part of a broader concern for the ability of refugees to assimilate into and to support British society. In the seventeenth century, the in-gathering of continental Protestant refugees had been had been discussed as a way to bolster trade as well as the Protestant faith. By the nineteenth century, Britons had shifted their attention from the material advantages offered by refugees and from their ability to assimilate into British society. Refuge's ideological assistance to liberalism on the global stage was emphasized instead. Yet, at the dawn of the twentieth century, the discourse of social and economic gain came back in full force. The selectively remembered Huguenots now served as an example of the ideal refugees. In contrast to the Russian Jews, many believed, the Huguenots had embraced English society, brought skills that would benefit the economy, and blended (if not without initial resistance on both sides) into the landscape.

Samuel Smiles, author of the immensely popular 1859 *Self-Help*, inadvertently led this new popularization of Huguenot history by penning two books on the French Protestants, one in 1867 and the other in 1873. The first mirrored Smiles's arguments in *Self-Help*. Fleeing an oppressive government that would have forced their conversion or killed them, the Huguenots arrived almost destitute on English and Irish shores. Although poor, they were not "idle." Like the ideal liberal that Smiles described in *Self-Help*, the Huguenots were independent, industrious, and duty-bound.[50] Smiles was not surprised that such a community went on to found so many industries in the British Isles. Members of the Huguenot Historical Society, formed at the bicentennial of the revocation of the Edict of Nantes in 1885, readily endorsed and promoted Smiles's depiction of their ancestors. Neither the Historical Society's publications nor Smiles's books addressed the relationship between new and old refugee groups. Smiles's publishers, however, appear to have recognized and exploited this parallel. They had a knack for republishing his 1867 text in moments of increased Eastern European Jewish immigration. Subsequent editions of the book appeared in 1881 and 1889—two such periods—and at the time of the Aliens Act debates in 1905.

Simply comparing the Huguenots and the Jews did not guarantee that a commentator was anti-Semitic or pro-restrictionist. Smiles did not sugarcoat the resistance the Huguenots met with from English workers. Moreover, the ex-president of the Huguenot Historical Society, W. J. C. Moens, provided expert testimony at the 1903 Royal Commission on Alien Immigration that could have been read either way. Moens confirmed the role of foreign trades in founding innumerable English industries. But these early alien immigrants were initially isolated from English society, lived together, and assimilated only over time.[51] Indeed, it could easily be argued that the Anglo-Jews themselves had imbibed a Huguenot model for their foreign coreligionists. They and other pro-alien commentators stressed Eastern European Jews' industriousness, sobriety, and contribution to trade. Indeed, Eastern European Jewish migrants proved generally upwardly mobile, despite fears to the contrary.

Whereas the Anglo-Jewish elite emphasized the similarity between Jewish refugees and the Huguenots, anti-alien commentators stressed Jews' inability to assimilate into their hosts' society. Increasingly, commentators understood assimilation as a process by which ethnic distinctions would eventually disappear entirely. In an 1893 novel, Sir Arthur Conan Doyle tapped into these popular concerns. In *The Refugees: A Tale of Two Continents,* he retells the history of the Huguenots in France prior to the revocation of the Edict of Nantes before returning to a familiar crime narrative in which bloodthirsty French Catholics pursue the Huguenot protagonists in the Americas. In a preface to the novel, Conan Doyle contrasts these refugee heroes with the contemporary Jewish migrants. "Each immigrant foreign Jew settling in this country joins, not the English community as the Huguenot and Hollander refugees from the Roman Catholic prosecutions of the seventeenth century joined us," Conan Doyle explains, "but a community proudly separate, racially distinct, and existing preferentially aloof." There were two options before the nation, he claimed. "England [was] either compelled to abandon her secular practice of complacent acceptance of every human being choosing to settle on these shores, or to face the certainty of the Jews becoming stronger, richer, and vastly more numerous."[52]

Accusations of "aloofness" enabled Conservative commentators to imply that successful Jewish trades would yield limited benefits for British society as a whole. It also gave commentators grounds for doubting whether Jews would, or could, intermarry with British natives and so melt into the mainstream, as the Huguenots had. Wilkins, for example, was disposed to believe that immigration into Britain was a good thing, provided that immigrants were "gradually absorbed into our national life, and become good and useful members of the community." "Such were the Huguenots," Wilkins explained. Destitute Eastern European Jews were different, he argued. Evans-Gordon described the Jews' "ghetto-habit," explaining the "vital difference between Huguenots and other Protestant immigrants and the Hebrew people" as the latter's "clannishness," which derived from "a sort of historical fear of separation from their co-religionists."[53] Whereas friendlier commentators cited Jews' ability (in the second generation especially) to learn English and thrive in English schools, anti-immigrant witnesses before the 1903 commission pointed to the formation of a "Jewish" East End in which English was hardly spoken.

Firm proponents of liberal individualism, the Anglo-Jews were confident that their coreligionists would assimilate in time, losing their distinctive orthodoxy, if not becoming entirely secular.[54] For Conservative proponents of restriction, however, blending in meant maintaining no religious or ethnic differences at all, though the state had abolished formal inequalities in public life on grounds of religious difference. In his testimony, Arnold White opined that the ideal refugees in this sense were "the Huguenots and Flemish whose second generation [in England] was a negligible element."[55] By contrast, the Jews "do not plant as the Huguenots did; that is my point . . . Holding fast to the faith of their fathers, [Russian immigrants] regard inter-marriage with the English as contamination; and assimilation, as involving tribal disgrace and religious delinquency."[56] In making this point, White harkened back to one of the dominant tropes of the classic refugee narrative. Though British welcome to foreign refugees had never before depended upon the possibility of their intermarrying, novelists had long depicted intermarriage as the second-best outcome of exile, after a return to a homeland freed of persecution. Indeed, the commissioners on alien immigration learned from the Reverend E. Canney, rector of a church in Holborn, Central London, that intermarriage was common even among Italian Roman Catholics. Canney explained that many of the less zealous Catholics—those more attached to Mazzini than to the Pope, for example—married English women.[57]

Anglo-Jews did not comment on this specific point, but Austro-Hungarian Theodore Herzl was forced to do so. When questioning the father of Zionism before the commission, Evans-Gordon demanded to know whether the assimilation of Jewish refugees was possible. Herzl used the example of the Huguenots as evidence in favor of assimilation. Evans-Gordon seized upon this point immediately, dismissing the analogy between Jews and the Huguenots. "The Huguenots," he explained, "were essentially an intermarrying people, and were speedily absorbed by marriage into the general population."[58] Herzl, whose larger sociopolitical views were separatist to begin with, could do little other than agree that full Jewish assimilation was unlikely if foreigners' assimilation or contribution to English society was so narrowly defined.

As powerful as this line of argumentation was in the public imagination, debate over the would-be refugees' character ran parallel to the core claim of the classic narrative. Refugees required special treatment, according to the moral politics of British refuge, because they had been persecuted. Their ability to assimilate into their hosts' society was beside the point. Yet, diminishing resources for open refuge made this core commitment more difficult to maintain. Rather than deny this moral imperative outright, officials and philanthropists began instead to hedge on the definition of persecution. As had the fugitive slave commissioners several decades prior, they sought to set a higher bar for what constituted persecution sufficient to merit refuge.

This was no easy task. Few in Britain denied that Russia treated its ethnic minorities unequally. The May Laws burdened Jews with civic and socioeconomic disabilities. Anti-Semitic hostility in the East led to intermittent pogroms. This was indisputable. But did this amount to persecution? After 1880, the ways in which philanthropists, officials, and public commentators determined which foreigners were refugees changed. Through the middle of the nineteenth century, any member of a persecuted group could be a refugee. Systems to check refugees' statements were generally limited to identifying that they were actually from said group and verifying that they were of good character. By the 1880s, activists and officials alike would be weighing new criteria. These were sufficiently narrow that fewer foreigners would be entitled to refuge.

Anti-alien commentators invented a host of reasons that the mistreatment of Russian Jews might not amount to persecution. In his 1892 *The Alien Invasion*, for example, Wilkins condemned the "hearsay tales" taken as proof of persecution, likening reliance on these tales to assuming that the annals of murder in the English court records accurately reflected the English character writ large. The Reverend

Reaney, in his contribution to White's edited volume of the same year, *The Destitute Alien*, demanded, "We must know more about them." Without knowing more about the character of the would-be refugees, Reaney argued sarcastically, the British could not satisfy themselves that "the only reason for their expulsion from Russia is because they are so pure and saintly and true to the best traditions of the remarkable race to which they belong." Reaney demanded pure victimhood—and purely religious persecution—from would-be Jewish refugees.[59]

By 1899, Arnold White took this skepticism further, blaming British officials for falsifying the refugee status of East European Jews. He accused English and Anglo-Jewish charities of enticing the "submerged tenth" from East European cities to British shores with their funds. White asserted that the Board of Trade had conspired to perpetuate the "idea that the dregs of Russian cities who remain here are mainly refugees," presumably because the Board of Trade hoped to dilute the market power of domestic laborers. Their "device" of terming these destitute foreigners "refugees" was an outright fiction used to convince the public and the House of Commons that refuge was necessary. Though this accusation has no basis in the records of the Board of Trade's 1894 investigation into alien immigration, Arnold White's 1899 *The Modern Jew* claimed to be addressing the public "frankly" at last.[60]

Whereas White fingered only the Board of Trade, Evans-Gordon, who headed the 1903 Aliens Commission, indicted the public at large. Perhaps the most overtly anti-Semitic of the anti-alien commentators, he questioned whether the public could identify "real" persecution at all. His 1903 *The Alien Immigrant* contained a chapter devoted to the notion of persecution, large sections of which were read into the commission hearings. In both venues, Evans-Gordon laid bare what he saw as inherent problems in popular outrage at alleged foreign despotism. Holding foreign governments to Britain's own liberal standards was wrong-headed, he claimed: "From an English point of view everyone in Russia is more or less persecuted." At the same time as he emphasized the equality (in misery) of Russian peoples, Evans-Gordon admitted that minorities were singled out, their lives made more difficult by attempts to Russianize them. He argued that, by applying their own standards to Russia's Jews, the British failed to notice that the Jews were treated on a par with all minority groups within Russia: "Quite apart from any special legislation against the Jews, it is a fundamental principle of Russian policy to Russianize, as far as possible, every subject of the Czar." Evans-Gordon asserted that Jews got off easily when compared with the Catholic Poles under Russian domination. The Jews might face civic and economic disabilities, but this did not amount to "distinctively religious persecution" sufficient to make this particular group actual refugees.[61]

Presumably, Catholic Poles could then be "real" refugees. But Evans-Gordon sidestepped this designation entirely. Rather than identifying what constituted persecution, he shifted his argument to assert that one would find similar efforts to assimilate minority groups in the Kaiser's Germany, in democratic America, and in liberal Britain.[62] In so doing, he endeavored to turn the logic of classical British refuge on its head. Outrage at the illiberal treatment of foreigners overseas was the root of interest in persecuted foreigners. Instead, Evans-Gordon reminded his audience that such experiences were the norm and that liberal Britain could do little to change the situation overseas.

Evans-Gordon tried to steer the royal commission toward the same conclusions during his questioning of Herzl. Exploiting ideological divisions between Herzl and the more assimilation-minded Anglo-Jewry, Evans-Gordon demanded of this Zionist leader what he meant when he said that the Jews were "persecuted." Pressed to define *persecution,* Herzl tried to explain that, though it took different forms, "everywhere the Jew is the scapegoat, the whipping boy; and one day he tries no longer to be a scapegoat, and he seeks other skies." Doubtful, Evans-Gordon fired back that not even the Jews themselves would uniformly call themselves "persecuted," to which Herzl explained, "You have definite outbreaks and persecutions which come occasionally, and then you have the far-reaching pressure every day. A man who does not know what it is to be a free man says: 'no, I am not persecuted,' because he has not got his head wounded." Laying a trap for Herzl, Evans-Gordon demanded whether "the economic conditions of overcrowding and so forth where there is great pressure, is a form of persecution which exists anywhere where people are overcrowded?" Herzl responded in the affirmative, adding quickly: "The Jew is not sure of his life to-morrow, and if his house is burnt and his windows are smashed, that is nothing; he lives in a perpetual fear with the madness of persecution." Pressing further, Evans-Gordon forced Herzl to admit that he did not have a precise definition of persecution. Defined generally, Herzl's term *persecution* included racist sentiments then on the rise in England proper. He explained that he "included in it even the slight anti-Jewish feeling in society where it exists." Stepping back, Evans-Gordon contended that this phenomenon was not persecution: "You say it produces persecution, but we will modify that, and say it produces anti-Jewish feeling or anti-Jewish action." Knowing that he had cornered Herzl, Evans-Gordon then asked if the desire to limit immigration to the East End amounted to persecution. Herzl might have been tempted to say yes. In the moment, however, he toed a fine line between highlighting the immorality of denying refuge to those in need and admitting that Britain had the sovereign right to defend her own population against mass immigration.[63]

Few ultimately endorsed Evans-Gordon's slippery views of what constituted persecution sufficient to warrant refuge. Nevertheless, activists too sought to narrow who counted as a refugee by refining their use of the term. Even the Anglo-Jewish MHF endorsed raising the threshold for foreigners seeking treatment reserved for bona fide refugees. In fact, it would be the MHF's revised criteria, devised in the 1880s, that would inform official deliberations over the definition of persecution, Evans-Gordon's virulent position aside. The fugitive slave commissioners had been the first to assert that not every foreign slave was necessarily entitled to British refuge, and that to be a refugee a slave had to be persecuted "in hot blood." After 1882, members of the MHF employed this model when classifying Jewish fugitives. Rather than relying on membership in the particular group, which would have meant counting all Eastern Jews as refugees, philanthropists emphasized the moment of flight as a means of distinguishing the immigrant from the refugee in cases where they were nearly indistinguishable from one another.[64]

Anglo-Jewish relief committees required proof that would-be refugees came from regions in Russia in which the Jews were being violently assaulted and that they had fled at a moment when persecution was actually taking place. The Mansion House committee insisted that they could only relieve those "who are strictly 'refugees' from violence and oppression.".[65] The Jewish Colonization Association similarly regretted that they could not help the Board of Guardians with "immigrants" from the East. Established to assist refugees, the association "cannot help with emigration where [those in question were] not from the country in which [Jews were being] being persecuted."[66]

Determining which foreigners fled "persecution" was a difficult task. The MHF committee continually lamented how difficult evidence of persecution was to gather as they found that "many Jewish families are daily arriving in London from the undisturbed districts in Russia and Poland, which they need not have left." The MHF committee concluded that these Jews had emigrated only "in the hope of being allowed to participate in the emigration afforded from the Mansion House fund." A "considerable number" of others could not easily be categorized as "refugees" as opposed to "immigrants," since they were "unable to produce the smallest amount of evidence, except their verbal statements, which are generally far from concise and apparently very unreliable, even of the districts from which they are, as they assert, fugitives."[67]

The MHF openly discussed whom it ought to exclude. For the first time in British history, the committee weighed whether economic in addition to political and religious oppression was sufficient "persecution" for foreigners to be admitted onto its refugee relief rolls. It became the first closely parsed distinction between political refugees and those now considered economic refugees. The MHF committee decided against this inclusion. Along with more conservative commentators, it dismissed this group of would-be refugees as parasites, often overlooking the distinction between active economic discrimination and inadequate opportunity. Jews could not be refugees simply because they sought "a better life" overseas. Reaney and Anglo-Jews tended to agree that life in the East End was not necessarily any better than Eastern Europe on that score. This view was akin to the one fugitive slave commissioners espoused in their 1876 report.

As ridiculous as it might seem to equate the East End with Russia, the point bore resemblance to some of the calculations the MHF found itself making in the cases at hand: Mansion House funds were not to be used by those simply trying to secure a better life. To deter applicants from doing so, the committee announced that "notice to this effect is being circulated [in continental newspapers] abroad, and will it is hoped, be strictly acted upon in turn by the intermediate committees, which have hitherto assisted many of such cases to London." There was no other means, the *Jewish Chronicle* lamented, "to nurse the funds and ensure the assisting of cases proved to be worthy of help, before aiding very doubtful ones." As the chairman of the Russo-Jewish Fund noted, the committee was already under fire from philanthropists in America "for not having been severe enough in the selection of *bona fide* Russian refugees for emigration."[68] In their effort to screen out free riders, MHF excluded two groups they deemed to be automatically morally suspect: men who left their wives and families behind and draft dodgers.[69] These "opportunists" were liable to be returned to Russia. Though the Jewish Board of Guardians did not have the legal ability to expel foreigners from Britain, the committee used its relief fund to pay return passage for "non-refugees."[70]

The Anglo-Jewish Association did not limit returns to foreigners classified as immigrants; indeed, the MHF repatriated some bona fide refugees in the same manner on the grounds that, even if they had had real cause to flee initially, they could return safely because the cause of their persecution was removed. The Anglo-Jewish elite has been much criticized by historians for returning Eastern European Jews. Without excusing the act, it is critical to see this behavior within the logic of British refuge. Though it often became permanent, refuge was meant to provide a temporary shelter from the political storm. The refugee's return was supposed to be triumphant, like that of Garibaldi to an Italy whose independence he had won. More often than not, however, foreigners returned home after receiving a general pardon or reprieve from the worst of the oppression that had forced them to leave in the first place.

At the founding of the MHF committee, Anglo-Jewish spokesmen had highlighted how optimistic they were that support of the Romanian Jews would soon become unnecessary. As an editor of the *Jewish Chronicle* noted, "the lives of Jews, the honour of their women have at least been safe in Roumania [*sic*]." Unlike the Russian Jews, the Jews of Romania "have no longer been commonly turned out of their houses in winter or in the dead of night. Their sufferings have ceased to be dramatic, although they have not been entirely terminated. . . . Slowly but surely [they are] being made citizens."[71] Note the insistence on relative improvements. It was not that the Jews were treated well, but rather that they were no longer "commonly" victimized in the most outrageous manner. Moreover, the *Jewish Chronicle*'s correspondent assumed that citizenship would surely give the Romanian government an interest in Jews' well-being. In short, the Anglo-Jewry need not concern itself with would-be Romanian refugees when the Russian case was more pressing.

By the beginning of 1883, however, the Anglo-Jewish community would turn from sharp critiques of Russian oppression to tentative hopes for Russian reform. As early as the summer of 1882, Jewish philanthropists expressed hope that the acute crisis in Russia was coming to a close and that it would thus be safe to stop refugee flight. While it is true that worst of the early 1880s pogroms were then in the past, the change in prognosis offered a reprieve from relief provision at a crucial moment. Most of the Russian refugees who had congregated at Brody on the Austrian border in 1881–1882 had been resettled. But, like other voluntary groups at work in the region, the MHF was at a loss over what to do with those who could not be forwarded to the

United States or elsewhere because they were too infirm or "demoralized" to make good settlers. Determining that their home districts in Russia were then safe enough allowed the MHF to help return three thousand of these remaining refugees to Russia.[72]

The following winter, the MHF also had on their hands several hundred Jewish migrants who "appeared to be quite unable to fight the battle of life away from their own country, amidst a people speaking a language unknown to them, and with habits somewhat different to their own." Despite the fact that many Anglo-Jewish charities were established for the express purpose of helping Eastern European Jews adapt to English society, the committee was relieved that "fortunately it was decided at the Vienna conference [of leading Jewish European philanthropists] that repatriation was possible." Thus, 510 adults and 114 children were returned home from Britain proper.[73]

Jewish Chronicle editors were circumspect in how they depicted this repatriation program. Knowing the wrong that they would be committing if they returned foreigners to face persecution, the MHF committee, via the *Chronicle,* was careful to state that the returnees were, in large part, those whose flight had been opportunistic. Moreover, they espoused a great deal of confidence in the rule of law in Russia. The *Chronicle* followed suit. In stark contrast to their earlier condemnation of Asiatic oppression in "Darkest Russia," the editors emphasized the end of violence and the prospect of legal reform. In February 1883, the *Chronicle* asserted: "Slowly, but as we would hope, surely, the condition of our Russian coreligionists is improving. . . . The government is beginning to see that Jews are being entrusted with the privileges [that] are enjoyed by the great mass of her people."[74]

When there was fresh violence six months later, the newspaper highlighted how keen Russian authorities were to suppress anti-Jewish sentiment. Quoting a correspondent in St. Petersburg, the *Chronicle* explained that "the Russian authorities have acted with great energy and severity in suppressing the anti-Jewish disorders. There has been no hesitation or loss of time in using military force against the rioters." Unlike in the previous year, the editors claimed, "there is, therefore, some hope that the agitation will not spread as it did before. The town is now reported to be quiet."[75] Nothing, it seemed, would bring a repeat of the level of violence that had accompanied the pogroms and May Laws of 1881–1882. The editors again implied that, if the czar and his officers promised reform in the future, the Jews need not be refugees now.

Beyond the Jewish circles, Anglo-Jewish philanthropists repeated this hope that the worst oppression was in the past. Hermann Landau testified before the Select Committee on Emigration and Immigration in 1888. Asked to comment on the cause of increased Jewish migration to Britain between 1882 and 1886, Landau, who ran the East End Poor Jews' Temporary Shelter, testified that Eastern European Jews had then been fleeing "persecution in Russia." When prompted, he added that the "acute part of it [the persecution] has ceased," assuring the committee that further flight would not be necessary. Landau went so far as to imply that, absent persecution, Russian and Polish Jews had little interest in leaving their homelands. Whereas there was a certain charm in emigration for the English, Landau explained, "when a young man in Poland or Russia leaves for abroad it is considered quite a disgrace to his family; I can assure you that is a positive fact."[76]

In the political sphere, the conversation followed this same pattern of downplaying persecution and narrowing the category of the refugee. The question before Conservatives and Liberals alike was not whether refugees would be exempted from the operation of a new aliens act, but how narrowly or widely the exemption would be defined: what sort of persecution was sufficient to warrant flight and trigger British asylum. The final shape of the opt-out clause was not a commitment to open asylum. Rather, it was an amendment that navigated carefully between a desire to maintain refuge for the persecuted and the sense that, without additional overseas outlets for refuge, the nation would be able to shelter only those who fled "in hot blood."

Parliamentary debate on an aliens bill began in earnest in April of 1904 and continued through the summer of 1905. Though members of both houses of Parliament continued to argue over the desirability of alien immigration in general, A. J. Balfour's Conservative administration was forced to deflect charges that the bill would end the tradition of asylum for refugees. MP Charles Dilke led the charge from the Liberal opposition, but Home Secretary Aretas Akers-Douglas denied that the government had any such intention: "This country has always been the asylum for the persecuted and the oppressed." He continued, "It would be a great breach of national hospitality if we were now, and for the first time, to close our doors against political refugees and against those who solely are the victims of political tyranny."[77] Indeed, he had already offered an amendment to the bill that, following the pattern of the 1870 Extradition Act, exempted those fleeing "prosecution for a political offence" whether or not they met the means test. Only one Conservative, Sir Carne Rasch, spoke against even this measure, defiantly stating that he "would welcome any Bill which would have the effect of keeping out political refugees of that [the French Communards'] sort, some of whom had succeeded in getting here, and had done the country more harm than good."[78]

By May 1905, politicians agreed that excluding religious refugees, like the sanctified Huguenots, from the bill's exemptions was troublesome. This was especially true in the wake of renewed violence against Jews in the course of the revolution in Russian that year. Even Evans-Gordon agreed that the "outbreaks of violence, such as have recently occurred at Kischineff, which the authorities took no immediate or adequate steps to prevent" were truly "deplorable."[79] The home secretary offered to add a clause that safeguarded those who fled religious prosecutions as well. For the next two months, the House of Commons debated whether asylum seekers deserved protection from "persecutions" or "prosecutions." As MP Charles Trevelyan argued, the refugee "rarely comes having escaped from a Bastille or the Siberian Mines. He has to fly beforehand."[80] When put forward as a question to the House, Conservatives found it unconscionable to disagree with Trevelyan's assessment. Lord Hugh Cecil poignantly insisted that no refugee could be told "that because he had not a certain property standard he was to be sent back whence he came." Cecil "was sure there was no body of Englishmen who would tolerate such a thing" and "invited the Government to adopt some remedy which would prevent this Bill from being used in a way that would be an outrage on the moral sense of every Englishman." Balfour too agreed that "there is not a man in the House who would not have the deepest sympathy for anybody of whom that [i.e., that he was a victim of religious persecution] could be truly said."[81]

As the home secretary put it, the difficulty with a new amendment that included "persecution" was that it might admit too many potential refugees, too many people who could arrive "saying they are suffering from political persecution." Balfour drew a line between political refugees and those who sought religious refuge. Although he did not deny that foreigners could be entitled to asylum on the grounds of religious persecution, Balfour did not know how to define religious persecution narrowly enough to bar foreign opportunists from Britain. Whereas Balfour dismissed much of Jewish life in Russia as merely "disagreeable," Trevelyan believed that it was precisely this general tendency toward bad governance and disagreement with a bad government that made the asylum a moral necessity. Rather than limit British refuge, Trevelyan sought to expand it to these Jews as well as those who opposed the military draft that had been in place for the unpopular Russo-Japanese War.[82]

In a manner reminiscent of the challenges of the previous thirty years, the debate revolved around whether refuge, when encoded in governmental policy, would be defined in broadly applicable terms, and whether that meant that slaves, violent political offenders, or a whole minority population would potentially qualify for shelter. The alternative at the turn of the twentieth century was to limit "persecution" to cases of flight from hot-blooded pursuit as the fugitive slave commissioners had stipulated in their 1876 report. Conservative proponents of immigration restriction argued the latter position in the course of the parliamentary debates, mirroring the refined definition of "persecution" developed by Anglo-Jewish philanthropists in the early 1880s. Several MPs, including Conservatives Henry Duke and J. F. Hope, suggested that "religious persecution" in the amendment apply only to a person who was "unable to live without danger to life or limb in the place of his domicile." Even Evans-Gordon acquiesced to the use of the word *persecution* in a new amendment if so qualified.[83] This did not go far enough for the opposition. Lord Asquith and trade unionist John Burns both argued that the amendment ought to include individuals facing "danger to life, limb or liberty."[84] For Conservatives, *liberty* was simply too broad a term. It would open the floodgates to those who fled in search of a better life, including morally suspect draft dodgers, as well as those who fled genuine persecution.[85]

Thanks to Conservative political majorities, the final act contained the more restrictive language. A destitute alien was to be considered undesirable unless able to prove that

> he is seeking admission to this country solely to avoid prosecution or punishment on religious or political grounds or for an offence of a political character, or persecution, involving danger of imprisonment or danger to life or limb, on account of religious belief. (5 Edw. VII. c.13, sect. 1[3][d])

The act thus preserved the tradition of asylum for persecuted foreigners. It offered a capstone to nineteenth-century humanitarianism and exemplified the moral stakes surrounding the politics of refuge. Developed in a British context, the moral power of the imperative was enough to make even unwilling politicians take note. But the victory was a mixed one. Though it enshrined a broad exemption for foreigners in law, one that was much broader than had been written into the

1870 Extradition Act, the amendment was significantly narrower than it might have been.

By the turn of the century, Liberals conceived of a broader, more inclusive humanitarian practice. In their quest to systematize refuge in a way that delimited the numbers of potential claimants on British hospitality, philanthropists and Conservative politicians alike checked these expansive claims. Despite national consensus on a commitment to refuge, refugee supporters were forced to compromise. For now at least, those who simply sought to escape from obnoxious governance would be considered insufficiently persecuted to belong to the refugee category.

Moreover, this legal codification shifted the location of the debate. It had the effect of bureaucratizing decision making about who was a deserving refugee. Officials would be the ones to take Britain's apparently diminished capacities for refuge into account. This worked; the number of persecuted foreigners who sought refuge in Britain shrank considerably in the following years. Few commentators took note of this change. Shifted out of the public arena into the world of bureaucrats, refuge was no longer the proud act of a morally demanding public. The moral force of refuge, which fed on public mobilization, thus faded into the background.

Conclusion

Moral Politics and the Quest for a Language of Right

Modern moral claims are "bounded only by our capacities to meet them," writes sociologist Allan Silver. Silver continues to explain that "because they are limitless, the ideal forms of helping contain an intrinsic failure. No matter what we may accomplish, there lies beyond the shimmering possibility of yet further achievements of disinterestedness, generosity, and helpfulness."[1] Moral emotions disdain the pragmatic concerns of scarcity, budgets, and power. Humanitarian relief as a real-world practice, however, does not have this luxury. This is what separates policy from the proud didactic narratives that made the refugee category potentially universal in scope, and the provision of refuge a powerful public commitment in the nineteenth century.

The disjuncture between moral emotions and considerations of scarcity parallels modern liberal societies' approaches to rights and laws. Liberal ideology assumes that issues of scarcity belong to the market, whereas the law houses the peremptory and unconditional demands of rights, the ultimate guarantee of an ethical commitment. There is a powerful thread of continuity between the largely nineteenth-century story of *Britannia's Embrace* and contemporary humanitarian politics.

The impression that law provides an absolute commitment has, if anything, become more powerful over the last half century. Activists and politicians worldwide have looked to the language of human rights as a means of transcending the political stalemates of the age, particularly during the Cold War and decolonization. Enshrine humanitarian commitments as legally enforceable rights, they contend, and an era of lasting peace ought to follow.[2] This "last utopia" of human rights law is all the more tantalizing for those concerned about refugees, for whom there is as yet no guarantee of asylum enshrined in international human rights law.[3] Seemingly less subject to the vicissitudes of public opinion or popular politics, a formalized code of rights holds out the possibility of transcending anti-alien sentiment and racism.

In fact, the history of British refuge demonstrates that there is a deep connection between resources and humanitarian commitments. It is hard to develop pride in and commitment to humanitarian promises if there is no ability to deliver on them.[4] Throughout the nineteenth century, Britain's political and economic ascendancy, including its resources of empire, made it increasingly plausible for Britain to pose as the refuge par excellence, the empire open to refugees of all races, classes, and creeds. Indeed, the seeming abundance of overseas refuges was what allowed the British to remain so welcoming of dissenters, Catholics, democrats, ex-slaves, and others whose long-term resettlement in the British Isles might have caused alarm. The sweep of the public's moral commitment to refuge thus increased during the period of Britain's waxing fortunes. Conversely, as the nation's relative imperial power began to wane, Britons began to hedge their moral commitments.

The decline of British asylum did not simply reverse the category's historical evolution. Britons scaled back on their moral commitments in a manner characteristic of moral politics. After 1870, when the British found it increasingly difficult to find destinations for refugee transmigration, they began whittling away at the scope of the refugee category. They did not default in an overt and carefully controlled manner, say, by promising refuge to one in three persecuted persons or whatever number they thought would realistically suit their available capacities. Instead, they narrowed the refugee category while claiming to be honoring it, by quibbling, for example, about the degree of persecution required to make someone a refugee. They thus sought to preserve the illusion that they were just as morally committed—and just as morally righteous—as ever. Yet, they were responding to the limitations of resources and of power. This pattern of manipulating categories foreshadows the problems with relying upon law as an ironclad guarantee of humanitarian action.

From a twenty-first-century vantage point, writing protections for refugees into law seems like a natural goal for humanitarian activists. In the nineteenth century, although public commentators came to assume that the British had an obligation to provide refuge, their quest to legally codify this commitment was somewhat accidental. New extradition treaties signed with the United States in the

1840s and with France in the 1860s raised concern about the status of refugees—refugee slaves in the first case, political offenders in the second. Activists and legal scholars sought to protect these persecuted foreigners, leading to the 1870 debut of a right to asylum in British domestic and international law. The same could be said of the 1905 Aliens Act. Activists and politicians sought to preserve British refuge by making it a legal right for the persecuted only when the passage of immigration restrictions seemed inevitable. As legal scholar and barrister Norman Wise Sibley noted in 1906, "probably the most important feature of the aliens act, the severest act on the subject of alien immigration in many respects, that has found a place on the statute book for eighty years," was that it "contain[ed] the most comprehensive declaration of the Right of Asylum that is to be found in the whole range of municipal legislation, not merely in the history of this country, but throughout the civilized world."[5] As Sibley observed, the scope of the 1905 exemption clause for the persecuted was unprecedented and remained exceptional in international human rights law for decades to come.[6]

By codifying asylum in law, refuge provision can be partly insulated from the vicissitudes of public opinion. It becomes bureaucratized and systematized. Codifying particular categories in law moves them from the emotionally charged world of narrative to a newly abstract and logically consistent plane, as John Stuart Mill, among others, discovered when he failed to find a legal formula that would exclude Irish Fenians from the category of political offenders in the late 1860s.

Activists and legal scholars sought to formalize refugees' rights in international law after the Second World War. French jurist René Cassin hoped to see a right to asylum in the 1948 United Nations Universal Declaration of Human Rights, but opponents argued that it undermined the right and duty of sovereign states to protect their own citizens. Furthermore, British delegates, among others, denounced the impossibility of obligating would-be hosts to accept all who sought refuge within their borders. The resulting language assured a right "to seek and enjoy asylum" but not to receive refuge in any given country.[7] Refugees' only guarantee in law is "non-refoulement," or immunity from direct repatriation to the jurisdiction where persecution took place, something today's humanitarian activists and scholars wish to remedy.[8]

While laudable, the quest for the perfect legal formula is subject to the same sort of illusion that categorical moral demands always entail. Legal guarantees are not, in fact, failsafe. Their actual execution will always hinge upon the troublesome practical problems of how and with what resources refuge will be provided. The history of nineteenth-century British refuge suggests that power and resources are always in a dialogue with categorical moral commitments, even if the emotional logic of those commitments constantly masks this. Simply enacting a legal right to refuge, the British experience suggests, would not itself guarantee the actual provision of refuge.

For example, the 1870 Extradition Act exempted all political offenders from deportation requests. In subsequent rulings, however, British judges narrowed the application of "political offences" to acts committed at times of open insurrection. This dynamic has been repeated in the vetting of asylum seekers across the globe and in other humanitarian crises as well. The case of genocide, which is linked to the strongest set of commitments in current international law, provides a tragic reminder. As the international response to the Rwandan genocide in 1994 illustrates, the onset of mass murder does not prevent onlookers from quibbling about definitions, proposing half-measures, and shifting responsibilities.[9]

The nineteenth-century British story further suggests that crystallizing refugees' rights in law can create uniformity of application and dedicated bureaucratic enforcement, but it can also have unintended consequences. When the provision, dramatization, and enforcement of refugee relief was removed from the public, Britons lost sight of the moral mission that linked refuge to the identity of the nation. Once members of the metropolitan public demobilized after the fugitive slave circular debate, believing the challenge to refuge had been eliminated, their attention waned over the ensuing decades. There was no public outcry when officials of the Imperial British East African Company returned escaped slaves to their masters. The passage of the 1905 Aliens Act, which extended an official welcome to all persecuted persons, whether or not they had the requisite £5 to their name, led the activist public to believe that the tradition of British refuge had been safeguarded. Yet the provisions of the act left determinations about persecution to officials. Such decision making has become part and parcel of the asylum-seeking process that increasingly takes place out of the public eye and reduces government willingness to mobilize the flow of resources necessary to provide refuge.[10] Much to activists' chagrin and often despite their best efforts, the public, having relinquished the process of judgment to distant and seemingly unaccountable officials, is just as likely to become exercised about excessive generosity as dishonorable refusals of hospitality. In the process, the British public's readiness to "remember the refugees" has become more the stuff of myth than contemporary reality.[11]

The forgotten history of Britain's nineteenth-century invention of modern refuge has several important analytical implications. First, nineteenth-century British refuge demonstrates the power of moral storytelling to kindle public enthusiasm for a broad-based humanitarian commitment. Second, it underscores the uneasy relationship between popular humanitarian movements and the institutionalization of the moral norms they create as legal categories and codified rights. Third, it emphasizes the importance of power and resources in creating and sustaining humanitarian moral fervor. The interaction between these three elements—cultural narratives, law, and resources—continues to shape humanitarian and human rights movements today.

Notes

INTRODUCTION

1. Lord Malmesbury to Lord Westmoreland, H. M. Ambassador at Vienna, on his first interview with Count Buol, London, March 8, 1852, in Malmesbury, *Memoirs of an Ex-Minister; An Autobiography* (London: Longmans, Green and Co., 1884), 313.
2. "Refugee, n," *The Oxford English Dictionary Online* (Oxford: Oxford University Press, 2014), http://www.oed.com/view/Entry/161121?rskey=W89aMP&result=1, accessed August 28, 2014; "Refugees," *Encyclopedia Britannica*, 3rd edn., Vol. 16, Pt. 1 (Edinburgh: A. Bell and C. Macfarquhar, 1796), 51.
3. Harriet Beecher Stowe, *Uncle Tom's Cabin, or Life among the Lowly* (Philadelphia: Henry Altemus, 1900), 281–282; *L'Homme*, October 31, 1855. "Car l'amoindrissement est quelque chose de plus triste encore que le bannissement, et le dédain de l'histoire ne vas pas au front haut, mais à la tête basse." ("Because dishonor [*amoindrissement*] is something sadder than banishment, and contempt for history does not proceed with its head held high, but lowered in shame.")
4. France and America offer the closest parallels in the development of refuge, as the language of republicanism and of democracy made European revolutionaries particularly sympathetic. Of these two, however, only the French systematically distinguished refugees from other foreigners prior to the end of the nineteenth century. The revolutionary Constitution of 1793 invited political allies to France, hoping that they would fight for the revolutionary order. In republican circles, revolutionary exiles were fêted into the 1840s. Nevertheless, refuge in France was a matter of state policy. The fate of refugees depended on the survival of the host government. Greg Burgess, *Refuge in the Land of Liberty: France and its Refugees, from the Revolution to the End of Asylum, 1787–1939* (New York: Palgrave Macmillan, 2008); Gérard Noiriel, *La Tyrannie du National: le droit d'asile en Europe, 1793–1993* (Paris: Calman-Lévy, 1991). American ideology did not develop a comparable cultural-political imperative to provide for refugees in particular. As a country of immigration unlike Britain or France, America's mythology collapses refugees into the broader category of foreigners; Emma Lazarus's "huddled masses" included all individuals seeking a better life, not just persecuted refugees. Marilyn Baseler's book on American asylum emphasizes America as a refuge for the persecuted during the colonial period, a point that I underscore in my discussion of British use of colonial outlets for refugees. More generally, however,

Baseler collapses "refugee" and "immigrant." *Asylum for Mankind: America, 1607–1800* (Ithaca, NY: Cornell University Press, 1998).

5. Andreas Fahrmeir, *Citizens and Aliens: Foreigners and the Law in Britain and the German States, 1789–1870* (New York: Berghahn Books, 2000), 238; David Feldman, "The Boundaries of Welfare," *History in Focus* 11 (Autumn 2006), available from http://www.history.ac.uk/ihr/Focus/Migration/articles/feldman.html.

6. Num. 35: 6–34; Deut. 19: 1–13; Josh. 20. With attempts to solidify state power since the Reformation, the willingness of the state to cede such powers to prosecute political enemies diminished greatly. Thomas John de Mazzinghi, *Sanctuaries* (Stafford, UK: Halden & Son, 1887), 101.
7. Patrick Joyce, *The Rule of Freedom: Liberalism and the Modern City* (London: Verso, 2003). For a recent taxonomy of liberalism as a behavioral norm and a political and economic ideology, see James Vernon and Simon Gunn, "Introduction: What was Liberal Modernity and Why was it Peculiar in Imperial Britain?," in *The Peculiarities of Liberty Modernity in Imperial Britain*, edited by Gunn and Vernon (Berkeley: University of California Press, 2011), 1–18.
8. J. S. Mill, *On Liberty* (London: Longmans, Green & Co., 1867); Samuel Smiles, *The Huguenots: Their Settlements, Churches and Industries in England and Ireland* (London: John Murray, 1867).
9. Colin Holmes's *John Bull's Island: Immigration and British Society, 1871–1971* (Houndmills, Basingstoke, Hampshire: Macmillan, 1988) opened a new field of study in this respect. Scholars have since explored individual migrant communities. See, for example, Todd Endelman, *Radical Assimilation in English Jewish History, 1656–1945* (Bloomington: Indiana University Press, 1990); David Feldman, *Englishmen and Jews: Social Relations and Political Culture, 1840–1914* (New Haven, CT: Yale University Press, 1994); Rosemary Ashton, *Little Germany: Exile and Asylum in Victorian England* (Oxford: Oxford University Press, 1986); Panikos Panayi, *German Immigrants in Britain during the Nineteenth Century, 1815–1914* (Oxford: Berg Publishers, 1995); Lucio Sponza, *Italian Immigrants in Nineteenth-Century Britain: Realities and Images* (Leicester, UK: Leicester University Press, 1988).
10. Davide Rodogno highlights Foreign Office reluctance to intervene in overseas crises even in the wake of massacres. His argument is part of a broader dispute over the role of public opinion, which he sets against that of Gary Bass who holds that public humanitarian pressure gave rise to governmental interventionism. *Britannia's Embrace* charts a different course, arguing that relief to refugees was a common denominator on which the Foreign Office and an exercised public agreed and worked together to create a viable humanitarian practice. Rodogno, *Against Massacre: Humanitarian Interventions in the Ottoman Empire, 1815–1914* (Princeton, NJ: Princeton University Press, 2012), 16–17; Bass, *Freedom's Battle: The Origins of Humanitarian Intervention* (New York: Alfred Knopf, 2008).

    Michael Barnett distinguishes between emergency and alchemical humanitarianism, the former treating crises, the latter treating underlying causes. While I grant that the two have become more distinct in the increasingly bureaucratized world of the twentieth and twenty-first centuries, the history of refugee support in the long nineteenth century demonstrates ably how interconnected the two were in origin, not just conceptually—as I think Barnett would agree—but in terms of relief organizations, as well. Barnett, *Empire of Humanity: A History of Humanitarianism* (Ithaca, NY: Cornell University Press, 2011), 10.

11. George Julian Harney, "Political Refugees," *The Vanguard, A Weekly Journal* (London: J. P. Crantz, 1853), 16.
12. Anthropologist Liisa Malkki rightly urges activists and officials to avoid this tendency to marginalize individual refugee voices, which remains problematic today. Malkki, "Refugees and Exile: From 'Refugee Studies' to the National Order of Things," *Annual Review of Anthropology* 23 (1995): 511–512.
13. Prakash Shah, *Refugees, Race and the Legal Concept of Asylum in Britain* (London: Cavendish, 2000).
14. Thomas Holt, *The Problems of Freedom: Race, Labor, and Politics in Britain and Jamaica, 1832–1938* (Baltimore: Johns Hopkins University Press, 1991); Catherine Hall, *Civilising Subjects: Metropole and Colony in the English Imagination 1830–1867* (Chicago: University of Chicago Press, 2002).
15. Liza Schuster, *The Use and Abuse of Political Asylum in Britain & Germany* (London: Frank Cass, 2003), 83–84.
16. Christian Joppke, *Immigration and the Nation-State: The United States, Germany, and Great Britain* (Oxford: Oxford University Press, 1999), 129. On rising racism, see Susan Pennybacker, *From Scottsboro to Munich: Race and Political Culture in 1930s Britain* (Princeton, NJ: Princeton University Press, 2009). English historians have largely rejected this past as self-serving nostalgia, a history used as a means of dismissing foreigners now seeking asylum. For critiques of this usage of the past see, among others, Tony Kushner, *Remembering Refugees: Then and Now* (Manchester: Manchester University Press, 2006), and Kushner, *The Battle for Britishness* (Manchester: Manchester University Press, 2014).
17. The exception to this trend is Greg Burgess's examination of refugees in France during the nineteenth and twentieth centuries. Burgess, *Refuge in the Land of Liberty.*
18. This is the core of Bernard Porter's argument, which has shaped the literature since its initial publication in 1979. Porter, *The Refugee Question in Mid-Victorian Politics* (Cambridge: Cambridge University Press, 1979); Porter, "Asylum of the Nations: Britain and the Refugees of 1848," in *Exiles from European Revolutions: Refugees in Mid-Victorian England,* edited by Sabine Freitag (New York: Berghahn Books, 2003), 43–58; John Garrard, *The English and Immigration, 1880–1910* (London: Oxford University Press, 1971); Bernard Gainer, *Alien Invasion: The Origins of the Aliens Act of 1905* (London: Heinemann Educational Books, 1972); Colin Holmes, *John Bull's Island* and *Immigrants and Minorities in British Society* (London: George Allen & Unwin, 1978); Kushner, *Remembering Our Refugees*; Michael Marrus, *The Unwanted. European Refugees in the Twentieth Century* (Philadelphia: Temple University Press, 1985); and Schuster, *The Use and Abuse of Political Asylum.*
19. Aristide Zolberg, "Who is a Refugee?," in *Escape From Violence: Conflict and the Refugee Crisis in the Third World,* edited by Zolberg et al. (Oxford: Oxford University Press, 1989), 5–10.
20. Zolberg draws on Michael Marrus's study of refugees and the development of international relief organizations in the postwar world. Claudena Skran focuses her account of the rise of an international refugee regime on the interwar era. Most recently, Peter Gatrell has offered a comprehensive account of the making

of refugee flights, their experiences, and their reception in the twentieth century. Marrus, *The Unwanted*; Skran, *Refugees in Inter-war Europe: The Emergence of a Regime* (Oxford: Clarendon Press, 1995); Gatrell, *The Making of the Modern Refugee* (Oxford: Oxford University Press, 2013).

21. See, for example, Peter Gatrell, *Free World?: The Campaign to Save the World's Refugees, 1956–1963* (Cambridge: Cambridge University Press, 2011); Gatrell, *The Making of the Modern Refugee*; Philip Marfleet, "Refugees and History: Why We Must Address the Past," *Refugee Survey Quarterly* 26, no. 3 (2007): 136–148; and Niklaus Steiner, *Arguing About Asylum: The Complexity of Refugee Debates in Europe* (New York: St. Martin's Press, 2000).

22. Norbert Gossman, "British Aid to Polish, Italian and Hungarian Exiles, 1830–1870," *South Atlantic Quarterly* 63, no. 2 (1969): 231–245; Porter, *Refugee Question* and *Exiles from European Revolutions*; Margot Finn, *After Chartism: Class and Nation in English Radical Politics, 1848–1874* (Cambridge: Cambridge University Press, 1993); Maura O'Connor, *The Romance of Italy and the English Political Imagination* (New York: St. Martin's Press, 1998); Jonathan Parry, *The Politics of Patriotism: English Liberalism, National Identity and Europe, 1830–1886* (Cambridge: Cambridge University Press, 2006); Laura Tabili, *Global Migrants, Local Culture: Natives and Newcomers in Provincial England, 1841–1939* (Houndsmill, UK: Palgrave Macmillan, 2011).

23. Alan Lester and Rob Skinner, "Humanitarianism and Empire: New Research Agendas," *The Journal of Imperial and Commonwealth History* 40, no. 5 (2012): 731. It is within this literature that an international as well as imperial frame has become increasingly important. See, among others, Frank Trentmann, Kevin Grant, and Philippa Levine, eds., *Beyond Sovereignty: Britain, Empire and Transnationalism, c. 1860–1950* (London: Palgrave Macmillan, 2007); Kevin Grant, *A Civilised Savagery: Britain and the New Slaveries in Africa, 1884–1926* (London: Routledge, 2005); Mark Mazower, *No Enchanted Palace: The End of Empire and the Ideological Origins of the United Nations* (Princeton, NJ: Princeton University Press, 2009); and Susan Pedersen, *The Guardians: The League of Nations and the Crisis of Empire*, (Oxford & New York: Oxford University Press, 2015).

24. While most scholars simply write about either humanitarianism or human rights, Samuel Moyn emphatically separates the two in *The Last Utopia: Human Rights in History* (Cambridge, MA: Harvard/Belknap Press, 2010), 72. Some historians have begun to address this disconnect. See, for instance, Michelle Tusan, "'Crimes against Humanity': Human Rights, the British Empire, and the Origins of the Response to the Armenian Genocide," *American Historical Review* 119 (February 2014): 47–77. Other social scientists, including scholars of refugee studies, have noted the tensions in this divide for some time. In a 2008 essay, sociologist Craig Calhoun notes the tensions in this distinction in refugee relief and more broadly within humanitarianism. The "imperative to reduce suffering" is about relief in crises and about bettering the human condition. As impossible as it is to distinguish between "complex emergencies" and long-term abuses—the one being the symptom of the other—Calhoun warns against discarding either form of relief. Calhoun, "The Imperative to Reduce Suffering: Charity, Progress, and Emergencies in the Field of Humanitarian Action," in *Humanitarianism in Question: Politics, Power, Ethics*, edited by Michael Barnett and Thomas G. Weiss (Ithaca, NY: Cornell University Press, 2008), 73–97, 74–75, 88, 90.

1. Marquis of Landsdown, December 21, 1792, in William Cobbett, *Parliamentary History of England* 30 (13 December 1792—10 March 1794), col. 150. These figures vary. Kirsty Carpenter cites a total of twenty to twenty-five thousand as more reasonable, but likely high. Carpenter, *Refugees of the French Revolution: Emigrés in London, 1789–1802* (London: Macmillian, 1999), 43, n. 61 on p. 217.
2. Samuel Romilly to M. Dumont, September 15, from *Romilly Memoirs*, quoted in E. M. Wilkinson, "French Emigrés in England, 1789–1802: Their Reception and Impact on English Life," thesis, 1952, 107.
3. Frances Burney, *Brief Reflections Relative to the Emigrant French Clergy: Earnestly Submitted to the Humane Consideration of the Ladies of Great Britain* (London: T. Cadell, 1793), 14.
4. Linda Colley, *Britons: Forging the Nation, 1707–1837* (New Haven, CT: Yale University Press, 1992).
5. These older communities had received the support of the Crown since the reign of Edward VI, whose support was likewise strategic, part of his interest in bolstering the nascent Anglican Church.
6. Estimates range from 200,000 to a million. Roy Sundstrom, "French Huguenots and the Civil List, 1696–1727: A Study of Alien Assimilation in England," *Albion* 8, no. 3 (Autumn 1976): 219–235, 220.
7. John Hintermaier, "The First Modern Refugees? Charity, Entitlement and Persuasion in the Huguenot Immigration of the 1680s," *Albion* 32, no. 3 (Autumn, 2000): 441.
8. Bernard Cottret, *The Huguenots in England: Immigration and Settlement, 1550–1700*, trans. Peregrine and Adriana Stevenson (Cambridge: Cambridge University Press, 1991), 185–186, quoting Bodleian Library, Rawlinson MSS A.478, f. 30; Daniel Statt, *Foreigners and Englishmen: The Controversy over Immigration and Population, 1660–1760* (Newark: University of Delaware Press, 1995), 54.
9. William A. Shaw, "The English Government and the Relief of Protestant Refugees," *The English Historical Review* 9, no. 36 (October 1894): 662–683, n. 2.
10. Sundstrom, "French Huguenots and the Civil List," 222; Robin Gwynn, *Huguenot Heritage: The History and Contribution of the Huguenots in Britain* (London: Routledge and Kegan Paul, 1985), 58.
11. Reginald Lane Poole, *A History of the Huguenots of the Dispersion at the Recall of the Edict of Nantes* (London: Macmillan, 1880), 81. The number tells us nothing about how many settled in England. Many were likely on their way elsewhere. Robin Gwynn cites eight to ten thousand as the number likely in England at this time. Gwynn, "James II in the Light of His Treatment of Huguenot Refugees in England, 1685–1686," *The English Historical Review* 92, no. 365 (October 1977): 820.
12. Gwynn, "James II in the Light of His Treatment of Huguenot Refugees," 822.
13. Hintermaier, "The First Modern Refugees?" 435.
14. Cottret, *The Huguenots in England*, 189–190, citing *Memorial from the English Protestants*, in a *Collection of State Tracts* 1 (London, 1705), 1–37; Poole, *A History of the Huguenots of the Dispersion*, 79.
15. William Shaw, "The English Government and the Relief of Protestant Refugees," n. 2.
16. Gwynn, "James II in the Light of His Treatment of Huguenot Refugees," 826.
17. Cottret, *The Huguenots in England*, 191.

18. Samuel Smiles, *The Huguenots: Their Settlements, Churches, and Industries in England and Ireland* (New York: Harper and Brothers, 1868), 214.
19. William Shaw, "The English Government and the Relief of Protestant Refugees," n. 3.
20. Sundstrom, "French Huguenots and the Civil List," 223.
21. Wilkinson, "French Emigrés in England, 1789–1802," 115.
22. Carpenter, *Refugees of the French Revolution*, 45; Minutes of the Committee of Subscribers for the Relief of the French Clergy, September 1792–November 1793, British Library Manuscript Collection (hereafter cited as BL MSS) 18,591, no. 1.
23. Wilkinson, "French Emigrés in England, 1789–1802," 116.
24. Donna Andrew, *Philanthropy and Police: London Charity in the Eighteenth Century* (Princeton, NJ: Princeton University Press, 1989), 5.
25. Adam Clarke, "The Nature, Design, Rules and Regulations of a Charitable Institution termed the Stranger's Friend" (London, 1798), 10. For Michael Roberts, this emphasis enabled Methodist charities to work more readily with local authorities. "Head versus Heart? Voluntary Associations and Charity Organization in England, c. 1700–1850," in *Charity, Philanthropy, and Reform*, ed. Hugh Cunningham and Joanna Innes (New York: St. Martin's Press, 1998), 72.
26. For example, speech of Lord Landsdown, December 21, 1792 in Cobbett, *Parliamentary History*, col. 151.
27. Margery Weiner, *The French Exiles, 1789–1815* (London: John Murray, 1960), 49–50; La Marquise de la Tour du Pin, *Recollections of the Revolution and the Empire from the French of the "Journal d'une Femme de Cinquante Ans,"* trans. and ed. Walter Geer (New York: Brentano's Press, 1920), 283.
28. Wilkinson, "French Emigrés in England, 1789–1802," 88.
29. Charlotte Smith, quoted by Loraine Fletcher, *Charlotte Smith: a Critical Biography* (Houndsmills, UK: Macmillan, 1998), 56.
30. Fletcher, *Charlotte Smith*, 196.
31. Nigel Aston, "Burke, Boisgelin and the Politics of the Émigré Bishops," in *The French Émigrés in Europe and the Struggle against Revolution, 1789–1814*, ed. Kirsty Carpenter and Philip Mansel (London: Macmillan, 1999), 197–198.
32. Thomas Macknight, *History of the Life and Times of Edmund Burke* 3 (London: Chapman and Hall, 1860), 660. See also Aston, "Burke, Boisgelin and the Politics of the Émigré Bishops," 208; and Carpenter, *Refugees of the French Revolution*, 108.
33. Frances Burney, *The Diary and Letters of Madame D'Arblay, Vol. 3, 1792–1840* (London: Vizetelly, 1891), 52; Linda Kelly, *Juniper Hall: An English Refuge from the French Revolution* (London: Weidenfeld and Nicolson, 1991).
34. Ian Haywood and John See, eds., *The Gordon Riots: Politics, Culture, and Insurrection in Eighteenth-Century Britain* (Cambridge: Cambridge University Press, 2012).
35. Advertisement for Foxe's *Book of Martyrs, Hampshire Chronicle*, Winchester, England, December 10, 1792, p. 2.
36. Hannah More, "Remarks on the Speech of M. Dupont, made in the National Convention of France on the Subject of Religion and Public Education. A Prefatory Address to the Ladies, &c. of Great Britain—In Behalf of the French Emigrant Clergy," in *The Works of Hannah More* (New York: Harper and Brothers, Publishers, 1852), 302.
37. James Epstein, *Radical Expression: Political Language, Ritual, and Symbol in England, 1790–1850* (Oxford: Oxford University Press, 1994), 6.

38. Ibid., 5.
39. Henry Dundas to Lord Kenyon, Lord Loughborough, and Lord Chief Baron, September 12, 1792, National Archives, HO 43/4, Domestic Letter Book, March 27, 1792–February 27, 1794, f. 95–96; E. P. Thompson, *Making of the English Working Class* (London: Penguin Books, 1990), chap. 5, especially 114–117.
40. Clive Emsley, "The London 'Insurrection' of December 1792: Fact, Fiction, or Fantasy?," *Journal of British Studies* 17, no. 2 (Spring 1978): 72.
41. Marianne Elliott, *Partners in Revolution: The United Irishmen and France* (New Haven, CT: Yale University Press, 1982).
42. Emsley, "The London 'Insurrection' of December 1792," 66.
43. Elliott, *Partners in Revolution*, 39–40.
44. Elizabeth Sparrow, *Secret Service: British Agents in France, 1792–1815* (Woodbridge, Suffolk, UK: Boydell Press, 1999), 24; Caitlin Anderson, "Britons Abroad, Aliens at Home: Nationality Law and policy in Britain, 1815–1870," (PhD diss, Trinity College, Cambridge, Faculty of History, 2004), 29.
45. Sparrow, *Secret Service*, 25. Sparrow cites this on the authorities of the secretaries to the Home Office William Wickham.
46. Sparrow, *Secret Service*, chap. 2; Anderson, "Britons Abroad, Aliens at Home," chap. 1, 25–30 especially; J. R. Dinwiddy, *Radicalism and Reform in Britain, 1780–1850* (London: Hambledon Press, 1992), chap. 8.
47. Aliens' Entry Books, National Archives, HO 5/1, Correspondence, 1794–1796.
48. Cobbett, *Parliamentary History* 30, cols. 201–202. Hardinge identified a third, "neutral" category of alien—the alien merchant and lamented the "necessary evil" of oppressing his movements.
49. Dundas to Sheffield, September 22, National Archives, HO 43/4, Domestic Letter Books, f. 100. See Aliens' Entry Books, National Archives, HO 5/1, Correspondence, for many instances in which émigrés were deemed to be of good character and to be assisted with passports at the ports, e.g., f. 253.
50. Rieko Karatani, *Defining British Citizenship: Empire, Commonwealth and Modern Britain* (London: Frank Cass, 2003) 64,n. 32.
51. Cobbett, *Parliamentary History* 30, col. 225.
52. Clive Emsley, "The London 'Insurrection' of December 1792," 69; Cobbett, *Parliamentary History* 30, cols. 398–399.
53. Petition from the Committee to the King, dated April 5, 1793, entered on April 8 into Minutes of the Committee of Subscribers for the Relief of the French Clergy, September 1792–November 1793, BL MSS 18,591, no. 1, f. 91–92, 93–94.
54. George R. to the archbishop of Canterbury, carried by HM's command by Dundas, April 17, 1793, reprinted in William Robert Wake, *Two Sermons Preached in the Parish Church of St. Michael, One on the Fast-Day, April 19; The Other on Occasion of Soliciting Relief for the Emigrant French Clergy, etc.* (Bath: W. Gye, 1793), 16–17.
55. Burney, "Brief Reflections," 26.
56. *The Welsh Freeholder's Farewell Epistles to the Right Rev. Samuel (Horsley) Lord Bishop, Lately of St. David's, Now of Rochester* (London: J. Johnson, 1794), vii.
57. William Williams (Rev.), A. B. of Worcester College, Oxford, *The Good Samaritan; or, Charity to Strangers Recommended. A Sermon Preached in the Parish Church of High-Wycombe, Bucks, for the French Refugee Clergy. On Sunday, the 2d June, 1793* (London: S. Cave, 1793), especially 19, 23, 25.
58. Williams, *The Good Samaritan*, 23.
59. Wilkinson, "French Emigrés in England, 1789–1802," 337.

60. Ibid., 177, 178; William Maxwell, "Dr. Maxwell's Address," *Times* (London),September 12, 1792, p. 1.
61. George Henry Glasse, "Art. 44: Preached at the Parish Church of Hanwell, Middlesex, June 16, 1793, after reading HM's letter in favor of the French Emigrant Clergy," *The Monthly Review* 13 (January–April 1794): 357–358.
62. Ibid.
63. Accounts of the Expenditure for the Relief of the French Clergy, 1792–1801, BL Add. MSS 18,593, no folio.
64. Cobbett, *Parliamentary History* 27 (February 14, 1788–May 14, 1789), col. 616.
65. As Wilmot wrote about the claims process, it should be confined to an Enquiry into the "*losses and services* of those who had suffered in their rights, properties, and professions, in consequence of their *Loyalty* to his majesty and attachment to the British government." Wilmot, *Historical View of the Commission for Enquiring into the Losses, Services and Claims of the American Loyalists, at the Close of the War between Great Britain and her Colonies, in 1783* (London: J. Nichols, Son, and Bentley, 1815), 42.
66. Wilmot, *Historical View of the Commission*, 70–71. For the Loyalist diaspora, see Maya Jasanoff, *Liberty's Exiles: American Loyalists in the Revolutionary World* (New York: Alfred A. Knopf, 2011); Christopher Moore, *The Loyalists: Revolution, Exile, Settlement* (Toronto: McClelland and Stewart, Inc., 1984); Mary Beth Norton, *The British-Americans: The Loyalist Exiles in England, 1774–1789* (London: Constable, 1974).
67. Committee for the Relief of the French Laity, Committee Resolution, October 17, 1792, BL Add. MSS 18,591.
68. Cobbett, *Parliamentary History* 31 (March 14, 1794–May 22, 1795), cols. 242–243; W. Wyndham, Minister in Tuscany for pensions and allowances to Toulonese and Corsican refugees, 1797–1807, National Archives, AO 1/851/7, Roll 7.
69. Cobbett, *Parliamentary History* 31, cols. 391–392.
70. Ibid., col. 1389.
71. Burney proposed a scheme whereby ten women were each to find ten more women to subscribe to the fund. The network would expand in this manner until it reached two hundred members. Although each woman was to donate no more than a guinea each, the campaign was to raise enough funds to prevent the émigrés from starving. Letter from Wilmot enclosing the following plan at the request of Dr. Burney, September 2, 1793, BL Add. MSS 18,591, f. 120.
72. Committee for the Relief of the French Laity, December 14, 1793, National Archives, T 93/1, f. 1–2.
73. Committee for the Relief of the French Laity, December 14, 1793, National Archives, T 93/1, f. 2–5.
74. Wilkinson, "French Emigrés in England, 1789–1802," 257.
75. William Cunningham, *Alien Immigrants to England* (London: S. Sonnenschein, 1897), 259; Carpenter, *Refugees of the French Revolution*, chap. 2; Minutes of the Committee of Subscribers for the Relief of the French Clergy, no. 2, December 1793–May 1796, BL MSS 18,592, f. 92–108.
76. Committee for the Relief of the French Laity, April 16, 1795, National Archives, T 93/1.
77. *The Cambridge Modern History, Vol. 8: The French Revolution*, ed. A. W. Ward, G. W. Prothero, and Stanley Leathes (London: Macmillan, 1904), 391.

78. Carpenter, *Refugees of the French Revolution*, 92.

79. Minutes of the Committee of Subscribers for the Relief of the French Clergy, No. 2, December 1793–May 1796, Rules and Regulations, dated March 24, 1796, BL MSS 18,592, f. 209–214, 227.

80. William Wordsworth, "Emigrant French Clergy," in his *Ecclesiastical Sketches* (1822), lines 6–11; Duncan Wu in *Wordsworth's Reading, 1770–1799* (Cambridge: Cambridge University Press, 1993), 128.

CHAPTER TWO

1. "Birmingham Political Union's 3rd General Meeting, July 30, 1832," *Polonia: Regulations of the Literary Association of the Friends of Poland* 1, no. 2 (September 1832): 106.

2. Gary Bass, *Freedom's Battle: The Origins of Humanitarian Intervention* (New York: Alfred Knopf, 2008), 373. Among other scholars who examine the role of public interest in overseas intervention, see Muriel Chamberlain, *'Pax Britannica'? British Foreign Policy, 1789–1914* (London: Longman, 1988); John Clarke, *British Diplomacy and Foreign Policy, 1782–1865* (London: Unwin Hyman, 1989); Maura O'Connor, *The Romance of Italy and the English Political Imagination* (New York: St. Martin's Press, 1998).

3. Davide Rodogno, *Against Massacre: Humanitarian Interventions in the Ottoman Empire, 1815–1914* (Princeton, NJ: Princeton University Press, 2012), 16–17.

4. The 1791–1792 sugar abstention campaign, for example, involved an estimated 300,000 participants; the 1792 petition to Parliament had 390,000 adult male signatories. Clare Midgley, "Slave Sugar Boycotts, Female Activism and the Domestic Base of British Anti-Slavery Culture," *Slavery & Abolition* 17, no. 3 (December 1996): 146; Christopher Leslie Brown, *Moral Capital: Foundations of British Abolitionism* (Chapel Hill: University of North Carolina Press, 2006); Seymour Drescher, *The Mighty Experiment: Free Labor Versus Slavery in British Emancipation* (Oxford: Oxford University Press, 2002), chap. 2.

5. Ruth Paley, "Imperial Politics and English Law: The Many Contexts of *Somersett*," *Law and History Review* 24, no. 3 (Fall 2006): 659–664; Parliamentary Papers, 1824 (442), Reports by the Commissioners on the State of Africans condemned under Acts abolishing Slave Trade and apprenticed in W. Indies, A joint letter from the commissioners, containing a report on the policy of condemning runaway slaves from the French Islands, dated May 31, 1822.

6. Thomas Laqueur, "Bodies, Details, and the Humanitarian Narrative," in *The New Cultural History*, ed. Lynn Hunt (Berkeley and Los Angeles: University of California Press, 1989), 177.

7. O'Connor, *Romance of Italy*, chap. 1; David Roessel, *In Byron's Shadow: Modern Greece in the English and American Imagination* (Oxford: Oxford University Press, 2002).

8. Jerome Reich, "The Slave Trade at the Congress of Vienna—A Study in English Public Opinion," *The Journal of Negro History* 53, no. 2 (April 1968): 130, 132–133.

9. Keith Hamilton and Farida Shaikh, eds., introduction to *Slavery, Diplomacy and Empire: Britain and the Suppression of the Slave Trade, 1807–1975* (Sussex, UK: Sussex Academic Press, 2009), 8.

10. John Thurston and Sanford Arnot, "The Polish Exiles," *Morning Chronicle*), August 17, 1833, p. 3.

11. "Situation of the Polish Refugees," *Morning Chronicle*, November 11, 1834, p. 3.
12. Douglas Dakin, *The Greek Struggle for Independence, 1821–1833* (Berkeley: University of California Press, 1973), 111 and chap. 4; Clarke, *British Diplomacy and Foreign Policy*, 162, 174–176.
13. "Sufferings of the Old Polish Provinces incorporated with Russia, Address of the States of Gallicia to the Emperor of Austria," *Polonia* 1, no. 1 (August 1832): 29–30.
14. "Apology of the Rt. Hon. Sir R. Peel for the Russian Government," *Polonia* 1, no. 1 (August 1832): 30; *Report of Proceedings of the Fourth Annual General Meeting of the London Literary Association of the Friends of Poland* (London: T. Brettell, 1836), 7.
15. "Apology of the Rt. Hon. Sir R. Peel for the Russian Government," 37–38. Patient to the last, the LASFP continued to agitate in their fashion into the twentieth century. They folded only (and prematurely, as it turned out) when Poland won independence in 1924. Maude Ashurst Biggs, *Literary Association of Friends of Poland, 1832–1924: A Retrospect* (London: Curwen Press, 1924).
16. Jonathan Sperber, *The European Revolutions, 1848–1851*, 2nd ed. (Cambridge: Cambridge University Press, 2005).
17. On British reactions to 1848, see John Saville, *1848: The British State and the Chartist Movement* (Cambridge: Cambridge University Press, 1990). Colonies across the British Empire, including Ireland and India, also erupted in revolutionary violence. Ireland aside, most Britons saw this as morally unrelated to the causes of continental liberals. In Chapters Five and Six, I address these colonial crises and their relationship to the reception of foreign refugees in greater depth. For the British Empire in 1848, see Miles Taylor, "The 1848 Revolutions and the British Empire," *Past & Present* 166, no. 1 (February 2000): 146–180; Fabrice Bensimon, *Les Britanniques face à la révolution française de 1848* (Paris: L'Harmattan, 2000).
18. "Spanish and Italian Refugees," *Examiner* (London), November 30, 1828, pp. 3–4.
19. "Having Lately Brought before the Public the Case of the Poor Italian Refugees. . ." *Times* (London), July 16, 1834, p. 2.
20. Gérard Noiriel, *La Tyrannie du National: le droit d'asile en Europe, 1793–1993* (Paris: Calman-Lévy, 1991).
21. Parliamentary Papers, 1828 (542), Correspondence with British Commissioners at Sierra Leone, Havana, Rio de Janeiro and Surinam on Slave Trade, 1827 (Class A); Correspondence with Foreign Powers on Slave Trade, 1827 (Class B).
22. Article VII of the Regulations for the Mixed Commissions, attached to the Treaty between Great Britain and Portugal (signed at Vienna, January 22, 1815).
23. Removal of Liberated Africans from Cuba, National Archives, CO 318/123, West India, Miscellaneous, 1835. The mixed commission courts organized by British treaties with Spain, Portugal, Brazil, and the Netherlands tried 528 cases between 1819 and 1845. An estimated 80,000 Africans were liberated; 65,000 were emancipated in Freetown, Sierra Leone, with a further 10,000 in Havana and 3,000 in Rio de Janeiro. Leslie Bethell, "The Mixed Commissions for the Suppression of the Transatlantic Slave Trade in the Nineteenth Century," *The Journal of African History* 7, no. 1 (1966): 79, 84, 89.
24. ""Sufferings of the Old Polish Provinces incorporated with Russia," 2.
25. "A Proposition for a Grant of 10,000/- to the Polish Refugees," *Times* (London), August 10, 1835, p. 2; "The Polish Refugees," *Times* (London), July 6, 1838, p. 5.
26. *Address of the Literary Association of the Society of Friends of Poland of Great Britain and Ireland* (London: E. Detkens, Booksellers, 1846), 43.

27. "A Proposition for a Grant of 10,000/- to the Polish Refugees," p. 2; "Polish Refugees," 5.
28. *Special Report of the Bristol and Clifton Ladies' Anti-Slavery Society; During Eighteen Months, from January, 1851, to June* (London: John Snow, 1852), 7.
29. Ibid., 58.
30. Ibid., 29.
31. For a summary of the copious work on the social bases of antislavery, see Seymour Drescher, "History's Engines: British Mobilization in the Age of Revolution," *William & Mary Quarterly*, 3rd Series, 66, no. 4, (October 2009): 737–756. On the midcentury revolutionaries, see O'Connor, *Romance of Italy*; Harry Rudman, *Italian Nationalism and English Letters* (New York: Columbia University Press, 1940); Norbert Gossman, "British Aid to Polish, Italian and Hungarian Exiles, 1830–1870," *South Atlantic Quarterly* 63, no. 2 (1969): 231–245; Iowerth Prothero's and John Saville's essays in *Exiles from European Revolutions: Refugees in Mid-Victorian England*, ed. Sabine Freitag; and Margot Finn, *After Chartism: Class and Nation in English Radical Politics, 1848–1874* (Cambridge: Cambridge University Press, 1993).
32. Typewritten notes about the life of Baroness Angela Burdett-Coutts, BL MSS 46,406, A and B.
33. "Neapolitan Exile Fund," *Times* (London, England), March 21, 1859, p. 12.
34. Norbert Gossman, "British Aid to Polish, Italian and Hungarian Exiles, 1830-1870."
35. BL Add. MSS 79,743, Vol. CLIII, f. 48–53; P. K. Martinez, "Paris Communard Refugees in Britain, 1871–1880" (PhD diss., University of Sussex, 1981), 66; Letter from Louis Blanc to Frederick Harrison, November 25, 1871, Special Collections of the London School of Economics, Harrison Collection, 1/21, Correspondence, 1870–1911.
36. On this general preference at the time to avoid facing the challenges of engineering a postslavery social order, see Catherine Hall, *Civilising Subjects: Colony and Metropole* (Chicago: University of Chicago Press, 2002).
37. *The Star of Freedom* (London), June 26, 1852, p. 1.
38. "Poland, Hungary and England," *Northern Star* (Leeds, England), December 21, 1850, p. 1. In the 1880s and 1890s, activists recapitulated this notion that refugees—in this case, Eastern European Jews—could regenerate British society.
39. Ibid. In the 1880s and 1890s, activists recapitulated this notion that refugees—in this case, Eastern European Jews—could regenerate British society.
40. Interaction with the democratic-socialist refugees after 1848 pushed middle- and working-class radical thinking in a more socialist direction, though the full effects of this influence would become obvious only decades later, as Margot Finn argues in *After Chartism*. Gregory Claeys argues that contact with Mazzini and Kossuth, who preached about duties as well as rights, helped temper the British radicalism in the 1850s. Gregory Claeys, "Mazzini, Kossuth, and British Radicalism, 1848–1854," *Journal of British Studies* 28, no. 3 (July 1989): 225–261. Most biographies of midcentury radicals mention refugees. See, for example, Miles Taylor, *Ernest Jones, Chartism, and the Romance of Politics, 1819–1869* (Oxford: Oxford University Press, 2003); Nigel Todd, *The Militant Democracy: Joseph Cowen and Victorian Radicalism* (Tyne and Wear: Bewick Press, 1991).
41. Refugees, 1853, National Archives, HO 45/4816.

42. *Report of the Proceedings of the Fourth Annual General Meeting of the London Literary Association of the Friends of Poland, held at their Rooms, No. 10, Duke Street, St. James's, April 26, 1836* (London: T. Brettell, 1836), 16.

43. *Address of the Literary Association of the Friends of Poland of Great Britain and Ireland* (London: E. Detkens, 1846), 34.

44. George Jacob Holyoake, "Kossuth-Mazzini Subscriptions," *Reasoner* 13 (July 28, 1852): 109–110.

45. O'Connor, *Romance of Italy*, 90; Lucy Riall, *Garibaldi: Invention of a Hero* (New Haven, CT: Yale University Press, 2007), 295. In 1857, Jessie White married nationalist fighter Alberto Mario; unlike Garibaldi's triumphs, the "last Polish insurrection" failed miserably. W. E. Adams, *Memoirs of a Social Atom* (New York: Augustus Kelley Publishers, 1968), 442–443.

46. Sir George Cornewall Lewis, *On Foreign Jurisdiction and the Extradition of Criminals* (London: John W. Parker and Son, 1859), 69, quoting Palmerston before the House of Commons on March 1, 1853.

47. W. E. Adams, author of *Tyrannicide*, escaped to America. Truelove was tried but the charges eventually dropped after Bernard was acquitted. Joseph Cowen's role in the affair escaped notice.

48. John Belchem, "Britishness, Asylum-Seekers and the Northern Working Class: 1851," *Northern History* 39, no. 1 (2002): 59–74.

49. *Hansard's Parliamentary Debates* 136, House of Commons Debate, December 22, 1854, c. 803.

50. Canning to Prince de Polinaque, November 12, 1825, National Archives, FO 27/345, France: Domestic Fugitive Slaves, 1824–1825, f. 8–9.

51. *Parliamentary Papers*, Papers respecting relations between Great Britain and Portugal, 1826–1829, (1829 [002]), Correspondence between Marquis de Palmella to the Duke of Wellington, December 3, 1828, 83.

52. "The Portuguese Emigrants," *Times* (London), December 9, 1828, p. 3.

53. Nigel Todd, *The Militant Democracy: Joseph Cowen and Victorian Radicalism* (Tyne and Wear: Bewick Press, 1991), 12. Parliament investigated the letter-opening affair and the apparent breech of the right to privacy for the next year. F. B. Smith, *Radical Artisan: William James Linton, 1812–1897* (Manchester, UK: Manchester University Press, 1973), 54; Petition to the Commons Signed Sarafino Calderara, William Lovett, W. J Linton, and Guisseppi Mazzini and Report of the Secret Committee on the Post Office Graham Papers, BL Add. MSS 79,743, Vol. CLIII, f. 48, 99–108; Edward Turner, "The Secrecy of the Post," *The English Historical Review* 33, no. 131 (July 1918): 320–327; A. P. Donajgrodzki, "Sir James Graham at the Home Office," *The Historical Journal* 20, no. 1 (March 1977): 97–120; David Vincent, "The Origins of Public Secrecy in Britain," *Transactions of the Royal Historical Society*, Sixth Series, 1 (1991): 229–248.

54. "Kossuth-Mazzini Subscriptions," *Reasoner* 13 (July 28, 1852): 109–110.

55. Antony Taylor, "Palmerston and Radicalism, 1847–1865," *Journal of British Studies* 33, no. 2 (April 1994): 165. Taylor is engaged in a project to rehabilitate Palmerston in the Liberal Party and accord to him a central role in solidifying popular and particularly radical support—a role typically accorded to Gladstone. Most historians who use British interest in European refugees during this midcentury period are engaged in this debate. See, for example, *Citizenship and Community: Liberals, Radicals and Collective Identities in the British Isles, 1865–1931,*

ed. Eugenio Biagini (Cambridge: Cambridge University Press, 1996); Eugenio Biagini, *Liberty, Retrenchment and Reform: Popular Liberalism in the Age of Gladstone, 1860–1880* (Cambridge: Cambridge University Press, 1992).

56. Bernard Porter, *The Refugee Question in Mid-Victorian Politics* (Cambridge: Cambridge University Press, 1979), chap. 6.
57. Giuseppe Mazzini, Letter to Louis Napoleon from the *Morning Advertiser* (London), March 29, 1858, Bishopsgate Institute Library, Charles Bradlaugh Collection, no. 54.
58. Edwin James quoted in George Holyoake, *Sixty Years of an Agitator's Life*, 2 vols. (New York: Garland Publishing, Inc., 1984), 32. Too bad, reminisced Holyoake, James turned out to be a scoundrel after elected to Parliament.
59. "The Queen against Simon Bernard," *Report of State Trials, Volume 8, 1850–1858*, new series (London: Eyre and Spottiswoode, 1898), 887.

CHAPTER THREE

1. *Hansard's Parliamentary Debates* 103, House of Commons Debates, April 20, 1852, 943–950. The popularization of the Hungarian cause worked to Palmerston's advantage, just as his apparent abandonment of refugees would cause his downfall at the decade's close.
2. "Kossuth not Allowed to Pass through France," *Newcastle Chronicle*, October 10, 1851, p. 3. See also extensive reporting in the *Hampshire Advertiser* from the fall of 1851. The *Advertiser* covered Southampton, among other port towns along England's southern coast.
3. Max Schlesinger, *Saunterings in and about London*, trans. Otto Wenckstern (London: Nathaniel Cooke, 1853), 3–6.
4. Alexander Herzen, *My Past & Thoughts*, trans. Constance Garnett, abridged by Dwight Macdonald (New York: Random House, 1974), 447; Schlesinger, *Saunterings in and about London*, 131.
5. Charles Dickens, *A Tale of Two Cities*, Penguin Classics edition (Newcastle upon Tyne: Cambridge Scholars Publishing, 2007), 22.
6. Donna Andrew, "'To the Charitable and Humane': Appeals for Assistance in the Eighteenth-Century London Press," in *Charity, Philanthropy. and Reform: From the 1690s to 1850*, ed. Hugh Cunningham and Joanna Innes (New York: St. Martin's Press, 1998), 88.
7. Whether foreign refugees were entitled to poor relief was a matter of debate. Generally, the laws seem to leave relief to the discretion of the individual parish. David Feldman, "The Boundaries of Welfare," *History in Focus* 11 (Fall 2006), available at http://www.history.ac.uk/ihr/Focus/Migration/articles/feldman.html.
8. "Spanish Exiles," *Times* (London), December 8, 1825, p. 2.
9. Ibid.
10. "A Fugitive Slave in Liverpool," *Times* (London), February 25, 1858, p. 8.
11. Frances Trollope, *The Refugee in America* (London: Whittaker, Treacher, and Co., 1832).
12. Letter of Introduction by Samuel May, reprinted in the *Report of the Bristol and Clifton Ladies' Anti-Slavery Society* (London: John Snow, 1852), 11.
13. Theresa Pulszky, *Memoirs of a Hungarian Lady* (London: Henry Colburn, 1850).

14. Artúr Görgey, *My Life and Acts in Hungary in the Years 1848–1849* (London: David Bogue, 1852); George Kmety, *A Refutation of Some of the Principal Misstatements in Görgei's 'My Life'* (London: William and Frederic Cash, 1853).
15. Luigi Bianchi, *Incidents in the Life of an Italian: Priest—Soldier—Refugee* (London: James Nisbet, 1859).
16. "Poland, Hungary, and England," *Northern Star* (Leeds, England), December 21, 1850, p. 1.
17. "A Fugitive Slave in Liverpool," *Times* (London), February 25, 1858, p. 8.
18. See, among others, "William and Ellen Craft," *Bristol Mercury*, August 30, 1851, p. 8; "The Fugitives William and Ellen Craft," *Gloucester Journal*, September 13, 1851, p. 4.
19. For instance: "They wandered in deserts and mountains, and in dens and caves of the earth" (Hebrews XI). Mrs. C. G. Hamilton, *The Exiles of Italy* (Edinburgh: Thomas Constable and Co., 1857), 193.
20. Hamilton, *Exiles of Italy*, 257.
21. Alfred Godwine, *The Refugee, A Novel Founded on Phrenological Observations* (London: R. Hirschfeld, 1857), 234.
22. Hamilton, *Exiles of Italy*, 496–497; Kossuth, *Memoirs of My Exile*, (London: Cassell, 1880), xxiv and 89.
23. Spurr to Cowen, May 17, 1851, Tyne and Wear Archives Service, Cowen Collection, A33.
24. Ladies' Society to Aid Fugitives from Slavery (London, 1855), 3–5, copy found in British and Foreign Anti-Slavery Society, Territorial Letters: The United States (1853–1897), Rhodes House Special Collections, Oxford.,
25. For instance, Hannah Kilham, *Report on a Recent Visit to the Colony of Sierra Leone* (London: William Phillips, 1828), 11ff.; Kilham, *Present State of the Colony of Sierra Leone, being Extracts of Recent Letters from Hannah Kilham*, 2nd ed. (Lindfield: C. Greene at the Schools of Industry, 1832).
26. "Isolées, surveillées, parquées, sans espoir, sans salaire et qui, pour garder la dignité des absents, sauront mourir au foyer, sans la plainte des agonies. [. . .] [C]'est notre sang, c'est nous-mêmes!" ["Isolated, under observation, caught, without hope, without income and who, for preserving the dignity of those absent, will die at home, without complaining of our agonies. [. . .] It's our blood, it's ourselves."] Charles Ribeyrolles, "Famine," *L'Homme* (St. Hélier, Jersey), January 11, 1854, p. 1–2.
27. There were occasional exceptions. Theresa Pulszky escaped with her children while her husband remained trapped behind. For the most part, when women did flee, their stories of persecution were told alongside those of their husbands, and not independently. See, for instance, "Spanish Refugees," *Times* [London], December 25, 1828, p. 2. Although revolutionary women were less prominent in the literature, individuals such as the French Jeanne Deroin were of immense importance within exile communities in the British Isles. Deroin established a school for refugee children.
28. Kossuth, *Memoirs of My Exile*, 89.
29. Letter of Charles Müller in Glasgow to Harriet Beecher Stowe, April 16, 1853, published in the introduction to *Uncle Tom's Cabin* (Boston: Houghton Mifflin, 1882), xxxiii–xxxiv.
30. Hamilton, *Exiles of Italy*, 172.

31. For example, "Fugitive Slave Bill, Working out of. . .," *Times* (London) October 31, 1850, 4.
32. Pulszky, *Memoirs of a Hungarian Lady*; Kossuth, *Memoirs of My Exile*, xxiv and 89.
33. "Landing in Liverpool of Hungarian Refugees," *Daily News* (London), March 6, 1851, p. 4.
34. Bianchi, *Incidents in the Life*, 200.
35. Ibid..
36. Charles Dickens, *A Tale of Two Cities*; Hamilton, *Exiles of Italy*, 385ff. The De Vere family, Hamilton explains, arrived in England with William the Conqueror (284).
37. For Dickens, Lucy Manette represents that domestic tranquility, at least while in London. Anna Maria Hall's St. Pierre (from *St. Pierre, the Refugee*, performed at St. James Theatre, London in February 1837) is ill-suited to English society and appears as a rather ridiculous character. Ultimately, the story revolves around his daughter, who marries into their newfound society. See also Anne Raikes Harding, *The Refugees, an Irish Tale* (1822), and, for earlier novels, Charlotte Smith, *The Banished Man* (1794), and Fanny Burney, *The Wanderers* (1814).
38. In the 1880s, Archbishop Manning became a constant feature at the Mansion House's meetings on the relief of Eastern European Jews.
39. Belchem, "Britishness, Asylum-Seekers and the Northern Working Class."
40. Reveling in such attention, Palmerston dispatched this resolution to Stratford Canning, counsel at the Sublime Porte, immediately. Palmerston to Canning, May 23, 1851, National Archives, FO 881/173, Dispatch no. 46, Enclosure no. 1.
41. "Abstract of the Meeting," *Anti-Slavery Reporter* 6, no. 8 (August 1, 1850): 135.
42. See Chapter Eight in this volume.
43. Gossman, "British Aid to Polish, Italian and Hungarian Exiles, 1830–1870."
44. "Liberation of Kossuth," *Newcastle Chronicle*, November 23, 1849, p. 6.
45. "Polish Insurrection," *Anti-Slavery Reporter*, New Series 1 (April–May 1846): 58.
46. Radical politicians spoke of the British working class as white slaves. By the 1840s, this rhetoric seemed less directed against the cause of abolition than earlier in the century, in the time of William Cobbett and through the 1830s. For this comparison, see Catherine Gallagher's "Workers and Slaves: the Rhetoric of Freedom in the debate over Industrialism" in her *The Industrial Reformation of English Fiction: Social Discourse and Narrative Fiction, 1832–1867* (Chicago: University of Chicago Press, 1985).
47. "Address of the Society of Friends of Italy," 1851, Tyne and Wear Archives, Cowen Collection, A134–135.
48. The names of those who attended various balls appeared in the national press, and helped to generate an aura of elite sociability. "Polish Refugees," *Morning Chronicle* (London), July 19, 1838, pp. 4–5. Balls and bazaars continued, though on a lesser scale, to help fund relief efforts.
49. In Newcastle, an 1851 concert featured songs like "The Slave," the battle song "Marching to Meet the Enemy," and the Polish national hymn "Poland is not Lost as Yet." Prograph for a June 3, 1851 concert, Tyne and Wear Archives Service, Cowen Collection, A50.
50. George Holyoake, "Kossuth-Mazzini Subscriptions," *Reasoner* 13 (July 28, 1852): 109–110.
51. Prince Czartoryski, Pulszki, Mazzini, Kossuth, and Garibaldi distributed the funds.

52. See appeals in the *Anti-Slavery Reporter* that were particularly commonplace in the wake of the Fugitive Slave Act and the publication of *Uncle Tom's Cabin.*
53. Internal memorandum of the Begging Letter Department regarding the "Russian" refugees, Mendleity [*sic*] Society, May 12, 1846, BL Add. MSS 40,591, Vol. CCCCXI, General Correspondence, f. 209–210.

54. Audrey Fisch, *American Slaves in Victorian England: Abolitionist Politics in Popular Literature and Culture* (Cambridge: Cambridge University Press, 2000), 92–95.
55. Refugee Circular, May 19, 1851, Tyne and Wear Archives, Cowen Collection, A37.
56. *Temperance Chronicle*, from April 1852, cited in Fisch, *American Slaves in Victorian England*, 93.
57. Wilhelmine von Beck, *Personal Adventures during the Late War in Hungary* (London: Richard Bentley, 1850), 320.
58. "The Late Baroness von Beck," *Liverpool Mercury*, October 14, 1851, 4; *Hungarian Impostors and Hungarian Patriots: The Case of Wilhelmina Racidula, Soi Disant 'Baroness Von Beck'* (Birmingham: J. F. Feeney, 1851), 1.
59. François, Duc de la Rouchefoucauld, "Hypocrisy is a Tribute that Vice Pays to Virtue," *Sentences et Maximes Morales*, no. 218.
60. Harriet Beecher Stowe, *Uncle Tom's Cabin, or Life among the Lowly*, new edition (Philadelphia: Henry Altemus, 1900), 281–282.
61. By the mid-1850s, similar stories became a selling point for the *Ladies' Newspaper* of London, which advertised that its "pink edition" would publish weekly stories on the issue (*Times*, October 10, 1856, p. 4). The novel also inspired spin-offs on the London stage. See Sarah Meer, *Uncle Tom Mania: Slavery, Minstrelsy and Transatlantic Culture in the 1850s* (Athens: University of Georgia Press, 2005), 134; Donald Ross, "Sunny Memories and Serious Proposals," in *Transatlantic Stowe: Harriet Beecher Stowe and European Culture*, ed. Denise Kohn, Sarah Meer, and Emily B. Todd (Iowa City: University of Iowa Press, 2006); Richard Huzzey, *Freedom Burning: Anti-Slavery and Empire in Victorian Britain* (Ithaca, NY: Cornell University Press, 2012), chap. 2.
62. Alphonse Esquiros, *The English at Home*, trans. Lascelles Wraxall (London: Chapman and Hall, 1861), 378; Fabrice Bensimon, "The French Exiles and the British," in *Exiles from European Revolutions*, ed. Sabine Freitag (New York: Berghan Books, 2003), 92.
63. Alexandre-August Ledru Rollin, *De la décadence de l'Angleterre* (Brussels: Société Typographique Belge, 1850); Friedrich Engels, *Die Lage der arbeitenden Klasse in England*, (Leipzig: Otto Wigand, 1845); Herzen, *My Past*, 502; Schlesinger, *Saunterings*, 125; Rosemary Ashton, *Little Germany: German Refugees in Victorian Britain* (Oxford: Oxford University Press, 1986), 225–256.

CHAPTER FOUR

1. Spanish Liberals (amnestied in 1834) and the French refugee clergy (1801) are the exceptions I have found.
2. George Julian Harney, "Political Refugees," *The Vanguard* (London: J. P. Crantz, 1853), 16.
3. Prakash Shah suggests that resettlement overseas was a means of offloading foreigners who were not welcome within Britain proper—hence, a means of denying sanctuary to fugitive slaves among others. *Refugees, Race and the Legal Concept of Asylum in Britain* (London: Cavendish, 2000).

4. Thomas James Mathias, *A Letter to the Lord Marquis of Buckingham . . . Chiefly on the Subject of the Numerous Emigrant French Priests and Others of the Church of Rome, Resident and Maintained in England at the Public Expense* (London: J. Owen, 1796), 9 and appendix.
5. "Religious and Polemical Section," *Monthly Review* 22, new and improved series (January–April 1797): 95–96.
6. Charles Stewart, F. S. A. Scot. (Pres), "Address to the 32nd Annual General Meeting of the H.S. of London," *Proceedings of the Huguenot Society* 11, no. 2 (1917): 11.
7. Letters and declarations regarding the Hartsinck Case, August 1805, BL Add. MSS 75,897, Aliens, October 1803–August 1806; National Archives HO/44/1, March 1820, f. 59, 20; HO 44/7, March 27, 1821, f. 234–235; HO 44/10, October 4, 1821, f. 25–28; and HO 44/11, March 27, 1822, f. 373–374.
8. Jones, *The Welsh Freeholder's Farewell Epistles*, 2.
9. Ibid., 7.
10. Krzysztof Marchlewicz, "Continuities and Innovations: Polish Immigration after 1849," in *Exiles from European Revolutions: Refugees in Mid-Victorian England*, ed. Sabine Freitag (New York: Berghahn Books, 2003), 107–110. The number of Polish refugees increased from a dozen to more than 400 between 1833 and 1834. The number fluctuated between 450 and 650 for the next decade and rose steadily after 1849, remaining above 700 through most of the 1850s. See table 7.1 in Marchlewicz, "Continuitities and Innovations," 105.
11. *Hansard's Parliamentary Debates* 103, House of Lords, March 19, 1849, c. 949. Other groups receiving funds from the government were the Toulonese and the Spanish.
12. See, for example, Parliamentary Papers (1840, 43-II), "Reports from Assistant Hand-Loom Weavers' Commissioners, Part III," 592.
13. "The Poles and the Citizens," *The Age* (London), November 16, 1834, p. 357.
14. "The Swindling Refugees," *The Age* (London), November 5, 1837, p. 363.
15. Ashton, *Little Germany*, 21.
16. Sylvie Aprile, "Voices of Exile: French Newspapers in England," in *Exiles from European Revolutions*, 149–163.
17. They were subjected to subsidies and custom duties (Cottret, *Huguenots in England*, 52). The legal theory (laid out by Edward Coke in 1608) made operative at the accession of James VI of Scotland or I of England set out that only the *postnati*—those born after the accession of James to the English throne—would be entitled to the full benefits of English subject status. This included the ability to hold office and, more crucially, transmit property. This meant that only the generation born in England would be able to hold or transmit property. Karatani, *Defining British Citizenship*, 40–41.
18. Cottret, *Huguenots in England*, 185–186.
19. Statt, *Foreigners and Englishmen*, 36; Cottret, *Huguenots in England*, 53.
20. Statt, *Foreigners and Englishmen*, 34–35.
21. P. K. Martinez, "Paris Communard Refugees in Britain, 1871–1880" (PhD diss., University of Sussex, 1981).
22. "An example for the authorities," *Refugee Circular*, April 16, 1851, p. 3; Belchem, "Britishness, Asylum-Seekers and the Northern Working Class: 1851."
23. William Linton, Letter (dated March 21) to *The Northern Star* (Leeds), April 5, 1851, p. 1.

24. Francis Newman suggested a similar plan for the Hungarians in London at the end of 1851. However, his plan was predicated on the reception of refugee "gentlemen" into the homes of their social peers. The insistence on class segregation was precisely the sort of thing that Chartists denounced in mainstream refugee assistance. See Newman's letter in the *Daily News* (London), January 1, 1852, p. 1.

25. "Hungarian and Italian Refugees—Meeting in Newcastle," *Newcastle Chronicle*, March 14, 1851, p. 6; "Polish and Hungarian Refugees," *Newcastle Chronicle*, May 23, 1851, p. 4. George Crawshay and John Fyfe advocated further removal to America in March, but were supportive of the refugees upon their arrival in Newcastle that May. Both sat on the committee for their relief; Cowen was secretary and treasurer.
26. The Polish Hungarian Refugees—to the Friends of Freedom and Humanity in Newcastle on Tyne, and its Vicinity, Tyne and Wear Archives Service, Cowen Collection, A41.
27. Belchem, "Britishness, Asylum-Seekers and the Northern Working Class: 1851," 70.
28. "Polish Refugees," *Newcastle Chronicle*, July 25, 1851, p. 4.
29. Adams, *Memoirs of a Social Atom*, 273.
30. Statt, *Foreigners and Englishmen*, 223.
31. Robin Winks, *The Blacks in Canada*, 2nd ed. (Montreal: McGill-Queen's University Press, 1997), 39–40.
32. Cobbett, *Parliamentary History of England* 30 (December 13, 1792–March 10, 1794), cols. 150–151.
33. Minutes of the Committee of Subscribers for the Relief of the French Clergy, December 7, 1792, BL MSS 18,591, no. 1, f. 52.
34. Wilkinson, "French Emigrés in England, 1789–1802," 353. Only thirty-four priests accepted British Treasury funds for removing to Canada.
35. Porter, *Refugee Question*, 82–83; John Sanders to Home Office, March 19, 1853, National Archives, HO 45/4816.
36. Parliamentary Papers, 1850 (134), Malta, Dispatches between the Governor of Malta and the Secretary of State for the Colonies, relating to the admission of foreigners into the island of Malta," 14, 28, 33; *Anti-Slavery Reporter* 6, no. 1 (January 1, 1851): 5; Bethell, "The Mixed Commissions for the Suppression of the Transatlantic Slave Trade in the Nineteenth Century," 79, 84, 89. On East Africa as well as refuge on board British ships and in consulates see Chapter Seven in this volume and Asylum for Political Refugees at HM Consulate at Santo Domingo, National Archives, FO 96/224. For India, see Parliamentary Papers, 1898 (8812), Government of India, Department of Revenue and Agriculture (Famine), Narrative of the Famine in India in 1896–97, by T. W. Holderness, I.C.S., Deputy Secretary (Famine) to the Government of India, 46–47. Official papers referred only to those from the Princely States as "refugees." Subjects of the British raj who left home were "wanderers," the implication being that they should not have left the famine camps designed for their relief.
37. Letter from Hector Minet at Dover, September 25, Minutes of the Committee of Subscribers for the Relief of the French Clergy, September 1792–November 1793, BL MSS 18,591, no. 1, f. 20.
38. Niklaus Steiner, *Arguing About Asylum: The Complexity of Refugee Debates in Europe* (New York: St. Martin's Press, 2000), chap. 4.
39. "Polish Refugees in Liverpool," *Weekly Dispatch* (Liverpool), March 3, 1851, p. 7.

40. Ibid.

41. Ibid.

42. "Hungarian Refugees at Southampton," *Daily News* (London), June 9, 1851, p. 4.

43. Elizabeth Elbourne, *Blood Ground: The Khoekhoe, Colonialism, Missions, and the Contest for Christianity in the Cape Colony and Britain, 1799–1853* (Montreal: McGill-Queen's University Press, 2002), 12–15.

44. CMS Central Minutes, *Church Missionary Society Archives*, vol. 2, reel 75, November 14, 1814 (Marlborough, Wiltshire: Adam Matthew Publications, 1997–); Christopher Fyfe, *A History of Sierra Leone* (Hampshire, UK: Gregg Revivals, 1993), 127.

45. Suggestions for the Improvement of the Social and Intellectual Condition of the Native Africans at Sierra Leone, CMS Printed Materials and Circular Letters (1799–1855), *Church Missionary Society Archives*, part 6, reel 63.

46. Mrs. Sherwood (Mary Martha), *Dazee, or the Re-Captured Negro*, new ed. (London: Houlston and Stoneman, 1850), 41, 72. First published in 1821, new editions appeared in 1822, 1831, and 1850.

47. Letter from the Rev H. Townsend to Capt. Trotter, RN on the African coast blockade, 1848, CMS Printed Materials and Circular Letters (1799–1855), *Church Missionary Society Archives*, part 6, reel 63.

48. Mary Church (pseudonym), *Sierra Leone; or The Liberated Africans, in a Series of Letters from a Young Lady to Her Sister, in 1833 & 1834* (London: Longman and Co., 1835), 24.

49. Fred Morton, *Children of Ham: Freed Slaves and Fugitive Slaves on the Kenya Coast, 1873 to 1907* (Boulder, CO: Westview Press, 1990), 53 and 98ff; *Church Missionary Society Archives*, vol. 40, reel 101, f. 269.

50. Settlements included the western district, Chatham, Ruiley, Sandwich, Anderton, Malden, Colchester, Gonfield, London, Hamilton, St. Catherine, Dawn, and Wilberforce. "At Toronto there are about 400 or 500 variously employed, principally as domestic servants," *Anti-Slavery Reporter* 6, no. 1 (January 1, 1851): 5.

51. Winks, *The Blacks in Canada*, 218ff; "Fugitives in Canada," *Anti-Slavery Reporter* 6, no. 10 (October 1, 1851): 162–163; "Visit to the Fugitive Slaves and People of Colour in Upper Canada," *Anti-Slavery Reporter* 7, no. 2, (February 2, 1852): 21–22; "Fugitive Slaves in Canada," *Anti-Slavery Reporter*, New Series 2, no. 5 (May 1, 1854): 102–103. For the Mennonites, see "Emigration of German colonists of Russia, from the Spectator," *The Friend*, New Series 14 (October 1874): 299. *The Friend* published articles on the Mennonites and their emigration from Russia and resettlement in the Americas from October 1874 through 1876. H. L. Sawatzky, *They Sought a Country: Mennonite Colonization in Mexico* (Berkeley: University of California, 1971).

52. Charles Hanson, Letter dated December 15, 1879, Constantinople Papers 1856–1888, BL Add. MSS 39,054, vol. CXXIV, f. 248–259.

53. The JCA, for example, though an international charity was incorporated in Britain, making the government technically responsible for its agents overseas. Immigration of Jews into Palestine, 1891–1905, National Archives, FO 78/5479, f. 75 and thereafter. See Case of Dr. Ginsburg, Complaints made by Jews, 1877–79, FO 99/189, for the difficulties attending cases of conversion. For British protection of Jews in the region, see Protection of Jews in Syria, 1871–1874, FO 78/2375A.

54. Robert G. Weisbord, *African Zion: The Attempt to Establish a Jewish Colony in the East Africa Protectorate, 1903–1905* (Philadelphia: The Jewish Publication Society of America, 1968); David Feldman, "Jews and the British Empire," *History Workshop Journal* 63 (2007): 81ff; Colin Holmes, *Anti-Semitism in British Society* (London: Edward Arnold, 1979), 118; David Glover, "Zionism, Territorialism, Race, and Nation in the Thought and Politics of Israel Zangwill," and Simon Rabinovitch, "Imperial Zion: Israel Zangwill and the English Origins of Territorialism," in *"The Jew" in Late-Victorian and Edwardian Culture: Between the East End and East Africa*, ed. Eitan Bar-Yosef and Nadia Valman (New York: Palgrave Macmillan, 2009).
55. "Agricultural Colonies in the Argentine Republic (Argentina)," *The Jewish Encyclopedia of 1906*, full text at JewishEncyclopedia.com. See also entries on agricultural settlements.
56. For example, *Hansard's Parliamentary Debates* 337, House of Commons Debates, June 14, 1938, c. 158.
57. Jewish refugees from Germany: settlement in British colonies, 1934, National Archives, CO 323/1271/1; Refugees: settlement by Jewish refugees in British Guiana, 1938, CO 111/756/2; Settlement of Jewish refugees from Central Europe in Tanganyika, June 3, 1938–January 20, 1939, CO 691/169/19; Bernard Wasserstein, *Britain and the Jews of Europe, 1939–1945*, 2nd ed. (Leicester, UK: Leicester University Press, 1999), 25; A. J. Sherman, *Island Refuge: Britain and Refugees from the Third Reich, 1933–1939* (Berkeley: University of California, 1973), *passim*; and Caroline Shaw, "A Hierarchy of Rights? Minority Rights versus Refugee Rights, 1920–1940," paper delivered at the North American Conference on British Studies in Montreal, November 9–11, 2012. On American involvement, see Mark Mazower, *No Enchanted Place: The End of Empire and the Ideological Origins of the United Nations* (Princeton, NJ: Princeton University Press, 2009), chap. 3; and Neil Smith, *American Empire: Roosevelt's Geographer and the Prelude to Globalization* (Berkeley: University of California Press, 2003).
58. Fyfe, *A History of Sierra Leone*, 263–265. For accounts of disease and death, see F. H. Rankin's *The White Man's Grave* (London: Richard Bentley, 1836). For an account of Sierra Leone and the impact of ex-slaves' experience on metropolitan abolition movements, see Bronwen Everill, *Abolition and Empire in Sierra Leone and Liberia* (Basingstoke, Hampshire: Palgrave Macmillan, 2012).
59. Missionaries and liberated Africans, it was hoped, would spread imperial interests without expense to the central government. Philip Curtin, *The Image of Africa: British Ideas and Action, 1780–1850*, vol. 1 (Madison: University of Wisconsin Press, 1973), 298.
60. Johnston Asiegbu, *Slavery and the Politics of Liberation, 1787–1861* (London: Longmans, Green and Co., 1969).
61. See Hall, *Civilising Subjects*; Elbourne, *Blood Ground*, 346–347, and chap. 10 more generally.
62. Church, *Sierra Leone*, 32.
63. Ibid.
64. By the 1850s, the colony's initial black settlers, including Loyalists and Caribbean transplants, had formed something of a Creole elite, and political strife increased. Joe Alfie, *A New History of Sierra Leone* (London: Macmillan Publishers, Ltd., 1990).

CHAPTER FIVE

1. Emphasis original. Sir Frederick Adam to Stratford Canning regarding captured neutral vessels and Greek refugees (1825) and Sir Frederick Adam to Col. Sir Charles Sutton, dated June 10, 1825, National Archives, FO 352/11 (3), f. 251–252.
2. Sir Frederick Adam to Stratford Canning regarding captured neutral vessels and Greek refugees (1825) and Adam to the Governor General of Calamos (modern day Kálamos), dated November 11, 1822, National Archives, FO 352/11 (3), f. 244.
3. Search of seagoing ships for arms; Spanish refugees, 1826–1831: James Rowan to George Don, dated October 8, 1830, enclosed with Dispatch no. 87 to the Colonial Office from Don, dated October 20, 1830; Don to Captain Burdett, April 2, 1831, and Don to Spanish General Ramirez, April 9, 1831, Enclosure 10 in Dispatch 55 to the Colonial Office, dated April 18, 1831, National Archives, CO 91/119.
4. Historians of antislavery movements have mentioned Anderson's case, as has David Turley, "'Free Air' and Fugitive Slaves: British Abolitionists versus Government over American Fugitives, 1834–61," in *Anti-Slavery, Religion and Reform: Essays in Memory of Roger Antsey*, ed. Christine Bolt and Seymour Drescher (Folkestone, UK: W. Dawson, 1980), 163–182. Paul Halliday mentions Anderson at the close of his account in *Habeas Corpus: From England to Empire* (Cambridge, MA: Belknap Press of Harvard University Press, 2010). There has been no scholarship on refugees on Malta. There is a third case of this nature during the 1850s, that of French refugees on the Jersey in the British Channel Islands. For more on that case, see Caroline Shaw, "Recall to Life: Imperial Britain, Foreign Refugees and the Development of Modern Refuge, 1789–1905," (PhD diss., University of California, Berkeley, 2010), chap. 4.
5. The "Peloro," for example, had 272 refugees, and the "Lycurgue" and "Ruben" had 150 and 124 refugees, respectively. Parliamentary Papers, 1850 (134) Malta, Copies or extracts of dispatches between the Governor of Malta and the Secretary of State for the Colonies, relating to the admission of foreigners into the island of Malta," 14, 28, 33.
6. Malta was ruled almost entirely by the Crown, a vestige of Lieutenant-General Thomas Maitland's military rule of the island during the Napoleonic Wars. The Crown-appointed governor formed a Council Board that shared power with Parliament in London. All directives, however, came from the Colonial Office. In addition to the governor, the board consisted of four Crown appointees, along with three Maltese appointed by the governor. Guglielmo Rapinet, *Lectures on the British Constitution and on the Government of Malta* (Malta: A. Aquilina, 1883), 175.
7. On Cephalonia, one of the British Ionian Islands, nationalists killed the colonial governor. Taylor, "The 1848 Revolutions and the British Empire," 172.
8. O'Ferrall immediately set out to make key constitutional reforms. He added an elected component to the Council Board, which had previously consisted entirely of appointees. This made local government partially representative. Rapinet, *Lectures on the British Constitution and on the Government of Malta*, 177; Hilda I. Lee, "The Development of the Malta Constitution 1813–1849," *Melita Historica: Journal of the Malta Historical Society* 1 (1952): 15; Confidential Memorandum on Malta Government in 1848 and 1849, National Archives, CO 325/31.
9. Michael Refalo, "Present (and Past) Concerns, Future Directions: Religion and the Church in the Writing of 19th-Century Maltese History," in *Religion,*

Ritual and Mythology: Aspects of Identity Formation in Europe, Vol. III, ed. Joaquim Carvalho (Pisa: University of Pisa Press, 2006), 218–219.

10. Confidential Memorandum on Malta Government in 1848 and 1849, no. 9: Extract of a Letter from Governor the Right Hon. O'Ferrall to Grey, dated June 2, 1849, National Archives, CO 325/31, f. 19.
11. O'Ferrall to Grey, May 17, 1849, Enclosure 2, "Instructions regarding Foreigners," signed Richard Plaskett, Chief Secretary to Government, January 1, 1818, National Archives, CO 325/31, no. 6, f. 14.
12. See correspondence on the Neapolitan deserters from the "Archimede" in CO 325/31, 19ff., 37ff., 41ff., and 64.
13. Letter to Palmerston, August 6, 1849, National Archives, CO 325/31, Enclosure in no. 9, f. 66.
14. "In the Midst of Our Self-Gradulatory Progress. . .," *Morning Chronicle* (London), September 8, 1849, p. 4.
15. O'Ferrall explained that he allowed Jesuits to land at the behest of the Sicilian government. When several of these men played active roles in the 1848 insurrectionary activities in Malta, this allowance was promptly discontinued, and the *dangerous* refugees removed. "Malta.—Mr. More O'Ferrall and the Italian Refugees," *Daily News* (London), April 15, 1850, p. 2; "Popery in Malta," *Belfast News-Letter*, April 23, 1850, p. 2.
16. "Popery in Malta," *Belfast News-Letter*, April 23, 1850, p. 2; "Malta.—Mr. More O'Ferrall and the Italian Refugees," *Daily News*, April 15, 1850, p. 4.
17. "Parliamentary Intelligence [from August 1]," *Times* (London), August 2, 1849, p. 3.
18. "From an Extract from the Globe," *Malta Times*, October 2, 1849, p. 4–5; "We Beg Leave to Inform the *Worthy* Correspondent of the *Daily News*," *Malta Times*, October 30, 1849, p. 4; "The Governor of Malta," *Times* (London), September 18, 1849, p. 3 (reprinted from the *Globe*).
19. O'Ferrall to Grey, December 11, 1849, National Archives, CO 158/148, Malta 1849, vol. 4, Refugees, Dispatch no. 24.
20. See, for example, The Report of the Superintendent of Quarantine and Marine Police on the English Barque "Michelina," with 87 Refugees, December 5, 1849, National Archives, CO 158/148, Malta 1849, vol. 4, Refugees, Enclosure 2, Dispatch no. 22, f. 53–54.
21. Archbishop of Malta to the Governor, July 26, 1849, National Archives, CO 158/148, Enclosure 4, Dispatch no. 16,.
22. Memorial of the Maltese to the Governor of Malta, July 22, 1849, National Archives, CO 158/148, Enclosure 3.
23. Grey to O'Ferrall, reported in "Malta—Mr. More O'Ferrall and the Italian Refugees," *Daily News* (London), April 16, 1850, pp. 4, 6.
24. *Daily News*, April 16, 1850, pp. 4, 6.
25. *Malta Times*, March 26, 1850.
26. Ibid..
27. The 1848 Aliens Act in Britain lapsed in 1849. Authorities had never invoked its powers.
28. Winks, *Blacks in Canada*, 168.
29. On the Extradition Clause of the Treaty of Washington," Memorial addressed to Aberdeen, February 13, 1843, Rhodes House Special Collections, Oxford,

Archives of the British and Foreign Anti-Slavery Society, E 2/19, Memorials and Petitions, f. 193.

30. "T. Clarkson memorial to Aberdeen forwarded to Palmerston," *Anti-Slavery Reporter* 6, no. 1, (January 1, 1851): 5. See also Chapter Four. Concerns over runaways in the Caribbean had been relatively commonplace, if not widely discussed, since the Haitian Revolution of 1793. For the most part, they were connected to concerns for international, rather than colonial, jurisdictions. In "Free Air," David Turley situates Anderson in a longer line of court cases involving slavery and the slave trade, including importantly the *Amistad* and the *Creole* cases of 1841. Each case involved slaves who rebelled against their captors on the seas and sought protection in a foreign territory. I focus on the Anderson case here because it tested the British commitment to refugees in a systematic way that the others did not.

31. Harper Twelvetrees, *The Story of the Life of John Anderson* (London: William Tweedie, 1863), 13.
32. Ibid., 25–26.
33. Winks, *Blacks in Canada*, 175–176.
34. Twelvetrees, *Life of John Anderson*, quoting Rev. Principal Willis, 43–44.
35. Minutes, January 25, 1861, Rhodes House Special Collections, Oxford, Archives of the British and Foreign Anti-Slavery Society, f. 142, 151.
36. Thomas Tapping, "Art. III. The Case of Anderson, the Fugitive Slave. The Application for the Writ of *Habeas Corpus* and Judgment Considered," *Law Magazine and Law Review* 21 (February 1861): 42.
37. Twelvetrees, *Life of John Anderson*, 67, citing the *Times* (London), January 5, 1861.
38. Ibid., 26. Lyons and Russell had been informed that Anderson was a "man of colour," but not that he was a slave. *Parliamentary Papers*, 1861 (2813), "Correspondence Respecting the Case of Fugitive Slave, Anderson," Correspondence between Irvine and Russell, October 8, 1860, No. 1 and Enclosure 1, p. 1; Lyons to Russell, April 8, 1861, no. 20, p. 46. According to this official correspondence, it would be another three months before Anderson was referred to as a "fugitive slave" in a letter from Downing Street dated January 9, 1861 (p. 2).
39. *Parliamentary Papers*, 1861 (2813), "Correspondence relating to [. . .]Anderson," Letter of the Duke of Newcastle to the Officer Administering the Government of Canada, January 9, 1961, no. 5, Enclosure 1, p. 3.
40. Edwin James as quoted in Twelvetrees, *Life of John Anderson*, 56–57.
41. Judgment of Lord Chief Justice Cockburn, cited in Twelvetrees, *Life of John Anderson*, 62–63.
42. Ibid., 63.
43. Tapping, "Art. III. The Case of Anderson, the Fugitive Slave," 53.
44. Ibid., 60, 63.
45. *The Upper Canada Law Journal*, March 1861, appended to Tapping, "Art. III. The Case of Anderson, the Fugitive Slave," 64.
46. Tapping, "Art. III. The Case of Anderson, the Fugitive Slave," 64.
47. Parliamentary Papers, 1861 (2813), "Correspondence . . . Anderson," Enclosure 3 in no. 19, Correspondence of Sir Edmund Head to the Duke of Newcastle, dated March 28, 1861, p. 37.
48. Twelvetrees, *Life of John Anderson*, 84.

49. Twelvetrees, *Life of John Anderson*, 76; Fred Landon, "The Anderson Fugitive Case," *Journal of Negro History* 7, no. 3 (July 1922): 242.
50. Bianchi, *Incidents in the Life of an Italian*, 282.
51. Twelvetrees, *Life of John Anderson*, 135.
52. Ibid., 157–179.

CHAPTER SIX

1. Hamilton, *The Exiles of Italy*, 317, 310. On the distance between the Scottish present and the past see, for example, Ian Duncan's *Modern Romance and Transformations of the Novel: The Gothic, Scott, Dickens* (Cambridge: Cambridge University Press, 1992).
2. To date, studies of refugee relief, extradition law, and political offenses have been separate fields. For British/European "political crime," see Barton Ingraham, *Political Crime in Europe: A Comparative Study of France, Germany, and England* (Berkeley: University of California Press, 1979); Leon Radzinowicz and Roger Hood, "The Status of Political Prisoner in England: The Struggle for Recognition," *Virginia Law Review* 65, no. 8 (December 1979): 1421–1481; Seán McConville, *Irish Political Prisoners, 1848–1922* (London: Routledge, 2003). The absence of overlap between these fields is particularly acute given the extent to which extradition and refugee relief factored into the Irish case. Nicholas Adams and Christopher Pyle alone attempt to tell the history of the political offender exemption clause in a way that touches upon British "traitors" and foreign refugees. Both authors focus on high politics and legal commentary. Adams, "British Extradition Policy and the Problem of the Political Offender, 1842–1914" (PhD diss., Hull University, 1989); Pyle, *Extradition, Politics, and Human Rights* (Philadelphia: Temple University Press, 2001).
3. Edward Clarke, *A Treatise upon the Law of Extradition* (London: Stevens and Haynes, 1888), 135; *Hansard's Parliamentary Debates* 122, House of Lords Debates on the Surrender of Criminals, June 8 and 25, 1852,: cc. 192–214 and cc. 1278–1284.
4. The status of the political offender was at issue in an 1865 case before the Canadian Courts. The United States demanded the extradition of Confederate soldiers who had raided a bank in St. Albans, Vermont, during the Civil War. The question was whether the robbery was political or not. While the substance of the case speaks to the subsequent debate over the line between the political and the criminal, it did not inform the conversation on the matter as far as I have seen.
5. Liberals remained fearful that France in particular would use a new treaty on extradition as a political tool. After all, this was a country known for her revolutionary temperament. Liberals were, however, willing to move forward with a new treaty. The liberalization of Louis Napoleon's Second Empire made the emperor a more palatable ally. Napoleon had amnestied the 1851 exiles in 1858, and the countries now enjoyed an expanded commercial alliance.
6. Prussian politics were also suspect on this score.
7. John Stuart Mill, *The Collected Works of John Stuart Mill, Volume XXVIII—Public and Parliamentary Speeches Part I November 1850—November 1868*, ed. John M. Robson and Bruce L. Kinzer (Toronto: University of Toronto Press, 1988), chap. 36; Pyle, *Extradition, Politics, and Human Rights*, 86–87. Mill compared the French treaty to the case of Jamaican General Eyre whose recourse to martial law in 1865

seemed to Mill equally likely to have abrogated the just rule of law even though the situation (in the wake of an uprising) was believed to have been a colonial emergency.

8. *Hansard's Parliamentary Debates* 184, House of Commons Debates, August 3, 1866, c. 2015.
9. Ibid., c. 2007.
10. Section 3.1 in The 1870 Extradition Act (33 & 34 Vict. c. 52).
11. This was perhaps an unintended consequence for Mill, who favored a definition of "political" that would enable the British to bring violent Irish nationalists to justice.
12. "Communist v. Fenian," *The Penny Illustrated*, June 17, 1871, p. 3.
13. Through the winter of 1870–1871, philanthropists sympathized with the ravages of the Franco-Prussian War, sending aid to Parisians whose situation was becoming desperate. That sympathy ended when Parisians took up arms against the National Guard and formed a commune that March. P. K. Martinez, "Paris Communard Refugees in Britain, 1871–1880" (PhD diss. University of Sussex, 1981).
14. James Epstein, *Lion of Freedom: Feargus O'Connor and the Chartist Movement* (London: Croom Helm, 1982); Bensimon, *Les Britanniques face à la révolution française de 1848*.
15. W. R. Greg, "*Suum Cuique*: The Moral of the Paris Catastrophe," *Fraser's Magazine* 4, no. 19 (July 1871): 117–118.
16. "British Subjects and the Commune," *Liverpool Mercury*, June 3, 1871, p. 7. For an example of this paranoia, see Samuel Hemyng, *The Commune in London: A Chapter of Anticipated History* (London: C. H. Clarke, 1871).
17. Frederick Harrison, "The Fall of the Commune," *Fortnightly Review* 10, no. 56 (August 1871): 129.
18. Anarchism was an outgrowth of a break within the International Working Men's Association between Karl Marx and Mikhail Bakunin. Bakunin disavowed Marxist participation in parliamentary politics as a means to socialist ends. Bakunin demanded the complete destruction of existing society and the formation of a "world-wide union of free associations for all existing authoritarian governments." Bakunin, quoted in Ernest Vizetelly, *The Anarchists* (London: John Lane, 1911), 33, 36–37.
19. Ultimately, the mainstream press painted communism as foreign phenomenon, though continental democratic-socialism, present in radical circles thanks to refugees, would inflect British socialism at the end of the century. Margot Finn, *After Chartism: Class and Nation in English Radical Politics, 1848–1874* (Cambridge: Cambridge University Press, 1993); Martin Crick, *The History of the Social-Democratic Federation* (Edinburgh: Edinburgh University Press, 1994), 70.
20. It was at the 1881 London Anarchists Conference that Prince Kropotkin advocated the use of dynamite. For British inattention to the conference, see Hermia Oliver, *The International Anarchist Movement in Late Victorian London* (London: Croom Helm, 1983), 17.
21. Militant Suffragettes later adopted Russian refugees' resistance methods when arrested. Kevin Grant, "British Suffragettes and the Russian Method of Hunger Strike," *Comparative Studies in Society and History* 53, no. 1 (2011): 113–143.
22. The French Foreign Minister quoted in Martinez, "Paris Communard Refugees in Britain," 55.

23. "Communist Refugees," *Liverpool Mercury*, May 31, 1871, p. 7.
24. Martinez, "Paris Communard Refugees in Britain," 55–56.
25. Ibid., 5, 55. Martinez dispels misconceptions on this front that were prevalent in the 1870s.
26. Ibid., 19.
27. Ibid., 53. "Foreign Intelligence," *Liverpool Mercury*, May 30, 1871, p. 7. The *Mercury* changed tenor within twenty-four hours. The May 29 issue detailed the supposed atrocities of the Parisian mob. By May 30, headlines described the brutal reprisals.
28. "Communist Trials," *Times* (London), September 7, 1871, p. 7.
29. In the fall of 1871, approximately 750 male communists and 1,000 women and children arrived in Britain. That number doubled in the ensuing years as the prosecutions continued (Martinez, "Paris Communard Refugees in Britain," 54). Estimates varied: 1,000 to 3,500 were said to be in London in 1875 (Martinez, "Paris Communard Refugees in Britain," 103; Communist Prisoners, 1872–1873, National Archives, HO 45/9303/11335).
30. "The Government has initiated a prosecution. . .," *Times* (London), April 1, 1881, p. 10.
31. Bernard Porter, "The *Freiheit* Prosecutions, 1881–1882," *The Historical Journal* 23, no. 4 (December 1980): 848.
32. *Hansard's Parliamentary Debates* 260, House of Commons Debates, April 28, 1881, c. 1312; *Hansard's Parliamentary Debates* 261, House of Lords Debates, May 19, 1881, cc. 785–789.
33. Porter, "The *Freiheit* Prosecutions," 847, n. 84 on 847.
34. John Quail, *The Slow Burning Fuse: The Lost History of the British Anarchists* (London: Paladin, 1978), 17; George Browne, *Narrative of State Trials, 1801–1830*, vol. I (London: Sampson Low, 1882), appendix B, abstract from *Reg.* v. Most (1881), 425–426; Porter, "The *Freiheit* Prosecutions," 846–847.
35. Martinez, "Paris Communard Refugees in Britain," quoting Harrison, 66. Harrison did not preserve detailed correspondence regarding this relief effort, nor was a final report published regarding the effort. Five pounds seems to be a large amount for a housekeeper.
36. Martinez, "Paris Communard Refugees in Britain," 37–38.
37. Ibid., 68. Although no one made the connection between their scheme and asylum for liberated Africans, the coincidence is interesting. Ironically, Marzial's small enterprise shared much in common with how Alice Bullard has characterized the French government's transportation of Communard prisoners to New Caledonia in *Exile to Paradise: Savagery and Civilization in Paris and the South Pacific, 1790–1900* (Palo Alto: Stanford University Press, 2000).
38. Ernest Vizetelly, *The Anarchists* (London: John Lane, 1911), 86.
39. Tom Corfe, *The Phoenix Park Murders: Conflict, Compromise and Tragedy in Ireland, 1879–1882* (London: Hodder and Stoughton, 1968), 249. Only the Venezuelan government complied with Britain's request for the extradition of Westgate, who boasted of his involvement in the murders. The claim proved false (Corfe, *Phoenix Park Murders*, 228).
40. I have found no post-1870 discussion of the United States's deportation of the Fenian leaders of an 1866 raid on Canada. More generally, the United States had a different policy regarding her neighbors. Extradition treaties with Mexico and

with Peru did not include an exemption for "political offenders." E. L. de Hart, "Extradition of Political Offenders," *The Law Quarterly Review* 2, no. 6 (April 1886): 186.

41. Jonathan Parry, "Cavendish, Spencer Compton, Marquess of Hartington and eighth duke of Devonshire (1833–1908)," *Oxford Dictionary of National Biography* (Oxford: Oxford University Press, September 2004), http://www.oxforddnb.com/view/article/32331, accessed May 16, 2009.
42. Hart, "Extradition of Political Offenders," 187. Hart drew from a report of the Institute of International Law, an organization founded in Belgium in 1873 by international jurists. Its meetings rotate; the report on the Political Offender Exemption was issued, in French, from Oxford.
43. "Treaties of Extradition," *Times* (London), July 28, 1886, p. 7.
44. "Another Extradition Fiasco," *Reynolds's Newspaper* (London), March 25, 1883, p. 4.
45. Spanish General Weyler was responsible for the first "concentration camps," the horrors of which made the term a loaded one by the time of the Second Anglo-Boer War. When Hitler used the term, however, it was part of his anti-British propaganda.
46. Spanish Atrocities Committee, *The Revival of the Inquisition* (London: J. Perry, 1897), 2, 3, and 19, as found in Foreign: Resolution re: tortures inflicted on Spanish political prisoners, National Archives, HO 45/9743/A56151C/3.
47. Sir John Rose, "Extradition of Alledged Political Offenders," *Times* (London), April 20, 1883, p. 4.
48. Among the members of the 1868 House of Commons select committee were J. S. Mill, Edward Egerton, E. P. Bouverie, William McCullagh Torrens, the solicitor general (Sir Charles Selwyn and then William Baliol Brett), W. E. Forster, Percy Wyndham, August Henry Layard, Sir Francis Goldsmid, Sir Robert Collier, and James Stansfeld. On the royal commission were Lord Chief Justice Sir Alexander Cockburn, Councillor Baron Selborn, Baron Blackburn (the Lords of Appeal in Ordinary), Russell Curney (recorder of City of London), Sir Richard Baggallay (judge of Court of Appeal), Sir William Baliol Brett (judge of Court of Appeal), Sir John Rose (Canadian jurist and diplomat, now permanently in England), Sir James Fitzjames Stephen (counsel), Sir William George Granville Harcourt (consul), William McCullagh Torrens (bachelor of laws), and Alfred Henry Thesiger (counsel). Only Torrens and Baliol Brett sat on both.
49. Testimony of the Rt. Hon. E. Hammond before the Committee, Parliamentary Papers, 1867–1868 (393) (393-I), "Index to the reports from the Select Committee on Extradition," pp.12–13, paragraph 207.
50. Mill in Parliamentary Papers, 1867–1868 (393), p. 13, paragraph 208.
51. Testimony of T. Henry, May 19, 1868, in Parliamentary Papers, 1867–1868 (393), p. 33, paragraph 620.
52. E. S. Roscoe, "Extradition of Criminals," *Fraser's Magazine*, New Series 14, no. 80 (August 1876): 167.
53. Parliamentary Papers, 1878 (2039) Royal Commission on Extradition, Report of the Commissioners, 7.
54. Ibid.
55. Ibid., 6.
56. Ibid., 8–9.

57. Harcourt to Selborne, February 22, 1885, HO 45/9606/A2566/17a, quoted in Adams, "British Extradition Policy and the Problem of the Political Offender, 1842–1914," 194.
58. As long as they did not conspire to murder—which was illegal—political revolutionaries were safe. It is unclear whether Britain would even have extradited a foreigner who conspired to murder as imprisonment within the United Kingdom was an option too.
59. Days after the Greenwich Park Explosion, Home Secretary Asquith assured concerned MPs that "the direction which International efforts can most fruitfully take is to be found not so much in an extension of the power of expulsion on suspicion." Such power "is apt to confound the innocent with the guilty, and to shift the burden and the danger from one country to another." Instead, protection would be found "in a more constant and concerted interchange of information" between the governments and the foreign and domestic police. *Hansard's Parliamentary Debates* 21, House of Commons Debates, February 19, 1894, c. 721ff.
60. Adams, "British Extradition Policy and the Problem of the Political Offender, 1842–1914," 241. The *Economist* was willing to see a new law implemented but would not hear of any interference with the political exemption. The *Times* thought any change highly impractical.
61. *See* Torrens's reasons for dissenting from Sect. VII of the 1878 Royal Commission Report (Section on Political Offense), *1878 Report*, (13–15), 14.
62. Pyle, *Extradition, Politics, and Human Rights*, 107ff.
63. "Queen's Bench Div., Nov. 10 and 11, 1890," *Law Times Reports* 64, no. 8 (May 16, 1891): 344–352.
64. Ibid., 346.
65. Ibid., 349.
66. Pyle, *Extradition, Politics, and Human Rights*, 94.
67. Meunier's bombing of Café Véry was timed with the French trial of anarchist Ravochol, who had been captured after bombings at the same café. John Merriman, *The Dynamite Club: How a Bombing in Paris Ignited the Age of Modern Terror* (New York: Houghton Mifflin Harcourt, 2009), 80.
68. "Queen's Bench Div., Monday June 11, Re: Meunier," *Law Times* 71 (November 17, 1894): 403, 405–406.
69. Adams, "British Extradition Policy and the Problem of the Political Offender, 1842–1914," 208.
70. The United States took its cue from British liberals. The 1866 debates over extradition in Britain also established the modern definition of "political offender" in the United States, Pyle explains. *Extradition, Politics, and Human Rights*, 83ff.
71. By the time of McKinley's 1901 assassination, even the United States seemed prepared to agree to anti-anarchist collaboration. America, however, like Britain, opted not to join renewed anti-anarchist meetings in 1904.
72. From November through December 1898, delegates from twenty-one European countries convened first to define anarchism, then to systematize international police collaboration, and finally to agree to the mutual extradition of anarchists between the states which signed the final accords. For a history of international policing, see Mathieu Deflem, *Policing World Society: Historical Foundations of International Police Cooperation* (Oxford: Oxford University Press, 2004), 65ff.

73. Conference on Anarchists, 1899–1904, Home Office Permanent Undersecretary Sir Kenelm Digby, Minute given on behalf of HM Government at the Conference in Rome in 1898, January 2, 1899, National Archives, FO 83/1970.

74. Marquis of Salisbury to Sir P. Currie, November 28, 1898, Correspondence Respecting the Anti-Anarchist Conference Held at Rome in 1898, National Archives, FO 881/7179, no. 7, f. 10.

75. Currie to Salisbury, December 5, 1898, Correspondence Respecting the Anti-Anarchist Conference Held at Rome in 1898, National Archives, FO 881/7179, no. 11, f. 17; Digby, Memorandum on Sir P. Currie's telegram of 5 December 1898 to Salisbury, Correspondence Respecting the Anti-Anarchist Conference Held at Rome in 1898, National Archives, FO 881/7179, no. 12, f. 19.

76. Digby, Memorandum on Sir P. Currie's telegram of 5 December 1898 to Salisbury, Correspondence Respecting the Anti-Anarchist Conference Held at Rome in 1898, National Archives, FO 881/7179, no. 12, f. 18–19.

77. "Anti-Anarchist Congress," *Reynolds's Newspaper*, December 4, 1898, 4; "Anti-Anarchist Conference at Rome," *The Graphic* (London), December 10, 1898, 28.

78. Edward Dutton Cook, *Doubleday's Children* (New York: G. P. Putnam's Sons, 1877), 161.

79. Ibid., 161–162, 266, 368.

CHAPTER SEVEN

1. See the case of Joah, who sought refuge on the British ship, the "May Frere" in 1873 in Parliamentary Papers, 1876 (1516), Royal Commission on Fugitive Slaves, Report of the Commissioners and Minutes of Evidence, xii, 166–167.

2. William Mulligan's "The Fugitive Slave Circulars, 1875–76," *The Journal of Imperial and Commonwealth History* 37, no. 2 (June 2009): 183–205 uses much of the same archival material. The first to describe the circulars, he never contextualizes the crisis in the history of asylum. Mulligan is surprised by the humanitarian protest on behalf of slaves and believes it to be the first expression of such interest since the 1830s and a harbinger of campaigns against new slaveries that began in the 1880s. Richard Huzzey, by contrast, uses the protest against the circular as evidence of continuing public antislavery sentiment. Huzzey, *Freedom Burning: Anti-Slavery and Empire in Victorian Britain,* (Ithaca: Cornell University Press, 2012), 71–72. For the history of slavery in the Indian Ocean world—Zanzibar, in particular—see Abdul Sheriff, *Slaves, Spices & Ivory in Zanzibar: Integration of an East African Commercial Empire into the World Economy, 1770–1873* (London: James Currey, 1987); and Robert Harms, ed., *Indian Ocean Slavery in the Age of Abolition* (New Haven, CT: Yale University Press, 2013).

3. These treaties were signed piecemeal, the first with Persian rulers the 1820s. It was the 1845 treaty with the sultan of Muscat and Zanzibar that renewed British antislavery work in the area. The treaty made the foreign trade illegal and gave the British right to patrol the coastline, including the sultan's territorial waters, for this traffic.

   The extent of territorial waters off any given coastline varied (and continues to vary) by country, but was generally determined by the line at which tidal waters began. Vattel found this determination to be a difficult one. Emer de

Vattel, *The Law of Nations* [1758] Book I, Ch. 23, §289. By twentieth-century conventions, the line can be drawn up to twelve nautical miles from the coast.

4. Parliamentary Papers, 1871 (420), Report from the Select Committee on Slave Trade (East Coast of Africa); together with the proceedings of the committee, minutes of evidence, appendix and index, vi. (Henceforward abbreviated as "1871 Committee Report")
5. 1871 Committee Report, vii.
6. Members of a House of Commons select committee on the eastern slave trade summed up the matter thus: "Assuming that an efficient squadron is maintained, [. . .] the disposal of the liberated slaves becomes a matter of large importance." 1871 Committee Report, ix.
7. Earl Russell's 1864 letter seeking to calm the sultan's concern for legal slavery as quoted in 1871 Committee Report, v, vi.
8. Edward Hutchinson, *The Slave Trade of East Africa* (London: Sampson Low, Marston, & Searle, 1874), 95. At a conference in Paris in 1867, representatives opened the meeting by recalling the "romance" of Sierra Leone and hoped that its history could be repeated for the Eastern slave. *Special Report of the Anti-Slavery Conference, Held in Paris in the Salle Herz, on the 26 and 27th August, 1867* (London: BFASS, 1867), 20–22, 49.
9. Confidential. Slave Trade on the East Coast of Africa (November 1871), BL Add. MSS 44,617, Vol. DXXXII (June–December 1871), f. 132, p. 1 of the memorandum. The author of this memorandum was likely H. C. Rothery, a high-profile barrister who later became a Conservative voice on the fugitive slave commission of 1876. He had, since 1860, been the Treasury's expert counsel on matters relating to the slave trade.
10. Ibid., f. 133, p. 3 of memorandum.
11. Ibid., f. 133, p. 4 of the memorandum.
12. Frere claimed that the objective was to advance abolition in a manner that demonstrated to the sultan that he was "being carried with us, and the native local authorities being carried with us in all that we do." Frere before the Committee, 1871 Committee Report, 25.
13. 1871 Committee Report, viii.
14. Parliamentary Papers, 1873 (820), Correspondence respecting Sir B. Frere's Mission to E. Coast of Africa, 1872–73, Treaty between HM and the Sultan of Muscat, signed April 14, 1873, Enclosure 1 in no. 48, Sir B. F. to Earl of Granville, dated April 14, 1873, 91; "On disposal of liberated slaves," no. 53 in 1871 Committee Report, Letter from Sir B. F. to Earl of Granville, dated May 7, 1873, 118–119.
15. Outside colonial territory, fugitive slaves were usually returned to their masters—a fact of which few in Britain were aware. Consular agents reportedly tried to ensure that masters did not subject fugitives to exceptionally severe punishment after their return to bondage. In settler colonies, individual fugitives could usually be accommodated without undue inconvenience to the government. India was different, however. More akin to the situation in East Africa, fugitives from domestic slavery taxed a colonial ideology that recognized both British law and local custom. The "Indian model" of abolition was designed to recognize local custom and to avoid the expense of emancipation incurred in the Caribbean. From 1833, slavery in India was outlawed, but administrators did not advertise this change in the hopes that emancipation would occur slowly.

Thus, only slaves who sought out freedom from British authorities were likely to receive it. Similar judicial authority developed in the Gold Coast and British East Africa after it became a protectorate in 1895. Radhika Singha, "Making the Domestic More Domestic: Criminal Law and the 'Head of the Household,' 1772–1843," *Indian Economic & Social History Review* 33 (1996): 311; Suzanne Miers, *Slavery in the Twentieth Century* (Walnut Creek, CA: Altamira, 2003), chap. 3; Howard Temperley, "The Delegalization of Slavery in British India," *After Slavery: Emancipation and Its Discontents*, ed. Howard Temperley (London: Frank Cass, 2000), 169–187.

16. 1871 Committee Report, Testimony of Henry Adrian Churchill, 24.
17. Parliamentary Papers, 1876 (1516), Royal Commission on Fugitive Slaves, Report of the Commissioners and Minutes of the Evidence, Qu. 173, p. 6; q. 365, p. 13; Q. 727, p. 27; Q. 754, p. 28; Q. 1002, p. 40; Q. 1181, p. 46; Q. 1228, p. 49; Q. 1250, p. 50; Q. 1310, p. 53. (Henceforward abbreviated as *"1876 Report"*)
18. The July 31, 1875, fugitive slave circular, reprinted in the *Anti-Slavery Reporter*, Third Series 19, no. 9 (November 1, 1875): 210.
19. Hutchinson, *The Slave Trade of East Africa*, 95; Hutchinson, *The Fugitive Slave Circulars; or, England the Protector of the Negro Slave. A Letter to the Baroness Burdett-Coutts* (London: Edward Stanford, 1876).
20. The *Times* reported townhall meetings in Birmingham (January 8), Worchester (January 10), Culper (January 17), Reading (January 17), Manchester (January 20), Salford (January 20), Brighton (January 24), Lambeth (January 26), and London (January 29); and association meetings for the Liberal Association in Oxford (January 10), the Chichester Conservative Association (January 10), the Heywood Conservative Association (January 13), Liberal meeting in Gloucester (January 17), Liberal Reform Association in Maidstone (January 19), Junior Conservative Club in Cambridge (January 18), and the Kiboworth Working Men's Constitutional Association (January 25).
21. "England and Slavery," *Newcastle Chronicle*, September 18, 1875, 4. James Somersett fled his American master, Charles Stewart, while traveling together in England. Having been recaptured, Somersett and abolitionist Granville Sharpe brought the case before the King's Bench. Lord Chief Justice Mansfield set Somersett free, declaring that there was no English law that permitted slavery. Popular understanding of the ruling in the decades thereafter often held that Mansfield referred to slavery in the British Empire as well. He did not.
22. Sir Henry James, letter to the editor, *Times* (London), October 27, 1875, 9. This Henry James was a lawyer and MP, not the novelist.
23. Historicus [pseudonym], "The Admiralty Circular," *Times* (London), November 5, 1875, 5. Historicus cites Theodore Ortolan, who issued a widely used guide for the French navy in the 1840s. There was no similar guide for the British, many bemoaned
24. George Davis, *The Elements of International Law* (New York and London: Harper & Brothers Publishers, 1887), 57, 71. Among others, Davis relies on the following for his point: French lawyer Théodore Ortolan; Henry Wagner Halleck, an American law expert; Sir Robert Joseph Phillimore, Lord Judge for the British Admiralty and a member of the Fugitive Slave Commission in 1876; Frederick De Martens, the Russian diplomat and jurist who dealt with international arbitration in this period; Travers Twiss, advocate-general to the British Admiralty and author on the law of nations; and the eighteenth-century Swiss theorist

Emer de Vattel, who was among the earliest international legal theorists and drew from Christian Wolff and Hugo Grotius. Vattel explains that this doctrine of the high seas had not always existed but was contested through the early eighteenth century as a part of the commercial conflict between expanding European empires—England and the Netherlands, in particular. *Law of Nations*, Book I, chap. 23.

25. "The Fugitive Slave Circular," *Pall Mall Gazette*, November 5, 1875, 1.
26. Vattel, *Law of Nations*, Book IV, chap. 7, §§ 92 and 93.
27. "Fugitive Slave Circular," *Times* (London), February 15, 1876, 8.
28. Arthur Cohen, Letter to the Editor, *Times* (London), February 24, 1876, 8.
29. "Letter from Ironside—Toryism and Slavery," *Newcastle Chronicle*, October 9, 1875, 4.
30. "Fugitive Slave Circular, *Daily News*, January 13, 1876, 2.
31. *Hansard's Parliamentary Debates* 227, House of Commons Debates on "Reception of Fugitive Slaves—The Circulars," February 24, 1876, c. 825.
32. *Hansard's Parliamentary Debates* 227, c. 735. Ashley was the son of the 7th Earl of Shaftesbury, a Tory who had also been a supporter of continental refugees (notably the Neapolitan refugees in the late 1850s) and fugitive slave supporter, especially in the wake of the American Fugitive Slave Act of 1850.
33. "Fugitive Slave Circular," *Times* (London), January 27, 1876, 4. For Gladstone's knowledge on this question and the evidence his administration gathered, see BL Add. MSS 44,617, Vol. DXXXII, f. 132.
34. "Fugitive Slaves and British Ships," *Liverpool Mercury*, February 17, 1876, 6.
35. "The Second Fugitive Slave Circular," *The Friend*, New Series 16 (February 25, 1876): 25.
36. "The Extinguisher Trick," *Punch, or the London Charivari* 70 (February 19, 1876): 59.
37. The commissioners included the Lord Chief Justices A. E. Cockburn (Duke of Somerset) and T. D. Archibald, several individuals with experience adjudicating cases of the illicit slave trade and others with particular expertise in international law and diplomatic policies more broadly. Sir Robert Phillimore, Leopold G. Heath, and H. C. Rothery each had expertise with the Admiralty. Phillimore had been admiralty general counsel. Heath was a retired rear-admiral who had served in the Near East. Rothery's experience was tied directly to the antislave-trade squadron, as legal adviser to the Treasury on matters relating to the slave trade. James Fitzjames Stephen, Montague Bernard, and Henry Maine were legal scholars. Stephen and Maine were experts in comparative and international law, and Bernard in diplomacy. Sir Henry Holland and Sir George Campbell had experience in the Colonial Office and Parliament. Holland, a Conservative MP, had been assistant colonial undersecretary (and would later be secretary of state). Campbell had just returned from India where he was lieutenant governor of Bengal. Upon his return he was elected as Liberal MP from Scotland.
38. 1876 Report, viii.
39. Casper Sylvest, "The Foundations of Victorian International Law," in *Visions of Global Order: Empire and International Relations in Nineteenth-Century Political Thought*, ed. Duncan Bell (Cambridge: Cambridge University Press, 2007), 51ff.
40. K. J. M. Smith, *James Fitzjames Stephen: Portrait of a Victorian Rationalist* (Cambridge: Cambridge University Press, 2002).

41. 1876 Report, xix–xx.
42. Ibid., xxv.
43. Ibid., xxv.
44. Cockburn, 1876 Report, xxx.
45. Ibid. In his 1883 *The History of English Criminal Law*, Stephen reiterated Cockburn's findings, using the fugitive slave question to explain the limit of British criminal law in the territorial waters of a foreign nation. (vol. II, chap. 16)
46. Cockburn, 1876 Report, xivi.
47. Stephen, 1876 Report, lx, lxi.
48. Stephen, 1876 Report, lx. See also p. lxi for more of Stephen's acknowledgement that this would necessarily cause "every humane person" to revolt.
49. Cockburn, 1876 Report, xxxii.
50. Here Cockburn draws from an 1820 case in which Lord Stowell argued that he knew "of no such right of protection belonging to the British flag, and that I think such a pretension is unfounded in point of principle, is injurious to the rights of other countries, and is inconsistent with those of our own." Cockburn, citing Stowell, 1876 Report, xxxv.
51. Admiralty officers confirmed that this slavery was "the mildest possible form," on the basis that they had never seen ill usage. Fugitive Slave Commission Hearings, paragraphs 75 (Rear Admiral A. Cumming, C. B. claims that they are well treated on the African coast and would not leave even if enticed), 247 (Captain George Sullivan, RN claims that "they laugh at everything, and . . . never see them unhappy"), 364 (none ran, even where policy was to free), 374, 526, 756, 817, 824, 1019, 1105, 1155, 1160, 1164, 1178, 1188, 1231, 1472, and 1483. Quoting Livingstone, the commissioners claimed that "it is the mildest possible form; the master lives with his slaves as the father of the family." Livingstone to Lord Clarendon, June 11, 1866, 1876 Report, xvi.
52. 1876 Report, xvii.
53. 1876 Report, points III, IV, VIII, p. xviii.
54. One would expect to find that the Aborigines' Protection Society (APS), concerned with coolie labor around the world, would have become involved in this question regarding the care of fugitive and liberated slaves in East Africa. Indeed, the APS shared a membership with the BFASS since their founding in the late 1830s. Despite these definite connections, I have not found evidence that the issues were openly linked at the time.
55. Reverend Edward Steere, "Slave Trade as at Present Existing," in the *Authorized Report of the Church [of England] Congress, held at Nottingham, 10–13 October 1871* (London: W. Wells Gardner, 1871), 179–181. Steere presented at an October 11 session on the "Duty of the Church in Reference to the Slave Trade." The charge was carried into the secular media as well. John Armstrong Challice of the Royal Navy wrote to the London *Times* on November 14, 1872, on the condition of life in British refuge.
56. Commission Testimony, 1876 Report, paragraph 254.
57. Ibid., paragraph 1703.
58. Ibid., paragraph 1702.
59. Ibid., paragraph 251.
60. Ibid., xvii.
61. Ibid.
62. Ibid.

63. Ibid.
64. Sir H. Bartle E. Frere, "Memorandum on the Establishments for Liberated Africans at Mombaza and Nyanza," Dated May 10, 1876, appended to the *1876 Commission Report*, 231.
65. Commission Hearing, 1876 Report, paragraphs 1704–1709.
66. 1876 Report, paragraphs 672, 935, 1704.
67. Edward Hutchinson, *The Slave Trade of East Africa*, 92. Naval officers who testified before the commission were also forgetful of the difficulties inherent in the Sierra Leone project. 1876 Report, 16.
68. "The New or Third Fugitive Slave Circular," *British and Foreign Anti-Slavery Reporter* (November 1, 1876): 160.
69. Morton, *Children of Ham*, 118–119.
70. R. T. Shannon, *Gladstone and the Bulgarian Agitation 1876*, 2nd ed. (Hassocks: Harvester Press, 1975).

CHAPTER EIGHT

1. *Hansard's Parliamentary Debates* 8, House of Commons Debate on "Destitute Aliens," February 11, 1893, c. 1157.
2. Ibid., c. 1156.
3. Gareth Stedman Jones, *Outcast London: A Study of the Relationship between Classes in Victorian London* (Oxford: Oxford University Press, 1971).
4. *Hansard's Parliamentary Debates*, House of Commons Debate on "Destitute Aliens," c. 1211. On the whole, the Board of Trade was not entirely immigrant friendly.
5. See, for example, Michael Marrus, *The Unwanted: European Refugees in the Twentieth Century* (Philadelphia: Temple University Press, 1985), chap. 1; Claudena Skran, *Refugees in Inter-War Europe: The Emergence of a Regime* (Oxford: Clarendon Press, 1995), 14ff; Liza Schuster, *The Use and Abuse of Political Asylum in Britain and Germany* (London: Frank Cass, 2003), 82; Colin Holmes, *John Bull's Island* (London: George Allen and Unwin, 1978); Porter, *The Refugee Question*; Tony Kushner, *Remembering Our Refugees: Then and Now* (Manchester: Manchester University Press, 2006); David Feldman, "Was the Nineteenth Century a Golden Age for Immigrants?," in *Migration Control in the North Atlantic World*, ed. Andreas Fahrmeir et al. (New York: Berghahn Books, 2005), 167–177; and, most recently, David Glover, *Literature, Immigration and Diaspora in Fin-De-Siècle England: A Cultural History of the 1905 Aliens Act* (New York: Cambridge University Press, 2012). Scholars who are more attentive to the language of the act itself tend, like Bernard Gainer, to attribute the entirety of the refugee opt-out clause to Liberals, and to Dilke in particular. Gainer, *Alien Invasion* (New York: Crane, Russak, and Co., Inc., 1972), 196. For Gainer, Dilke's victory has little to do with British involvement with foreign refugees—though he cites this tradition in the debates. Rather it is more to do with the struggle between free trade ideology and protectionism (Gainer, *Alien Invasion*, chap. 7). I agree that the debate has much to do with this ideological and policy concern. However, this does not help us to understand the distinction between refugees and immigrants within the debate or within liberal ideology more generally.

6. Carole Fink, *Defending the Rights of Others: The Great Powers, the Jews, and International Minority Protection* (New York: Cambridge University Press, 2004), prologue.
7. See Chapter Four in this volume. On the emergence of transnational movements, see Frank Trentmann, Kevin Grant, and Philippa Levine, eds., *Beyond Sovereignty: Britain, Empire and Transnationalism, c. 1860–1950* (London: Palgrave Macmillan, 2007); Kevin Grant, *A Civilised Savagery: Britain and the New Slaveries in Africa, 1884–1926* (London: Routledge, 2005); Akira Iriye, *Global Community: The Role of International Organizations in the Making of the Contemporary World* (Berkeley: University of California Press, 2002).
8. Cariclee Zacaroff, "The Turkish Compassionate Fund," in *The Congress of Women*, ed. Mary Kavanaugh Oldham (Chicago: Monarch Book Company, 1894), 618–622, accessed online at http://digital.library.upenn.edu/women/eagle/congress/zacaroff.html; H. Mainwaring Dunstan, *The Turkish Compassionate Fund: An Account of its Origin, Working, and Results* (London: Remington and Co., 1883).
9. Israel Davis, *The Jews in Roumania* (London: Trübner and Co., 1872). Romania naturalized Jews at an appallingly slow rate. International pressure eased when outright violence against Jews ebbed, though such violence would surge again at the turn of the century.
10. Simon Dubnow, *History of the Jews in Russia and Poland*, trans. I. Friedlaender (Bergenfield, NJ: Avotaynu Inc, 2000), 260 especially.
11. Resolutions drawn up at a meeting of the Anglo-Jewish Association on May 27 for the May 30 Mansion House meeting, Roumanian Committee Minute Book, 1872–1876, University of Southampton Special Collections, Anglo-Jewish Association Archives, AJ 37/6/2/7, f. 9.
12. "Bigotry in Roumania," *Times* (London), May 31, 1872, p. 8.
13. Recalling the 1872 meeting, one writer admitted that oppression in Romania had not ended, but he argued that the Romanian government had "taken care that their grievances should fall short of the measure which was sufficient to call forth the protests then publicly made in the city of London as well as elsewhere in Europe and America." Similar results, he implied, could be expected in the wake of public remonstrance against Russia. "Mansion House Meeting," *Jewish Chronicle* (London), February 3, 1882, p. 9.
14. "Persecutions of Jews in Russia," *Jewish Chronicle*, February 10, 1882, p. 10–11; Dubnow, *History of the Jews in Russia and Poland*, 347.
15. John Klier, "The Times of London, the Russian Press, and the Pogroms of 1881–1882," Paper no. 308, *The Carl Beck Papers in Russian and Eastern European Studies*, ed. Wm. Chase and R. Linden (Pittsburgh: University of Pittsburgh, 1984), 14–15. Regional newspapers republished the proceedings of each meeting and added notes on local approval of humanitarian outreach, a move that helped to raise relief funds in turn. For a sampling of the national press coverage, see "Persecution of the Jews in Russia," *The Belfast New-Letter*, February 2, 1882, p. 5; "Persecution of the Jews in Russia," *Birmingham Daily Post*, February 2, 1882, p. 5, and February 15, 1882, p. 8; "Anti-Jewish Agitation in Russia," *Bristol Mercury*, February 2, 1882, p. 8; "District News," *Bristol Mercury*, June 22, 1882, p. 6; "Persecution of the Jews in Russia, *Glasgow Herald*, February 2, 1882, p. 5, and February 3, 1882, p. 7; "Persecution of the Jews in Russia" and "Mansion House

Meeting," *Hampshire Telegraph*, February 4, 1882, pp. 3–4; "Jewish Persecution in Russia," *Western Mail*, March 10, 1882, p. 3; "Exodus of the Jews from Russia," *Western Mail*, June 1, 1882, p. 3.

16. Gladstone's letter was reprinted throughout the press, as were the proceedings of meetings in favor of Jewish settlements overseas, in Palestine, in particular. For Gladstone's letter, see *Birmingham Daily Post*, May 29, 1891, p. 5; *London Daily News*, May 29, 1891, p. 5; *Liverpool Mercury*, May 29, 1891, p. 5; and the *Northern Echo*, May 30, 1891, p. 3, to name a few of the publications. For examples of meetings on resettlement in Palestine, see (among others) "Society for the Relief of Persecuted Jews," *The Graphic* (London), June 13, 1891, p. 31; "Colonisation of Palestine by Jews," *Liverpool Mercury*, July 6, 1891, p. 3; "Refugee Jews in Palestine," *London Daily News*, November 13, 1891, p. 3 (The paper covered Jewish migration to the region extensively that fall.); and "The Persecution of the Jews in Russia," *Western Mail* (Cardiff, Wales), June 22, 1891, p. 6.
17. "Mission to the Czar," *Jewish Chronicle*, January 2, 1891, p. 13.
18. Grant, "British Suffragettes and the Russian Method of Hunger Strike," 125.
19. "Russian Outrages," *Jewish Chronicle*, February 24, 1882, p. 1.
20. Eugene C. Black, *The Social Politics of the Anglo-Jewry, 1880–1820* (Oxford: Basil Blackwell, 1988), 255, table 9.2.
21. "Russo-Jewish Refugees," *Jewish Chronicle*, January 19, 1883, p. 10.
22. For request to the baroness, see, for instance, n. 441 in the Anglo-Jewish Association's Executive Committee Meeting Books (September 1874–November 1909) as found in AJ 95/ADD/5 of the University of Southampton Special Collections. The *Jewish Chronicle* also reported on her immense contributions to refugee Jews.
23. *Persecution of the Jews in Russia, Mansion House Relief Fund, Liverpool Commission* (Liverpool: Egerton Smith and Co., 1882), 7; Joseph Jacobs, *Statistics of Jewish Population in London, etc., 1873–1893* (London: E. W. Rabbinowicz, 1894), 5.
24. Dubnow, *History of the Jews in Russia and Poland*, 321; *Jewish Chronicle*, May 19, 1882,–5, and this issue of the *Chronicle* more generally; and *Mansion House and JBG Report of Proceedings, 1883*, 70, as found in the University of Southampton Special Collections, MS 173, Jewish Care 1/12/4, Jewish Board of Guardians, Annual Reports, 1880–1886.
25. Letter of Lewis Emmanuel printed in the *Jewish Chronicle*, May 26, 1882, p. 4. Days later, Hermann Kisch, permanent under-secretary of state at Calcutta, joined the MHF. Kisch does not seem to have been sent to Brody. Nevertheless, Emmanuel felt "sure that Mr. Kisch will be able to afford the precise kind of technical knowledge derived from his experience during the Indian famine."
26. "The Russian Refugees at Brody," *Jewish Chronicle*, July 14, 1882, p. 10.
27. Edward Manson, "The Admission of Aliens," *Journal of the Society of Comparative Legislation* New Series 4, no. 2. (1902): 114–127; "Emigration to South Africa," *Jewish Chronicle*, February 6, 1903, p. 11.
28. Moritz Ellinger, "The Emigration of Russian Jews"(An address by of the Hebrew emigrants' aid society of NY), *Jewish Chronicle*, January 27, 1882, p. 11. See also scholarship and contemporary media coverage on Baron de Hirsch's schemes to resettle Jews in Canada and in South America. The concern was whether Jews would thrive as agriculturalists. The question tended to be answered in the negative.
29. "Mansion House Fund," *Jewish Chronicle*, June 2, 1882, p. 10.

30. "Russian Jews in America," *Jewish Chronicle*, June 30, 1882, p. 7.
31. W. H. Wilkins, *The Alien Invasion* (London: Methuen and Co., 1892), 11.
32. Chapter Four in this volume.
33. Immigration of Jews into Palestine, 1891–1905, National Archives, FO 78/5479, f. 75 and thereafter. Arnold White even suggested Armenia, which was particularly odd given the massacres of Armenian Christians then taking place (Gainer, *Alien Invasion*, 127).

34. Initially, the groups making these claims were small. At the time of the Boer War and the 1901 Khaki Election, popular organizations emerged (Gainer, *Alien Invasion*, 60). Deborah Cohen highlights that this strident emphasis on Jewish distinctiveness derived from concern over how similar they were to native-born subjects. Cohen, "Who Was Who? Race and Jews in Turn-of-the-Century Britain," *Journal of British Studies* 41 (October 2002): 461.
35. W. H. Wilkins, *The Alien Invasion* (London: Methuen and Co., 1892), 47; Arnold White, *The Problems of a Great City*, 3rd ed. (London: Remington and Company, Ltd., 1895 [1886]), xxvi.
36. William Evans-Gordon, *The Alien Immigrant* (London: William Heinemann, 1903), 3.
37. Feldman, *Englishmen and Jews: Social Relations and Political Culture, 1840–1914* (New Haven, CT: Yale University Press, 1994), 142.
38. White's testimony in *Parliamentary Papers*, 1888 (305), Report from the Select Committee on Emigration and Immigration (foreigners), p. 93, paragraph 1906.
39. Wilkins made the connection to unfree labor explicit (Wilkins, *Alien Invasion*, 44).
40. J. A. Hobson, *Imperialism: A Study* (London: J. Nisbet, 1902), 64. For the impact of this line of argument in literature, see Nadia Valman, "Little Jew Boys Made Good: Immigration, the South African War and Anglo-Jewish Fiction," in *The 'Jew' in Edwardian Culture*, ed. Eitan Bar-Yosef and Nadia Valman (London: Palgrave, 2008), 45–64.
41. Holmes, *Anti-Semitism in British Society*, 68. Military recruiters found that two-thirds of urban would-be soldiers were physically unfit for service. James Vernon, *Hunger: A Modern History* (Cambridge, MA: Harvard University Press, 2007), 87. This could have fueled anti-Semitism. White tended toward this point in his testimony (1903 [Cd. 1742] Royal Commission on Alien Immigration, *Minutes of Evidence, Vol. II*, 50). But this revelation led instead to a fear for the British race that ran parallel to the fear for the growth of a racially other East End. Ironically, the 1904 Committee on Physical Deterioration studied the Jewish parents as models for good parenting: their children appeared to be stronger despite growing up in the same environment as their Christian counterparts. Mitchell Hart, *The Healthy Jew* (Cambridge: Cambridge University Press, 2007), 185.
42. Judith Walkowitz, *City of Dreadful Delight: Narratives of Sexual Danger in Late-Victorian London* (Chicago: University of Chicago Press, 1992), 200ff.
43. See Gainer, *Alien Invasion*, 183, for a discussion of the stroke of luck for the anti-alienists. They dominated the royal commission with only legal expert Kenelm Digby and Lord Rothschild as countervailing forces.
44. Rev. G. S. Reaney, "The Moral Aspect," in *The Destitute Alien in Great Britain*, ed. Arnold White (London: Swan Sonnenschein, 1892), 83.
45. White, *Modern Jew*, 195–196.

46. Evans-Gordon, *The Alien Immigrant*, 293.
47. This change dovetailed with international relief organizations' emphasis on humanitarianism as nonpolitical. Both activists and the their iconic charitable subject are meant to be neutral players—the latter innocent victims of the chaos around them. This too has remained critical to nongovernmental organizations' personas.
48. I. A. Williams, "Cadbury, George (1839–1922)," revised by Robert Fitzgerald, *Oxford Dictionary of National Biography*, Oxford University Press, 2004, online edition, May 2006, available at http://www.oxforddnb.com/view/article/32232.
49. See, for example, George Cadbury, "The Stundists," *The Friend*, New Series 32 (February 12, 1892): 115.
50. Smiles, *The Huguenots*, 111. Smiles would have admired Jews' ability to live on little at a time when elite society had become so dependent on its riches. John Garrard, *The English and Immigration: A Comparative Study of the Jewish Influx 1880–1910* (London: Oxford University Press and the Institute of Race Relations, 1971), 95ff.
51. Tony Kushner, "Meaning Nothing but Good: Ethics, History and Asylum-seeker Phobia in Britain," *Patterns of Prejudice* 37, no. 3 (2003): 266–267; Moens testified on May 18, 1903, [Cd. 1742] Royal Commission on Alien Immigration, *Minutes of Evidence*, Vol. II, 847, paragraph 23,062. (Henceforward abbreviated as "1903 Royal Commission")
52. Arthur Conan Doyle, *The Refugees: A Tale of Two Continents* (London: Longmans, Green, 1893), xii–xiii.
53. Wilkins, *Alien Invasion*, 6; Evans-Gordon, *Alien Immigrant*, 8.
54. For a concise history of Jewish thought on assimilation, see Walter Laqueur, *A History of Zionism*, 3rd ed. (New York: Tauris Parke Paperbacks, 2003), chap. 1.
55. 1903 Royal Commission, Vol. II, p. 16, paragraph 332.
56. Ibid.
57. Ibid., p. 430, paragraph 12,676. George Eliot's 1876 *Daniel Deronda* anticipated this line of thought, posing the same question vis-à-vis Britain's Jews. Though not about refugees as such, the novel explores the fate of characters who marry—for love or money—in and out of the Jewish faith. Deronda, once aware of his heritage, marries the Jewish Mirah Lapidoth. Eliot does not deny that individual Jews might prefer to marry outside the faith—Deronda's mother, after being forced into marrying her first husband (Daniel's father), converts to marry her second husband.
58. 1903 Royal Commission, Vol. II, p. 217, paragraph 6364.
59. Wilkins, *Alien Invasion*, 11; Reaney, "Moral Aspect," 79.
60. Arnold White, *The Modern Jew* (London: William Heinemann, 1899), 188, 191.
61. Evans-Gordon, *Alien Immigrant*, 50–53; 1903 Royal Commission, Vol. II, p. 450, paragraph 13349. Even Evans-Gordon had to admit that the government compelled Jews to leave Romania, given their refusal to naturalize Jews. This, he admitted, was persecution. Evans-Gordon viewed Romanian Jews as a cut above their Russian and Polish coreligionists. They were well suited for emigration, though he hoped they would settle in Argentina, not London. 1903 Royal Commission, 460ff.
62. Evans-Gordon, *Alien Immigrant*, 52.
63. 1903 Royal Commission,Vol. II, pp. 215–216, paragraphs 6290–6309.

64. Standard accounts of the Anglo-Jewry highlight the parallel between their elite's response to foreign coreligionists and broader British attitudes toward the poor. The elite tended to view poverty as moral failure, emphasizing work as the solution and rationalizing/rationing their charitable activities thus. Their activities thus followed the changes to charities attempted by the Charity Organisation Society. See, for example, Feldman, *Englishmen and Jews*. Among historians, Feldman alone notes the distinction between Anglo-Jewish relief for refugees and the Anglo-Jewish Board of Guardians' work with the Jewish poor.

65. "Russian Refugees," *Jewish Chronicle*, March 31, 1882, p. 11.
66. Jewish Colonization Association Letter, dated November 9, 1896, University of Southampton Special Collections, MS 173, Jewish Care, 1/11/2, Letter book, January 1890–December 1900, f. 210.
67. "Russian Refugees," *Jewish Chronicle*, June 2, 1882, p. 6.
68. Ibid.; "Russian Refugees," *Jewish Chronicle*, July 21, 1882, p. 7.
69. Ibid.; Anglo-Jewish Association Archives, Minutes 1901–1911, dated June 19, 1905, University of Southampton Special Collections, MS 173 1/1/3, f. 133. This is in contrast to the Russian Mennonites, for example, with whom British Quakers readily identified for their shared pacifism.
70. This form of relief was typical for foreigners (non-refugees) in distress. The Society of Friends of Foreigners in Distress (begun in 1806) used this as one of its standard models of relief because they assumed a) it would be less expensive, and b) that the foreigner had better support networks in his or her home country. See accounts of the Society for 1814, 1817, 1819, 1823–1825, 1828, 1847, 1866, 1892, in the British Library's Rare Books Collection.
71. "Mansion House Meeting," *Jewish Chronicle*, February 3, 1882, p. 9.
72. "Jews in Russia," *Jewish Chronicle*, July 14, 1882, p. 10.
73. "Russo-Jewish Refugees," *Jewish Chronicle*, January 19, 1883, p. 10.
74. "Notes of the Week," *Jewish Chronicle*, February 23, 1883, p. 3.
75. "Anti-Jewish Riots in Russia," *Jewish Chronicle*, August 10, 1883, p. 7.
76. *Parliamentary Papers*, 1888 (305), Report from the Select Committee on Emigration and Immigration (foreigners), p. 112, paragraphs 2264–2265.
77. Akers-Douglas in *Hansard's Parliamentary Debates* 133, House of Commons Debates, April 25, 1904, cc. 1145–1146.
78. Carne Rasch in *Hansard's Parliamentary Debates* 133, House of Commons Debates, April 25, 1904, c. 1160.
79. Evans-Gordon in *Hansard's Parliamentary Debates* 133, House of Commons Debates, April 25, 1904, c. 1085.
80. Trevelyan in *Hansard's Parliamentary Debates* 145, House of Commons Debates, May 2, 1905, c. 704.
81. Cecil in *Hansard's Parliamentary Debates* 149, House of Commons Debates, July 10, 1905, c. 173; Balfour in *Hansard's Parliamentary Debates* 145, House of Commons Debates, May 2, 1905, c. 800.
82. Akers-Douglas in *Hansard's Parliamentary Debates* 145, House of Commons Debates, May 2, 1905, c. 752; Balfour in *Hansard's Parliamentary Debates* 149, House of Commons Debates, July 10, 1905, cc. 179–180; Trevelyan in *Hansard's Parliamentary Debates* 145, House of Commons Debates, May 2, 1905, c. 704.
83. Hope and Evans-Gordon in *Hansard's Parliamentary Debates* 149, House of Commons Debates, July 10, 1905, c. 175–176, c. 180–181.

84. Asquith and Burns in *Hansard's Parliamentary Debates* 149, House of Commons Debates, July 10, 1905, c. 180–181.

85. Balfour in *Hansard's Parliamentary Debates* 149, House of Commons Debates, July 10, 1905, c. 180; Cecil in *Hansard's Parliamentary Debates* 149, House of Commons Debates, July 17, 1905, c. 950.

CONCLUSION

1. Allan Silver, "The Lawyer and the Scrivener," *Partisan Review* 48, no. 3 (Summer 1981): 422–423.

2. Samuel Moyn, *The Last Utopia: Human Rights in History* (Cambridge: Harvard/Belknap Press, 2010). Moyn's argument is twofold. He argues that the turn to a "human rights regime" since World War II and especially since the 1970s was part of a last (or the latest) quest for a new solution to persecution, other alternatives having failed. His second argument—that concerns with human rights and the quest for such a regime began only in this moment—is untenable given, among other things, nineteenth-century discussions of a "right to refuge."

3. Moyn popularized the phrase "the last utopia" with his book of that title. See Moyn, *The Last Utopia*.

4. Here I draw upon historian William H. Sewell, Jr.'s explanation of the dual relationship between schema and resources in his "A Theory of Structure: Duality, Agency, and Transformation," *American Journal of Sociology* 98, no. 1 (July 1992). The essay is reprinted as chapter 4 of *Logics of History: Social Theory and Social Transformation* (Chicago: University of Chicago Press, 2009).

5. Norman Wise Sibley, *The Aliens Act [Stat. 5 Edw. VII. c.13], and the Right of Asylum: Together with International Law, Comparative Jurisprudence, and the History of Legislation on the Subject, and an Exposition of the Act* (London: W. Clowes and Sons, 1906), 130.

6. Alison Bashford and Jane McAdam, "The Right to Asylum: Britain's 1905 Aliens Act and the Evolution of Refugee Law," *Law and History Review* 32, no. 2 (May 2014).

7. The right "to seek" asylum is not without practical value. It has come to mean the right to be considered for asylum through a standardized process. United Nations, Commission on Human Rights Drafting Committee, Second Session, Summary of the Thirty-Seventh Meeting, May 18, 1948, United Nations Document E/CN.4/AC.1/SR.37, 8ff; Thomas Gammeltoft-Hansen and Hans Gammeltoft-Hansen, "The Right to Seek—Revisited. On the UN Human Rights Declaration Article 14 and Access to Asylum Procedures in the EU," *European Journal of Migration and Law* 10 (2008): 446; and G. Daniel Cohen, "The 'Human Rights Revolution' at Work: Displaced Persons in Postwar Europe," in *Human Rights in the Twentieth Century*, ed. Stefan-Ludwig Hoffmann (Cambridge: Cambridge University Press, 2011), 52–60, especially.

8. Unable to encode a right to asylum in human rights law, refugee conventions have turned instead to lesser rights. In addition to the right "to seek and enjoy asylum," there is a right not to be returned to a home state in which persecution remains unchecked. This non-refoulement appeared first in the 1933 League of Nations Convention on Refugees. It became a critical tool in the 1951 United Nations Refugee Convention and in the 1967 Protocol Relating to the Status of Refugees. This innovation became all the more important as the 1967 Protocol

extended the category of refugee beyond the specific groups named in earlier conventions. In this respect, the 1967 Protocol was the first international law to match the breadth of the 1905 British exemption clause, which applied to any asylum seeker facing political or religious persecution. See Gammeltoft-Hansen and Gammeltoft-Hansen, "The Right to Seek—Revisited," 441.

Refugee scholars and activists continue to bemoan the increasing separation between human rights and refugee law. The proposed solution to this problem tends to be an urgent appeal to enshrine a right to asylum more securely within the evolving arsenal of human rights guarantees. See Vincent Chetail, "Are Refugee Rights Human Rights? An Unorthodox Questioning of the Relations between Refugee Law and Human Rights Law," in *Human Rights and Immigration*, ed. Ruth Rubio-Martin (Oxford: Oxford University Press, 2014),19–21; "Message from Louise Arbour: United Nations High Commissioner for Human Rights," *Refugee Studies Quarterly* 27, no. 3 (2008): 14–15. For an additional bibliography, see Chetail, "Are Refugee Rights Human Rights?," n. 3 (p. 19–20), n. 4 (p. 20), and n. 7 (p. 20–21).

9. A. Dirk Moses, "The United Nations, Humanitarianism, and Human Rights: War Crimes/Genocide Trials for Pakistani Soldiers in Bangladesh, 1971–1974," in *Human Rights in the Twentieth Century*, ed. Stefan-Ludwig Hoffmann (Cambridge: Cambridge University Press, 2011). As Moses highlights, the international community was quite reluctant to apply the term *genocide*. Perpetrators of mass murder were first tried successfully for "genocide" only in the aftermath of the Rwandan Genocide. Moses, "The United Nations, Humanitarianism, and Human Rights," 260.

10. Refuge has become more bureaucratized and removed from the public gaze in the century after the Great War with the proliferation of governmental and nongovernmental agencies dedicated to refugee relief and the asylum-seeking process. On the domestic level, members of the European Union have—since the 1980s—fined airline companies for bringing undocumented foreigners to their borders. These companies have become a de facto part of the asylum-seeking process, forced to screen closely those they take on board, as was the case for shipmasters in the wake of the 1905 Aliens Act (Gammeltoft-Hansen and Gammeltoft-Hansen, "The Right to Seek," 450–451). On the international scene, the professionalization that accompanies the proliferation of humanitarian agencies likewise fragments authority for refugee relief even among those determined to help. For example, the 1967 Protocol on Refugees recognized the need to distribute responsibility for refugees among different organizations. The Protocol specifically excluded refugees already attended to by other United Nations Agencies. Palestinian refugees were thus not covered under its terms as they fell within the purview of the United Nations Relief and Works Agency for Palestine Refugees in the Near East rather than the High Commission on Refugees. Office of the UN High Commission for Refugees, "Introductory Note" to the Text of the 1951 Convention Relating to the Status of Refugees and Text of the 1967 Protocol Relating to the Status of Refugees," December 4, 2010, accessed online at http://www.unhcr.org/3b66c2aa10.html. For the best synthetic account of the origins of these shifts in policy and their implications for refugees in the twentieth century, see Peter Gatrell, *The Making of the Modern Refugee* (Oxford: Oxford University Press, 2013).

11. Tony Kushner, *Remembering Refugees: Then and Now* (Manchester: Manchester University Press, 2006), and Kushner, *The Battle for Britishness: Migrant Journeys, 1685 to the Present* (Manchester: Manchester University Press, 2014). There were major exceptions to this in the twentieth century, including examples that echo the tactics of the nineteenth century. For example, the United Nations' World Refugee Year of 1959 involved an immense campaign initially begun by the British Conservative Party's magazine *Crossbow* to end the world's refugee problem. The editors unleashed a torrent of global sympathy for European, Middle Eastern, and Asian refugees, a drive that would be brought to the fore by celebrities, just as local and national notables had supported similar efforts for more than 150 years. Even fitful media attention boosts refugees' causes. Peter Gatrell, *Free World?: The Campaign to Save the World's Refugees, 1956–1963* (Cambridge: Cambridge University Press, 2011), 10, 145–168.

Select Bibliography

PERSONAL PAPERS AND ASSOCIATIONAL ARCHIVES

British Library Manuscript Collection, London (BL MSS)

Additional Manuscript (Add.) 18,591, 18,592, and 18,593: Accounts and Minutes of the Committee of Subscribers for the Relief of the French Clergy, 1792–1801

Additional Manuscript 75,897: Althorp Papers

Additional Manuscript 79,743: Graham Papers

Additional Manuscript 44,617: Gladstone Papers

Additional Manuscript 39,054: Layard (Austen Henry) Papers

Additional Manuscript 46,406: A and B: Osborne Papers

Additional Manuscript 40,591: Peel Papers

Bishopsgate Institute Library, London, United Kingdom: Charles Bradlaugh Collection and George Holyoake Collection

London School of Economics and Political Science, London, United Kingdom: Special Collections: Harrison [Frederick] Collection; Armenian Leaflets 1896–1897; London Positivist Society Collection; Collections on the Revolution of 1848 in Germany

Rhodes House Library, Oxford, United Kingdom: Collections of the British and Foreign Anti-Slavery Society

Society of Friends, Friends House Library Collections, London, United Kingdom.

Tyne and Wear Archives Service, Newcastle, United Kingdom: Cowen [Joseph] Collection

University College London, United Kingdom: Special Collections Library: Huguenot Collection

University of Southampton, United Kingdom: Special Collections, Hartley Library: Wellington Papers Collection; Collections of the Anglo-Jewish Association and the Jewish Board of Guardians

GOVERNMENT PUBLICATIONS AND OFFICIAL AND SEMI-OFFICIAL RECORDS

Cobbett, William. *Parliamentary History of England from the Norman Conquest in 1066 to the Year 1803*. 36 vols. London: T. C. Hansard, 1806–1820. Continued as *Cobbett's Parliamentary Debates* from 1806–1812.

National Archives, Kew
Colonial Office Records: CO 91/119, CO 111/756/2, CO 158/148, CO 318/123, CO 323/1271/1, CO 325/31, CO 691/169/19
Foreign Office Records: FO 27/345, 78/5479, 78/2375A, FO 83/1970, FO 352/11, FO 881/173, FO 881/7179
Home Office Records: HO 5/1, HO 43/4, HO 44/1, HO 45/4816, HO 45/9303/11335, HO 45/9743/A56151C/3

Parliamentary Papers, 1824 (442). Reports by the Commissioners on the State of Africans Condemned under Acts abolishing Slave Trade and Apprenticed in W. Indies.

Parliamentary Papers, 1828 (542). Correspondence with British Commissioners at Sierra Leone, Havana, Rio de Janeiro and Surinam on Slave Trade, 1827 (Class A); Correspondence with Foreign Powers on Slave Trade, 1827 (Class B).

Parliamentary Papers, 1829 (002). Papers respecting Relations between Great Britain and Portugal, 1826–1829.

Parliamentary Papers, 1840 (43-II). Reports from Assistant Hand-Loom Weavers' Commissioners, Part III.

Parliamentary Papers, 1850 (134). Malta. Dispatches between the Governor of Malta and the Secretary of State for the Colonies, relating to the Admission of Foreigners into the Island of Malta.

Parliamentary Papers, 1861 (2813). Correspondence Respecting the Case of Fugitive Slave, Anderson.

Parliamentary Papers, 1871 (420). Report from the Select Committee on Slave Trade (East Coast of Africa); Together with the Proceedings of the Committee, Minutes of evidence, Appendix and Index.

Parliamentary Papers, 1873 (820). Correspondence respecting Sir B. Frere's Mission to E. Coast of Africa, 1872–1873.

Parliamentary Papers, 1876 (1516). Royal Commission on Fugitive Slaves, Report of the Commissioners and Minutes of Evidence.

Parliamentary Papers, 1878 (2039). Royal Commission on Extradition, Report of the Commissioners.

Parliamentary Papers, 1888 (305). Report from the Select Committee on Emigration and Immigration (foreigners).

Parliamentary Papers, 1903 (1742). Royal Commission on Alien Immigration, Minutes of Evidence, Vol. II.

MAIN PERIODICALS

The Age
Anti-Slavery Reporter
Belfast News-Letter
Bristol Mercury
Daily News
Examiner
The Friend
Gloucester Journal
The Graphic

Hampshire Advertiser
Hampshire Chronicle
Jewish Chronicle
L'Homme
Law Times Reports
Liverpool Mercury
Morning Chronicle
Newcastle Chronicle
Northern Star
Pall Mall Gazette
Penny Illustrated
Polonia
Proceedings of the Huguenot Society
Punch, or the London Charivari
Reasoner
Refugee Circular
Reynolds's Newspaper
Star of Freedom
The Times (London)
The Times (Malta)
Weekly Dispatch

PRINTED PRIMARY AND SECONDARY SOURCES

Adams, W. E. *Memoirs of a Social Atom*. New York: Augustus Kelley Publishers, 1968.

Address of the Literary Association of the Friends of Poland of Great Britain and Ireland. London: E. Detkens, 1846.

Alfie, Joe. *A New History of Sierra Leone.* London: Macmillan Publishers, Ltd., 1990.

Andrew, Donna. *Philanthropy and Police: London Charity in the Eighteenth Century.* Princeton, NJ: Princeton University Press, 1989.

Arbour, Louise. "Message from Louise Arbour: United Nations High Commissioner for Human Rights." *Refugee Studies Quarterly* 27, no. 3 (2008): 13–15.

Ashton, Rosemary. *Little Germany: Exile and Asylum in Victorian England.* Oxford: Oxford University Press, 1986.

Asiegbu, Johnston. *Slavery and the Politics of Liberation, 1787–1861.* London: Longmans, Green and Co., 1969.

Authorized Report of the Church [of England] Congress, held at Nottingham, 10–13 October 1871. London: W. Wells Gardner, 1871.

Barnett, Michael. *Empire of Humanity: A History of Humanitarianism*. Ithaca, NY: Cornell University Press, 2011.

Bar-Yosef, Eitan, and Nadia Valman, eds. *"The Jew" in Late-Victorian and Edwardian Culture: Between the East End and East Africa*. New York: Palgrave Macmillan, 2009.

Baseler, Marilyn. *Asylum for Mankind: America, 1607–1800*. Ithaca, NY: Cornell University Press, 1998.

Bashford, Alison, and Jane McAdam. "The Right to Asylum: Britain's 1905 Aliens Act and the Evolution of Refugee Law." *Law and History Review* 32, no. 2 (May 2014): 309–350.

Bass, Gary. *Freedom's Battle: The Origins of Humanitarian Intervention.* New York: Alfred Knopf, 2008.

Beck, Wilhelmine von. *Personal Adventures during the Late War in Hungary.* London: Richard Bentley, 1850.

Belchem, John. "Britishness, Asylum-Seekers and the Northern Working Class: 1851." *Northern History* 39, no. 1 (2002): 59–74.

Bell, Duncan, ed. *Visions of Global Order: Empire and International Relations in Nineteenth-Century Political Thought.* Cambridge: Cambridge University Press, 2007.

Bensimon, Fabrice. *Les Britanniques face à la révolution française de 1848.* Paris: L'Harmattan, 2000.

Bethell, Leslie. "The Mixed Commissions for the Suppression of the Transatlantic Slave Trade in the Nineteenth Century." *The Journal of African History* 7, no. 1 (1966): 79–93.

Biagini, Eugenio, ed. *Citizenship and Community: Liberals, Radicals and Collective Identities in the British Isles, 1865–1931.* Cambridge: Cambridge University Press, 1996.

Biagini, Eugenio. *Liberty, Retrenchment and Reform: Popular Liberalism in the Age of Gladstone, 1860–1880.* Cambridge: Cambridge University Press, 1992.

Bianchi, Luigi. *Incidents in the Life of an Italian: Priest—Soldier—Refugee.* London: James Nisbet, 1859.

Birmingham Ladies' Society for the Relief of British Negro Slaves, 1825–1919. 2 Microfilm Reels. East Ardsley, Yorkshire,UK: Microform Academic Publishers, N.D.

Black, Eugene C. *The Social Politics of the Anglo-Jewry, 1880–1820.* Oxford: Basil Blackwell, 1988.

Bolt, Christine, and Seymour Drescher, eds. *Anti-Slavery, Religion and Reform: Essays in Memory of Roger Antsey.* Folkestone, UK: W. Dawson, 1980.

Braidwood, Stephen. *Black Poor and White Philanthropists: London's Blacks and the Foundation of the Sierra Leone Settlement, 1786–1791.* Liverpool: University of Liverpool Press, 1994.

Brock, Peter. "Joseph Cowen and the Polish Exiles." *Slavonic and East European Review* 32, no. 78 (December, 1953): 52–69.

Brock, Peter. "The Polish Revolutionary Commune in London." *Slavonic and East European Review* 35, no. 84 (December 1956): 116–128.

Burgess, Greg. *Refuge in the Land of Liberty: France and its Refugees, from the Revolution to the End of Asylum, 1787–1939.* New York: Palgrave Macmillan, 2008.

Burney, Frances. *Brief Reflections Relative to the Emigrant French Clergy: Earnestly Submitted to the Humane Consideration of the Ladies of Great Britain.* London: T. Cadell, 1793.

Burney, Frances. *The Wanderer; Or, Female Troubles.* 5 Vols. London: Longman, Hurst, Rees, Orme & Brown, 1814.

Calhoun, Craig. "The Imperative to Reduce Suffering: Charity, Progress, and Emergencies in the Field of Humanitarian Action." In *Humanitarianism in Question: Politics, Power, Ethics.* Edited by Michael Barnett and Thomas G. Weiss, 73–97. Ithaca, NY: Cornell University Press, 2008.

Carpenter, Kirsty, ed. *The French Émigrés in Europe and the Struggle against Revolution, 1789–1814.* London: Macmillan, 1999.

Carpenter, Kirsty. *Refugees of the French Revolution: Emigrés in London, 1789–1802.* London: Macmillian, 1999.

Cesarani, David, and Tony Kushner, eds. *Internment of Aliens in Twentieth-Century Britain*. London: Frank Cass, 1993.

Chatterton, D. *The Commune in England. The Organ for Smashing up Kings, Queens, Princes and Priests, Policemen, Prigs and Paupers, Land and Money-Mongers, and Rogues and Rascals of All Degrees.* London: D. Chatterton, 1882.

Church, Mary (pseudonym). *Sierra Leone; or The Liberated Africans, in a Series of Letters from a Young Lady to Her Sister, in 1833 & 1834.* London: Longman and Co., 1835.

Church Missionary Society Archive. Microfilm. Marlborough, Wiltshire, UK: Adam Matthew Publications, 1996.

Claeys, Gregory. "Mazzini, Kossuth, and British Radicalism, 1848–1854." *Journal of British Studies* 28, no. 3 (July 1989): 225–261.

Clarke, Edward. *A Treatise upon the Law of Extradition.* London: Stevens and Haynes, 1888.

Clarke, John. *British Diplomacy and Foreign Policy, 1782–1865: The National Interest.* London: Unwin Hyman, 1989.

Cohen, Deborah. "Who Was Who? Race and Jews in Turn-of-the-Century Britain." *Journal of British Studies* 41 (October 2002): 460–483.

Colley, Linda. *Britons: Forging the Nation, 1707–1837.* New Haven, CT: Yale University Press, 1992.

Cook, Edward Dutton. *Doubleday's Children.* New York: G. P. Putnam's Sons, 1877.

Corfe, Tom. *The Phoenix Park Murders: Conflict, Compromise and Tragedy in Ireland, 1879–1882.* London: Hodder and Stoughton, 1968.

Cottret, Bernard. *The Huguenots in England: Immigration and Settlement, 1550–1700.* Translated by Peregrine and Adriana Stevenson. Cambridge: Cambridge University Press, 1991.

Crick, Martin. *The History of the Social-Democratic Federation*. Edinburgh, UK: Edinburgh University Press, 1994.

Cunningham, Hugh, and Joanna Innes, eds. *Charity, Philanthropy, and Reform.* New York: St. Martin's Press, 1998.

Cunningham, William. *Alien Immigrants to England.* London: S. Sonnenschein, 1897.

Davis, Israel. *The Jews in Roumania.* London: Trübner and Co., 1872.

Dickens, Charles. *A Tale of Two Cities*. Penguin Classics edition. Newcastle upon Tyne: Cambridge Scholars Publishing, 2007.

Donajgrodzki, A. P. "Sir James Graham at the Home Office." *The Historical Journal* 20, no. 1 (March 1977): 97–120.

Doyle, Arthur Conan. *The Refugees: A Tale of Two Continents.* London: Longmans, Green, 1893.

Drescher, Seymour. "History's Engines: British Mobilization In the Age of Revolution." *William & Mary Quarterly.* 3rd Series, 66, no. 4, (October 2009): 737–756.

Drescher, Seymour. *The Mighty Experiment: Free Labor Versus Slavery in British Emancipation*. Oxford: Oxford University Press, 2002.

Drew, Benjamin. *The Refugee: Or the Narratives of Fugitive Slaves in Canada. Related by Themselves with an Account of the History and Condition of the Colored Population of Upper Canada*. Boston: John P. Jewett and Company, 1856.

Dubnow, Simon. *History of the Jews in Russia and Poland*. Translated by I. Friedlaender. Bergenfield, NJ: Avotaynu Inc, 2000.

Elbourne, Elizabeth. *Blood Ground: The Khoekhoe, Colonialism, Missions, and the Contest for Christianity in the Cape Colony and Britain, 1799–1853.* Montreal: McGill-Queen's University Press, 2002.

Emsley, Clive. "The London 'Insurrection' of December 1792: Fact, Fiction, or Fantasy?" *Journal of British Studies* 17, no. 2 (Spring 1978): 66–86.

Endelman, Todd. *Radical Assimilation in English Jewish History, 1656–1945.* Bloomington: Indiana University Press, 1990.

Epstein, James. *Lion of Freedom: Feargus O'Connor and the Chartist Movement.* London: Croom Helm, 1982.

Epstein, James. *Radical Expression: Political Language, Ritual, and Symbol in England, 1790–1850.* Oxford: Oxford University Press, 1994.

Esquiros, Alphonse. *The English at Home.* Translated by Lascelles Wraxall. London: Chapman and Hall, 1861.

Evans-Gordon, William. *The Alien Immigrant.* London: William Heinemann, 1903.

Everill, Bronwen. *Abolition and Empire in Sierra Leone and Liberia.* Basingstoke, Hampshire, UK: Palgrave Macmillan, 2012.

Fahrmeir, Andreas. *Citizens and Aliens: Foreigners and the Law in Britain and the German States, 1789–1870.* New York: Berghahn Books, 2000.

Fahrmeir, Andreas, Olivier Faron, and Patrick Weil, eds. *Migration Control in the North Atlantic World.* New York, Berghahn Books, 2005.

Feldman, David. "Jews and the British Empire." *History Workshop Journal*, no. 63 (2007): 70–90.

Feldman, David. "The Boundaries of Welfare." *History in Focus* 11 (Autumn 2006), available from http://www.history.ac.uk/ihr/Focus/Migration/articles/feldman.html.

Feldman, David. *Englishmen and Jews: Social Relations and Political Culture, 1840–1914.* New Haven, CT: Yale University Press, 1994.

Fink, Carole. *Defending the Rights of Others: The Great Powers, the Jews, and International Minority Protection.* New York: Cambridge University Press, 2004.

Finn, Margot. *After Chartism: Class and Nation in English Radical Politics, 1848–1874.* Cambridge: Cambridge University Press, 1993.

Fisch, Audrey. *American Slaves in Victorian England: Abolitionist Politics in Popular Literature and Culture.* Cambridge: Cambridge University Press, 2000.

Fletcher, Loraine. *Charlotte Smith: A Critical Biography.* London: Macmillan, 1998.

Freitag, Sabine, ed. *Exiles from European Revolutions: Refugees in Mid-Victorian England.* New York: Berghahn Books, 2003.

Fyfe, Christopher. *A History of Sierra Leone.* Hampshire, UK: Gregg Revivals, 1993.

Gainer, Bernard. *Alien Invasion: The Origins of the Aliens Act of 1905.* London: Heinemann Educational Books, 1972.

Gallagher, Catherine. *The Industrial Reformation of English Fiction: Social Discourse and Narrative Fiction, 1832–1867.* Chicago: University of Chicago Press, 1985.

Gammeltoft-Hansen, Thomas, and Hans Gammeltoft-Hansen. "The Right to Seek—Revisited. On the UN Human Rights Declaration Article 14 and Access to Asylum Procedures in the EU." *European Journal of Migration and Law* 10 (2008): 439–459.

Garrard, John. *The English and Immigration, 1880–1910.* London: Oxford University Press, 1971.

Gatrell, Peter. *Free World?: The Campaign to Save the World's Refugees, 1956–1963.* Cambridge: Cambridge University Press, 2011.

Gatrell, Peter. *The Making of the Modern Refugee.* Oxford: Oxford University Press, 2013.
Gibney, Matthew. *The Ethics and Politics of Asylum: Liberal Democracy and the Response to Refugees.* Cambridge: Cambridge University Press, 2004.
Gilley, Sheridan. "The Garibaldi Riots of 1862." *Historical Journal* 16, no. 4 (December 1973): 697–732.

Glasse, George Henry. "Art. 44: Preached at the Parish Church of Hanwell, Middlesex, June 16, 1793, after Reading HM's Letter in Favor of the French Emigrant Clergy." *The Monthly Review* 13 (January–April 1794): 357–358.
Glover, David. *Literature, Immigration and Diaspora in Fin-De-Siècle England: A Cultural History of the 1905 Aliens Act.* New York: Cambridge University Press, 2012.
Godwine, Alfred. *The Refugee, A Novel Founded on Phrenological Observations.* London: R. Hirschfeld, 1857.
Görgey, Artúr. *My Life and Acts in Hungary in the Years 1848–1849.* London: David Bogue, 1852.
Gossman, Norbert. "British Aid to Polish, Italian and Hungarian Exiles, 1830–1870." *South Atlantic Quarterly* 63, no. 2 (1969): 231–245.
Grant, Kevin. "British Suffragettes and the Russian Method of Hunger Strike." *Comparative Studies in Society and History* 53, no. 1 (2011): 113–143.
Grant, Kevin. *A Civilised Savagery: Britain and the New Slaveries in Africa, 1884–1926.* London: Routledge, 2005.
Greg, W. R. "*Suum Cuique:* The Moral of the Paris Catastrophe." *Fraser's Magazine* 4, no. 19 (July 1871): 115–134.
Gunn, Simon, and James Vernon. *The Peculiarities of Liberty Modernity in Imperial Britain.* Berkeley: University of California Press, 2011.
Gwynn, Robin. *Huguenot Heritage: The History and Contribution of the Huguenots in Britain*. London: Routledge and Kegan Paul, 1985.
Gwynn, Robin. "James II in the Light of His Treatment of Huguenot Refugees in England, 1685–1686." *The English Historical Review* 92, no. 365 (October 1977): 820–833.
Hall, Anna Maria. *St. Pierre, the Refugee.* London: John Macrone, 1837. Performed at the St. James's Theatre, February 20, 1837.
Hall, Catherine. *Civilising Subjects: Metropole and Colony in the English Imagination 1830–1867.* Chicago: University of Chicago Press, 2002.
Halliday, Paul. *Habeas Corpus: From England to Empire.* Cambridge, MA: Belknap Press of Harvard University Press, 2010.
Hamilton, Mrs. C. G. *The Exiles of Italy*. Edinburgh, UK: Thomas Constable and Co., 1857.
Hamilton, Keith, and Farida Shaikh, eds. *Slavery, Diplomacy and Empire: Britain and the Suppression of the Slave Trade, 1807–1975.* Sussex, UK: Sussex Academic Press, 2009.
Harding, Anne Raikes. *The Refugees, an Irish Tale.* London: Longman, Hurst, Rees, Orme, and Brown, 1822.
Harms, Robert, ed. *Indian Ocean Slavery in the Age of Abolition*. New Haven, CT: Yale University Press, 2013.
Harrison, Frederick. "The Fall of the Commune." *Fortnightly Review* 10, no. 56 (August 1871): 129–155.
Hart, E. L. de. "Extradition of Political Offenders." *The Law Quarterly Review* 2, no. 6 (April 1886): 177–187.

Haywood, Ian, and John See. *The Gordon Riots: Politics, Culture, and Insurrection in Eighteenth-Century Britain*. Cambridge: Cambridge University Press, 2012.

Herzen, Alexander. *My Past & Thoughts.* Translated by Constance Garnett. Abridged by Dwight Macdonald. New York: Random House, 1974.

Hintermaier, John. "The First Modern Refugees? Charity, Entitlement and Persuasion in the Huguenot Immigration of the 1680s." *Albion* 32, no. 3 (Autumn 2000): 429–449.

Hoffmann, Stefan-Ludwig, ed. *Human Rights in the Twentieth Century.* Cambridge: Cambridge University Press, 2011.

Holmes, Colin. *Anti-Semitism in British Society*. London: Edward Arnold, 1979.

Holmes, Colin. *John Bull's Island* and *Immigrants and Minorities in British Society.* London: George Allen and Unwin, 1978.

Holt, Thomas. *The Problems of Freedom: Race, Labor, and Politics in Britain and Jamaica, 1832–1938.* Baltimore: Johns Hopkins University Press, 1991.

Holyoake, George Jacob. *Sixty Years of an Agitator's Life.* 2 Vols. New York: Garland Publishing, Inc., 1984.

Hungarian Impostors and Hungarian Patriots: The Case of Wilhelmina Racidula, Soi Disant "Baroness Von Beck." Birmingham: J. F. Feeney, 1851.

Hunt, Lynn. *Inventing Human Rights: A History*. New York: W. W. Norton, 2007.

Hutchinson, Edward. *The Fugitive Slave Circulars; or, England the Protector of the Negro Slave. A Letter to the Baroness Burdett-Coutts*. London: Edward Stanford, 1876.

Hutchinson, Edward. *The Slave Trade of East Africa.* London: Sampson Low, Marston, and Searle, 1874.

Huzzey, Richard. *Freedom Burning: Anti-Slavery and Empire in Victorian Britain.* Ithaca, NY: Cornell University Press, 2012.

Ingraham, Barton. *Political Crime in Europe: A Comparative Study of France, Germany, and England.* Berkeley: University of California Press, 1979.

Iriye, Akira. *Global Community: The Role of International Organizations in the Making of the Contemporary World*. Berkeley: University of California Press, 2002.

Jacobs, Joseph. *Statistics of Jewish Population in London, etc., 1873–1893*. London: E. W. Rabbinowicz, 1894.

Jasanoff, Maya. *Liberty's Exiles: American Loyalists in the Revolutionary World.* New York: Alfred A. Knopf, 2011.

Jews of Roumania. Report of the Public Meeting Held at Mansion House, on Thursday, May 30, 1872. London: Asher I. Myers, office of the "Jewish Chronicle," 1872.

Jones, David. *The Welsh Freeholder's Farewell Epistles to the Right Rev. Samuel (Horsley) Lord Bishop.* London: J. Johnson, 1794.

Jones, Gareth Stedman. *Outcast London: A Study of the Relationship between Classes in Victorian London.* Oxford: Oxford University Press, 1971.

Joppke, Christian. *Immigration and the Nation-State: The United States, Germany, and Great Britain*. Oxford: Oxford University Press, 1999.

Joyce, Patrick. *The Rule of Freedom: Liberalism and the Modern City.* London: Verso, 2003.

Karatani, Rieko. *Defining British Citizenship: Empire, Commonwealth and Modern Britain.* London: Frank Cass, 2003.

Kay, Diana, and Robert Miles. *Refugees or Migrant Workers?: European Volunteer Workers in Britain, 1946–1951*. London: Routledge, 1992.

Kelly, Linda. *Juniper Hall: An English Refuge from the French Revolution.* London: Weidenfeld and Nicolson, 1991.

Kilham, Hannah. *Present State of the Colony of Sierra Leone, being Extracts of Recent Letters from Hannah Kilham*. 2nd Edition. Lindfield, West Sussex, UK: C. Greene at the Schools of Industry, 1832.

Kilham, Hannah. *Report on a Recent Visit to the Colony of Sierra Leone*. London: William Phillips, 1828.

Klier, John. "The Times of London, the Russian Press, and the Pogroms of 1881–1882." Paper No. 308, *The Carl Beck Papers in Russian and Eastern European Studies*. Edited by Wm. Chase and R. Linden, 1–26. Pittsburgh: University of Pittsburgh, 1984.

Kmety, George. *A Refutation of Some of the Principal Misstatements in Görgei's "My Life and Acts in Hungary in the Years 1848–1849."* London: William and Frederic Cash, 1853.

Kohn, Denise, Sarah Meer, and Emily B. Todd, eds. *Transatlantic Stowe: Harriet Beecher Stowe and European Culture*. Iowa City: University of Iowa Press, 2006.

Kushner, Tony. "Meaning Nothing But Good: Ethics, History and Asylum-Seeker Phobia in Britain." *Patterns of Prejudice* 37, no. 3 (2003): 257–276.

Kushner, Tony. *Remembering Refugees: Then and Now*. Manchester: University of Manchester Press, 2006.

Laqueur, Thomas. "Bodies, Details, and the Humanitarian Narrative." In *The New Cultural History*. Edited by Lynn Hunt, 176–204. Berkeley and Los Angeles: University of California Press, 1989.

Laqueur, Walter. *A History of Zionism*. 3rd Edition. New York: Tauris Parke Paperbacks, 2003.

Lattek, Christine. *Revolutionary Refugees: German Socialism in Britain, 1840–1860*. London: Routledge, 2006.

Ledru Rollin, Alexandre-August. *De la décadence de l'Angleterre*. Brussels: Société Typographique Belge, 1850.

Lee, Hilda I. "The Development of the Malta Constitution 1813–1849." *Melita Historica: Journal of the Malta Historical Society* 1 (1952): 7–18.

Lester, Alan, and Rob Skinner. "Humanitarianism and Empire: New Research Agendas." *The Journal of Imperial and Commonwealth History* 40, no. 5 (2012): 729–747.

Lewis, Sir George Cornewall (Bart. MP). *On Foreign Jurisdiction and the Extradition of Criminals*. London: John W. Parker and Son, 1859.

Linton, W. J. *The Plaint of Freedom*. Newcastle-Upon-Tyne: G. Bouchier Richardson, 1852.

Malkki, Liisa. "Refugees and Exile: From 'Refugee Studies' to the National Order of Things." *Annual Review of Anthropology* 24 (1995): 495–523.

Malmesbury, Earl of. *Memoirs of an Ex-Minister: An Autobiography*. London: Longmans, Green and Co., 1884.

Marfleet, Philip. "Refugees and History: Why We Must Address the Past." *Refugee Survey Quarterly* 26, no. 3 (2007): 136–148.

Marrus, Michael. *The Unwanted: European Refugees in the Twentieth Century*. Philadelphia: Temple University Press, 1985.

Mathias, Thomas James. *A letter to the Lord Marquis of Buckingham . . . on the Subject of the Numerous Emigrant French Priests and Others of the Church of Rome, Resident and Maintained in England at the Public Expense*. London: J. Owen, 1796.

Mazower, Mark. *No Enchanted Palace: The End of Empire and the Ideological Origins of the United Nations*. Princeton, NJ: Princeton University Press, 2009.

Mazzinghi, Thomas John de. *Sanctuaries.* Stafford, UK: Halden and Son, 1887.

McConville, Seán. *Irish Political Prisoners, 1848–1922.* London: Routledge, 2003.

Meer, Sarah. *Uncle Tom Mania: Slavery, Minstrelsy and Transatlantic Culture in the 1850s.* Athens: University of Georgia Press, 2005.

Merriman, John. *The Dynamite Club: How a Bombing in Paris Ignited the Age of Modern Terror.* New York: Houghton Mifflin Harcourt, 2009.

Miers, Suzanne. *Slavery in the Twentieth Century.* Walnut Creek, CA: Altamira, 2003.

More, Hannah. *The Works of Hannah More.* New York: Harper and Brothers, Publishers, 1852.

Morton, Fred. *Children of Ham: Freed Slaves and Fugitive Slaves on the Kenya Coast, 1873 to 1907.* Boulder, CO: Westview Press, 1990.

Moyn, Samuel. *The Last Utopia: Human Rights in History.* Cambridge, MA: Harvard/Belknap Press, 2010.

Noiriel, Gérard. *La Tyrannie du National: le droit d'asile en Europe, 1793–1993.* Paris: Calman-Lévy, 1991.

Norton, Mary Beth. *The British-Americans: the Loyalist Exiles in England, 1774–1789.* London: Constable, 1974.

O'Connor, Maura. *The Romance of Italy and the English Political Imagination.* New York: St. Martin's Press, 1998.

Oliver, Hermia. *The International Anarchist Movement in Late Victorian London.* London: Croom Helm, 1983.

Paley, Ruth. "Imperial Politics and English Law: The Many Contexts of *Somersett.*" *Law and History Review* 24, no. 3 (Fall 2006): 659–664.

Panayi, Panikos. *German Immigrants in Britain during the Nineteenth Century, 1815–1914.* Oxford: Berg Publishers, 1995.

Parry, Jonathan. *The Politics of Patriotism: English Liberalism, National Identity and Europe, 1830–1886.* Cambridge: Cambridge University Press, 2006.

Persecution of the Jews in Russia, Mansion House Relief Fund, Liverpool Commission. Liverpool: Egerton Smith and Co., 1882.

Poole, Reginald Lane. *A History of the Huguenots of the Dispersion at the Recall of the Edict of Nantes.* London: Macmillan, 1880.

Porter, Andrew. *Religion Versus Empire? British Protestant Missionaries and Overseas Expansion, 1700–1914.* Manchester: University of Manchester Press, 2004.

Porter, Bernard. "The *Freiheit* Prosecutions, 1881–1882." *The Historical Journal* 23, no. 4 (December 1980): 833–856.

Porter, Bernard. *The Origins of the Vigilant State: The London Metropolitan Police Special Branch before the First World War.* Woodbridge, Suffolk: Boydell Press, 1987.

Porter, Bernard. *The Refugee Question in Mid-Victorian Politics.* Cambridge: Cambridge University Press, 1979.

Pulszky, Theresa. *Memoirs of a Hungarian Lady.* London: Henry Colburn, Publisher, Great Marlborough Street, 1850.

Pyle, Christopher. *Extradition, Politics, and Human Rights.* Philadelphia: Temple University Press, 2001.

Quail, John. *The Slow Burning Fuse: The Lost History of the British Anarchists.* London: Paladin, 1978.

Radzinowicz, Leon, and Roger Hood. "The Status of Political Prisoner in England: The Struggle for Recognition." *Virginia Law Review* 65, no. 8 (December 1979): 1421–1481.

Rankin, F. H. *The White Man's Grave.* London: Richard Bentley, 1836.

Rapinet, Guglielmo. *Lectures on the British Constitution and on the Government of Malta.* Malta: A. Aquilina, 1883.

Refugees' Benevolent Fund. *The Final Report of the Acting Committee Made to the Grand Committee and General Body of Subscribers, at a Meeting Held at the Mansion House, City of London, September 8, 1871.* London: Jas. Truscott and Son, 1871.

Report of the Bristol and Clifton Ladies' Anti-Slavery Society. London: John Snow, 1852.

Report of the Proceedings of the Fourth Annual General Meeting of the London Literary Association of the Friends of Poland, held at their Rooms, No. 10, Duke Street, St. James's, April 26, 1836. London: T. Brettell, 1836.

Rodogno, Davide. *Against Massacre: Humanitarian Interventions in the Ottoman Empire, 1815–1914.* Princeton, NJ: Princeton University Press, 2012.

Roscoe, E. S. "Extradition of Criminals." *Fraser's Magazine.* New Series 14, no. 80 (August 1876): 163–175.

Rubio-Martin, Ruth, ed. *Human Rights and Immigration.* Oxford: Oxford University Press, 2014.

Rudman, Harry. *Italian Nationalism and English Letters.* New York: Columbia University Press, 1940.

Saville, John. *1848: The British State and the Chartist Movement.* Cambridge: Cambridge University Press, 1990.

Schlesinger, Max. *Saunterings in and about London.* Translated by Otto Wenckstern. London: Nathaniel Cooke, 1853.

Schuster, Liza. *The Use and Abuse of Political Asylum in Britain and Germany.* London: Frank Cass, 2003.

Sewell, William H. "A Theory of Structure: Duality, Agency, and Transformation." *American Journal of Sociology* 98, no. 1 (July 1992): 1–29.

Shah, Prakash. *Refugees, Race and the Legal Concept of Asylum in Britain.* London: Cavendish, 2000.

Shannon, R. T. *Gladstone and the Bulgarian Agitation 1876.* 2nd Edition. Hassocks, UK: Harvester Press, 1975.

Shaw, William A. "The English Government and the Relief of Protestant Refugees." *The English Historical Review* 9, no. 36 (October 1894): 662–683.

Sheriff, Abdul. *Slaves, Spices & Ivory in Zanzibar: Integration of an East African Commercial Empire into the World Economy, 1770–1873.* London: James Currey, 1987.

Sherman, A. J. *Island Refuge: Britain and Refugees from the Third Reich, 1933–1939.* Berkeley: University of California, 1973.

Sherwood, Marika. *After Abolition: Britain and the Slave Trade Since 1807.* London: I. B. Tauris and Co., Ltd., 2007.

Sherwood, Mary Martha. *Dazee, or the Re-Captured Negro.* New Edition. London. Houlston & Stoneman, 1850. First published in 1821.

Sibley, Norman Wise. *The Aliens Act [Stat. 5 Edw. VII. c.13], and the Right of Asylum: Together with International Law, Comparative Jurisprudence, and the History of Legislation on the Subject, and an Exposition of the Act.* London: W. Clowes and Sons, 1906.

Silver, Allan. "The Lawyer and the Scrivener." *Partisan Review* 48, no. 3 (Summer 1981): 409–424.

Silverman, Jason J. *Unwelcome Guests: Canada West's Response to American Fugitive Slaves, 1800–1865.* Millwood, NY: National University Publications, Associated Faculty Press, Inc., 1985.

Singha, Radhika. "Making the Domestic More Domestic: Criminal Law and the 'Head of the Household,' 1772–1843." *Indian Economic & Social History Review* 33 (1996): 309–343.

Skran, Claudena. *Refugees in Inter-War Europe: The Emergence of a Regime.* Oxford: Clarendon Press, 1995.

Smiles, Samuel. *The Huguenots: Their Settlements, Churches and Industries in England and Ireland.* London: John Murray, 1867.

Smith, Charlotte. *The Banished Man.* London: T. Cadell and W. Davies, 1794.

Smith, F. B. *Radical Artisan: William James Linton, 1812–1897.* Manchester: Manchester University Press, 1973.

Smith, Neil. *American Empire: Roosevelt's Geographer and the Prelude to Globalization.* Berkeley: University of California Press, 2003.

Society of Friends. *Anti-Slavery Collection: 18th–19th Centuries from the Library of the Society of Friends.* London: World Microfilms Publications Ltd., 1978.

Sparrow, Elizabeth. *Secret Service: British Agents in France, 1792–1815.* Woodbridge, UK: Boydell Press, 1999.

Special Report of the Bristol and Clifton Ladies' Anti-Slavery Society; During Eighteen Months, from January, 1851, to June, 1852. London: John Snow, 1852.

Sperber, Jonathan. *The European Revolutions, 1848–1851.* 2nd Edition. Cambridge: Cambridge University Press, 2005.

Sponza, Lucio. *Italian Immigrants in Nineteenth-Century Britain: Realities and Images.* Leicester: Leicester University Press, 1988.

Statt, Daniel. *Foreigners and Englishmen: The Controversy over Immigration and Population, 1660–1760.* Newark: University of Delaware Press, 1995.

Steiner, Niklaus. *Arguing about Asylum: The Complexity of Refugee Debates in Europe.* New York: St. Martin's Press, 2000.

Stowe, Harriet Beecher. *Uncle Tom's Cabin, or Life among the Lowly.* Philadelphia: Henry Altemus, 1900. First published in 1852.

Sundstrom, Roy. "French Huguenots and the Civil List, 1696–1727: A Study of Alien Assimilation in England." *Albion* 8, no. 3 (Autumn 1976): 219–235.

Tabili, Laura. *Global Migrants, Local Culture: Natives and Newcomers in Provincial England, 1841–1939.* Houndsmill, UK: Palgrave Macmillan, 2011.

Tapping, Thomas. "Art. III. The Case of Anderson, the Fugitive Slave. The Application for the Writ of *Habeas Corpus* and Judgment Considered." *Law Magazine and Law Review* 21 (February 1861): 42–73.

Taylor, Antony. "Palmerston and Radicalism, 1847–1865." *Journal of British Studies* 33, no. 2 (April 1994): 157–179.

Taylor, Miles. "The 1848 Revolutions and the British Empire." *Past & Present* 166, no. 1 (February 2000): 146–180.

Taylor, Miles. *Ernest Jones, Chartism, and the Romance of Politics, 1819–1869.* Oxford: Oxford University Press, 2003.

Temperley, Howard, ed. *After Slavery: Emancipation and Its Discontents.* London: Frank Cass, 2000.

Thompson, E. P. *Making of the English Working Class.* London: Penguin Books, 1990.

Todd, Nigel. *The Militant Democracy: Joseph Cowen and Victorian Radicalism.* Tyne and Wear, UK: Bewick Press, 1991.

Trentmann, Frank, Kevin Grant, and Philippa Levine, eds. *Beyond Sovereignty: Britain, Empire and Transnationalism, c. 1860–1950.* London: Palgrave Macmillan, 2007.

Trollope, Frances. *The Refugee in America.* London: Whittaker, Treacher, and Co., 1832.

Turner, Edward. "The Secrecy of the Post." *The English Historical Review* 33, no. 131 (July 1918): 320–327.

Tusan, Michelle. "'Crimes against Humanity': Human Rights, the British Empire, and the Origins of the Response to the Armenian Genocide." *American Historical Review* 119 (February 2014): 47–77.

Twelvetrees, Harper. *The Story of the Life of John Anderson*. London: William Tweedie, 1863.

Vincent, David. "The Origins of Public Secrecy in Britain." *Transactions of the Royal Historical Society.* Sixth Series, 1 (1991): 229–248.

Vizetelly, Ernest. *The Anarchists.* London: John Lane, 1911.

Wake, William Robert. *Two Sermons Preached in the Parish Church of St. Michael, one on the Fast-Day, April 19; the Other on Occasion of Soliciting Relief for the Emigrant French Clergy, etc.* Bath, UK: W. Gye, 1793.

Walkowitz, Judith. *City of Dreadful Delight: Narratives of Sexual Danger in Late-Victorian London.* Chicago: University of Chicago Press, 1992.

Wasserstein, Bernard. *Britain and the Jews of Europe, 1939–1945.* 2nd Edition. Leicester: Leicester University Press, 1999.

Weiner, Margery. *The French Exiles, 1789–1815.* London: John Murray, 1960.

Weisbord, Robert G. *African Zion: The Attempt to Establish a Jewish colony in the East Africa Protectorate, 1903–1905.* Philadelphia: The Jewish Publication Society of America, 1968.

White, Arnold, ed. *The Destitute Alien in Great Britain*. Londón: Swan Sonnenschein, 1892. White, Arnold. *The Modern Jew.* London: William Heinemann, 1899.

White, Arnold. *The Problems of a Great City.* 3rd Edition. London: Remington and Company, Ltd., 1895. First published in 1886.

Wilkins, W. H. *The Alien Invasion.* London: Methuen and Co., 1892.

Williams, William (Rev.). *The Good Samaritan; or, Charity to Strangers Recommended. A Sermon Preached in the Parish Church of High-Wycombe, Bucks, for the French Refugee Clergy. On Sunday, the 2d June, 1793.* London: S. Cave, 1793.

Wilmot, John. *Historical View of the Commission for Enquiring into the Losses, Services and Claims of the American Loyalists, at the Close of the War between Great Britain and her Colonies, in 1783.* London: J. Nichols, Son, and Bentley, 1815.

Winks, Robin. *The Blacks in Canada.* 2nd Edition. Montreal: McGill-Queen's University Press, 1997.

Zolberg, Astride, Astri Suhrke, and Sergio Aguayo, eds. *Escape From Violence: Conflict and the Refugee Crisis in the Third World.* Oxford: Oxford University Press, 1989.

UNPUBLISHED SECONDARY SOURCES

Adams, Nicholas. "British Extradition Policy and the Problem of the Political Offender, 1842–1914." PhD diss., Hull University, 1989.

Anderson, Caitlin. "Britons Abroad, Aliens at Home: Nationality Law and Policy in Britain, 1815–1870." PhD diss., Trinity College, Cambridge, Faculty of History, 2004.

Martinez, P. K. "Paris Communard Refugees in Britain, 1871–1880." PhD diss., University of Sussex, 1981.

Shaw, Caroline. "A Hierarchy of Rights? Minority Rights versus Refugee Rights, 1920–1940." Paper delivered at the North American Conference on British Studies, Montreal, November 9–11, 2012.

Shaw, Caroline. "Recall to Life: Imperial Britain, Foreign Refugees and the Development of Modern Refuge, 1789–1905." PhD diss., University of California, Berkeley, 2010.

Vo, Quyen. "The scope of British refugee asylum, 1933–93." PhD diss., Jesus College, University of Cambridge, 2011.

Wilkinson, E. M. "French Emigrés in England, 1789–1802: Their Reception and Impact on English Life." B. Lit Thesis, Lady Margaret Hall, Oxford, 1952.

Index